THE
UNCOMFORTABLE
TALKS

30 PRINCIPLES FOR ESSENTIAL PRACTICE

A Special Collection of Transcripts
from Inspired Talks Between

2008 - 2017

BILL SKILES

To order additional copies of this book, contact:
Bookwhip
1-855-339-3589
https://www.bookwhip.com

CONTENTS

Foreword by Bill Skiles v

Class 1. Even So Must The Son Of Man Be Lifted Up..........1
Class 2. The Narrow Path of Impersonalization.................. 10
Class 3. The Conscious Awareness of the Living Christ.......27
Class 4. Surrender... 41
Class 5. The Father Within He Doeth the Works.............56
Class 6. Seek Incorporeality.......................................71
Class 7. Why Seek Ye The Living Among The Dead...........88
Class 8. No Illusion Is Ever Externalized 105
Class 9. Leave Your Nets 127
Class 10. Spiritual Alchemy.......................................138
Class 11. Enter The Sabbath...................................... 155
Class 12. The Inner Christ 170
Class 13. A New Heaven And A New Earth..................... 191
Class 14. The Great Secret...213
Class 15. Crucifixion..234
Class 16. All That I Have Is Thine...............................250
Class 17. Behold I Make All Things New 273
Class 18. Conscious Union With God............................288
Class 19. One Immortal Self 300
Class 20. Time Shall Be No More 315
Class 21. Ascension Into The Soul Realm 329

Class 22. Ascension Into The Soul Realm 347
Class 23. My Kingdom Is Not Of This World....................364
Class 24. Spiritual Resurrection...388
Class 25. From Law To Grace.. 410
Class 26. Impersonalize God 434
Class 27. Equal With God...446
Class 28. The Temple Of The Living God 463
Class 29. To Him That Hath 474
Class 30. As We Forgive 489

FOREWORD
BY BILL SKILES

"I have yet many things to say unto you, but ye cannot bear them now."

"Howbeit when he, the Spirit of truth, is come, he will guide you into all truth: for he shall not speak of himself; but whatsoever he shall hear, that shall he speak: and he will shew you things to come."

– John 16:12-13

These talks are called "The Uncomfortable Talks," because they are designed to kill the false self, and practicing the principles revealed in these talks will make humanhood dissolve. This of course is very uncomfortable, so much so that Joel Goldsmith in the "Wisdoms" in the original Infinite Way book stated simply that: "I die hard," indicating that he also experienced the difficulty of dying to self.

Elsewhere, Joel said, *"I am going to give you the real secret of life. God is not with mortals. Take it from there."* A statement that when contemplated leads us to the conclusion that we cannot add God to our humanhood but must instead rise up into the consciousness of the Kingdom, here and now.

Herb Fitch stated this uncomfortable principle: "The Son of God does not walk in material streets or in a material body, or have material friends. Think of that. The Son of God has no material friends. The Son of God has one Friend – the Son of God. The Son of God – where forms appear. The Son of God, where Mother appears and Father appears and Son appears and Brother appears and 'personal self' appears. Only the Son of God walks this earth."

Every one of these talks came forth within from that Spirit which was promised to us by Christ Jesus and only the death of personal self will usher in the Kingdom, the Son of God. But you must be willing to lay down your personal life to be ground into nothingness in order that the Truth may live Itself where you walk. God bless you who find the real hidden Life Eternal.

Bill Skiles
Robbinsville, NC
05/14/20
Link: *http://www.mysticalprinciples.com*

CLASS 1

EVEN SO MUST THE SON OF MAN BE LIFTED UP

Bill: Good morning!

I received a very specific message last night. I'm going to try to get it across. But first, take a deep breath; let it out; relax and close your eyes. If you're not in a position where you can close your eyes, then you need to turn this talk off and come back to it later when you can be still, when you can close your eyes and be receptive.

The Spirit that flows through me flows through you and it is the Spirit that makes intercession for us. Now, let us begin with a meditation that we have probably had before, one that we may have memorized, and yet, even though we've heard it, we may never have heard it. So, let us close our eyes, relax back in a comfortable chair or seat, and let us go through this together as one. With your eyes closed, wiggle your toes. Don't open your eyes keep them closed.

Alright. Now are you in those toes? Ask yourself the question. Am I in these toes? Am I down there in the toes? Or do these toes belong to me? Am I in these feet? Am I? Or do these feet belong to me? How about these ankles, these shins, these calves, these knees? Am I down there? Am I? Although we know a surgeon can look inside and not find me. So am I down there in those shins and calves and knees? Or are those mine? No, those are mine. I move them where I will. And most of the time I'm not even aware of them. How about these thighs? Am I aware of these thighs in the back of the leg? Or anywhere in the legs or the feet? Or are these mine? These are mine. I am not there. I am not in those legs. I move them, but I am not in them.

How about your organs, your abdomen, your seat, your waist, your diaphragm? Are you there? Is that you? Am I in that? No! I am not in that; I use them, I digest, I eliminate, I breath but I am not in them. How about the stomach, the chest? the back? How about the heart? Am I in that heart? No! Most of the time, I'm not even aware that it's beating. I am not in that heart. I am not in that chest. I am someplace else. How about the neck? Am I in the neck? Am I in the Adam's apple? Am I in the spinal cord? No. No, I'm not there. Am I in the head? Am I in the ears in the mouth or the nose? Am I even in the eyes? No! No, I look out through the eyes but I am not in the eyes. And even if these eyes weren't here, I would still be here, wouldn't I? And now, what about this brain, this skull? Am I in the brain? No. I am not in the brain; the brain is mine. Am I in this body anywhere? I am not in this body? I move this body around; I use this body, but I am not in this body.

Now, we have been told to say the word "I" within our being, gently; "I". And pull ourselves up about six inches above our head and six inches behind our body. And so I pull myself up, six inches above my head and six inches behind the body and I realize, "I".

I am the Way. Live by way of Me. I look down upon the body. I look at this human body. This is mine to move to do with as I will. This brain, this human mind, this is mine. I am the thought. I am the thinker. And when this body is still and this mind is quiet, I function it. There is no life in this body unless I give it life, for I up here, above the head, behind the body I am the life. I have the power to lay this body down or to pick it up again. This body, this mind has no power, and of itself, it is nothing, of itself it cannot function. I, the I up here, human existence. But not you! Not ye! *"That which is born of the flesh is flesh and that which is born of the Spirit is Spirit. Marvel not that I said unto thee, ye must be born of the Spirit."*

And so imagine, if you will, my coming out of this meditation opening my bible, going directly to where I was told to go and reading: *"Just as Moses lifted up the serpent in the wilderness, even so must the son of man be lifted up,"* or, must you be lifted up into an awareness of the I.

My beloved friends, you must practice lifting up the son of man into the son of God. You must practice have the actual experience of living in it and it living - you. You must have the experience of the Father speaking to the I that you are. You must have the experience of resting back knowing that I am the way and allowing Me to live you. You must have the experience of taking your entire attention off of any belief any universal belief in the human existence and trust the I of you to out-picture itself.

Now there's one other thing I wanted to read to you from Joel because it also caught my attention. See if this is not what we are doing.

"Sooner or later you must come to the realization that God has fulfilled itself in you, not today, and not tomorrow and not since you have studied the Infinite Way. Before Abraham was I am you. I am the fulfillment of you. Before Abraham was, I have come in the midst of you that you might be fulfilled. I am come that you might have life and that you might have life more abundant, or life eternal."

"This message is not to make you spiritual, but to reveal the spiritual origin of your nature, the I am nature of your individual being. Therefore at some time or another, you must find yourself in the position of Moses, where he was on the mountain top and suddenly realized: I am that I am. I already am. I understand that for a while you were studying with a hope of becoming spiritual but sooner or later in the message there must come an awakening as Paul had on

7

the road to Damascus. It may shock you, blind you for a moment, but it must knock the wind out of you as you realize: 'My God, I am.' And then there is a relaxing a resting an abiding in the word: 'all that God is, I am'."

You see, the exact instructions were given two thousand years ago, but perhaps we did not have ears to hear. Now today, this day, can be your rebirth out of mortality into your spiritual existence as you realize: I am that I am; that I am is living me. All that God is, I am. All that God has, I have. I am the Way. "I" am the Way.

It's time you live by that I and in that I. Abide in Me, I say, and I shall abide in you. I in the Father and the Father in me, and I in you and you in I, and the Father in us, and in the Father. And all that the Father is, I am.

It's time to step behind the veil, live here in the invisible I of your being. This is the rebirth that must come to each of us. And I, if I be lifted up, will draw all others to this same level. Of course it wasn't true when you said, 'all that the Father has is mine' and were living a human life. That is why we were told you cannot add God to that human life. But now as you have minutes, moments maybe even days and you live here in the inner I, you can declare with absolute authority: I am the Life and all that the Father has, I have, and all that God is, I am, for we are one and I am that One.

And now I say unto you I want you to dwell in this I. Abide in this I; let this I abide in you. This is your work and this is your blessing. Dwelling in this I, resting in this I, being open to receive of your Father the blessings. Everything you see, hear, taste, touch and smell, will be transformed by this inner renewing, and lifted up, and lifted up, and lifted up, until that which I am, the I of you, out-pictures as the harmonious perfect creation of your Father.

And yes, where two or more are gathered together to do this, there am I in their midst, in their very midst. And I will reveal myself to them. And I will reveal myself to you. Know ye not ye are the temple of the living God? The I of you is the temple and the living God lives in that temple and here in the I of you, I and the Father commune and are one. And the I of you and the I behind all living form and the I behind every living one, that I that I am, is the I of all. And the I of all, and the I that I am, and the Father, are one I.

And so follow the instructions of Joel and Paul and "*henceforth know no one after the flesh*," for that is nothing. That can have no power no life that I don't give them. And so know no one after the flesh. As you have recognized the I of you, recognize the I of them, for this is one I and this I is the Father and the Son, one. Now you have found the Secret Place of your most high Father. Now you have found the Christ. And as you have your being in Christ, you will experience the Father individualized as the I of you.

Do not speak of this; do not talk about this. Follow the instructions. Dwell in the I that I am. I am the Way. I am the Truth. I am the Life, All that is. And I, and the Father, are one Being, one Presence, one Mind, one Life, one I.

So be it!

CLASS 2

THE NARROW PATH OF IMPERSONALIZATION

Bill: *I in the midst of you am mighty. Rest back now in this I in your very midst. Realize that I have come that you might have life and life more abundant. My life; infinite eternal abundance.*

We are going to discover this day how to come into the conscious awareness of our true identity. We are going to discover how to awaken to the kingdom of heaven here and now. And we are going to do this as it was laid out for us by the consciousness that appeared and is appearing on earth as The Infinite Way.

We are going to start with that passage from "The Infinite Way" book, which by now you probably feel you know very well. And yet, I submit unto you, unless this has become the springboard from which you are set free, you do not know it.

So here is the first paragraph of "The New Horizon" yet once again:

The sense which presents pictures of discord and inharmony, disease and death, is the universal mesmerism which produces the entire dream of human existence.

That means, your entire life from the cradle to the grave is mesmerism, hypnotism, illusion.

Therefore, inside of your being, you must understand *that there is no more reality to harmonious human* pictures *than to discordant human* pictures. You must *realize that the entire human scene is mesmeric suggestion, and* you *must rise above the desire for even good human conditions.*

You must understand completely *that suggestion, belief or hypnotism is the substance, or fabric,* out of which *the whole mortal universe, and human conditions of both good and evil* is made. Therefore, they are *dream pictures having no reality or permanence.* You must *be willing for the harmonious as well as the inharmonious conditions of mortal existence to disappear from your experience in order that reality may be known and enjoyed and lived.*

And this last line is the secret. We might say, **when** the *harmonious as well as the inharmonious conditions of mortal existence disappear,* **then** *reality may be known and enjoyed and lived.*

So we say, well, I've heard that before. Yes, but how do you do that? How do you see through the harmonious as well as the inharmonious pictures presented to you by world mind? How do you see through your entire human life?

Now, I'm going to read something else to you—some of you have heard it, most of you haven't—because it tells us the secret. Actually, it tells us four secrets that the world does not know. But you who choose to awaken out of this dream of mortality, you are going to be given the opportunity and the precise instructions today on how to awaken.

Now this was written on June 13th in 1960 at 7 PM by Joel Goldsmith when he was staying at the Hotel Wellington. And I have a copy in my hand, in his handwriting, where he spelled out for all time what these secrets are that were given to very few over the centuries. If you catch this message today, you will be blessed indeed. And so, at 7 PM, in the Hotel, possibly before a talk, in meditation, this came to him and he grabbed this Hotel stationary and wrote it down and it says:

There are four secrets the world does not know:

1. *That all evil has its rise in the universal belief in two powers, this belief operating as a universal mental malpractice. This we sum up as the activity of the carnal mind or mortal mind—originally called devil or Satan.*

And so here he is recognizing and revealing to us that there is a universal belief that operates as a universal mind or a world mind, a carnal mind; a mortal mind, an impersonal devil or Satan.

2. *That this malpractice has no power in and of itself beyond that of tempter, but it operates as power where it is not known and understood.*

In other words, there is a mental malpractice, a world mind, bombarding you with mental images which operates on you and through you as a power until you see it and know what it is. If you do not see it and know what it is, you have no hope of ever awakening.

3. *Further, that the human scene—good or evil—is the product of this universal malpractice or world mind or carnal mind and has no contact with God* whatsoever, *and is not under the law of God.*

And so you have a universal mental malpractice or world mind bombarding you with mental images that operates as power until you see it and cast it out. And the entire human scene—good or evil; beautiful for spacious skies, lovely little darling just born, three minutes old; ugly, cancerous cells all over the body; meteors falling to the earth and smashing an entire small town—both of these, all of these pictures are products of this universal world mind.

The entire human scene that the senses report to you, your life from the cradle to the grave, has no God contact and is not under the law of God. You know that's true because, well, turn on your television and see what's happening to these mental images —good or bad.

Oh, the beautiful but unfortunate Princess Di. What happened? It turned ugly. This beautiful tropical paradise, this tsunami destroyed it. Yes, it turned ugly. First it looked beautiful, then it turned hideous.

They are both, forever, mental images broadcast by this impersonal world mind, world thought, carnal mind, devil or Satan and never contact God and never come under the law of God.

4. *Harmony of a permanent nature can only be attained as the spiritual Self is realized through impersonalizing and nothingizing of the carnal mind.*

You will not attain harmony nor will you realize your spiritual identity until you see; there is one narrow path to the realization of oneness, to a realization of your spiritual Self and that path is through impersonalizing and nothingizing this mental malpractice; this impersonal world mind, devil or Satan.

It is **through** the impersonalizing and nothingizing that your spiritual Self is realized. That is why you cannot add God to your humanhood. That is why you cannot stay in humanhood and realize your spiritual identity. Humanhood must be given up, seen through, impersonalized and nothingized, *then* your spiritual identity is revealed.

And he left himself a final note, a number 5 actually:

5. *Then there is another unknown that is responsible for world discords:*

The secret of harmony is not in using power—but in refraining from the use of power—since Omnipotence recognizes no power to overcome or destroy. This recognition of non-power establishes harmony in the human scene.

And today, I understand why. Because when you have successfully impersonalized and nothingized the world mind mental images, including your personal life span, and stand there in the stillness, not using any power at all to try to change the pictures, then your spiritual Self reveals Itself as harmonious being and appears as harmonious forms.

Now, just so that we have this clear, let's read this through as he wrote it without interruption and let this go within you, enter your Consciousness.

Hotel Wellington, June 13, 1960, 7 PM:

There are four secrets that the world does not know:

1. *That all evil has its rise in the universal belief in two powers, this belief operating as a universal mental malpractice. This we sum up as the activity of the carnal mind or mortal mind—originally called devil or Satan.*
2. *That this malpractice has no power in and of itself beyond that of tempter but operates as power where not known or understood.*
3. *Further, that the human scene—good or evil—is the product of this universal malpractice or carnal mind and has no contact with God, and is not under the law of God.*
4. *Harmony of a permanent nature can only be attained as the spiritual Self is realized **through** impersonalizing and nothingizing of the carnal mind.*

5. *Then there is another unknown that is responsible for world discord: The secret of harmony is not in using power—but in refraining from the use of power—since Omnipotence recognizes no power to overcome or destroy. The recognition of non-power establishes harmony in the human scene.*

I suspect that many of you have had the same kind of conversation, perhaps late at night, sitting by yourself alone. "Alright, I recognize that there is an illusion. Alright I know that God is all there is in Reality, but how, how do I make this transformation? How does it come about? How do I awaken out of this dream and into Reality? How do I step across? How do I get across?"

We have already been told and that is through impersonalizing and nothingizing these mental images, this mortal dream, this personal life.

So, we must start with our own personal life. *He who loses his life shall find life eternal.* We have been told from the beginning that if we lose this personal sense of life, personal sense of self, we can awaken to an eternal Self. So we must begin with this personal life.

Now, if you close your eyes for a moment, look at your life when you were 5 or 6 years old. You remember that? I do. I recall being in kindergarten and my sister and her girlfriend from the playground, singing "kindergarten baby born in the gravy." I can see that mental image. But wait a minute—mental image? Mental image, that was a mental image produced by this world mind. Why that was never a person at all. That was this impersonal something projecting pictures. That is not my life. I am not in that picture. I was never in that picture. That's a mental image and because it's a mental image, it's nothingness. It has no God contact, it's not under the law of God. There's no God in that picture. Otherwise, it would have been eternal and where is it? It's dissolved; it's dissolved. That same mental malpractice, that same world mind is now showing me other pictures.

And what about when we were in our early teens? I remember going to school dances, picking out the prettiest girl in the room and asking her to dance. I can see it clearly in the mind, this mental image. But wait a minute—mental image? Mental image, that's right. That was projected by this universal world mind. There's no life in it, there's no God in it. It is not in God and God is not in it. It's a nothingness.

And on up we go through young adulthood, possibly middle age if we're there. When these images come to your mind, you must now turn on them and say, "Get thee hence. Get thee hence. That's not a life. That's a mental image. I know thee not. Thou art nothing."

We can only come into a *realized* spiritual identity *as* we impersonalize and nothingize our personal sense of life. And so as you look at this personal life that you supposedly had, from the cradle up to this moment, everything you thought you saw, the good as well as the bad, never happened.

And as you look at yourself today, whether you appear to have good health or bad health; whether you appear to have a good body or a bad body, that's this world mind. Those are the images it is showing to you. You cannot come into the realization of your spiritual identity **until** you turn on those images and say, *"Get thee behind me. This is that impersonal world thought presenting a picture as an identity. I know it for what it is. A nothingness. Yet, right here in my very midst is the I, the invisible I, and I rest in It. Now, I, Christ, reveal your Self."* And be still.

You might be seeing in your mind's eye, an adequate income. You might be above average, even wealthy or you could be lacking, below the poverty line. You might have a mansion with several rooms, several automobiles, a pool and a tennis court. You might have maids and servants. You might even have a chauffeur. You might have businesses in several parts of the world. You are wealthy.

On the other hand, you might be just barely existing on a fixed income. Who says it's fixed? Perhaps you live in a three room flat or four rooms if you count the bathroom. Perhaps you aren't able to afford right now an automobile or you might not be able to afford right now the price of gasoline. You can't go very many places. You're limited. Perhaps you go to the grocery store and you have to settle for 83% lean meat instead of the 93% or 97% that you really want. Perhaps you have to settle for cube steak instead of sirloin steak. Perhaps you have to settle for imitation crab meat instead of the shrimp and crab that you really want. Maybe you have to settle for local fruits grown in your area when you would really like something exotic like kiwi or mango. Perhaps you have to settle for generic brands when really the name brands taste the best.

What are you looking at? You're looking at mental images, wealthy or poor; affluent or lacking, rich or poor. They are both the same mental images. The *substance* and the *fabric* is the world mind and you will not recognize and realize your spiritual identity unless you go to work and in your inner being, turn on these images.

"Get thee hence. Get thee behind me. This is a mental image. It's impersonal. God made no such life. This has no God contact. This has no God. There's no Presence flowing into this. It's not under the law of God. There's no Spirit in this. This entire human life I have been living and seeing, why this is a branch of a tree that is cut off and no wonder it withers and dies and no wonder the beauty turns to ugly and no wonder the live turns to dead. It's a branch that is cut off. Aw, but wait. I want to awaken. So let me look in these Infinite Way books and see, what are the instructions, how do I awaken?"

In this one called, "Realization of Oneness," it says:

17

The secret lies in knowing the nature of error. And the nature of error can be summed up in such words as "carnal mind," "suggestion," "appearance," or "hypnotism." In other words, says Joel, *the moment you see God **and**, you are hypnotized.*

That doesn't say the moment you see God *and* evil or God *and* devil. It says the moment you see God *and*, **and anything**. The moment you see God *and* you, God *and* good, God *and* evil, God *and* them, God *and* it, you are hypnotized.

The moment you see a mortal, material world—of any kind— *you are hypnotized; and from then on, there is no possible way to get rid of the appearance.*

Well, so there you have it in "The Realization of Oneness." If you see God *and* a 'you life', you are hypnotized.

Continuing in the same chapter, which is "No And!"

*If you can agree that there is God, which means that you accept an infinite power of good, certainly then you must be able to understand there cannot be error, disease, or death. In fact, not since time began has there ever been a single death **in the kingdom of God.***

*So whatever you see in the nature of sin, disease, or death is a part of the hypnosis, and furthermore, **whatever you see as good humanhood is also a part of the same hypnosis.** Even the healthy human being of thirty or forty will some day be an old human being of seventy or eighty. When you see a young, healthy person, you are just being fooled by an* appearance. *Until you can become dehypnotized to the degree that you can know that there are no good human beings or bad human beings, no diseased human beings or healthy human beings, there is only God, the one Life, the one Soul, the one Spirit, the one Substance, the one Law and the one Activity—until you can* do that, *you will have to experience death.*

Well, that's pretty plain, isn't it? Hopefully we have made it clear, the road to awakening to your spiritual Self, spiritual reality, to the kingdom here and now, the road —what is your part in this, what do you have to do? You, *you,* must pick up the principles of impersonalizing and nothingizing.

And yet that's not enough. There must be a further step. Maybe this further step is the one you missed. There's three parts to this. What is the third step?

The only way to be dehypnotized, he says, *is to quiet the physical senses, to be still inside, and* in the stillness *spiritual awareness reveals the truth of being that enables us to see that which is not visible* with the human eyes, *to hear that which is not audible* with the human ears, *to know that which is not knowable with the human sense.*

Do you understand that? No, of course not. We have to explain it now. So, we're going to do that.

The road to spiritual awakening is narrow and few there be that enter. Yet, by the end of this talk, you will know precisely what to do to enter. If you do not do this, do not say that you want, above all things, to find God or your spiritual identity because it isn't true. And if you do this, you will find your spiritual identity, you will know God aright, whom to know aright is to discover your own life eternal. So it's imperative that you follow this narrow path which has been given to us in modern language by The Infinite Way.

Once you have grappled with the truth that everything you see, hear, taste, touch and smell—good or bad—is a part of this mental malpractice, this world thought, this universal illusion and that it is taking place in your mind and not outside of it; once you have grappled with that, and you've grown weary, tired, "God, how do I wake up? Please show me." Then you are ready for these steps.

In your meditation, you are going to have to look at your personal life and every square inch of it, every iota must be impersonalized and nothingized. And so, in your mediation, you must look at this personal life and say:

"This is not that life eternal. This is a mental image, a series of universal beliefs woven together to appear as a life. Yet, there is no life in it. This human life has no contact with God; this one, right here. It has no contact with God, is not under the law of God and it is not a life at all. I have been dreaming and so this is not a personal life. This belongs to no one. This is a series of many of the millions of mental images being broadcast by this something called a world mind. But I want to [come] home, I want to awaken."

Now, it is said in the story of the prodigal son that once the prodigal son decided to return to the Father's house, that the Father met him halfway, before he was halfway home—before he was halfway—the Father met him, fell on his neck and kissed him and gave him the ring and the robe and the abundance that was his inheritance. This beautiful story is the story that you must experience. For when you have seen and grappled, wrestled and come to the understanding—because remember we started this off reading that quote from the Hotel Wellington: 'it must be known and understood'— when you know and understand to the depth of you, that your individual personal life is nothing more than a series of mental images, when you have impersonalized it in your meditation and you have nothingized it, seeing there is no life in it, it's a branch of a tree cut off, a nothingness, then is when you say, "I will go to the Father. I will return to the Father Consciousness, to that *I* in the midst of me. Now I am still. I have turned away from these mental images. Father, reveal spiritual Truth. Father, reveal the *I*, and the Christ life." And then wait upon God.

In that determination, in that single-pointed, one-minded focus, I will return that I may awaken—in that state of receptivity which only comes when you have laid down this false sense of self, God *does* respond.

You see, when you pick up the principles, and work them and impersonalize and nothingize this personal life, not only yours but everyone you see, the Father says, "Oh, so you're coming home are you? Well then, welcome home. Here is the robe, here is your ring, here is your inheritance." The Father sees *by your devotion* to the narrow path that you have decided to return and in your decision, which you have put into action by practicing these narrow principles, and in your resting, leaning back in the *I* in the midst, so that It can reveal the truth, It *does* respond; It *does* flow out; It forms Itself as a brand new life, the Christ life, the Son of God life, the abundant life. It forms Itself. It reveals Itself.

There is a *release* within you. You *feel* it and that release sets into motion the activity of Spirit which then appears as fulfillment, as an infinite everywhere Self. And you see it, you know it, you experience it. You are awakening to your spiritual Self and that Self appears before your very eyes. It's like magic. It appears; that Christ life appears. You have fulfilled the conditions. You are walking the narrow path. You are practicing impersonalizing and nothingizing *you* and in the resting, *I* appear, *I* form my Self as the fulfillment of your life. Then you can finally say, as you behold this life appearing, "Thou seest my life, thou seest the Father manifesting."

Now, I'm assuming, of course today, that in your meditations you have reached that level where you *feel* the Presence, you *feel* this *I* in the midst of you.

And so there are three parts to this: impersonalizing, nothingizing your personal sense of life and all these mental images and the personal sense of any life you see around you. And the second part of resting, after that impersonalizing and nothingizing is done. For in this resting is where you invite the Father, where you show the Father you're coming home to the Father Consciousness, that that Father Consciousness may reveal your real identity. And so in the resting in It, in that *I*, you let the *I* form Itself as your experience.

21

You see, if I go not away, if the personal sense of you goes not away, then you cannot receive the Comforter, even the Spirit of Truth or your spiritual Self. First, I, me, you must go away. Then the Comforter comes and blesses you with an infinite abundant eternal Self which becomes an ongoing experience.

And so praying without ceasing means now to impersonalize and nothingize and then rest back in *I* without ceasing. This must become your being. You must be this very impersonalizing and nothingizing and resting in *I*. This is what is called being receptive.

And so, to pray without ceasing you must impersonalize, nothingize and rest back in *I* without ceasing. So shall you return home to the conscious awareness of your Christ identity; so shall you awaken to the kingdom of heaven, here and now.

You see, you do not awaken yourself. You, in this resting from a personal life, you become aware of that which already is. Now, we've known for a long time, intellectually, that God already is, but we haven't known how to become aware of it. What do we do? Well, now we know.

This third part, this resting back is important. So I want you to understand—I feel you must, by now, understand—the need to impersonalize, nothingize, any personal life, any human life—good or evil—especially your own. It must start with your own. You're unable to impersonalize and nothingize anybody else's until you have impersonalized and nothingized your own. Once you have had that experience, then you can begin with the others that you see. But you must start with your own.

So, I am feeling that by now you understand the narrow path to—the only way to—a realization of your spiritual Self is through impersonalizing and nothingizing a personal self, your self and after that comes this rest. And it's important that you understand this rest because in the rest is when the Father rushes forward to meet you and Christ manifests; forms Itself as your new life revealed.

And so it says here:

This Presence cannot be felt until you are free of the barrier: The barrier is the belief in two powers; the barrier is the belief in something apart from God.

And so do you see why you must impersonalize and nothingize a personal sense so that you no longer have two, no longer have God *and?* Then you can rest back and then you can feel this Presence which is the second part; the third part is where the realization dawns; the manifestation happens; Christ appears.

So, it's important that you understand this resting. *You can rest in the Word waiting for the Spirit of the Lord God to be upon you and when it comes, it breaks the mesmerism or hypnotism.*

Alright so, your part is to impersonalize, nothingize a personal you; to sit in the silence and rest until the Spirit or the Presence or the Christ is upon you. And then It breaks or dissolves the personal you and reveals in Itself, your Christ identity.

The stone is cut out of the mountain without hands. You cannot break it, you cannot dissolve it because the very you that would, is the you that is the personal self. But in the silence, It rushes forward.

The weapon against error—our offense and defense—is something that is neither physical nor mental, no action, no words, no thoughts—only the awareness of God.

So again, I repeat, the resting means that after you have impersonalized and nothingized a personal sense of you, you sit back, rest in the feeling of this Presence, this *I* in your midst. *It* then dissolves a personal you and in its place stands the risen Christ.

As you carry this out in practice, he says, *watching the stone being formed in and of your Consciousness while you stand to one side as a witness or a beholder, a state of peace will come. Then you will catch a glimpse of God as* **Is**—*not a power over anything, just* **God Is**.

The principle behind this process is that, inasmuch as the activity of the human mind is the substance and the activity of world hypnotism, world mind, when the human mind is not functioning, there is no more hypnotism. When you are not thinking thoughts or words, when you are in a stillness, the human mind is stopped—the hypnotism is gone. When you experience this, you will feel something which transcends the human dimension of life.

You can sit in meditation and you will feel the descent of the Spirit, the Holy Spirit; *you will feel the peace that passes understanding; you will feel a divine Presence and a release from fear or discord.*

You will understand that God is not a word, *God is much more even than a long list of thoughts; God is an experience.*

So, do we understand this? Let us end this talk the same place we began it, sitting with Joel in his hotel room, after the revelation in meditation came to him, before he was about to give a class, which should now be a revelation that has come to you.

There are four secrets the world does not know and will never know:

All evil has its rise in the universal belief in two powers, this belief operating as a universal mental malpractice or as world mind. *This we sum up as the activity of carnal or mortal mind—originally called devil or Satan.*

This devil or Satan has manufactured a personal self and has you convinced, hypnotized that that's who you are. But be of good cheer. You can overcome the world.

This mental *malpractice has no power in and of itself beyond that of tempter.* It tempts you to believe in a second self, a second creation. *But* it does *operate as power where it's not known and understood.*

Further, that the human scene, all of it—good or evil—is a product of this universal mental *malpractice or carnal mind* or world mind *and has no contact with God* whatsoever, *and is not under the law of God.*

Do you really want to live in a personal life, manufactured by world mind, that has no contact with God?

Harmony of a permanent nature can **only** *be attained* **as the** *spiritual Self,* your true identity, *is realized* **through** *impersonalizing and nothingizing of the carnal mind.*

Ah, but then there is another part, isn't there? The resting back after that, which he puts next.

There is another unknown that is responsible for world discord: The secret of harmony is in not using power—but in refraining from the use of power—since Omnipotence recognizes no power to overcome or destroy. The recognition of non-power establishes harmony in the human scene.

What that means is that you must rest. You must, well if you would awaken to your spiritual Self, according to the revelation that has become The Infinite Way Consciousness, then there is one narrow path. You must come to terms with the fact that everything you thought was your individual, personal life, is not yours. That's why you have so little control over it. Today it's good; tomorrow it's bad. Today it's healthy; tomorrow it's ill. Today it's alive and tomorrow it's dead. What control do you have over this personal sense of self that's being broadcast to you, into your mind, by world thoughts?

So the way is narrow and few there be that find it. But you cannot say that you do not know the way, for the way has been revealed; The Infinite Way. You must impersonalize, nothingize this personal sense of life. You must commit suicide. You must die to this personal sense of life. Now, I don't mean you go out there and kill your body. I mean you must die to a personal belief. You must impersonalize and nothingize yourself. Then you must sit back, rest in the understanding, well you can even say,

"Father, reveal your Self. Reveal the glory I had with you before this personal sense was. Reveal the glory I had with you before the world was." And then you rest. You wait upon the Lord.

Then, then comes the glorious moment when the Father says, *"Oh, my beloved! You have returned. Welcome home. Now Son, now child, let me show you the glory I had with you before this dream of a mortal existence. Did you know that you have all that I have? Look! Here it is, flowing continuously. Did you know that all that I am, thou art? Look! Here I am, flowing, as your very life, as the substance of your form. Did you know that all that I know, you know? Here it is, flowing. Receive the wisdom of the ancients. Oh, my child! Have the ring of authority for you are the Son of a king. And know that you have dominion over all the kingdom. Oh, my beloved one, receive the robe, your forever Christ Consciousness. Watch as it expresses, manifests, flows out to every corner of the kingdom. Awakening everyone on whom it touches. Oh, my son, my daughter, my child, my very essence, I love you."*

All of it is for you, awaiting your decision, which is not a decision until put into action. It is your living these principles that summons the Father to your side. It is the living of these principles that shows you are willing to lay down your life that you may pick up your eternal Life. It is the living of these principles that shows you have decided to return to your Father's house.

Blessings, blessings, blessings.

[Silence]

26

CLASS 3

THE CONSCIOUS AWARENESS OF THE LIVING CHRIST

Bill: Good afternoon.

This is the 16th of December 2012, according to the calendar on my computer. The Mystical Principles site has started up once again, by request, and I thought we'd make it a limited number this time instead of inviting just the general public. I thought we'd have a smaller group with just the more serious students. And how do you know the more serious students? Well, those are the students that may occasionally ask for some help but pretty much have sure footing in these principles and on this path. And so rather than making a human life better, they're more interested in what are the principles? And that's how I see a serious student. They've gotten past the place where they want a little better supply or a little better health or a little better companionship. Not that they don't ask for help once in a while in those areas, but for the most part, they're serious about the principles and more interested in what is the correct principle behind this? How do I practice it? Knowing that these other things are the added things which come from the practice of the principles.

So, here we are and we're a small group and I'm sure they'll be some others joining us as the nudge comes. And this is a talk that, this talk I'm making this afternoon, that is only going to be available to the small group. It's not going to be available to the general public and I feel that in this smaller group, I can be a little bit more explicit, a little bit, well, we can talk about some things that perhaps the beginner might be shocked at. So let us just get right down to the nitty-gritty and see where we're at, each of us individually and you can ask yourself too, while listening or reviewing, "where am I at with this?"

Now unless you've been hiding in a cave somewhere, surely you are aware by now of the unfolding tragedy in Connecticut. What's the name of that? Sandy Hook, Connecticut. Twenty children and six faculty, I guess it is, gunned down, killed by an individual that it appears has a mental illness or had a mental illness because then he shot himself and if you're like me and something like this happens, you ask yourself why or how? How could this happen?

Now, I hate to be brutal but we all read or hear in the news all the time about elementary-aged students in Afghanistan walking down the street and the religious zealots drive by and throw a bottle of acid in her face, permanently disfiguring her because she has the audacity to want an education and that's perhaps so far away from home that we don't, well, we're sort of a few steps away from that and we kind of impersonalize it and don't think too much about it. I'm sure we don't agree with it and I'm sure perhaps our hearts cry out, "There must be something better. Surely, we must do something about this." But it doesn't bother us the same way as when a tragedy hits us in our own backyard. And so, when it hits close to home, if you're like me, your thought goes to, "How could it? Where was God? God is Omnipresent." We repeat that to ourselves. We read it in the message of The Infinite Way and in other messages. We read it in the Bible.

And so, if God is Omnipresent, where was God standing while this this deranged person was shooting innocent children?

We have to face this. We can't just hide our heads under a rock. Where was God? How could this happen? This is, I'm sure, the very thing that these parents are asking themselves. I would be. But those of us that have been in The Infinite Way for any length of time, surely know the principles that answer this.

Let's go to, well if you've read the articles or listened to the news reports out of Sandy Hook, then you know what a frightening experience that must have been. Now in contrast to that, listen to David in Psalm 91 and tell me what the difference is.

David says:

He that dwelleth in the secret place of the most High shall abide under the shadow of the Almighty. I will say of the Lord, he is my refuge and my fortress. In Him will I trust.

And down a little farther:

A thousand shall fall at thy side and ten thousand at thy right hand, but it shall not come nigh thee. There shall be no evil befall thee neither shall any plague come nigh thy dwelling. For he shall give His angels charge over thee, to keep thee in all thy ways.

He that dwelleth in the secret place of the most High shall abide under the shadow of the Almighty.

Now, in The Infinite Way or perhaps in your own experience, you have learned or I have learned, that the secret place of the most High is the conscious awareness of the living Presence of God, here and now. And so if you dwell in the conscious awareness of the living Presence, the living Omnipresence of God, here and now, none of these things shall come nigh thy dwelling place.

Well, what happens if you don't dwell in that? Well as you know only too well, you're a human being or as Paul puts it, you're in the flesh and they that are in the flesh cannot please God. But you're not in the flesh but in the spirit if the Spirit of God dwells in you. Turn that around and it says, if the Spirit of God, if the conscious awareness of the Presence of God does not dwell in you, then you are not in the Spirit. you're not in the awareness of the Spirit, you are only in the awareness of the flesh and of course, if you dwell only in the flesh, he says, its death. So, if you dwell in the conscious awareness of the living Presence of God, then you are led by the Spirit of God and "As many as are led by the Spirit of God, they are the sons of God."

Alright, so what does this mean? This means you either have a conscious awareness of the living Presence of God and you dwell in the Spirit and abide under the shadow of the Almighty and none of these things come nigh your dwelling place or you do not have the conscious awareness of God, you only have the awareness of a fleshly existence, a material world, you only have a material sense of body, a material sense of life, a material sense of supply, a material sense of companionship, a material sense of power, a material sense of health. And so you're dwelling in material sense or in matter or in flesh and of course the wages of that is death.

Now, ask yourself this: If Jesus Christ had manifested at that school or on the road in Afghanistan, walking beside that child, if Jesus Christ had sat down to tell a story to these children in that classroom and this boy had walked up, would he have shot all those children? Could he have shot all those children? And you know the answer; of course not.

Well, what makes Jesus Christ so different? How does he have the power to stop this? He doesn't and he'll tell you that himself *"I, of my self can do nothing."* Then, what of him? What in him makes the difference so much so that when a man possessed with a demon walked up to him, he never made an attempt to do anything. The demon itself said, "Well, what are you going to do with us? If it's okay with you, can we go into that sheep?" Now you know something similar would have happened. What do you want me to do? "Lay that down and come over here."

Well, what is the difference? What is the difference between Jesus Christ and say, one of the teachers or the principal which was plenty brave? What is the difference? The difference is the conscious awareness of the living Presence of the Almighty God, here and now, wherever you stand. The difference is that Jesus, having the consciousness of Omnipresence, of the Omnipresence of God, anything and everything that entered that conscious awareness stepped into the Omnipresence of God.

But now take him out of that picture, no Jesus there, what happens? No one has anything except a material sense of existence and the drama unfolds as it always does, sometimes good, sometimes bad; sometimes wonderful, sometimes horrid. That's the nature of life lived on only a material plane.

So let us go back here and see, If I want to abide under the shadow of the almighty, if I want to be covered by His feathers and let His Presence be my shield and buckler, if I want to stand still and see the salvation of the Lord, even though a thousand fall at my side and ten thousand at my right hand, if I want it to not come nigh my dwelling place, I have to find a way to dwell *consciously* in the secret place of the most High, to dwell consciously in the conscious awareness of Omnipresence Itself. That is the secret. Or to be led by the Spirit which makes me the Son of God, which makes me aware of Omnipresence.

Now, how do I do that? If so be the Spirit of God dwells in me, then I am in the Spirit. I walk in another dimension and I take it with me wherever I go, whether I travel to Afghanistan, Iraq, North Korea, Hawaii, California or Connecticut or South Africa or China or New Zealand or Australia or Japan, I take the conscious awareness with me. It is my Consciousness and those that enter my Consciousness come under the shadow of the Almighty. Just as they do when they step into the Consciousness of Jesus Christ. So, they do when they step into the Consciousness of Barbara Christ or Bill Christ or Laura Christ or Linda Christ or Miranda Christ.

Whoever has that Consciousness becomes the sons of God. "If so be the Spirit of God dwell in you, then are ye the Sons of God" right? So, that's why I can say you're Barbara Christ or Jesus Christ or Linda Christ or Bill Christ and whoever steps into that Consciousness comes into contact with the Omnipresence of God. It is true, in the absolute, God is Omnipresent, but unless someone is consciously aware of that Omnipresence, *God isn't there.* This is what started Joel on his search when he realized God is not in the human scene.

One person is a majority if they have the conscious awareness of Omnipresent God. One person becomes the son of God or Christ. One person becomes the only power in that consciousness or that room or that family or that town. Do you see that?

And so *you* have to be the difference maker in your community. You have to be the one, if you have children enrolled in a school, you have to be the one that going to that school, takes that consciousness of the living Christ, the Omnipresence of God, into that school. You have to be the one, that coming home knows that that consciousness stays there and goes with you wherever you go. That consciousness includes you and what you are aware of because it's entering your consciousness and so you have to be the one that makes a difference in your community, by carrying the living Christ. You see that?

Now, here's another principle: "Not by might, nor by power, but by my Spirit." See? We're saying again, not what you can do physically. Well, we'll just set up a bunch of barriers and put guards around and we'll issue a proclamation or a law that nobody can carry any weapons in this town and we'll do this, that and the other and make all these physical preparations to safeguard ourselves. We get all those in place and we feel pretty good about ourselves, we've made all these material, physical preparations and along comes a disease and wipes out the same children. How could this have happened? Because we were trying to save things by might.

Well, okay, so now we try on the other shoe and we try it by power. Let's take a lot of positive thought, let's give everybody a free psychoanalysis and let's put in a lot of positives, a lot of positive thoughts and positive sayings. Let's treat this town for the disease and make sure that we know that no disease has power and we'll throw these truths at it and we'll set aside a time to work on this and we'll give it a lot of thought and a lot of energy and we will try by power to protect this community.

And sure enough the community doesn't get any disease. Wow, we're successful. But wait! A law is passed which affects the economy in that area and it's devastated and people are laid off by the thousands. Nobody can find work and now they're losing their houses; now they're going hungry. But wait! We thought we had it fixed by power. No. "Not by might, nor by power, but by My Spirit." It doesn't say as many as are filled with physical abilities they shall be the sons of God. It doesn't say as many as are filled with intellectual power and acuity and mental power, those are the Sons of God. No, it says you give both of those up and you're filled with the Spirit and then you become the sons of God.

And so not by might, not by something you can do physically. That's not an answer. Not by power, not by something you can think or reason out or come to a logical conclusion on or agreement with. No. That's not the way either. The way is by Spirit, by My Spirit.

In other words, again, the answer, the only answer that God says is the right answer, is the conscious awareness of the living Spirit of God, the conscious awareness of Omnipresent God, here and now. So if you have this conscious awareness, you are protected. It's promised. It's promised. A thousand shall fall at thy side, ten thousand at thy right hand, but it shall not come nigh thee - *thee.*

Now Joel says here in his first talk of the 1955 Kailua Study Series, the very last paragraph:

"Eventually you are going to see it's just as much of a sin to believe that there is power in good thought as to believe that there is power in bad thought. That was the original discovery that started The Infinite Way on its way when I realized in 1932, that a good thought isn't any more powerful than a bad thought. Why? Because a good thought is just as human as a bad thought and a human thought isn't power."

You see? "Not by might, nor by power, but by My Spirit." Not by anything human, but only by Spirit and spiritual awareness, do you become the son of God, the child of God, that Consciousness that anything that steps into is protected. And so, you and your community have got to find a way to not use thought, not use any thought – good or bad. Not use any physical answer, good or bad. But only stand so still that you're lifted into the awareness of the living Christ. Then that, that governs your Consciousness and everyone that steps into it and it does not come nigh thy dwelling place. Because if you're led by that spiritual experience, then you are the son of God and if the son of God, then you're an heir of God, joint-heirs with Christ to all the heavenly riches. You see?

So now let us start again, those of us who are serious students, and let us look again. What is the answer? How could such a thing happen? And the answer: No one had the conscious awareness of the living Presence of God. All were living by a material sense of existence. That's not anybody's fault, by the way. That's the nature of "this world". "This world" is made up of individuals living solely in a material sense of existence, of personal sense.

But you, you know now. In your community, you must be the one willing to sit down with this Kailua Study Series, one talk at a time, perhaps one paragraph at a time, like we saw today, until you have thrown off the letter which is a mental exercise and will not bring you the Spirit of God, thrown off the letter and moved and been lifted up by the Spirit. You, each of you, in your community, must be that one, lifted into the conscious awareness of the living Omnipresence of God and this you do first, in your meditations.

If you have not yet read and studied the Kailua Study Series, chapter ten, "How to Pray" and chapter twelve which is, "Experiencing the Christ" and chapter 23 which is called, "Experience of the Christ," if you have not yet read those, studied those, live with them and practice them to the point of stepping out of the material sense of existence, stepping out of a mental concept and simply resting back until you feel the inner movement and are lifted into the conscious awareness of the living Christ, here and now, if you have not done that, then that's what you need to do so that you can be the difference maker in your community. So that you can be the son of God on earth. So that you can have the Consciousness into which those that step into it experience a measure of the Spirit of God, a measure of the Christ, a measure of the shadow of the Almighty, of the cool resting place. You must be the Christ in your neighborhood, in your community, in your house, in your family, on your street.

You have said that you are serious about learning these principles. Well then, stop coasting. Stop coasting. If you have the conscious awareness, then do as Joel suggested and take little moments throughout the day and evening and perhaps one or two times at night, and just for three minutes, dwell in It. Because what you're aiming for is the constant, conscious awareness of the living Presence, even while going about your daily activities. Sometimes in the foreground and sometimes in the background, but always an area of your consciousness is consciously aware. That is what you're, what we are, walking towards.

And if you don't and have not had the conscious awareness of the Presence of God, then perhaps you might want to pick up "The Art of Meditation" and read it again and put that into practice, because if you know the principles and are practicing meditation, the Christ must lift you up at some point, you must let go, stand still, and see and experience the living Omnipresence of God, if only for a moment.

This is the consciousness that makes the difference. Christ Consciousness, which is nothing really fancy, it simply means that you are consciously aware of the living Christ; you feel it, you know it, you see it through discernment.

And so my friends, there's only eighty five of us right now. I'm sure there will be more as we move forward. This is the [3rd] talk, maybe the last talk. Then again, we may go forward and have a little community of serious students, making a difference in their own communities. Let me know what you think, or what you feel rather, not what you think. I'm not interested in what you think. Let me know what you feel about this. Does it feel right to you? And if it does, then post a message, we're all here together and let us know that this is something that feels right.

Again, the only one to which it is true that a thousand will fall at thy right hand and ten thousand at thy left, but it shall not come nigh thy dwelling place. The only one to which that is true is he or she that dwells in that secret conscious awareness, it's the secret place of the Most High because it's the conscious awareness that nobody knows, saving he or she that *received* it. And it is the Consciousness of the Most High, the Omnipresence, the living Omnipresence of God. And so dwelling there, in that, it cannot come nigh thy dwelling place and you become a law unto your little community. Whithersoever thou goest, the conscious awareness goes and the Christ goes with you, as you.

I hope in the days and weeks and months to follow, that we can cover some more principles in a serious way and not be afraid to look at things that perhaps would be upsetting to a newer student. Let us see how we can die to an individual material sense, fleshly sense or intellectual sense of existence and come into the conscious awareness of the living Presence, right here and now, so that we may be born into this new awareness. We can't wait for this to happen somewhere down the line for God to wave His magic wand and lift us up into Christhood. We can't even depend on teachers to come to our neighborhood and give classes. This is an inner work that each of us must do. No one can do it for us and none of it can happen if we're still working on "Well, how can I double my income or get the right partner, or improve my health?"

Again, I repeat, it's not that we can't occasionally say, "Hey, I need a little help here. I'm falling back into a material sense of supply and of course, it's not working." But as soon as possible, stop asking for that kind of thing and instead let us see what principles we're missing. What principle am I missing here? How could this happen to me? What principle have I missed? And let us not be afraid to look at it. If you dwell in only the flesh, you are going to die. You can look for an experience that's pretty bad because you have no conscious awareness and these things will come to your dwelling place.

On the other hand, if you're fearless and you say, "Well, okay, okay, what principles must I practice?" And you take it in your hands and you say, "I'm going to use these tools. I'm going to find a way to be lifted up into the conscious awareness of the living Christ, here in my midst, as my midst."

Then, for you, it won't come nigh thy dwelling and you don't know how or where that awareness of Christ is going to move you, into what community and into what action and into what work. But trust me, it'll be something you've never dreamed of, you never thought of, because it won't be of thought, it'll be of the Spirit - If so be that the Spirit dwells in you, then you become a son of God.

Now, let us look at this first chapter of John because this is what we're really talking about. It says:

"As many as **received** *him,* that is, the Spirit *to them gave he power to become the sons of God. Which were born now, not of blood,* that is, not of the flesh, *nor of the will,* that is, not of the mind, *nor of the will of man, but of God.*

And the Word, or the Spirit, *was made flesh, and dwells among us, and we behold his glory, the glory as of the only begotten of the Father, full of grace and truth."*

And this is exactly what happens to you. If you will let go of material sense of existence, if you will let go of a mind sense of

38

existence, if you will stand still until you are lifted up into that quiet place where you receive the Spirit of God or the conscious awareness of the living God, then you become the son of God and now you are no longer born of the flesh. You're no longer born of the mind. You are born of God and now the Word has become your flesh, the Spirit has become your experience and standing still, you behold His glory, that is the secret place of the Most High, the only begotten of the Father, full of grace and truth. This becomes your living experience and into this Consciousness, anyone that steps into this Consciousness that is not of God, cannot exist very long. It will run, they will flee from you, but it will not come nigh your dwelling place nor any that dwell there with you.

So can we answer the question now? Even though perhaps we don't enjoy looking at it? Can we now answer the question? How could such a thing happen? Such a thing always happens where there is no conscious awareness of God. If there is only a conscious awareness of flesh, then you have good and you have evil which is what makes up flesh. But where the Spirit of the Lord is, there is liberty from good and evil - both. Now you have neither. You have conscious awareness of the Omnipresence, the living Omnipresence of God, neither good nor evil, only God.

Well, I don't know if I'm going to talk to you again before Christmas, which is in nine days, (December of 2012). Let's see, that'll be a week from Tuesaday. And then Christmas Day would be Wednesday I guess. I don't know if I'll talk to you before then, but I hope you all understand now what Christmas really is.

It's the birth in you of this *conscious awareness* of the living Christ and so I wish for all of you, all of us, a wondrous Christmas experience, so that we may see and know and believe and trust and feel the Omnipresence of the living Christ.

Let's have a meditation for a moment....

Right here in our midst, in my midst, is the living Presence of Christ. Christ, take over this meditation. I am still. I am listening. I behold, Christ. And I feel the living Christ and I hear, "Son, thou art ever with me and all that I have is thine." My friends in Christ, Merry Christmas!

CLASS 4

SURRENDER

Bill: Good morning.

Well, I just finished my walk for a mile and here in the mountains there is no level ground, so you walk up and you walk down, and you walk up and you walk down, but it was a beautiful walk. The birds were out. The sun was out. Although it was only 24 degrees out, it was still quite nice. I walked past the creek and heard the water running and looked at the little waterfall and looked up at the deep blue sky and it was peaceful.

Last year my wife got for me a very wonderful shirt. It is flannel on the outside and fleece on the inside, and *it is warm*, so I'm able to take those walks and everything is warm except my ears, which I'm working on. Going to get one of those hats with the flaps that come down and hopefully Santa will bring it to me in a couple of days and I'll have my ears warm as well when I go out on these walks.

But anyway, I went out on this walk and during the walk I was thinking of a principle, and the principle is "surrender." Now I don't know if you know much about surrender or how important it is. I know Joel has a chapter in <u>A Parenthesis in Eternity</u> called *Self Surrender*, and in that chapter he talks about the new students feeling that they should mount up in the seventh heaven and have servants and students and all sorts of things. But he points out that the opposite is true: *The higher you go, the more of a servant you become.* And so, self surrender, he says, is very important.

Now I had a man tell me back when I was 22 and he was 80, he said to me: *"There will never be a time when we don't have to surrender to God. We will **always** have to surrender."*

And I wasn't too keen on that idea, in fact, when I was 19 years old and searching for God and searching **hard** for God, trying to find God, and I couldn't find him anywhere. I had read The Art of Meditation and perhaps The Art of Spiritual Healing and Practicing the Presence, and I *tried* to meditate. I *tried* to pray, but I couldn't feel God anywhere. And so for all intents and purposes, it was as if God didn't exist.

Oh, I had a concept of God, and I believed in that concept, but I didn't have any experience, any feeling, any conscious awareness of the living Presence. But I tried. I really tired. And eventually after a year and a half of hard labor I became so frustrated, so angry at myself, feeling I must be a failure and angry at God - why was he playing hide-and-seek with me? And then I started to wonder: "Maybe there **is** no God. Maybe these people are calling it God, but it's not really God. And I just, I just was so frustrated and perhaps that's not a bad place to be, because you remember in several of the books, in many places in the writings Joel talks about having to get rid of every concept of God we ever had in order to experience God, and that that **can** be a painful process, and it was for me.

And eventually at the height of the frustration, when I felt I could take no more, I just broke down one night at two in the morning - three in the morning. I lived in Pasadena, California in the County of Los Angeles, and I sat out on my front porch steps in the middle of the city, and the dam broke. I just, I just started to sob, and I cried out to the universe and I said:

"God - Jesus - Buddha - Christ - *anyone - anywhere* - I'll do **anything** if you just show me how to live." And I meant it from my longest toenail to my longest hair on my head - I would do *anything*.

And see, something happened to me at that moment, because I became *teachable*. Up until then I was full of the letter of truth, and I mean *full of it*: I could quote it to you and spout it off at any moment and often did, sometimes when people didn't even ask! Of course, that didn't win friends and influence people, but I knew the letter backwards and forwards, and yet - I knew **nothing** about God. Nothing. Zero. Was not even sure God existed. But when I cried out to the universe, when I cried out to God: I'll do *anything* if you just reveal yourself really is what I meant; if you just show me how to live.

Well, at that exact moment in time, that split second I realized I did not know anything in spite of all the letter I had memorized and I became teachable. Inside myself I became receptive for the first time, and although I didn't feel anything sitting there on my front porch steps, in the days that followed all sorts of remarkable miracles began to take place because inside myself I had *surrendered*.

I surrendered a personal sense of knowing the truth. **My** understanding of truth I surrendered. I **had** no understanding. **My** prayers I surrendered. I **had** no prayers. No prayers were left. Just an emptying out, just a surrender. And when that kind of a vacuum is created, we all know if by no other means but by reading, we know that when you create a vacuum, **God happens.**

God is constantly *Is-ing*, and that is perhaps the only truth that we can say is absolute. God **Is**.

Yet, to experience the Isness of God, to experience God Is-ing, there must be a complete surrender of self, of a false sense of a personal self. And then into that vacuum rushes the living Presence of God. The living Presence of God was always omnipresent, but never felt until the vacuum, until the surrender.

And so in that state of surrender, standing in that **unknowing**, God began to reveal itself in my experience. And miracle after miracle after miracle took place.

And then something else happened, and that is the personal sense of self slowly took control again and took back everything and started to try to run things. "Well, that's **my** money, so I'll invest how I want to. Well, that's **my** marriage, and I'll direct it the way I want to. Well, that's **my** career, and I'll...," and so on and so forth. So a personal sense of self exerted itself again, and although I thought at the time of that surrender on my front porch steps, I thought: "Oh, I'm so glad <u>that</u> happened and I never have to do <u>that</u> again" - it turned out that my friend was right. There will **never** be a time when we don't have to surrender.

Now I told you that a little while after this, I told you in the last talk that my wife left me, and she did. And while I was there alone, again another surrender, a deeper surrender took place in which I asked God to take all of me, all of me.

I realized that the scripture: *"Not by might nor by power, but by My Spirit"* was an act of surrender.

Not by personal, physical might because that personal, physical might is nothing. And not by personal, mental power because that, too, is nothing. But in the surrender of that and the standing still from that, My Spirit functions.

And then, too, I began to realize Joel's right. If we only know within ourselves that God is omnipresent, if we only bear witness to God, then we only have half of the package. That's only half of it. We have to have the <u>total</u> package in order to have what he calls the demonstration to which we are entitled, or to which we can *have*, is the way he puts it. We rob ourselves of that complete demonstration if we only have half the package.

And so the complete set of principles are:

When I recognize the nothingness of a personal sense of a material life, and I recognize that a personal sense of mind thinking thoughts of truth, or the truth as I understand it, is also nothing, then I surrender a personal sense of self, a personal sense of physical life, a personal sense of mental life, a personal sense of truth - the truth I understand - that must go too. A personal concept of God. God as I understand God. That must go too.

In the practice of the principle of bearing witness to the nothingness of self - of a personal sense of self - a surrender happens. I surrender out of that personal sense of self. I surrender it, and standing there still, standing there naked, standing there open and receptive, God **Is**, and I become aware of God Is-ing.

One of the most beautiful scriptures to me is: *"And the Spirit of God moved over the face of the deep."* I love that because that's how it feels. When you stand there in complete surrender or rest - rest in complete surrender from a personal sense of body or mind or life or truth or being and surrender. Then just like this moment, the Spirit of God moves over the water and you *feel* it. You become consciously aware of it. It's a living thing.

It was there before, but you *weren't*. You were *inside* of a personal sense of existence. But when you see the nothingness of a personal sense of life, you surrender. You stand still. You watch. You bear witness to the nothingness of a personal sense of self and standing still, *"Behold - I come quickly."* The Spirit moves over the face of the deep. There is a flowing. There is a presence. There is an invisible spiritual Being moving, and you feel it, you feel it. You are conscious of it. And now you are practicing the second half of the principle: *Bearing witness to God in action.*

So there's two parts: You bear witness to the nothingness of a personal sense of self. You surrender, and in the surrender, in that attitude of resting from a personal sense of self, the Infinite

Invisible Self moves through your being, reaching right up through you out into the world.

This principle of surrender is very important. After my wife left, while I was by myself I was lying down to sleep one night. I wasn't yet asleep, but I wasn't awake - I was in that in between stage, and lying there peacefully in the state of surrender, I heard a voice, an internal voice. It wasn't the mind, of that I am certain, but the voice said this:

"God needs no prayer. God already Is. Man needs prayer in order to let God Is."

And so startling was that that it woke me up, and I jumped out of bed and ran for a piece of paper and a pencil, and I wrote that down, and now of course, it is in the book <u>Steps to Mystical Experience</u>, but it became the foundation for my life of prayer: *God needs no prayer. God already Is.*

See, most of us pray to God for this or that or the other. Send me health. Give me wisdom. Give me that, give me this. Take away this, take away that. But God needs no prayer. Not **that** prayer, because God already Is.

There is nothing you can do to influence God. Who can influence, or what can influence the Infinite? One thing alone, and it doesn't *influence* the Infinite, it simply provides an opening, and that is surrender.

God needs no prayer. God already Is. Man needs prayer in order to let God Is.

And so you see, I discovered that night Paul's injunction that we must pray without ceasing. I never knew what it was until that night. I used to think: "Wow, how can we pray without ceasing and do our jobs at work every day? How could I possibly pray without ceasing and be attentive to my wife? How could I pray without ceasing and do a good job with the children? How can I pray without ceasing and even drive my car?" And I didn't understand it for a long time, but you see, prayer becomes now an act of surrender.

Prayer is an act of surrender. Again, we are told that we don't know how to pray. The Spirit makes intercession, but the Spirit makes intercession when you **surrender**. So, I discovered how to pray without ceasing, and that is by practicing throughout the day, and if I awaken in the night, *staying surrendered*.

Now Joel tells us and told us in the Kailua study series that at least 12 times a day we need to pause for two or three minutes and just invite God: Father, reveal Thyself, or anything else that reminds us just to rest, just to be still, just to surrender. And then pause and wait one minute or two minutes and see if we feel that movement … if somehow or another the Presence of God reveals itself or flows through our being.

And - if it does - well, it's a beautiful thing. We open our eyes and go about our business. And if it doesn't that's okay too, he says, because he points out that the goal is what? You remember? The goal is to create a consciousness that is consciously aware of the living Presence of God and has an area of consciousness set aside for listening. In other words, this act of surrender must be a **continuous** act of surrender.

So we pray without ceasing. We take the Kailua study series seriously, and we practice 12 times a day. Joel says he practices this 30 or more times a day. I used to wonder how could he possibly sit down for an hour or even 15 minutes of meditation and heal or work on 300 cases of the flu in a day, and now I recognize that's not what he did. He didn't do that. He practiced praying without ceasing. He practiced these moments of listening so much so that his consciousness became constantly open to that movement of Spirit, of Christ within.

And I have found that even while driving my car a part of my consciousness can be listening, can be surrendered, can be open, can be receptive. The first time I became aware that I was doing this was way back when the movie Star Wars came out, and George Lucas did an excellent job with that movie. And I was watching the movie. I took my 8-year-old son to see it, and we were enjoying - I was enjoying the movie: C-P3O and R2-D2 and all the characters and robots and whatnot and Han Solo and his Wookiee - remember?

Well, I was enjoying the characters and not even thinking of anything in particular, and all of a sudden I felt a flooding of the Presence in the middle of the movie theater, in the dark movie theater. And I pulled my attention within myself at the speed of light because I wanted to know *what was going on*! And when I pulled it within I realized, I recognized for the first time ever that while I was watching the movie, totally caught up in the characters, an area of my consciousness was praying. Some part of consciousness was surrendered - there was an opening.

And so I had inadvertently not even known that I was saying: "Father, fulfill Thyself. Thy Will be done" and watching the movie. And the answer came - I was flooded with the Presence. So I discovered from that, that Joel did not sit down. Sometimes he sat down, but more often than not he even says in the Kailua study series he could be out swimming and at the same time praying. He could be mowing the grass and praying. He could be eating and praying. Because an area of consciousness was surrendered, was open, was receptive, was still. You see that?

And so praying becomes an act of surrender. It's an attitude of surrender. An altitude of stillness and silence.

The principle we're looking at today is surrender and how vitally important it is, and so Chuck was right. There is never a time when we don't have to surrender - or - I would say it this way now: There is never a time when we don't have to **be** surrendered.

And I also discovered that - you know, I used to get into some trouble and then stop and say "Uh oh! What happened!" and then I'd walk back through my day, sort of take myself a little inventory of my day and walk backwards until I could see - "Uh oh! Look, there. I, I went after that again instead of trusting God, or I forgot that God was on the scene and I wanted to fix that, or whatever the problem was.

And I used to say: "Now how did I do this **again**! I'm *tired* of doing this. There must be a better way." And that's when I discovered, or reinforced the idea: If I *stay surrendered*, then I don't have to confront these huge problems that *make* me surrender. I don't like to feel pain or uncomfortable, and so I look for ways that I can practice principles and not have to end up that way. I know they say, and I've been hearing all my life, that pain is the touchstone of growth.

But my experience is you **don't** have to wait until you're in pain to grow. You don't have to carry that touchstone around with you. *You can grow just as much out of love as you can out of problems.* And I know this, because love of God will motivate you to stay surrendered in order to stay close to the experience of this movement of Spirit. Once you love that with all your mind, heart, and soul, that will motivate you to stay surrendered - to pray without ceasing. To continually have an area of consciousness that's listening for Thy Father's voice.

All right...so it is a complete package, and there's two parts to one experience. And the first part is, as he says in the Kailua study series: Bearing witness to the nothingness of error. Or let's just call it like it is - bearing witness to the nothingness of a person or a personal sense of self.

It really *is* nothing. It really is. And when you see it where you stand, when you see the nothingness of a person or a personal sense of self, then the surrender happens. You surrender. You stand still and you bear witness to God, to God *Is-ing*. Joel says: "Is alone overcomes the world."

Now he didn't mean *Is* and you helping, and he didn't mean *Is* and your praying, and he didn't mean *Is* and your personal view of truth or your personal understanding or your personal knowledge of truth. No. Is *alone* overcomes the world. That's a complete sentence.

And so we surrender and bear witness to God Is-ing, and the *Is* alone dissolving the world and a personal sense of self. Every time we surrender and the *Is* happens - we become *aware* of the *Is* is a better way of saying that, because the *Is* is already Is-ing - but we're not aware of it when we're in a personal sense of life.

Surrendering the personal sense of self and seeing its nothingness and standing still before the lord, we become aware - consciously aware of God Is-ing, and that Is-ing dissolves a little deeper this personal sense of self. And standing there in the cloud of *unknowing*, the *Is* reveals itself. So do you see the importance of surrender and the principle of surrender?

All right, let's have a little silence now.

[Silence]

I surrender this personal sense of self that I thought had wisdom, understanding, knew truth. All it had was a letter - a letter of truth - and the letter of truth **kills** because it's nothing, and this personal sense of truth is nothing.

And so I surrender. I stand here still - empty - open. Father, reveal Thyself.

Reveal God Is-ing. And now I wait.

[Silence]

And sometimes there is the movement of Spirit across the water, and it reminds me of when I was on Lake Michigan real early one morning before I started my boat. I looked out across the water and it was smooth as glass. Smooth - not a movement at all. Very, very still. And then very slowly there was a few - yes - a, a light breeze blew across my face, and I looked and there was a tiny ripple moving in the water, across the water. And sometimes it feels that way - the movement of Spirit.

And you may feel the Presence in another way, but this Presence that you feel is the only Self that's here. You are not aware of it when you're living as a false self, a personal sense of self. When you surrender that and stand still, the real, infinite invisible Self reveals Itself and moves Itself and lives Itself and is Itself.

And so we pray without ceasing. We surrender unceasingly. We train ourselves to have an area of consciousness that is always open to the Divine impulse.

I found this in the original book The Infinite Way, and it's the very last chapter. I don't think it was here in the beginning. I think he added it when he added *The New Horizon*. And this chapter is called: *The New Jerusalem*, and I'm going to read it because it's only two pages, two pages and a little bit, a few lines, and I want to read it to you because in it you can feel - I can feel - we can feel - Joel's surrender. You can actually **feel** it.

And so listen. Be still and listen. Just close your eyes. Surrender any personal sense of this chapter you thought you knew and listen. Listen for the surrender.

THE NEW JERUSALEM:

"*The former things have passed away,*" and "*all things are become new ....*"

Now you see, that's just what we're talking about. In this surrender, the recognition of the nothingness of a personal sense of self - and the subsequent surrender - in the standing still all things are become new. This invisible Spirit reveals a new Self, a new kingdom, a new *being*, a new life.

"Whereas I was blind, now I see," and not "through a glass, darkly," but "face to face." Yes, even in my flesh, I have seen God.

And that's the experience of surrender. As you surrender, in that moment of silence, into that silence God pours Itself.

The hills have rolled away, (and the hills are a false sense of self). *The hills have rolled away, and there is no more horizon, but the light of heaven makes all things plain.*

Long have I sought thee, O Jerusalem, but only now have my pilgrim feet touched the soil of heaven.

And if you surrender daily, if you feel the movement of Spirit, then your feet are touching the soil of heaven.

The waste places are no more. (He says). *Fertile lands are before me, the like of which I have never dreamed. Oh, truly "There shall be no night there." The glory of it shines as the noonday sun, and there is no need of light for God is the light thereof.*

See, you don't need a personal sense of understanding. You know you do not have to know any truth anymore? Think of that. This personal sense of mind that had to know all this truth - NO MORE! No more. I surrender the personal sense of self, a physical, material self, and I surrender a personal sense of mind, a personal sense of mental truth, a personal sense of the letter. I don't have to know any truth anymore EVER with the mind. No, no, no - for God is the light thereof, and in the surrender of a false personal sense of self, the invisible Spirit flows through me, and *I* am the truth it declares. *I* am the truth. Bear witness to me.

He says:

I sit down to rest. In the shade of the trees, I rest and find my peace in Thee. Within thy grace is peace, O Lord. In the world I was weary - in Thee I have found rest.

*In the dense forest of words I was lost; in the **letter** of truth was tiredness and fear, but in Thy Spirit only are shade and water and rest.*

And see - in a personal sense of truth - which is the letter of truth - there is tiredness and fear, and it doesn't work. You can repeat it over and over and over as vain repetitions, but it doesn't work. There is still a personal sense of self practicing a personal sense of truth.

Oh! No - no - no! We are to transition into Christhood. That's what **this** group is about. And so - in the surrender of that self, in the standing still - Thy Spirit reveals itself, and it is shade and water and rest.

How far have I wandered from Thy Spirit, O Tender One and True, how far, how far! How deeply lost in the maze of words, words, words! But now (after the surrender) am I returned, and in Thy Spirit shall I ever find my life, my peace, my strength. Thy Spirit is the bread of life, finding which I shall never hunger. Thy Spirit is a wellspring of water, and drinking it I shall never thirst.

And do you recall Jesus sitting on the edge of the well and the lady there, and he said: *"If thou knewest the gift and who it is that I am, and if you would have asked, I would have given you living water, and you never would have thirsted again."* Remember? This is the Spirit that sits on the well of your consciousness, waiting for your surrender. And that's how you ask. You don't ask with your lips. You ask with an action, and that action is surrender. In the surrender of a personal sense of self, into that vacuum God Is-es, and you become consciously aware that that Spirit is moving over the face of the water.

And so he says:

As a weary wanderer I have sought Thee, and now my weariness is gone. Thy Spirit has formed a tent for me, and in its cool shade I linger and peace fills my Soul.

That's exactly what happens. My Peace floods your being.

Thy presence has filled me with peace. Thy love has placed before me a feast of Spirit. Yea, Thy Spirit is my resting place, an oasis in the desert of the letter of truth.

And if you have lived on the letter and in the letter - and by a personal sense of self and a personal sense of truth, then you know what that desert is like. Ah - but in the principle of surrender, *I* will lift you up, and you will feel this Spirit. You will feel My Spirit, and you will find the resting place, and you will be filled with the living water.

In Thee will I hide from the noise of the world of argument; in Thy consciousness find surcease from the noisomeness of men's tongues. They divide Thy garment, O Lord of Peace, they quarrel over Thy word - yea, until it becomes words and no longer the Word.

And see, the words are what you now surrender. Any personal understanding must go. In the silence, in the stillness, in the surrender - the Word becomes flesh and you see it, you feel it. Yes, Thy Word becomes flesh.

As a beggar have I sought the new heaven and the new earth, and Thou hast made me heir of all.

How shall I stand before Thee but in silence? (and in surrender). *How shall I honor Thee but in the meditation of mine heart?*

Yes, not in the meditation of mine **head**. Not in the meditation of what I memorize. Not in the meditation of a personal sense of self. No! No! **Surrender**, surrender, and in the silence the heart is felt. And the Spirit enters the heart.

Praise and thanksgiving Thou seekest not, but the understanding heart Thou receivest.

The empty heart. The surrendered heart Thou receivest.

I will keep silent before Thee. My Soul and my Spirit and my silence shall be Thy dwelling place.

Yes, your surrender will be the dwelling place of God Is-ing.

Thy Spirit shall fill my meditation, and it shall make me and preserve me whole. O Thou Tender One and True - I am home in Thee.

Yes, it shall make me and preserve me whole, or holy. Do you, dear one, wish to bear witness to the Word becoming flesh and dwelling among you and dwelling in you and as you?

Then surrender, surrender.

Surrender that which you thought you knew. Surrender a physical sense of self. Surrender a mental sense of self. Surrender a mental knowing of truth. Surrender in the recognition of the nothingness of a personal sense of self and stand still, trying to do nothing physically, trying to do nothing with the mind. Just stand still and be receptive. And in this stillness, the Spirit moves over the face of the deep. The Word becomes flesh and dwells in you.

This is the true meaning of Christmas. This is the Christmas I know is within you, and I recognize is yours by inheritance.

And so, my friends, this is the principle of surrender. Always. There will never be a time when we don't have to surrender. Always we maintain a certain area of consciousness that is open, receptive, silent, and surrendered. Into this, God pours Itself. The invisible Isness of God, and that Is transforms the world into the living manifestation of the Word made flesh, and Christ is born again.

Blessings, and all my love.

[Silence]

CLASS 5

THE FATHER WITHIN HE DOETH THE WORKS

Bill: Good morning.

This morning we're going to take a look at the principle: The Father within me, He doeth the works. Now I know some folks have reported being uncomfortable with these recent talks, and I'm sorry to say that today's talk is not going to be any better. The Christ said: *There are many things I have to tell you, but you cannot bear them now* – some 2000 years ago. And we now, 2012 years later, surely we must be ready to hear them even if they do make us uncomfortable. So we're going to take a look at this principle and how we might practice it and how we might live it and how we might let it live us.

Recently someone online thanked me for the website and sent me some documents which contained quotes from the German man, Jacob Boehme (**Bay**-meh is the way it's pronounced. I looked it up. The dictionary says it's **Bay**-meh). Jacob Boehme from the 1500s and 1600s – 1624. He lived until 1624. Anyway, this was the shoemaker if you remember. All he did all day was repair shoes, and yet he had some mystical experiences, and because he localized them and put them in writing, the church at the time became very upset and wanted to burn him at the stake for heresy. But that never happened and he lived out his normal life. Close to the end the church became roused up again and he had to leave for a little while, but he came back within the year, and it is said he lived a normal life. He had a wife and he had 4 children, 4 sons I think it was, and he was a shoemaker, a shoe repairer.

Jacob Boehme, and he said this: (Listen carefully today. Put on your listening ears. Listen with your soul – that's me talking, not Jacob. I want you to listen to what Jacob has to say, because it's the Christ speaking in and through Jacob).

He says:

"No man can make himself a child of God. But he must throw himself entirely into a state of complete obedience to God."

Now that means surrender, doesn't it. It means being in a state of complete obedience or receptivity to God. So again:

"No man can make himself a child of God. But he must throw himself entirely into a state of complete obedience to God. Then will God make him his child. He must be dead to all sense of self. Then will God in the Christ live in him."

And you can see that's all about surrendering and being receptive, isn't it? Now we all know that Jesus said, Jesus Christ said: *"I can of mine own self do nothing, but the Father that dwelleth in me, he doeth the works."* Does that not again seem like standing still and being a witness?

Now in the Kailua study Joel goes into more detail. He takes this principle and he - he puts flesh on it. He expands it, and he does so in our modern language. He says this. And again, I remind you to <u>listen</u>.

Now, the point that I am making is this: (This is the 1955 Kailua study series. This is chapter 12, and it is called <u>Experiencing the Christ</u>. It's one of my favorite all-time chapters. And this is, we're starting on second paragraph of page 10). All right.

"Now, the point that I'm making is this: In being aware of the discords of human existence, instead of drawing on this head for your

denials and affirmations, instead of drawing on your head, on your thinking, on your **memorization** *of truth, now I want you to stand stock still, and let the Father give you the necessary truth for the situation. Because this is the way I have to do it when I'm called upon for help. I can't turn to a single soul. I can't turn to any memorized statements from my writings. Because if I thought they had power I'd just let them do the work. No. I never go back to draw on anything in the writings or anybody else's writings, not even from Scripture."*

"When I am called upon for help for any problem, I sit down in an atmosphere of expectancy, if I have to sit down. Sometimes I'm walking or I'm out here under the trees. Sometimes I'm at the table eating. But I am so in a state of receptivity a receptive state of consciousness that regardless of what presents itself to me, I wait for the Father to give me the answer."

And Christ Jesus said: *"The Father that dwelleth in me, He doeth the works."*

And Joel says:

"I wait for the Father to give me the answer. I don't rush into speech. I don't rush into answering letters on my desk. I read them and I sit down and I listen, and if the answer isn't there, I put the letter aside until later that day or that night or tomorrow. But when I answer a letter, *it has to be the Father answering*."

The Father that dwelleth in me, He doeth the works. It has to be the Father answering.

"And so it is, when I am asked for help, you all notice my attitude. It's always one of listening, and then if I have anything to say, I say it. Now this is to bring you (you that are listening today) to the point of experiencing the Christ. You experience the Christ every time a discord or inharmony appears to you, and instead of you making a statement of truth or thinking a thought of truth, thinking a truth, you just turn within and wait until something comes to you. It doesn't have to come in words. It doesn't have to come in thoughts. Eventually you will discover it comes in just a feeling of release, and you know all is well.

That is the experience of the Christ, and that is the point I am trying now to see if all of you can embody. The method?"

What's the method? Well, what does our good friend Jacob say? *"No man can make himself a child of God. He must throw himself entirely into a state of complete obedience to God. Then will God make him his child. He must be dead to all false sense of self. Then will God in the Christ live in him."*

And furthermore, Jacob says: *"It's not that I know these things, but God knows them in me."* You see, Jacob has discovered it's useless for him with his mind to know truth. God must know truth in him. *"Listen, he says, oh blind men. You live in God and God is in you. If you live holy, that is, in obedience and surrender and receptivity, then will you yourselves be God, and wherever you look, there will be God."* You see that? That's what he says.

Jesus Christ says: *"I can of my own self do nothing. The Father that dwelleth in me, He doeth the works."*

Paul says: *"I live yet not I; Christ liveth my life."* Is that not the same thing? I live – yet not I. Christ liveth my life.

And Joel says: *"Do not engage in any controversy with any error. Stand still."* And the highest to aim for is to take no thought and **wait** for the Father that dwelleth in you to doeth the work. *"If you must think a thought,"* he says, *"at least think something that has nothing to do with the problem."*

Let's say someone presents to you a problem: "I have a cold." And then you, if you must think something, you can think: *"I have meat the world knows not of."* Well, that has nothing to do with it! Yes, exactly. *"Anything like that,"* says Joel, *"will do. Anything like that will keep thought occupied so that your thought isn't directly meeting or responding to or refuting the problem."*

Do you see that? And that gives the Christ, or the Father within, an opportunity to come to you in experience. You see that? He is adamant that you take no thought in regards to the problem.

So if someone presents to you with a problem: "I'm experiencing lack – can you please work on my supply?" is how they usually say it. You will turn within, take no thought, and wait for an experience of release, which lets you know that God Is – and God is Is-ing. If it doesn't come right then, you do this again in an hour or two, and again and again until it does come. And when that release comes and you know that God Is and God is Is-ing right here omnipresent, then you're done. The work is done. You didn't do it you bore witness to this experience.

Now if you're not there where you can wait upon the Lord, if you really must take thought, then take thought on something that has **nothing** to do so you're not meeting the problem. See – we're not allowed now to live on affirmations and denials. Yes, they worked in the past and we used them quite a bit. No more. Not if you would experience the Christ. If you want to stay on the level of affirmations and denials, you'll discover they no longer work.

You must come up higher to *be* the living Christ.

You must put aside childish things. And so when a problem is presented to you, you are not allowed now to deny it and say: "This has no power. It's not a part of God. God never made it." Those are denials, and you're not allowed to do that. Because if you do that, you're relying on a mind, a human mind, which is supposed to be dying daily. And if you rely on affirmations and say: "Only God is present. God is Is-ing right here. God is the only presence, the only power." Again, you're trying to meet this problem which is being presented to your mind on the level of the mind.

And Joel says – what? *"You can't meet a problem on the level of the problem?"* Where is this problem? You have it in your mind and you're trying to meet it with the mind, whether denials or affirmations. And this part is supposed to be dying. You're supposed to be dying to a material sense of self. You're supposed to be dying to a mental sense of self. So why are you trying to use the mental sense of self to meet this problem? You see the dilemma don't you? Joel's trying to lift us up higher in this Kailua study series.

Jesus Christ was trying to give us the principle to come up higher. You can almost see him saying: Come up higher, come up higher. Let the Father doeth the works.

And Jacob, our good friend Jacob, in 1620 is saying: You must be dead to all sense of self, standing still, not using the mind, and then will God in the Christ live in you.

See, we're in agreement. And what is the goal? Really—is the goal to heal someone? Is that why we're practicing these principles? No. That's just sort of a fringe effect, isn't it?

The goal is to live as Christ.

The goal is to die.

The goal is to experience: I live, yet not I, Christ liveth my life. Christ liveth in me.

The goal according to Jacob is: If you live this way, then will you yourselves be God, and wherever you look, there will be God.

And so the goal is to enter Christ consciousness really, isn't it? That's the goal. That's the path we're walking. To die to self, a false sense of self and awaken in Christ consciousness. And Christ consciousness is the spiritual awareness of Christ or God everywhere, omnipresent.

Now, we said that today's talk may make us uncomfortable. And now we enter the part where that uncomfortability might take place. You see, we have all for many years desired to meet problems with spiritual principles and watch them dissolve, and we took joy when that happened. But along comes our good friend, Jacob, who says that you must be dead to *all* false sense of self. Then only will God in the Christ live in you. And along comes Paul who says: *"Henceforth know we no man after the flesh."* And

Jesus Christ says: Believest thou not that I am in the Father and the Father is in me? And that's also true of you?

And our good friend, Joel, spells it out without any reservations. Here's the pure truth – like it or lump it! This is the truth. And so now listen – really, really listen. He says if you do this with the problems that are presented to you, if you take no thought, if you stand still, that gives the Christ an opportunity to come to you in experience.

"Later on," says Joel, *"you will follow the same method with all of the <u>harmonies</u>, because once you have achieved the slightest degree of success in meeting discords, the next thing that will present itself to you is this: If you look at a 12-, 15-year-old child and think how beautiful, how sweet, how innocent, how nice—your thought will rush ahead a little to 10 years from now or 20 or 50, and you'll say: "Oh, this just a temporary good. This pure, innocent, sweet, clean, healthy child is going to be a doddering old woman or a sinful man.""*

*"Do you see what I'm getting at? Because you know right well that the human good of this moment won't remain. And so you will learn to follow the same principle, same practice when you see youth, health, vitality, wealth. You will learn to look right through it and not rejoice in it, but clear your thought in the same spiritual way and stand still so that the Christ can show you the truth about what appears even as human good. Just as you want Christ to reveal the truth about a discord and an inharmony, you had better, **you had better** want the Christ to reveal the truth about good human appearance, or it's only a question of time when it's going to change to bad human appearance."*

"The nature of all human good is to become evil, isn't it? Youth becomes age. Health becomes sickness. Strength becomes weakness. Abundance becomes lack. And so forth. And finally, life becomes death. That's the history of the human world. By first training ourselves with the evidences or appearances of discord and inharmonies, to close our mind to that picture and permit the Christ to reveal the true nature

of being, we then prepare ourselves for the next step, and the next step is to look out at beautiful trees, beautiful plants, beautiful animals, wonderful youth, beautiful sunsets, mountains, and be able to not think good thoughts. But wait patiently for the Christ to reveal the truth about them."

Now, that is exactly the same as: *He must be dead to all false sense of self. Then will God in the Christ live in him.*

That is the same as: *Henceforth know we no man after the flesh. I live, yet not I. Christ liveth my life.*

That is the same as: *I of myself am nothing. The Father that dwelleth in me, He doeth the works.*

Do we not see that the next step that we have to take, **we literally have to *unsee* the entire world in which we thought we were living.** We have to allow the Father within to doeth the works. Again, Jacob says to us: *"No man can make himself a child of God, he must throw himself entirely into a state of complete obedience or receptivity to God, and then God will make him His child. He must be dead to all false sense of self, and then God in the Christ will live in him."*

Do you see this? We have said for years maybe that we want to live as Christ. We want to be instruments for Christ. We want to experience Christ consciousness. Now that Christ consciousness says to us: You must die completely to all false sense of self *everywhere*. Well, this seems okay when we're meeting discords, doesn't it? Oh yes, this is—this is good. Yes. I can—I can stand still and God reveals Itself where the discord appears to be, and the discord dissolves and I become aware of God everywhere.

Ahhh, but now Christ says: You must know this truth about the harmonies and the good of human existence. You must turn and look at your spouse, your partner, your wife, your husband, even your son and daughter, your grandchild, your parents – you must be able to look right at your spouse whom you love, and recognize – *this is an appearance*. It's just as much an appearance as that inharmony. I have not seen what's here. I am in love with a mental image. A nice image … but still an image.

What is the truth here? I must turn within with the same principle. I can of mine own self not see what's here. I can bear witness. I can stand still. I can be receptive. Father, what is the truth? And then *wait, wait*. Take no thought. Don't try to put something there with your mind: Oh, this is a child of God and God is here. No. You cannot meet the harmony either with the mind.

"*No man can make himself a child of God. He must throw himself entirely into a state of complete obedience or receptivity.*"

"*We prepare ourselves for the next step,*" says Joel, "*which is to look out at beautiful trees, beautiful plants, beautiful animals,* a wonderful spouse, beautiful partner, *and be able to think no thoughts about them. But wait patiently for the Christ to reveal the truth.*" You see? We have to give up all our childish toys, even the good ones. We in this class must be willing to go to any length to awaken to Christ consciousness, to awaken to Christ everywhere. We have said that like Jacob we want to live in God and experience God living in you. We want to live this spiritual life so deeply that then will you yourselves be God, and wherever you look *there will be God.*

That's what we've said we wanted. Well, you cannot have *that* and hang onto humanhood. Not your humanhood, not her humanhood, not his humanhood. In order to stand or rest in Christ consciousness you must die to all false sense of self. Now Joel says, "*there is no literature in all the world, ancient or modern, that reveals this truth. There is none. Search for it and see if you can find it. There's no literature, ancient or modern, that reveals the way to attain Christhood.*" And he means in specific, exact instructions like he's giving today.

So do you want to lay down your life, or are you going to be like Peter? "*I will lay down my life for you!*" Will you, Peter? "*Will you lay down your life for me?"* Most of us say that, but like Peter we won't really give up all false sense of self because we're enjoying him too much, we're enjoying her too much.

This is not for the fainthearted or the weak. Narrow is the path, and Joel tells us again how to do it: "Stand aside. You don't refute appearances. You don't enter into a mental argument with it. *Stand aside and realize: "I am the way." You say; "That's meaningless! Good!" says Joel. The more meaningless it is, the better. So let it be, because we do not want through the power of our thought or reason to meet a situation—but through the Christ. Remember that statement."*

"We do not wish even through reason to meet a case, but through Christ. The Christ which passeth all human understanding." You see that? You can't have this experience of the Christ when you're taking thought because the Christ is hidden. It's hidden. And you can't experience the Christ, well do you really think you can experience the Christ when you have your eyes closed in meditation and then open your eyes and look lovingly and longingly at her? Where is the Christ then? You're looking lovingly and longingly at her or him, and now the Christ is hidden. You've gone back into a mental image. You're living in humanhood. It's good humanhood, but Joel says we reach the place where we have to take that step.

"He says Christ is the activity that takes place in your consciousness when no thinking is going on." And I might add – no human feelings either. "Oh, he's so precious, my little grandson!" What are you looking at? What are you looking at? Yes, it is true Joel says you lose some of the good things in life, but what you gain more than compensates for it when you are able to see Christ everywhere. When you are able to like Jacob says – when you are able to –when you yourselves are God and wherever you look, there will be God.

I will lay down my life for you, Christ! Will you? Will you lay that down too? Will you lay down her and him and it? Will you lay down not just the inharmonies, but the harmonies as well? Will you let God within doeth the works? Will you let God reveal what is really there? Can you be Christ part of the time and human part of the time? Do we not reach this jumping off place where we have to go for broke, where we have to say: "I'm willing to go all the way. I may not be real good at it yet, but I'm willing to go, and I'm going to start practicing. I'm going to start seeing not just the discords, but the harmonies as well as nothing, or nothingness. I'm going to stand still, stock still. Not think any thoughts of truth about it. But wait … wait upon the Lord."

And if you wait upon the Lord it is said, *"you will mount up with wings as eagles."* Eagles, of course, are symbols for messengers of God because they fly up high close to God according to Native Americans. Do you want to mount up and be the instrument for a message of God? Then you must wait upon the Lord.

We talked about it last week and the week before. Waiting on that ***movement***, and the *Spirit breathed over the face of the deep.* I love that. That's exactly how it feels, but that feels that same way not just releasing the discord and standing still, but also releasing the harmony and standing still. This must be a constant state of consciousness, or as our good friend, Jacob, puts it: *"He must throw himself entirely into a state of complete obedience to God,"* which is what Jesus Christ was living when he said: *"I can do nothing, but the Father that dwelleth in me, He doeth the works, and I bear witness to that."*

Yes, and that's what Joel says here is pretty much what was just said.

"When you (can) *come to that point of absolute humility where Jesus found himself when he said "I can of mine own self do nothing." When you come to that point of absolute humility, you will stand still in thought with your ear wide open, your inner ear, waiting and giving God the opportunity to come out into expression,* (and

that) *is when Christ will have the opportunity to fulfill Itself in (our) experience."*

You see that? We can't make it any plainer. But what we have to know now is to complete the picture, it has to be in **all** of our affairs. Yes, even with sweet little Johnny. Even with lovely Madalyn. You see that? Even with that beautiful mountain range. Even with the wonderful sunset. Even with those billions of stars.

Joel told us many years ago we have to convert the entire, this entire – well – this world has to be reinterpreted into omnipresence, and you don't do the reinterpreting. You stand still.

Remember, he told us. He told us even in this part we're reading here up above where he, well – let's see if we can find it so we can use his words. If you remember, he was standing before the bed of someone that was dying and nothing would come to him, and he didn't think any thoughts. He just stood there speechless. He knew the guy was going to die if something didn't come. And he says, *"I can assure you you can keep out the Christ by speech and thought. All the recitation of nice metaphysical statements, even Scriptural promises – those are hindrances to the activity of this invisible Christ. Unless they come forth spontaneously as the activity of the Christ, just as they did as I stood at that man's bed in the hospital, standing there in a state of receptivity. Then the Voice said: Man does not live by bread alone."*

Now remember – he was on an iron lung, the man, and the words that came from within when the Father did the works were *"Man shall not live by bread alone,"* and Joel understood instantly, that's right, that's right. We don't live by breath. We live by Christ. It's Christ. It is I. Be not afraid. And instantly the man signaled for the nurse and they took away the iron lung and he left the hospital a couple days later. Remember? That's what he's saying.

"Now we can heal wherever there is a receptive consciousness. We can reform. We can redeem. We can renew. We can regenerate. But

only in one way, and now you know the truth of being. Now that you have the letter of truth, and you have to keep reminding yourself of it – when you're actually living about your business all the rest of the day: Don't think thoughts! Keep yourself receptive to an inflow of thoughts so that it breaks through into your consciousness, and thereby you have the experience of the Christ."

"Now eventually, as I said before, you will go through this same procedure when you witness the harmonies of life, when you witness a beautiful sunset you will turn also and open a way for the Christ experience to come so that you can rightly see the sunset as it is or the mountain scene as it is. This will ultimate in the activity of the Christ being a **constant** *experience, one not achieved, one not attained at certain moments of the day or night, as when you sit down to meditate and then the other 90 percent of the time you're back in this humanhood, this human state of consciousness. No, no – it will be a* **constant** *state of be-ing, so that at any time necessary you can blink the eye and the activity of Christ will consciously be realized. But it isn't even necessary that that be done."*

Now listen. *"The time eventually comes"* – this is for all of us, and hopefully you're still listening – *listen. "The time eventually comes, and I call that in all the writings a point of transition where you pass from living your own life to having your life lived for you and through you. Where you become nothing more than an instrument for this divine experience – and you go where you're sent and when you're sent, and you have no will of your own. No wish of your own. No desire of your own. You never have supply of your own and you never even have health. It is always an It that is living Its own life, and you go along for the ride."*

All right?

[Silence]

He says, "*we engage our minds while we wait, and by refraining from taking a statement of truth or thinking truth, the Christ announces Itself.*" And so this transition is what Jacob means when he says: *Listen, oh blind men. You live in God and God is in you. If you live* (this) *holy* (way), that is, waiting upon the Christ, *then will you yourselves be God, and wherever you look, there will be God.*

And Christ Jesus says: "*Believest thou not that I am in the Father and the Father is in me? I can of mine own self do nothing, but the Father that dwelleth in me, He doeth the works.*"

And our friend, Paul, says: "*I live, yet not I. Christ liveth my life,*" and henceforth I know no one after the flesh. I know only God. I know only Spirit everywhere.

Now, we must take this step. It's a hard saying, bitter in the belly, yet we must take this step. The principle is: The Father within doeth the works. This must be our experience not only with the inharmonies. Not only do we stand still and become beholders as God reveals Itself where the inharmony was appearing; now we must take the more difficult step and stand still even while eating or walking or swimming or driving and allow God to reveal Itself where the harmony appears. In this way the entire human scene is transformed into Heaven here and now. But it means you have to let go of some of these cherished mental images, doesn't it? Yes sir, it sure does. Yes ma'am, it sure does.

I will lay down my life for you, Master! Will you lay down your life for Christ? Will you? Yes, this is the point of transition. This is the point where Christ liveth our lives in all of our affairs. This is the point where we completely die to any false sense of self as Jacob told us, and God lives in us and we see God everywhere. Christ lives Itself.

Let us be still for a moment and see if this completes today's talk. Father, you doeth the works. I stand still and listen.

[Silence]

And so I wish for you, all of you – a new Self. As in our human world 2012 turns to 2013, I wish for you that you step out of that and into the flow of eternity in which Christ liveth Its life. Not by might. You cannot make the change yourself physically nor mentally with any statement of truth that you think. And it's really not about meeting problems by being still and letting Christ consciousness speak.

It's really about meeting this world in its entirety with nothing but silence and allowing Christ to reveal God's omnipresence, or the Isness of God. Not evil, not good. The pairs of opposites must go. On this path in this new Consciousness the pairs of opposites cannot exist. You cannot have evil anymore. Ahh, but also you cannot have good anymore. You can only have what God reveals as Its Isness.

I will lay down my life for this Isness. Well, if this is true then you know what you must do. Completely die to the world of opposites and be reborn into a new awareness of whatever Christ, the Father within you, reveals as that which Is, as that which *I* Is.

Blessings to you my dear friends. May we rest back in the Oneness of Christ Consciousness and see the heaven of here and now. Thank you so much for drawing this forth today.

Blessings.

CLASS 6

SEEK INCORPOREALITY

Bill: Good morning.

We are continuing our series of talks. I guess we could call them <u>The Uncomfortable Talks</u>, and today's is going to be called "Seek Incorporeality." Now we discussed in previous talks how we look out with our five physical senses and see only images in thought, and then we love or we fear or we hate these images and never see the reality. And I know it's uncomfortable to think that you've been living with someone for 20 or 30 or 40 years and never seen the reality of them and perhaps only loved an image in the mind. Yet, if we would see reality, if we would come up over this world, if we would stand in the heaven of here and now, we must be willing to be transformed by the renewing of our mind, that is, by the renewing of our vision.

Now we need to discuss incorporeality, and I know that's kind of perhaps difficult to conceive, but I don't want you to conceive of it. That's not going to help. What we need is the conscious awareness of our own incorporeality and then the conscious awareness of the incorporeality of *all* life. And so we'll look at Joel's chapter in the book <u>Beyond Words and Thoughts</u> called Chapter 10: Incorporeality: God, Man, and Universe. It's probably the best chapter ever on giving you hints on how you can go about catching a glimpse of incorporeality. We are also going to look at the Kailua study series, Chapter 7, called: [Understanding The

Body]? And we're going to look at our good friend, Jacob Boehme, our German friend from the 1500s and 1600s.

Okay, so let us get started with this chapter in <u>Beyond Words and Thoughts</u>, which should tell you something right there. That you're going to have to go beyond words and beyond thoughts. Now, he says:

"Incorporeal God cannot give birth to a corporeal man, only to incorporeal man. An incorporeal man has no physical structure, therefore in your meditation, prayer, and treatment, those on the mystical path must remove from thought the image-man, the corporeal man, the man who has physicality because that man is not the man of God's creation. For this reason, prayer, which is the communion between God and man can never take place between incorporeal God and corporeal man."

And we know that, well, elsewhere I remember Joel saying that when you sit down to do healing work, you must first eliminate the patient and then you must eliminate yourself, and what is left can receive the word or commune with God. You remember that? Remember him saying that? And so you see, whenever he sat down to meditation he eliminated any corporeal sense of self and any corporeal sense of another. Then, standing in his own incorporeality – which is the one incorporeality of *all* life – It revealed Itself to his awareness. He became aware of it as a present reality, and he did that in every single meditation. And he says here:

"If I look out at a group of persons with my eyes, I can be aware only of corporeal man. The "natural" part of me, the five physical senses, can be aware only of the five physical senses of you. If I am limited to that consciousness, however, I have no right to be a metaphysical practitioner or a teacher, and I have no right to claim to have attained any degree of the mystical consciousness."

And so do you see how he is saying here that if I am dwelling in a natural mind with five physical senses and I'm looking out,

I can be aware only of the five physical sense self of you, or the corporeal sense of you, which is *nothing?* Do you see where he says that in order to have the mystical consciousness we must step out of that? Here I am living in a five physical sense of self, looking at you saying: "I love you," a five physical sense of self.

All of this is taking place in the realm of mental images, and God didn't create any of it. You see the depths or the heights we have to attain? We must die to all that even if it's painful to let it go. We must rise into mystical consciousness where we become aware of a real incorporeality of ourselves and others. So, he says here on the next page:

"*The point is that each of us is in part a physical being* (that's the five physical sense self); *each of us is a mental being* (that's the thinking self); *and each of us is an incorporeal, spiritual being, and the reality of us is that incorporeal, spiritual Selfhood which is born of God.*"

And so you see, not by might, not by a physical sense of self can you do anything or help anyone. Not by power. Not by any mental sense of self can you do anything. But when all of that is stopped and you're standing in a cloud of unknowing, then the incorporeal self of them, which is your incorporeal self, which is the incorporeal self, can reveal itself to your awareness.

"*The other part of us* (he says) *is that creation described in the second and third chapter(s) of Genesis, which was made, not by God, but by mind, by the mind of man, by what is called Lord God.*"

"*If I am to acknowledge God, I must acknowledge incorporeal God, and that means not only that I cannot embrace It in a figure or a form, I cannot even embrace It in a mental image. And I dare not even name it.*"

See he's instructing us to go beyond words and thoughts if we would know our partner, if we would know our spouse, if we would know our child, if we would know our parent, if we would know our sibling, if we would know our neighbor, if we would know our friend, if we would know our enemy, if we would know our beloved – then we must be willing to set aside the creation of mind. Yes, it's kind of sad, but I may have been in love with a creation of mind which was not made by God, which means it has no real existence other than a universal series of concepts. Well, then what am I to do? I can't sit down and just think – well, here is the Christ. That doesn't help anything. That doesn't give me the awareness. That's using the mind. I have to do <u>something</u> and he says here, the answer is:

"How you can ever embrace in your mind what omnipotence and omnipresent mean? You cannot! Therefore, release all concepts; let them go. Do not try to understand God. Do not try to embrace God in your mind."

"Well, how, then, are you to know God aright? Ah, (says Joel) *that you can do. You can know God aright. God is. Then let God define itself. And so you come to the realization* (he says) *that in the final analysis you cannot know God with your mind, but God can announce Itself to you. God can say, "I will be with thee to the end of the world. I will never leave thee, nor forsake thee.""*

Yes, he says:

"All you will ever know about God is the word I," and how do you define I? Can you define it? Can you define your incorporeality? Can you put it in a box? Can you explain it? Explain your incorporeal I, would you please? You can't! You can't. And so if you are willing to stop using the senses and stop using the mind, first in your meditation, then the incorporeal I of the universe, of yourself, of herself and his self – will announce Itself. It will reveal Itself. It will move into your awareness, and when that happens to you, *"you have reached that state of consciousness where you are ready for the mystical life,"* he says.

Now, *"this is the reason,* (says Joel), *it's been possible to write or cable me from any part of the world and be healed before the message reached me physically, because I have recognized my incorporeality. I have recognized that I am not in a body: I am speaking through the body, but I am not in the body."*

And I have a little note here in the margin: *As per Kailua, Chapter 7.* Let's go over there now and see what that says, because I made that note some years ago. It says: <u>The body is the Word made flesh</u>. Now let me explain to you. When you sit still and attain that silence and know that your mind – with your senses and with your mind you cannot know the reality of your spouse of your partner of your beloved, and when you are willing to sit still, "Father, reveal Thyself." What is this Word made flesh? Then into your awareness will spring an incorporeality, an incorporeal self, an incorporeality of I, and you won't be able to explain it or pin it down in your mind, but you won't be functioning in your mind at that point you'll be in mystical consciousness, resting in the awareness of the Isness of incorporeality.

And so he says here in Chapter 7:

"The body is the Word made flesh." That is the body that you experience here in this meditation. The incorporeal body, your real body, your real Self, and your spouse's real Self, and the real Self of all life – **that** is the Word made flesh. *"But because the physical sense has intervened, all you can see* (with your eyes) *is the concept of body,"* and so you look out at incorporeality, and the mind shows you a concept of that incorporeality which is called your spouse, your love. Now, I'm not saying that you can't love that. I'm saying that if you love the concept, then you're loving that which God did not make, and Joel tells us repeatedly: In the mystical path you cannot love, fear, or hate that which is appearing. But in your meditation you can go beyond that. You can commune

with the incorporeality being that is your spouse. And **that** you can love with all your mind, heart, and soul and being. And that automatically, *automatically* when you are loving **that** with all your heart, mind, soul, and being – it automatically manifests as loving action out here. It's automatic.

So in Chapter 7 he says: *"The concept must die."* Well, that's pretty plain, isn't it? The mental concept you have entertained all these years of your spouse, your son, your granddaughter, your mother – that mental concept must die. It **has** to die! You can't go beyond it until it does. When it dies, simultaneously there's a resurrection of the incorporeality of them, which is the resurrection of the incorporeality of you. And so, *"Even the concept that you entertain of yourself,* (says Joel), *must die for that concept can never know God. As you entertain a concept of yourself as man* (or woman), *as effect, as sinful* or *sickly* (or healthy or wealthy), *as human, that concept of yourself must die until you become aware:* "No, I Am that I Am," *and that is what I Am. When that realization comes your old concept of yourself has died. You have fulfilled Paul's statement:* "Ye must die daily. You must be reborn of the spirit.""

Now, do you see? You see the point to which we're leading here in this group? We have said we want to live in Christ Consciousness. Okay fine here is the way. Concept of the Word made flesh, your concept of the invisible incorporeality - you have been loving that concept, or in the case of an enemy, perhaps fearing that concept. But they're all concepts, and they must die including the concept you've had lo these 30, 40, 50, 60, 70, 80 years of yourself! That concept must die because that concept can never know God. Your physical sense of self, which is the concept of your own incorporeality, is not your own incorporeality. It's a concept, and it cannot know your own incorporeality. And your concept of mind and all the concepts that are in your mind also must die, because a concept in the mind is never going to be incorporeality, and so to think that you can think of Christ or visualize Christ or draw a picture of Christ in your mind – even if it's a beautiful picture – it's not Christ – it's not the incorporeality of I.

So this must die too, and it must die in every meditation from now on. If you're sitting down to help someone, as he said, first you must eliminate the patient. You must eliminate a physical sense of them and a mental sense of them in order to be so still that you can wait on the Lord to reveal the incorporeality that is there. And once you're eliminated them, then you must eliminate yourself, says Joel. I of myself can do nothing. I of myself am nothing, and so now I let the concept of a physical self or the concept of a mental self - I let that go.

And now I stand still, and if God doesn't reveal incorporeality, I can go no further. This is the point at which I leave the letter and enter the Spirit. This is the point in which I leave the mind and enter the awareness or consciousness. This is the point that I leave behind mind and I rest back in infinite consciousness. And if I will do this repeatedly until the experience comes, I will have the experience of incorporeality. And then the person that reached out to that consciousness touches their own incorporeality, the reality of them, and they say: "Wow! I feel better. Thank you." But concepts have improved over there. You know the reality is still the incorporeality, and so you're not buying the fact that they're sick and you not buying the fact that they're well. You know you have touched – you have the awareness of the incorporeality of them.

And so he says in Chapter 7:

"That concept must die. Even the concept that you entertain of yourself must die, for that concept can never know God, it can never know reality. (It can never know incorporeality.) *It is only as you refrain from judging by appearances."*

Remember, *Judge not by appearances* – means quite a bit more, now doesn't it? It's quite a bit deeper than "don't believe what you're seeing with your eyes."

"*It is only as you refrain from judging by appearances* (or from standing in the mind), *and through a transformation of consciousness: Be ye therefore transformed through the renewing of your mind. (And) Let God define what you are and who you are, that the answer will be, "This is my beloved Son in whom I am well pleased.""*

It doesn't mean that you'll just think that. No! Thinking that has never done anything for you. It means, you die to the concept of a physical sense of self. You die to the concept of a mental sense of self. You stand still in consciousness, naked as it were, with nothing to lean on. No props. And you 'wait upon the Lord', and as he says here: You *"let God define what you are and who you are."* Then comes the living awareness: *"This is my beloved Son in whom I am well pleased."* Then comes the living awareness, *"the Father and I are One."* Then comes the living awareness—*the Word is my invisible flesh. My incorporeality."*

And so he says:

"*In reality, you are the beloved Son, the Word made flesh. But that flesh is an infinite* (invisible) *individuality and an infinite body that is eternal. In this spiritual realization* (that is – spiritual discernment) *of your individual embodiment – you can truly say*: "*In my flesh I see God.*" And so now comes the admonition which we heard over the years many, many thousands of times, now it means something, spoken from God within yourself. Spoken from God as your invisible Self, it says to the senses and to the mind: "You, be still and know I am God." And so the incorporeality of you reveals itself to your awareness, and you become aware of what you are.

Now, our friend Jacob says it this way and you have to realize these words were written in 1500, 1600, so you have to – probably in the early 1600s, so you have to listen with spiritual discernment in order to see that he is saying exactly what Joel said, and he says:

By means of the introduction of the divine will, man becomes reunited to God and reborn in his nature. He then begins to die relative to the selfishness of the false desire[s] (in him) *and to be regenerated in new power. There is then still attached to him the carnal quality, but in the spirit he walks with God, and thus there is born within the earthly man of flesh a new spiritual man with divine perception and with divine will, killing day by day the lust of the flesh, and by divine power rendering the world – i.e., the external life – heavenly, causing heaven – i.e., the inner spiritual world – to become visible in the external world, so that God becomes man and man God, until finally the tree reaches its perfection, when the external shell will drop off, and it then stands there as a spiritual tree of life in the Garden of God.*

This imbibing of the "Elixir of Life" no man can accomplish by his own mental power. All he can do is to render himself receptive for the divine power. The rest is done by the Spirit of God.

Now you see that? You can feel the consciousness is the same. He is saying that you are reborn, regenerated. You walk in the Spirit with God and you have divine perception or spiritual discernment which reveals to you the life heavenly and *causing heaven, the inner spiritual world – to become visible in the external.* In other words, as you become consciously aware through this rebirth of your own incorporeality, it then manifests itself where before there was only concepts. But he says you can't do this yourself. The mind can't do this. *No man can accomplish this by his own mortal power. All he can do is to render himself receptive.* See? In meditation, in your attitude, and *the rest is done by the Spirit of God.* And so he's in agreement with Joel that the Spirit of God is what brings to your awareness incorporeality when you step out of a personal sense of self or a mind sense of self.

Now to continue in Incorporeality of God, Man and Universe, Joel says:

"In one of my deeper meditations, when I was in full awareness of the incorporeality of my Self, I saw that I could incarnate as a male or

a female. That is because I, God, is neither male nor female. There is only one I. You have never had a beginning. You cannot coexist with God and have a beginning or an ending. You have always lived, you have always lived somewhere, but you may not have lived in the part of the world where you're now living."

So, this incorporeality that you must become aware of, this has always existed. Before the mind formed this concept which you thought was your life, you existed in the invisible. And you exist now in the invisible. In fact, you never left the invisible, and when this concept dies you find yourself standing again in the invisible incorporeality of I, your being, the Father's being, all being.

Now I say to you this: When your day of passing comes, if all you have is a physical sense of self and a mental sense of self, and you're standing in that as it dies, then you will experience death, will you not? That will come to an end. But if you've already died to that, if you've died to that false sense of self, then, well … you're already standing in incorporeality, watching the concept dissolve. And in fact, in fact … if you have died to this physical sense of self, if you have died to a mental sense of self, and if you are standing in your own incorporeality, feeling it with full awareness of it, then what is there to die? When that moment of passing comes, you step out without leaving any of you behind. People may see their concept of you die, but for you there will be no death. You'll be standing in your eternal life. Right?

Now let's see if I can find this other part I wanted to read. Okay, we go back over to Chapter 7 here in the Kailua study series, and he says:

"Our work is not to get rid of the body, but rather <u>to be clothed upon</u> with a new concept of body," or I like better, a new awareness of body. And, *"at some time we will all put off this outer envelope and step out into a higher heritage, for we know <u>that if our earthly house of the tabernacle</u> were dissolved, we have a building of God: <u>An</u>*

house not made with hands eternal in the heavens." That's what we just said. *"Some will die after the flesh, and some will voluntarily lay down this form for a higher one, that mortality might be swallowed up of life."*

Now, you see that? We here in this group have the opportunity to lay down this concept voluntarily here, now. Step into an awareness of incorporeality, of an incorporeal Self, of an incorporeal Supply, of an incorporeal Life, of an incorporeal friend. We will find incorporeality. All right?

Now back over to the book, Incorporeality of God, Man, and Universe.

"Do you understand the point to which I am leading? (Joel asks). *You will never do good spiritual healing work until you attain the inner awareness, not the thought or the belief or the faith — but the inner awareness of the incorporeal nature of man's being. The only image there is of God is man. God appears as man. But since God is incorporeal, man is incorporeal. The fact that man has a corporeal body does not make him corporeal. The fact that he travels in an airplane does not make him an airplane. And the fact that he uses a body does not make him a body? Man himself is the same incorporeality that God is, because they are One, not two. It is God Itself that is living man's life. "Son, thou art ever with me, and all that I have is thine."*

All right? But this must be an inner experience, first in your meditation and later with eyes open. So I put in the margin here some years ago: Joel is telling us in each meditation we must drop the structural life of man including patient and including our self. Then comes the awareness of the truth of being, or incorporeal being, and we rest in that, and healing follows.

But what is it really? Is it really healing? No. We know better now. As he put here: *"A higher concept appears."* That incorporeality dissolves the false concept of self and reveals a little more of the reality, and we call that a healing. So Joel says, *"to live mystically you not only must live as I, but you cannot teach or heal except as you recognize that you are I, whether it's sitting on this side of the table or the other."*

Now, "w*atch the difference, (says Joel), when you begin to accept not only the incorporeality of God, but the incorporeality of man. Then everyday that you live you become younger and stronger because the more of incorporeal life you use, the more you have. You are dealing with an incorporeal God manifest as an incorporeal man. You are living, moving, and have your being in the conscious awareness of this."*

That's the key word – the **conscious awareness** of this. You have the conscious awareness that God is your incorporeal being. God is your incorporeal body. First in your meditation, later with eyes open. And you look at your spouse, your child, your mother, your father – you have the conscious awareness of the incorporeality of their being, which is the incorporeality of your being. "*But—says* Joel—*if you are a human being who has nothing more than a physical body and a mind, then of course what I'm saying to you cannot make sense because you have no capacity with which to receive it."*

And so in this ministry or in the spiritual life you must have this additional faculty of discernment, or none of this can make sense, which is why the wisdom of God is foolishness to man. You go out there on the street and say: "Hey, hey listen Mr. Mailman! Did you know that you're invisible being and all this walking around here is just a concept? And he'll probably say, "well, that's fascinating," and scratch his head and walk away. Or in Mr. Jacob's time, the Church said: "Why this is heresy!" and wanted to burn him at the stake. At any rate, they have no capacity with which to receive it because they haven't had the experience or the awareness of it in meditation.

And Joel says:

"I had a really hard time with business. (He says): *I ended up as broke as anyone has ever been because I was trying to live in a corporeal sense of supply and demonstrate incorporeal supply, and it cannot be done. To attempt it is to tear yourself to pieces!"*

You understand what he is saying there? He is saying this word, this silly little word, incorporeality, a lot of syllables. It must become, we must have this spiritual discernment, this inner capacity, or the Father within must reveal to us the incorporeality of our being, of our mate's being. The incorporeality of our supply. The incorporeality of our health, our life. The incorporeality of our beloved. We really must step out of corporeality into incorporeality. So he says:

"We're carrying forward the unfoldment of the incorporeality of God into the incorporeality of man, the incorporeality of body, and the incorporeality of supply." Now, *"you must know that all supply is incorporeal,* (he says). *When it appears visibly, we attach a corporeal sense to it, but it's just as present now as it ever will be* (in the invisible). *As it manifests, we attach a corporeal sense to it, but it does not necessarily have to be that way."*

"Many persons, in moments of spiritual discernment, have witnessed the incorporeal form of man. I, too, have beheld the incorporeal form hundreds of times, because when a person is in the Spirit, that is all he can behold."

Now that should tell you right there that as you live and move and have your being in Spirit, the only thing you can behold is the incorporeality of those coming to you or those appearing to you.

And so I repeat again where we started: We must be willing to let go of the concept of person and in its place stand still until the incorporeality of them is resurrected in our consciousness and comes out of that tomb. Then, when we see, when we behold, when we are consciously aware of the incorporeality – this then is what we can love forever with all of our mind, heart, and soul.

And by seeing this, it then begins to manifest, and Joel said he did this hundreds and hundreds of times. Sometimes with eyes closed, sometimes with eyes open.

So he says:

"*Unless you have the spiritual vision* (not the mental thought, not the belief – but the spiritual vision) *that can perceive beyond the physical senses and see the incorporeal man and woman, see fruits and trees and crops all as incorporeal, even though you entertain a material sense of them,* (well, unless you can do that) *the crippled man is going to stay crippled.*"

"*The metaphysician who has not succeeded in the spiritual ministry, in healing persons or demonstrating supply or bringing forth fruit has failed because he has had an incorporeal God called Spirit, and he was trying to make It manifest corporeally. And there is no corporeal creation.* Now I have that triply underlined. ___**There is no corporeal creation**___. *It is we who entertain a* **corporeal sense** *of an incorporeal creation!*"

See, we entertain a concept of the invisible. We entertain a concept of incorporeal being, and we love the concept and not incorporeal being. But you are to have no other Gods before me.

So he says:

"*To know God aright you must be unknowing, but to know man aright* (or to know your spouse aright) *you must be equally unknowing. (And) to know supply aright you must be unknowing. You must never deal with corporeality in your spiritual ministry. The fabric of life, which is consciousness, is incorporeal.*" Although it appears as corporeal form, it is really incorporeal form. So if you focus on the concept appearing as form, then of course you'll have to go through the loss of that concept. But if you focus on the incorporeality and the incorporeal form, the word made invisible flesh – ah, this then is eternal and you will – well – "*I will never leave thee nor forsake thee.*"

"*Rising to mystical consciousness in prayer and treatment means rising into incorporeality. You must begin* (says Joel) *with an incorporeal God that you cannot see, hear, taste, touch, smell, or think. Be sure of that last point: you cannot think it. You can know God aright as long as you are not thinking. But if you stop with incorporeal God, your ministry will bring forth only the fringes of healing. The moment you have incorporeal man and you drop his structural appearance, you will stop trying to reduce fevers and lumps. You will stop trying to arrest the aging process, because incorporeal man has none. He was never born and he will never die; he was never born, and he cannot age.*"

"*When you have that man as your ministry, you must have healings.*" And when you have that One, that incorporeal being as your spouse, then you must have love, an eternal love. You must have companionship, an eternal companion. You must have – well, more of that incorporeal being appearing as healings.

"*This is the ultimate truth* (says Joel). *There is nothing left to teach. You cannot go beyond incorporeality. You cannot. You have to* (you—each of you hearing this) *you have to bring forth incorporeality out of your consciousness, bring forth incorporeal man out of your consciousness, incorporeal body and incorporeal supply.*"

Do you see the importance now of why we should seek incorporeality? See the purpose for this talk today? This is a very important principle, incorporeality. And so I suggest that you look at that chapter in Beyond Words and Thoughts, Incorporeality: God, Man, and Universe. I suggest you review, perhaps listen if you have the talks, otherwise read the talk in the Kailua study series, Chapter 7. The talk is called: Understanding the Body, and I suggest you go into meditation and ask that the Father within, or the Presence, or the Christ – whatever you call it – the "I" of your being – reveal incorporeality to you.

Now, let us be still for a moment and see if there's anything else to say.

[Silence]

I of myself am nothing. Yet, there is an incorporeality here. Let it reveal itself.

[Pause]

This is again one of those sayings that surely comes from "*I have more to tell you, but you cannot bear it now*," and perhaps now we're in a way of spiritual discernment where we <u>can</u> bear it. And so you see, the way to eternal life is now in your hands. You can lay down the concept, all of these concepts willingly. You can step right out of the concept, right out of the mind that entertains concepts and stand still, and the Christ of your being will lift you into an awareness, a consciousness of your own incorporeality, which of course, is the incorporeality of all being. And that's all there ever was to the practice of spiritual healing. Simply to recognize this that I am seeing is a concept, and the one seeing it is a concept, and now I let that go and stand here, and I am still, and I would know the incorporeality of God. And then stand there or rest there until incorporeality reveals itself to you. And when incorporeality reveals itself to you and you stand in it and you feel the humming of it, you feel the movement of it, you feel the vibration of it – it melts the concept, and It Itself takes form.

And so it's up to each of you individually to decide: I will die to these concepts and step into my own incorporeality before I leave here. I will do it right here, right now, perhaps in little ways in my meditations at first, yet greater and greater as I go along until I can stand in my incorporeal Self, in my own incorporeality. In the incorporeality of *I*, I stand. Or in the incorporeality of *I*, I rest. And behold God makes all things new. And standing there I never have to taste death again.

And so I wish for you a whole new, happy new self – an incorporeal Self which you can tell no man about, but which you can experience and love with all your heart, mind, and soul and rest in, and it will never leave you because it is you. I wish for you this whole new incorporeal Self.

Blessings.

[Silence]

CLASS 7

WHY SEEK YE THE LIVING AMONG THE DEAD

Bill: Good morning.

This is the first talk of 2013, Sunday morning, January 6th, and it's another Uncomfortable Talk. And if you're not uncomfortable during this talk at some point, I'm pretty sure you're not listening – not deeply listening. Because we're going to discuss some things today that are uncomfortable. I don't like them either. I don't like to look at them. But I need to look at them. I must know the truth, and the truth will set me free. I cannot pretend, and quite frankly, I'm not sure where to start.

I will give you the name of this talk. The principle of this talk is: Why seek ye the living among the dead? And as you recall, that's what the angel said to those that looked into the tomb and were trying to find Jesus Christ and his body, and it wasn't there. The angel said: *"Why seek ye the living among the dead?"* And I'm afraid that when we're practicing the letter of truth, that's what we do. We seek the living among the dead. We try to demonstrate spiritual principles in our human lives, and it will not work. It does not work.

Now, before you sat down and started this talk, what were you thinking about? Let's be honest with yourself now. Take a look, climb up here into the mind and see what were you thinking about? Were you thinking like me that tomorrow's Monday and the children go back to school, and it should be quieter around here? Were you thinking about some chore you had to do today or thinking about returning to work tomorrow? Were you thinking about your body and how you need to go do some exercise or some walking or swimming, take some vitamins? Were you thinking about doing some yoga? Perhaps you were thinking about your finances and paying off those gifts you just bought. Or maybe you're thinking of something you need to do around the house or maybe a repair.

All these thoughts are normal thoughts. Nothing wrong with them. Except for one little thing … what are these thoughts about? All of these normal thoughts are about the world, aren't they? Things you need to do in the world? Maybe things you did in the world. And so these are thoughts about the world, about this world. And of course we know the scripture. We've heard it hundreds of times: "*My kingdom is not of this world.*" Now who's saying that exactly anyway? "*My kingdom is not of this world.*" Who is saying that? Is that some man 2000 years ago saying that to 12 other men and to a handful of women?

Where is Christ? What is Christ? If you have discovered that Christ is the I within you, then you know that that I is saying: "*My kingdom, my realm, is not of this world.*" And yet, when we checked our thoughts a moment ago, all of them were about this world. What do we know about the Christ? If the Christ is not of this world, is the Christ going to have thoughts of this world? No.

The Christ does not function in this world. "*There is no God in the human scene,*" says Joel. No God in this world.

Then if Christ is not having thoughts about this world, who *is* having thoughts about this world? And that would be the mind that thinks about this world, or the world mind. Now, I ask you … how close is that world mind? Was that not the mind that was just functioning in you, the world mind … looking at the world and something of the world? In fact, the world mind while that was going on was functioning as you.

Let's just lay it out there. The world mind was *you*. Because it certainly wasn't the mind which was in Christ Jesus, you know the mind that hears the still small voice. And that mind, that world mind takes a scripture or a truth and attempts to practice it intellectually. That's known as the letter of truth. And of course it may get a comfortable little feeling, but it doesn't demonstrate My kingdom, does it? Because it's trying to pull spirituality and the spiritual kingdom into this world, saying: "Thy Grace is my sufficiency. Thy Grace is my sufficiency. Thy Grace is my sufficiency 300 times a day and thinking that by saying that many times it will produce a miracle out here. All this is the world mind.

Isn't that something? The world mind has been living you and me and all of us. If we have thoughts about this world, concerns about this world, loves of this world, fears of this world, hates of this world then you can be sure that you're listening to the world mind operating your mind. So how close is the world mind? Wow! Pretty close! Therefore, the angel says: "*Why seek ye the living among the dead?*" Why are you still looking at this world? Why are you still hoping to fix this world? Why are you still listening to the mind that speaks of this world? And why aren't we listening to the Christ. Why aren't we seeking the Christ among the living, which is deep within? Which is in Consciousness, not in world mind.

Maybe we don't know how. Maybe we never learned. Maybe we thought that thinking about these truths was sufficient. But if we've been paying attention these last few weeks we know thinking and speaking and writing and reading and listening to truth statements are not the truth. Which is why the voice among the living says: "*I am the truth.*" And so we know we must come out and be separate from the mind thinking about the world, and we know we must be still. We must be silent so that the Christ in us can rise up. That same angel said: "*He is not here. He is risen.*" Stop looking in the tomb of the world mind and expecting Christ to function there. *He is risen*, and so you must rise out of world mind, and in the silence and in the stillness He is risen in you. Christ is risen and you hear its voice.

And that voice says: "(But) w*hosoever drinketh of the water that I shall give him shall never thirst; but the water that I shall give him shall be in him a well of water springing up into everlasting life.*" And that is one of the scriptures that has really haunted me lately because it occurred to me the Christ of me is saying that the conscious awareness of Itself – my conscious awareness of the living Christ within rising up – is in me a well of water springing up into everlasting life.

But what is life? It's not this form. It's not this world. It's not anything in this world. **Life in not in this world** because everything in this world can die. So that's not life when he says springing up into everlasting life. Life existed somewhere before this form appeared, and after this form disappears life will still be somewhere. Life existed before this world. Before Abraham was I AM. Before the beginning I AM. And even unto the end and after the end of the world, I AM. So life is not this world or anything in it.

And so if I have a life in this world, whose life am I looking at? I'm looking at an artificial world mind personal sense of self, and it's not life. Yet, the voice says within, "*If you drink this water*", if you become consciously aware of I, "*then it shall be in you a well of water springing up into everlasting life.*" It shall spring up into a life that the senses have never known. When that world mind is silent something springs up in you, and that something is the life that I AM. It's the real life.

Now, we've all heard this story, but perhaps it's time to hear it again. It's from <u>Practicing the Presence</u>, Chapter 4: The Infinite Nature of Individual Being. And it begins:

There is an old, old story about a great spiritual teacher who knocked at the gates of heaven for admission into paradise. That's what we're doing and have been doing. We've been knocking at the gates of our consciousness wanting to demonstrate Christ. After some time, God came to the door and inquired, *"Who is there? Who knocks?"*

To this query, came the confident response, *"It is I."*

"Oh, I'm Sorry, I'm very sorry. There is no room in heaven. Go away. You will have to come back some other time." Is that not what happens when we try to demonstrate the Christ in this world in a human life, in a world mind life? We hear the same thing or experience the same thing. *Go away.*

The good man, surprised at the rebuff, went away puzzled. After several years, spent in meditating and pondering over this strange reception, he returned and knocked again at the gate. Most of us, if not all of us, have several years attempting to practice these principles and still we stand without in this temporary human, mortal dream life. So after several years in meditation he returned and knocked again. He was met with the same question and gave a similar response. Once again he was told, *"There is no room in heaven; it's completely filled at this time."*

"In the years that passed—now we have more years. It's a long time to live in the letter, isn't it? The teacher went deeper and deeper within himself. You see where he went? Deeper and deeper beyond the world mind to that mind which was in Christ Jesus.

In the years that passed, the teacher went deeper and deeper within himself, meditating and pondering. After a long period of time had elapsed, he knocked at the gates of heaven for the third time. Again God asked, "Who is there?" This time his answer was, "Thou art." *And the gates opened wide* and *God said, "Come in."* Come in. *There never was room for Me and thee."*

And of course we read that and we, as a human being, living in this mortal mind, we read that and we think it's kind of cute and we chuckle at it. Yes, that's right. We might even remind ourselves *"I and the Father are One,"* but nothing happens. We have no real conscious awareness of this, this water that Christ has to give us. We don't drink it. We stay in the mind.

In this same chapter on page 57, Joel says: *"Let God be the only presence."* We read right over that, too, don't we? We think it means that if I just walk around saying, "I and my Father are One, or I am the Life, or I am the Way, or I am the Truth, or I am the Bread," and repeat that to ourselves 315 times a day something will happen in our human experience. This doesn't say that. This says: *"The water that I shall give him shall be in him a well of water springing up into everlasting life,"* everlasting *I.* It doesn't say it'll spring up into a good human experience, does it? And so we see the world mind is the mind in which we live almost all the time, except that we have a little 5-minute or 10-minute excursion into consciousness and hoping to bring up this water, this wellspring of water.

Now we read this last week, but I want to point it out something to you. This is the New Horizon in <u>The Infinite Way</u>. Pay attention to how many times he says *entire* or intimates the word *entire*.

"The sense which presents pictures of discord and inharmony, disease and health – and now we know harmony, health, disease, death, life, a human life, all of these opposites are coming from the same world mind – *is the universal mesmerism which produces the entire* (that's one – the entire) *dream of human existence."* Now that means human existence is, or the entire human existence is a dream, does it not? Doesn't mean just the bad. It means when we were thinking well, tomorrow I believe I'll head on into work, but

first I need to pick up a loaf of bread. It means all of that thinking about this world is a dream. It's a dream, and if we act on it, then world mind is moving our body around, or world mind is moving its body, since this body is not our real body.

World mind is living here because we're permitting it, because we're acting on world thought. World mind says, "Okay, this is what you're gonna do with the rest of today. You still have to get out there and clean up the yard and you have to run that errand and then you need to get home. You have to get dinner on." And so on and so forth. All this is world mind. This is not the mind which was in Christ Jesus. Not listening to a still, small voice. You're not drinking of the water within that springs up into everlasting I. You're acting out world mind. So how close is world mind? World mind is you at that point, isn't it? And so he says:

"*The sense which present pictures of discord and inharmony, disease and death, is the universal mesmerism which produces the entire dream of human existence.* (That's one). *It must be understood that there is no more reality to harmonious human existence than to discordant world conditions. It must be realized that the entire* (that's two) *human scene is mesmeric suggestion, and we must rise above the desire for even good human conditions.*" (All right?) "*Understand fully that suggestion, belief, or hypnotism is the substance, or fabric, of the whole* (which means entire, so that's three) *the substance, or fabric, of the* (entire) *mortal universe and that human conditions of both good and evil* (that's all of them, or the entire conditions) *have no reality or permanence.* So, *be willing for the harmonious as well as the inharmonious conditions of mortal existence to disappear from your experience.*" (That's what you have to do. That's exactly what we're talking about. You have to), "*be willing for the entire mortal existence, good and bad, to disappear from your experience.* (So that's four) *in order that reality may be known and enjoyed and lived.*"

"Above this sense-life there is a universe of Spirit governed by Love." Now that means above this sense-life. Where are the senses? The five senses are taking place in the brain. The brain is this world mind, this - yes, the brain is this world, the world mind. That's where this sense-life is taking place, so above this is a *"universe of Spirit governed by Love, peopled with children of God living in the household or temple of Truth."* And now those that were standing not in this world mind, but above it in Spirit, in consciousness, in the awareness of everlasting I, they were able to see Christ.

They were part of the 500 that saw Christ after the resurrection, because they weren't standing where they saw a dead body, which is all the world mind can see. They weren't thinking about what am I gonna do with that body or can I take it away, can I clean it up? Can I do this, can I do that? No. They were standing above that world mind in Spirit, in consciousness. And there they were able to behold the living Christ. *"He is not here. He is risen. Why seek ye the living (Christ) among the dead?"* Well, that's because I've never learned how to live outside of this world mind. So he says:

"This world is real and permanent: Its substance is eternal Consciousness." Or we might say, everlasting I. Right? *"In it there is no awareness of discords and no awareness of good."* Now there you have it. So, *"The first glimpse of Reality—or the Soul-realm—comes with the recognition and realization of the fact that all temporal conditions and experiences are products of self-hypnotism."* So all temporal conditions might be the same as the entire human scene. Right? *"With the realization that the entire human scene"* (that's number five he uses that word) – *"its good as well as its evil – is illusion, comes the first glimpse and taste of the world of God's creation and of the sons of God who inhabit the spiritual kingdom."*

So when you reach that state that is above the world mind and you're standing in the conscious awareness of that everlasting I, or the living I, then you become consciously aware of that dimension and all who are in it, which is why you can commune with Joel, because he never died, and you can commune with Herb and you can commune with Jesus. And you could commune with Buddha and you could commune with Lao Tzu and you could commune with Shankara, Krishna. You can commune with these beings because they exist there.

"Why seek ye the living among the dead?" You will never find and never be able to demonstrate the living in something that's not alive. Oh, now there's a shock! Because it means that this world mind life that we allow to live us, is dead. *"Why seek ye the living among the dead?"* And again Christ says: *"Let the dead bury the dead."* You come, come up higher and follow Me. And so I submit to you that this personal life that you've been living, that you've been thinking about is nothing more than world thought operating right there where you are.

That's the tomb in which you've been buried, standing there watching world mind live itself. And that's the tomb in which you will be buried if you don't climb out of that tomb. And how do you come out of that tomb? Joel gave us the way in his Kailua study series, and I know you know it. But listen again. Maybe you'll hear it a little differently. He says: *"Achieving that state of consciousness"* (and that's the consciousness where you are come out of the world mind life, and you live out from the living waters, the everlasting I, the immortal Self).

"Achieving that state of consciousness begins in this particular way. First, because the discords and inharmonies of our existence are the most irritating to us and therefore announce themselves more forcefully to us, in those moments we will now train ourselves to resist the temptation to deny or affirm or think thoughts, even good ones." Because we know that's all in the realm of mortal world thought. *"But we will give ourselves an opportunity for the Christ to announce Itself in us and through us, and if necessary to engage that mind while*

waiting for Christ, we will take any one of the Christ messages that begin with the word I, such as "I will never leave you nor forsake you" or "Thy grace is my sufficiency.""

"*Anything, anything that reveals our awareness of the fact that there is a Christ, and that if we give it an opportunity it will come into expression.*" You know, "*I have hidden manna. I have meat to eat the world knows not of.*" That's if you have to entertain this world mind because it won't shut up and you're trying to get still and create an opening through which the everlasting I can manifest, can be, can express, can reveal itself. And so to attain this state of consciousness where the everlasting I is living itself, he says first you meet the discords in this new technique where you don't meet it with any words or thoughts, where you meet it just with silence. Then, he says, "*eventually as I said you will go through this same procedure when you witness the harmonies of life. When you witness a beautiful sunset you will also turn and open a way for the Christ experience to come so that you can rightly see the sunrise and sunset as it is, or the mountain scene.*"

You see that? In the beginning we start with the discords because they press upon us. And so the world thought life discords pressing upon us, and we don't want them, and so we find after passing through the letter of truth – which takes years and years – we return again in our consciousness, so we knock at the gate and Christ within says, "Who's knocking?" And if we are still, all that we can say is, "Thou art" or "It is I" or "Flow, Father. I am listening. I'm still. I'm nothing. Reveal Thyself."

And then in that, the door opens, and he says, "*this will ultimate in the activity of the Christ being a constant experience,*" because after we learn to do that with the so-called discords and inharmonies, now we also have to do it when we catch ourselves saying, "Oh, isn't that beautiful!" Wait a minute what am I looking at? I'm still looking at world thought. What's really here? I don't know. Well, let me go within. Be still. Let me allow Christ to reveal itself here. And so we learn to do it with the discords, we learn to do it with the inharmonies, but then we also start to practice this same thing with the harmonies.

Oh look! A check came in the mail today for $1500! I didn't even know that the government owed it to me, and yet there's a check, a tax refund. Wow! Isn't that wonderful! Yes, God's grace. Wait a minute, what am I doing? What am I doing? This is world thought again trying to color this as something good, but this is not what it seems. What is really here? Let me turn within. Close my eyes for a moment. Father, reveal Thyself. And I listen. Always, always, always I'm creating that opening. I'm creating that opening with the discords, with the inharmonies, with the good things, with the loving things, with the abundant things, with the beautiful things, I am creating an opening with either one, because the good and the bad - well - look again. This is the directions.

Be willing, (you hearing this!), "*be willing for the harmonies as well as the inharmonies to disappear from your experience in order that reality may be known and enjoyed and lived,* because *above this sense-life, there is a universe of Spirit governed by love,*" and so do you want the kingdom, the Spirit governed by love? You want the conscious awareness of the living waters, the everlasting I? Then you must dissolve both the good and the evil of world thought. And this you do by not participating in it anymore, by constantly turning within.

And so now listen. Eventually, as I said, "*you will go through this same procedure when you witness the harmonies of life, when you witness a beautiful sunset,*" says Joel. "*You will turn also and open a way for the Christ experience to come so that you can rightly see the sunrise or sunset as it is or the mountain scene. This will ultimate in the activity of the Christ being a constant experience,*" not one achieved or attained at certain moments of the day or night when you sit down to meditation. No, *"it will now be a constant state of being so that at any time necessary it's only necessary to blink the eye and the activity of Christ will be realized. But it isn't even necessary to do that."*

"The time eventually comes," and I talk about it in all of the writings - there comes a point of transition. NOW LISTEN! *"There comes a point of transition where you pass - you pass from living your own life to having your life lived for you and through you, where you become nothing more than an instrument for the divine experience and you go where you're sent and when you're sent, and you have no will of your own and you have no wish of your own, no desire of your own, and you have no supply of your own, and you never even have health of your own. There is always an It, a Christ, that is living Its own life, and you are going along for the ride."*

So there comes eventually a point, an exact point of transition, where you pass - you pass away. This mortal world thought life passes, and this everlasting *I* lives Itself where you stand. There actually comes, as it did for Joel, an exact point where you pass. This mortal life, this sense-life, this seeing good and evil, this world thought living you passes. It passes away. It dies. And in its place there is a resurrected Christ living. He is risen! And now everlasting I lives Itself, and I am the Bread and I am the Way and I am the Life.

Everlasting. I looked it up. Everlasting means in the old sense - today we think it means everlasting from this point forward, but in the old sense it meant no beginning and no ending. Everlasting was everlasting. No beginning also.

So this life that had a beginning is dissolved at a certain point and everlasting life takes over. That life that has no beginning and no ending, that life that existed before this world thought life was formed. That life that will exist after this world thought life is dissolved. No beginning, no ending, and no interruption. You never come back to living a world thought life.

Now this Christ within you, if you haven't had the conscious awareness of it, it is because you've been listening to world thought, which is pretty easy to do since it's operating as the human mind, your human mind. But if you can become still, if you can listen, if you can practice with the bad - so-called bad and the so-called good things - this turning away and listening and not trying to think a statement of truth, but listening, then you will be fed the bread of life.

"And it came to pass, as he sat at meat with them, he took bread, and blessed it, and broke and gave to them. And their eyes were opened, and they knew him." And this is, of course, after the resurrection. These two gentleman had not risen out of world thought. It was still functioning them and they're walking along discussing Jesus' body and how it was crucified and it was buried and maybe it'll rise and they didn't even know that they're focused on world thought. They thought they were being spiritual. And right in their midst is the living Christ, and they didn't see it. But when they became still and it began to teach them, it took them through the letter until they reached that point where we are – tired of the letter.

After years of meditation he came and knocked again. "Who's there?" Who are you? And he fed them bread, and their eyes were opened. *"Thou art."* And they knew him.

This is your resurrection. This is your transition. Come out of the tomb. *"Why seek ye the living among the dead?"* Come up here into another realm. Come up here and see the living. Come up here into the Christ. Open the gate. Come into heaven.

You must rise in consciousness. You must be lifted up, and as our friend, Jacob, told us last week: It is God in us that must do the lifting. You're totally and completely at the mercy of your own inner Christ. No one can do it in this world. No one can do it that is world thought formed, not even your world thought formed, which is your human life. This must die. *"A corn of wheat"* must be buried, *"but if it die it bringeth forth much fruit."* If it's buried, if you stand in your inner chamber, then you bringeth forth much fruit or you bringeth forth a wellspring of water springing up into everlasting life.

Now we've heard this before too, but let's listen with a new ear, shall we?

"In the beginning was the Word, and the Word was with God, and the Word was God. The same was in the beginning with God."

Now we understand what the Word is, don't we? It's that living water, that everlasting *I*. Before the beginning, I Am. And so the Word was God. This I in the midst of you existed before the world mind formed this human life. And this Word, this everlasting I, *"All things were made by Him; and without Him was not any thing made that was made."* And so this invisible everlasting I made all things, and anything made such as the world thought form was not made. It's an imitation. It's not everlasting. *"In Him was life; and the life was light of men. And the light shineth in darkness; and the darkness comprehended it not."* This light, this everlasting *I*, shines in consciousness, but living in world thought life, we are unaware of it. We don't see it. We don't feel it. We don't know it. We're the dead. Right?

And now let's skip down here a little bit: *"The true Light (which) lighteth every man that cometh into the world. (And that light) was in the world, and the world was made by him, and the world knew him not. He came unto his own, and his own received him not."* See? Nobody could receive that. Not for a long, long time. Years and years.

And a third time he returned to the gates and knocked. *"Who's there?"* To you comes that response now. *"Who's there?"* And are you able to receive Him? Are you able to say, "I am nothing. Thou art" and stand in that or rest back in that? Are you able to stand in the infinite invisible nothingness that you cannot comprehend and simply know "Thou art"?

Because if you can, here's what will happen. *"(But) as many as received him, to them gave he power to become the Sons of God, even to them that believe on his name:"* Or experience his nature. So if you can receive that everlasting *I*, then you will be given power to come out of the world thought form and stand as a Son of God, *"Which are born, not of blood, nor of the will of the flesh, nor of the will of man, but of God."*

You see, there comes an exact transition, an exact point of transition in which you are born of God. You're reborn. *"And the Word is made flesh, and dwells among us."* It's at that point of transition, the Word that existed before the world thought form and that will exist after the world thought form is passed or dissolves, that Word is made flesh **if you can receive it**. If you are one who has come to this point after thousands of years that you can receive this – difficult as it is – uncomfortable as it is – **if you can receive it**, you will be born of God. You will become the Son of God. You will be the Word Itself made flesh, full of grace and truth.

And so today's principle is: Why seek ye the living among the dead? Come up higher. Come up higher and seek the living in the realm of the soul.

"Above this sense-life, he says, there is a universe of Spirit governed by Love, peopled with children of God living in this household, in this temple of truth. This world is real and permanent: Its substance is eternal Consciousness. In it there is no awareness of discords" and no awareness of good. *"Now, in this moment of uplifted consciousness,* when you're standing in it, *"you are able to see yourself free of material, mortal, human, and legal laws. The fetters of finite existence (begin to) fall away."*

"We glimpse the unlimited boundaries of eternal life, infinite consciousness, everlasting I. *The experience at first is going to be*

like watching the world thought form *disappear over a horizon and drop down from before us. There is no attachment to it, no desire to hold onto it – probably because to a great extent (this) experience does not come until a great measure of your desire for the things of "this world"* or this world thought *has been overcome."*

"*At first you will not be able to speak of it. You will have the sense of Touch me not, for I have not yet ascended."* No, I'm not up here permanently, not yet, but I know, I know it's coming. For now "*I am still between the two worlds, so do not make me speak of it because it may drag me back. Let me be free to rise; then when I am completely free of (this) mesmerism,* this world thought form, when I am standing in everlasting I, *I will tell you of many things eyes have not seen nor ears heard."*

And so, "*The first glimpse into the heaven here and now is the beginning of the ascension for us. And the ascension is understood now as a rising above the conditions and experiences of "this world,"* thought life *where you behold the "many mansions" prepared for you in spiritual Consciousness or in the awareness of Reality."* And finally at the end of this it says, "this is the I speaking from that realm." It says:

"*I am breaking the sense of limitation for you as an evidence of My presence and My influence in your experience. I—the I of you—am in the midst of you revealing the harmony and infinity of spiritual existence. I—the I of you—never a person, never a personal sense of I, but the I of you am ever with you. Look up!"*

And so we are promised from one that went before us that made this transition, that rose above the world thought form and rose into the everlasting I and rested there and reached that point of transition where it took over and Christ lived, we are told from one that has completed that: This is the way! Follow me. Walk in this way.

Start with the meeting of discords with the mind which was in Christ Jesus, not with the world mind, and then go on to meeting the harmonies, the opposite side of the world mind, with the same silence, with the same consciousness of Christ, awareness of Christ, and nothing else. Don't meet it with a thought from that thought mind, meet it with the silence, with the awareness of Christ. And then through the practice and the continued practice, we will come again to the third visit where we knock within ourselves, and the Voice says: "Who's there?" and we're able to say, "Thou art." And we will reach that point of transition where Thou, I Christ, the living awareness, the everlasting I, will live where we stand.

And so are we ready? Are you ready to come out of the tomb? To seek the living among the living? Are you ready to die? Are you ready to make this point of transition? I think you are. I feel you are. I know I am. And so let us resolve to walk this way, to follow that Me which has laid it down before us.

But, *"Whosoever drinketh of the water that I within shall give him shall never thirst; [but] the water that I shall give him shall be in him a well of water springing up into everlasting life."* And I am the life, so springing up into everlasting *I Am.*

We thank you, Father, for this hidden path that the world does not know about. Even the world that has read your words, because the world read them while standing in world thought. We thank you that Thou has lifted us out of that world thought where we may hear the word and witness the Word made flesh.

My friends, I love you, and God speed in your journey.

[Silence]

CLASS 8

NO ILLUSION IS EVER
EXTERNALIZED

Bill: Good morning.

The subject for today, the principle of this talk is "No illusion is ever externalized," and that's a quote from Joel's book <u>A Parenthesis in Eternity</u> and the chapter *Reality and Illusion*, which we're going to cover this morning. And I feel it's important, and I don't know if you have the book, so if I read a lot of it, I apologize. I just don't know any better way of getting the message across than to use the words that float out to describe the truth about reality and illusion.

All right, so let's begin right at the beginning of the chapter. I have the book here. Mine's all marked up. I don't know how you do with your books, but mine get marked up. All right, now... the chapter is *Reality and Illusion*, and it's very important because in it he explains that no illusion is ever externalized, and if you think of that, if you look at that, and again I repeat that some of these things really stick with me and they haunt me for a while, and that was one that did.

No illusion is ever externalized.

And the reason why it did is because so many times we hear the expression ... well, this world is an illusion and this world is just not real and this world is a world of universal hypnotism and this world but all the time that we're saying that, we're pointing to a world out here, and if we believe the statement which came through Joel that no illusion is ever externalized, then <u>there is no world out here.</u>

No world of illusion exists out here.

You're not moving through a world of illusion, and if you see that illusion as taking place out here, you've missed the whole point. But he explains it better than I can, so let's get into the chapter, and I'm going to stress parts of it. I didn't want to stress it all, but as I read it again for the umpteenth time this morning, I found that I was underlining practically everything, so I'm sorry (chuckles). But we're gonna look at this chapter. He starts right off with a bang. He says:

To recognize that we live in two worlds, the world created by the five physical senses and the world of Consciousness, is to bring ourselves closer and closer to illumination. Now, the five physical senses take place as we said in the brain, in the mind. So, *to recognize that we live in two worlds, the world created by the* mind *and the world of Consciousness, is to bring ourselves closer to illumination.*

Now we have said that we're going from the letter to the Spirit. Those are perhaps archaic terms, and so to put it in more modern scientific language, we are moving from the mind to Consciousness. And then he gives an example in our Bible. He says:

In the first chapter of Genesis, God made man in His own image and likeness, without any help from anyone. This pure spiritual birth, this immaculate conception, is God manifesting and expressing Himself and His qualities, Consciousness revealing Itself as form. This is the pure, unadulterated, spiritual creation, the immaculate conception of man and the universe, God, the infinite Life expressing Itself individually without any material forms, processes, or systems.

Now you notice he says up here one sentence before this that the first chapter of Genesis is Consciousness revealing Itself as form. Then in the very next sentence he says God expressing Itself individually without any material forms. And there we have the whole secret. There are two kinds of forms! There are two kinds of creation. There are two kinds of body. There are two kinds of whatever. One is the pure, immaculate, invisible form, and one is the forms as seen with the eyes and felt and heard and tasted and touched.

In other words, one is invisible form which you behold while you're standing in Consciousness in that high mountain of transfiguration you behold Consciousness formed. Or down here in the human mind you behold the mind and its many forms. You see? Which is why he gave us the Kailua talk, talk #8 I believe, on Flesh and Flesh. *Yet, I will behold God in my flesh* means in the invisible Consciousness formed. But *all flesh is grass* means the mental images.

And so no illusion is ever externalized. There is no illusory world out here. It's all taking place in the human mind, and it gets worse than that. I told you these talks are uncomfortable.

So, in the first chapter of Genesis we see Consciousness formed. But:

In the second chapter of Genesis, God not only creates, but He miscreates, and because of His mistakes He has to do it over and over again. He "forms man of the dust of the ground," and then, He brought forth woman from man's rib, and finally He decided to bring forth man and woman for the purpose of creation. This man of earth, "the natural man" which is what the second chapter of Genesis is talking about, created by Lord God, which is mind, the human mind, is not under the law of God, and "neither indeed can be," in fact, it is not a man at all: it's a mythical creation of the human mind.

Now there you go. And so are you standing in the human mind, looking out and believing all these images are out there, or are you standing in Consciousness, beholding the one infinite spiritual body of God?

Now, let us turn the page. There's nothing else underlined here. Let's see;

If we could erase from our thought everything that we have ever heard or read about a person—We talked about this last week or the week before—*If we could erase everything we've ever heard or read – everything and every opinion that we ourselves have formed* and say, "Father, wipe all this away. I'm willing to start all over. Here's a blank slate. Show me, Father. *Show me this man as he is. Show me his nature. Reveal him to me.* If we could do that *we would find that by turning within with a listening ear, the truth would be revealed to us. In this way we would know him aright. The I of him would be born in us immaculately.*

That's how healings happen. Joel didn't set out to heal. He set out to attain spiritual Consciousness, which is standing in Consciousness beholding the One. And when people came to him and said, "Would you help me please? I have a headache." And he turned within and said, "Well, Father, I don't know how I can't help anybody, and I can't even change this picture." So he stopped right there. Joel stopped, and in that silence, in that vacuum, in that listening he calls it, in that standing still in Consciousness he beheld and beholds the one infinite being. And that one infinite being and its form, because of his awareness of it, appears. And the person taps Joel and says, "Oh, thank you!" And Joel did nothing except stand still and behold.

And so, as we said a week or two ago: If you have love or fear or hate of anything in this world, then you're loving or fearing or hating a mental image. Yes, even that includes your wife, your spouse, your partner, your husband, your children, your grandparents. Remember? And that's kind of uncomfortable. That's really uncomfortable. Yet, we are entertaining concepts which are within. No illusion is ever externalized.

All these people are not out there! I'm sorry! (chuckles). It's true! No illusion is ever externalized. All of this is a creation of the human mind. Your entire world that you've been living in is taking place in the mind. You've never gotten outside of the mind unless through meditation you've stepped out briefly and you beheld the spiritual creation or Consciousness formed.

And so he recommends that you turn to God. Say, "I don't know her. I don't know him. Let me drop all those mental images now. What's really here, Father? What's really here? Show me. Reveal him, reveal her as they are." And then in that stillness, if you attain that silence and the mind stops functioning temporarily, even briefly, only even for a glimpse, you will behold Consciousness formed, the first chapter of Genesis. See that? And so he says:

Are you beginning to see how much we all have accepted about God and about one another without any real knowledge? Or awareness, or recognition, or realization? All right here we go:

The world that we see, hear, taste, touch, and smell is the world the Master overcame, but it's not a real world. Now you can't say that and hang onto part of it. You can't say, "well, it's not a real world, but I like this. I'm gonna hang onto this part. I've known him for a long time, and he's my best friend, and I like the way he does this and he does that, although he has some character defects which I don't really like. You know, sometimes he overeats a little bit." Now wait a minute! You can't say this world is an illusion – hang onto part of it because you like it!

This is all or nothing. <u>All or nothing</u>. No illusion is ever externalized. So when he says here it's not a real world, it's a world formed by our sense impressions or by the mind. He is saying **it's in the human mind**. There's no world out here. It's in the human mind.

What's out here, what's everywhere in and out is Consciousness formed. You're standing in the kingdom, dreaming your life away in a this world that's only internal and all the characters in it. Remember – this world is a stage and we're all characters says Shakespeare? He wasn't kidding. He wasn't being just poetic. He was declaring the truth. "Nothing is good or bad but thinking makes it so." Right? The world is a stage, and we're all actors, all characters on the stage.

And so if you've fallen in love, isn't that terrible to contemplate? Doesn't it make you really squirm in your chair like it does me? If you've fallen in love, you have fallen in love with a mental image that isn't even out there. Ah, but are you brave enough to face that and say, "Well, wait a minute now. Come on! I want to awaken. I want to awaken. Show me! Show me the truth, Father. What's really here?" If you're brave enough to do that, then - well - how did he put it? The I of them will be born in you immaculately. Which means you'll have awareness of it. You'll have feeling of it, and that is the eternal life that you can love forever.

Now, let's read this paragraph uninterrupted, because I feel it's important.

The world that we see, hear, taste, touch, and smell is the world [that] the Master overcame, but it is not a real world: it is a world formed by our sense impressions, by the mind, *by what we like or dislike at the moment. So it is that this world of the second chapter of Genesis, the world of a man created out of dust, [of a] woman created out of a rib, and (of) children created from the union of man and woman – this is not a world, this is a dream.*

You can't make it any plainer than that. You know, I don't know how people read over these paragraphs in these pages in these chapters in these books and just go on down the street. I mean it shocks the heck out of me! It makes my thinking stand still, which is what it was designed to do, I suspect. And in the stillness I have seen many things which eyes and ears have not seen. Now:

This world of sense impressions is not under the law of God.

Now doesn't that make you kind of shake a little bit, kind of fearful? It did me the first time I saw it. Wait a minute, wait a minute! I'm living in this world created by the senses. I never get outside of my mind, and that world is not under the law of God. Anything can happen! **Anything!** I could get hit by a train tomorrow. Lightning could strike the top of my head. That person I love the most could die and never return. Yes, anything can happen. It's a horrible dream. I don't think it's very nice.

Oh, there are nice parts to it. You can say, well, isn't that rainbow lovely? Isn't that bubbling stream nice? But tomorrow the rainbow becomes a hurricane or a tornado, and the bubbling stream becomes contaminated with ingredients spewing forth from a factory a mile away. Now, that's not a world. Oh, and the woman that you love can run off with another guy. I mean this is—you're spending your whole lifetime and I am spending my whole lifetime and all of us are spending our whole lifetimes believing that we're living lifetimes!

And as he gets into this chapter, the whole point is to try to take one of the opposites and change it. Well, we'll get into it in his words.

The world that we can see, hear, taste, touch, and smell is not under the law of God, and yet this very world that we are living in, which is the kingdom, is under the grace of God when we see through the appearance to Reality.

And so I submit to you, here is the whole answer. All these books comes down to this. If you can see through the mind world and stand still, get out of that even for a moment, catch a glimpse of the world of Consciousness formed, of My kingdom of Spirit, of the Light, of the one Self, then you come under grace.

So In this world created by the senses, the unreal world of mental images, we are deceived by appearances because in "this world" we are faced always with the pairs of opposites. Unlike My kingdom everything in this world has its opposite: up, down; health, sickness, life, death; wealth, poverty; good, evil; purity, sin; white, black; gain, loss.

There is nothing in the world of sense that does not have its opposite, and if we analyze our experience, we will see that life is just a continuous effort—Human life is just a continuous effort—*to change one of the pairs of opposites into the other(s).*

Haven't you analyzed it? Haven't you looked at this human life you were living and seen that you're trying to change, you're trying to get just enough supply or put away enough for retirement, and that's trying to change lack into abundance. You're trying to find the right partner, the right mate, the right spouse, right husband, the right wife, and that's trying to change loneliness into companionship, or aloneness into companionship. Or you're trying to go to the right doctor or find the right herbs or the right yoga positions or the right exercises or the right diet to make your health good, change it from bad health to good health. And we do this over and over and over. We try to find the right job. We try to find the right career. We try to find the right this, the right that, and always they're changed from right to wrong. We're in the middle of a job that we love and suddenly it gets worse. Somebody comes in there that becomes our supervisor that's really horrible to work for. Now we have to leave that one and go looking again for the right..., and a whole lifetime passes and – Bam! 60 years are over. Ten or twenty more years, you're dead.

You lived a whole series of mental images and never got outside and never stepped foot into My kingdom. Oh, you may have read about it. You may have read about it a lot, but you have no awareness of it. In the kingdom of God we not only do not have all these pairs of opposites, we do not have even one of them. We do not have life any more than we have death. Now, I think I've told you this, but if I did, I'll repeat and if I didn't, then listen.

In the kingdom of heaven we do not have life any more than we have death. Now you and I, we have been thinking in terms of the only life we knew, which is this individual human life. Right? And we read the words everlasting life, eternal life, and we think of this life going on, going forward. But in the kingdom of heaven we don't have death, but we also don't have life.

What? That's right, that's right. Well then, what is meant by the word everlasting life? What is everlasting life? This everlasting thing that is never changing, never changed, never born, never dying. It's not alive, it's not dead. What? Yeah it's not alive, it's not dead. It's something else. There's a third choice. We don't know what that is. We give it names. We say "being." That doesn't mean anything. What is it, Father. Reveal to me. What is this everlasting life? What is life? I don't even know what that word means. You see? And I'm not gonna tell you what's been revealed to me. You need to take that in your own meditation.

On the next page he says: *The kingdom of God is the realm of being.* Isn't that weird that I'm explaining things to you and it's coming out exactly what's next in the book, and I have no way of knowing. I didn't memorize it. Anyway, *The kingdom of God is the realm of being, divine being — not live being because life has its opposite, death; but being — possessing no degrees, amounts, quantities, or qualities. "The darkness and the light are both alike to thee."* That's another one that can haunt you. *"The darkness and the light are both alike to thee."* That means the bad weather, the bad relationship, the bad health, and the good health, the harmonious weather, the harmonious relationship, the harmonious supply — they're both alike to thee who has seen through them. So he says:

In this world of the senses, there is good and evil, and there is the centering of attention on changing the evil into good. But, *In "My kingdom," we ignore the appearance(s) and seek to realize spiritual truth, to realize God's grace, and God's presence, and God's power.*

The moment that we feel a conscious oneness with God, the appearance changes. And now, to our human sense, the evil appearance now has a good appearance, the appearance of lack has an abundant appearance, and the sick appearance has a well appearance. But we are not fooled by the changed appearance. We know that in seeking the kingdom of God within, we are merely beholding Reality, or Consciousness formed. *We are merely beholding Reality appearing. We come face to face with God; and we see Him as He is, and we are satisfied with that likeness.*

So you see, again and again and again what he did was not healing work. What he did was he shut out the senses. He created a vacuum. He said he has in the Kailua study, he said I have a knack for resting. That means resting out of the mind and just waiting upon the Lord. Standing still in Spirit. Remaining silent and receptive to Consciousness. And then there's the movement. Consciousness reveals itself, reveals Its form, and he said in the Kailua study, said Joel, I myself have beheld that spiritual form dozens and dozens of times. Remember? And catching the awareness of that, then the appearance changes and more of Reality, more of God appears.

Why? **Because you live in your awareness.** You're not doing these tricks like waving a magic wand and healing somebody. You're living in your awareness, and if you're aware only of the mind and its images, then that's what you see – good and evil. Sometimes good, sometimes evil. But if you've learned *"not by might,"* no physical effort, *"nor by power,"* no taking thought, but *"by My Spirit,"* by Consciousness revealing Itself, and if you've learned how to meditate according to the Kailua study series, chapter 10 and chapter 12, then you are beginning to catch glimpses of Consciousness formed. And when you catch glimpses of that when you have **awareness,** not thinking or thoughts or ideas or theories but outside of the mind, you catch a glimpse. You have an awareness of Consciousness, then it appears. And when you have awareness of only the mind and good and evil, then it appears.

You stand and you live and you move and you have your being in your awareness.

All right? So, now listen to this next part. This next part is so very important.

This page and a half is the reason for this entire talk.

To understand the illusory nature of the finite world is to grasp the kernel of all mystical teaching to understand the illusory nature and the fact that it's not externalized *but if it is misunderstood, it can act as a deterrent to progress as it has in India which has one of the noblest spiritual heritages of any nation on earth.*

Perhaps the greatest of all the Indian seers was Gautama the Buddha whose revelation of absolute truth was so profound that while there are other revelations equal to it, there are none which have surpassed it. He had the full realization of the one Self, the one I which constitutes the Consciousness of the universe, and he himself understood and proved that the appearance-world is maya, or illusion. And Because of its fruitage, his message spread like wildfire across all of India.

Now the fruitage was his awareness appeared as harmonious being inside and out, his awareness of this. Like Joel, he had the awareness of the nothingness of the hypnotic mind, but he also had the awareness of the allness of Being, and resting in that awareness, people that came around him felt it and were lifted up, and some received healings and some received awareness themselves. And so the fruitage—that's the fruitage. And, *because of the fruitage, his message spread like wildfire across all of India, but*—listen to this, because many of us in The Infinite Way make this mistake:

But his teaching of maya or illusion was misunderstood. The belief that the world is an illusion led to a do-nothing attitude, a passive acceptance of the evil conditions in the world. His followers failed to see that it's not the world that is illusion.

Before we do that, before we go there, I want to point out what he's referring to. If you've ever seen pictures and photographs or talked to people from India and that part of the world who misunderstood Buddha's teaching of maya and illusion, then you'll hear such statements as, "Well, it's just my karma. I can't do anything about it. I guess it'll just take 2 more lifetimes or 10 more, however many it takes for this karma to be lifted." And so he says it leads *to a do-nothing attitude, a passive acceptance of the evil conditions* and it does. I have a friend from India in Florida, another friend in Australia, and another friend—well, I call him a friend, but he's the author of I Am That. I guess his name is hmm, hang on a minute. I'll look it up. I Am That, and his name is Sri Nisargadatta Maharaj.

Anyway, he's a mystic, and I have no doubt about the authenticity of his experiences because he explains things you can't know unless you are experiencing I am That. But he also suffered from lung cancer because he chain smoked. He had a tobacco store, and he chain smoked, and he had cancer. And he says in there himself it's just something the body's going through and it's no big deal. It's an illusion all the time talking about God and his very real realization of God. So you see, my friend in Florida, he does the same thing. He has a drinking problem. He also has deep experiences of God in his meditation, and his wife is saying, "You need to stop drinking! You have to stop. You have to take responsibility. You have to get a job. You have to do this. I mean, I'm supporting, I'm raising the kids." And he's going on with "Well, it's just an illusion. It's just an illusion. What's the big deal? You should eat, drink, and be merry." And then my friend in Australia says the same thing. This is an illusion. It's just something the body is going through. It's just karma. It's the karma of the body. Don't worry about it. You just attain your single focus on I am That.

Now – Joel says that's a misinterpretation! He says that's a misperception. So he says:

His teaching of maya was misinterpreted. The belief that the world is an illusion led to a do-nothing attitude, a passive acceptance of the evil conditions in the world. His followers failed to see that it is not the world that is an illusion. The world is real. It has to be real. You're standing in the kingdom. *The world is real: the illusion is in the misperception of the eternal, divine, spiritual universe which is the only universe there is, and which is here and now.*

You see that? Where is the illusion? **Get this concrete!** Get this! Well, get this.

No illusion is ever externalized. Every time you catch yourself saying, "Well, that's an illusion out there," **STOP IT!** Correct yourself. No—this is mind. This is the human mind. I want to step outside of this. Father, what's really here? You can ask <u>that</u> in your meditation. And when He reveals Himself, you'll know that you're standing in Consciousness formed in My kingdom. And so Joel says here:

Because of an illusory sense of a spiritual universe, the mortal scene appears as mortality with all its errors, whereas it is in reality [a divine kingdom], a divine universe. This world is God's world; it is the temple of the living God; but when we see it with finite eyes and ears, we see and hear an illusory picture of the reality that is there. The illusion is in the mind that is falsely seeing the kingdom as this world: the illusion is never out in the world. An illusion cannot be externalized. An illusion is a deceptive state of thought, and it can take place only within a person's mind, not outside of it.

He mentions also elsewhere that it's taking place only in the human mind, and there's only one human mind, and I'll leave that with you to look at deeper. There is only one human mind.

Now, do you see the principle? No illusion is ever externalized.

I've done some work in mental hospitals because I got a degree in counseling, and I used to go into mental hospitals, some of the state hospitals. I've been to Camarillo in California and other places, and the people that are there really believe what they tell you. If you walk up and you say, "Hi. My name's Bill Skiles and I'm a therapist. I'm gonna run a group today." You might get somebody very nice sticking out their hand and saying, "Hi. My name is Napoleon Bonaparte," and the other hand's stuck inside of their shirt, you know. Or you might get someone saying, "Oh, that's very good my child, and my name is Jesus." Now they're living in that delusion in their mind, are they not? Yes, they are. Now, <u>but so are you</u>! You thought you were well and healthy. Ha-ha! Surprise!

You're just as insane, which is why we have to be restored to sanity. We have to have a spiritual awakening and awaken out of the insanity of the illusion. So, the illusion, pinpoint it where it is is in the human mind and the mental images. When we said last week this makes you uncomfortable when you ask how close is the world mind, only to discover the world mind has been <u>your</u> mind, and you've been living it and allowing it to live as you.

Ah, but now here comes this person doing all these healings and the message is spreading like wildfire, and you get a hold of it and what is this, what is this all about? And you discover first: "Hey, I can apply some of these principles and turn lack into supply, and I can turn loneliness into companionship, and I can turn ill health or sickness into harmonious physical health." And you think that that's the whole purpose of The Infinite Way. Ah, but then you dig deeper and the years pass, and maybe these principles stop working as Joel says in the original book, <u>The Infinite Way</u>. They stop working.

Let's see if we can find that. Hang on - Yes, he says in *Our Real Existence*:

The advancing student will gradually relinquish his attempts to improve humanhood or to improve beliefs in order that the truth of spiritual existence may unfold in his consciousness. You see that? And he says in *Putting On Immortality*:

The first years of a student's search are devoted to overcoming discords and healing disease through prayer to some higher Power. The day arrives, however, when he perhaps discovers that the application of truth to human problems does not "work" or does not work as it once did. Eventually, he is led to the great revelation that mortals only put on immortality, as mortality disappears—they do not add immortal spiritual harmony to human conditions.

You see that? So, the day eventually comes when you have the great revelation – and hopefully you've had it – that you cannot add Consciousness formed to this human life. You cannot add Consciousness formed to the mind's images! Stop trying! It never was what it's about. In fact, he says here in *Our Real Existence*:

There is a constant warfare between the flesh and the Spirit and maybe you're experiencing that, *and this will continue as long as we entertain any degree of corporeal sense.* That is, material forms. If you have any degree of material forms – if you still see a he, a her, an it, a corporeal creation, then you're going to be involved in this warfare, and *the attempt to bring Spirit and its laws to bear upon material concepts constitutes this war. Peace can only come when the structural sense of universe and the corporeal sense of man have been overcome.*

And Jesus says, "I have overcome the world." And in the Kailua study series, Joel says he did it in one fell swoop. Yes, he did. He stepped out of the mind concept and beheld the glory of the father. Consciousness formed. Again and again and again. Perhaps you're called upon to do healing work. That's good, because that means that you will have the opportunity to behold Consciousness formed.

Now back to *Reality and Illusion* we're almost done with it in <u>A Parenthesis in Eternity</u>. He says, I'm gonna read this paragraph again. It's probably the most important paragraph you'll ever read on illusion.

"Because of an illusory sense of the universe the mortal scene appears as mortality with all its errors, whereas it is in reality a divine universe. This world is God's world; it is the temple of the living God.

Now, that's all that's out here. So if you ever see anything other than the temple of the living God, other than Consciousness formed, you are living in an illusion in your mind, which is the only place illusion can be. So:

This world is God's world; it is the temple of the living God; but when we see it with finite eyes and ears, what we see and hear is an illusory picture of the reality that is really there. The illusion is in the mind, falsely seeing the world or the kingdom: the illusion is never out in the world. An illusion cannot be externalized. An illusion is a deceptive state of thought, and it can take place only within a person's mind, not outside it.

With our human eyesight we see a world constantly changing. All of this is an illusory picture in the human mind, but because there is only one human mind, it's an illusory picture in your mind and mine. And Such a world has no externalized existence.

And neither do any of the people in that world! Neither do any of the corporeal forms, the material forms. He says over and over there is no structural universe, and we nod our heads and smile. Isn't that spiritual, isn't that nice, and then go live in a structural universe! What's going...? **LISTEN! OPEN YOUR EYES! HEAR IT!**

We are aware of the world through our senses, but what the senses cognize is illusion, an illusion not outside the mind but in it. And to be able to understand and grasp this idea is also to be able to grasp the idea that this illusion cannot be corrected out here. That's why prayer fails. People are trying to improve an illusion which – he says trying to improve or add God to our humanhood in The Infinite

Way – *They're trying to improve an illusion which, if they succeeded in doing, would still be an illusion except it would be a good illusion instead of a bad one.*

So, *God is not in "this world,"* which is taking place in the mind.

Now he says there is a theory or a belief called pantheism which teaches that God is manifesting Himself as this world, and that's not true. God's not manifesting Himself as these mental concepts, which is why they can be smashed and changed and destroyed. He says if this were true, if this world were really a manifestation of God – now remember, this world is the world in the mind – there's no "this world" out here. There's only My kingdom out here.

THIS WORLD, THIS WORLD, THIS WORLD IS IN THE MIND, THE MIND, THE MIND.

So, *If this were true and this world and the mind were a manifestation of God and made in the substance of God, it would be eternal.*

People would live forever. You could drive your car; it would never wear out. You'd have trees forever. Okay?

But the substance of the forms we behold are not that substance which is God. Right? That which is made is not made of that which doth appear *and once we perceive that, we shall understand the true meaning of the word "illusion," which is that our perception of what we behold constitutes the illusion.*

So, this world is what? Perception! And perception in the mind constitutes the illusion. You're standing in the Kingdom, living lifetime after lifetime in the mind. We're not moving from letter to Spirit. We're moving from mind to conscious awareness. We're moving from mental images, thoughts, my thoughts to Thy thoughts. We're moving from thinking to awareness of Consciousness formed. We are undergoing a transformation, a transfiguration. Now listen. Other than pantheism there is also one called theism. And that: *regards God and the world as two distinct substances* and he says: *How impossible it would be for God, the creative Principle, to create anything unlike Itself.*

So see there's not God and this world out here. You've got to stop that! You'll never get out of it if you think it's out here. So, he says:

The next question is: What about this physical universe? And, *The answer to that is, "My kingdom is not of this world." "This world" is the Adam dream; this world is mortal concepts; this world is mental projections. When we recognize this and are able to close our eyes and realize*—become aware, recognize, have the awareness of—*I in the midst of us, then this body loses its sense of mortality*—or corporeality, and I have overcome the world. See that? *And it becomes what God's world really is—harmonious and perfect.*

And so he says: *The truth is that God is Spirit, Consciousness, and therefore all that really exists is God formed, or God in manifestation.*

So the world that you see with the senses and everyone in it is a world in the mind, and it's illusion in the mind. If you can step outside of that even for a moment and behold My kingdom, then your awareness will be what you're living. But he says you can't do this with the mind because that's the very one that's hypnotized.

It takes spiritual discernment to know the things of God. So he says: *Let us not look [out] at this visible world and call it spiritual,* because we're not really looking <u>out</u> on a physical world; we're looking <u>in</u> at mental images of a physical world. So let's not call it spiritual and let's not *call it a creation apart from God. Let's cleave to the Middle Path which leads back within our spiritual center* where we can say, "Father, what is really here?" And we see the Christ of God. *No human being can look upon physicality* with his mind and detect Christ. Only the Christ can reveal the Christ.

When the Master asked, "Having eyes, see ye not? Having ears, hear ye not?" he was referring to spiritual discernment or Christ-consciousness. If you can look through the appearance to

the Christ, the Christ ever-present, or Consciousness formed –
although not apparent to your eyes, you will be able to break the
mesmerism and when you break the mesmerism through your
spiritual discernment, you will behold the spiritual nature even of
a dying person. Which is how Lazarus came forth. All right? We
in The Infinite Way must learn to look *through the appearance with
inner discernment and there behold the invisible, spiritual child of
God who was never born and will never die, eternal right here* now.

Miracles can be performed by the person who does not try to heal.
You see that now? Where is there to heal? You need to step
outside of the images that say they need healing. You need to step
outside of the belief that you can do anything. You need to step
into this eternal silence, into a Sabbath from thought taking and
allow God to reveal Itself. And so he says:

On the spiritual path, we do not try to change an external world
because there isn't one! There's only My kingdom out there. *We
seek nothing of the world: we seek only the realization of My kingdom.*

*When we see fruit on the trees, we are seeing the fruitage of
an invisible life* and that's what we want to become aware of.
Remember in The Infinite Way, well, in the Kailua study talks
he talks about in The Infinite Way discussing the orange tree in
that chapter on supply and how not very many people that he has
met in The Infinite Way have connected that up with the truth
of being? Remember that? Well here he's saying it again because
he must have had a profound experience looking at a fruit tree,
because he discusses it a lot. So he says here:

*When see fruit on the trees, we are seeing the fruitage of an
invisible life, an invisible activity* and that's what we have to become
aware of *an invisible unfoldment appearing visibly.*

We have to become aware of Consciousness formed, and this
awareness comes to you first in your meditation, later with eyes
open. So finally he says, to wrap this up:

When enlightenment has been attained, the temporal picture is recognized for what it is: maya or illusion. Then when we are faced with evil people or erroneous conditions, we don't fight them and we don't try to get God to do something to them.

We relax! Again he says he has a knack for relaxing. We relax out of the mind. We relax out of the body and we relax out of the mind, knowing that this is an illusion in the mind.

And when we awaken from beholding the mortal dream we will see one another as we are we will discover that our neighbor is our Self. Because we will see there is only one Self, and I am That Consciousness formed.

All this will become apparent to us, not through knowledge, but because we have developed a deep inner spiritual awareness. The object of The Infinite Way is to develop this spiritual awareness.

The goal is attaining the spiritual vision, so that we can behold God's universe we can commune with Him, walk and talk with Him, live with Him - Okay?

The attaining of some measure of this spiritual vision is enough. It is an awareness that reveals that God is Spirit, that all that really is must be spiritual, and there will never be any confirmation of this through our eyes because Spirit [or Consciousness] cannot be seen with the eyes. The eyes must be closed to sense so that we can inwardly behold God's creation. It is a matter of attaining a depth of inner awareness, says Joel, *an awareness that expresses itself not so much in words or thoughts as in feelings.*

And feelings doesn't mean emotions. It means intuition or awareness. I like awareness better than feelings.

Now do you see the principle today? The principle is: No illusion is ever externalized. Right? Now listen. A couple of things. A Hindu friend of mine sent me a poem from Shankara, which as you know – or maybe you don't – but Joel really liked Shankara. And here's the poem, and it came to me just today, which was really quite fantastic because, well, it's just that there's no way that he could know I was going to have this topic: No illusion is ever externalized, and yet, out of Consciousness formed comes this poem to us today. And it says:

When one sees the image of the world within him,
The world appears as if it is outside.
It is similar to his seeing due to illusion,
During the state of sleep, the one real fact appears as many different truths,
And he realizes, when he wakes up and sees the reality,
That he is really the one and only one soul.

Isn't that beautiful? That's just exactly what we were talking about. Just exactly it. And when you have that inner awareness, when you have the inner consciousness, the inner seeing and knowing and beholding of Consciousness formed, or My kingdom, then you will have that inner experience which is portrayed in the mount of Transfiguration. You see, the mount is a high level of consciousness in which you behold Consciousness formed, or the Body of God, or the one Soul, or the one Self. And here's how it was explained.

And after six days, Jesus took Peter, James, and John and bringeth them up into a high mountain apart, And was transfigured before them: and his face did shine as the sun, and his raiment was white as the light.

Now that was Matthew's interpretation. Here's Mark's.

And he said unto them, Jesus said unto them, *"Verily I say unto you, That there be some of them standing here, which shall not taste of death, till they have seen the kingdom of God come with power."*

And after six days took them with Peter, and James, and John, and leadeth them up into a high mountain apart by themselves: and he was transfigured before them. And his raiment became shining, exceedingly white as snow; so as no fuller on earth can white them.

You see that? Both of these people had that inner experience when Jesus took them up higher and lifted them high into Consciousness **out of the mind** – they saw the Body of Christ, and that's your body. There's only one Self, one Soul. When you're lifted out of the mind of these many forms – which now you know aren't out here – they're only in the human mind. When all of that is released, if only even for a moment, you will experience the transfiguration and you will see Consciousness formed, the first chapter of Genesis. You will see the Body of Christ and you will see a face shining as the sun and raiment white as the light. This is what you will see, and you will be beholding Consciousness formed, the real creation, My kingdom, in which you stand now.

Now I had a similar experience, as I've said many times in my talks, when I attended Herb Fitch's seminar in Avila Beach, northern California, and in that experience he was speaking on stepping outside of time and I was in meditation. I felt lifted up on a high mountain you might say. It was a high experience of Consciousness, and when I opened my eyes everywhere my eyes looked I could feel myself in that and that in me. I could feel that I am That, and the entire world, the entire creation was in my being, and I could feel it. But I could also feel that I was the only being appearing as all that. And so I lived and moved and had my being in the awareness of Consciousness formed. And since then it has happened in meditation many times.

Well, we're out of time. This talk is gonna run out this tape, so just let me say the principle is: No illusion is ever externalized. And wrestle with that until you make some progress and come into the awareness of Consciousness formed, the perfect spiritual creation of God.

Blessings.

[Silence]

CLASS 9

LEAVE YOUR NETS

Bill: Good morning, my friends.

I don't know if today's talk is going to be very long or not. It may be just only 15 minutes. I don't know.

I wish I could just close my eyes, get that feeling of the Presence of the Christ, feel that inner humming, and transmit that through this talk. And then there would be nothing to say, because that's the whole purpose of The Infinite Way is to bring the seeker to that point of contact, and then in a moment of resting, in a moment you think not, to that experience called communion, union with the I with God.

I don't know how it is for you, and I might have mentioned this before, but if I didn't I'll say it now. There are some things that I hear, some things that I read, and even some things that come to me as a thought that stop me in my tracks. They short circuit my thinking. It comes to a stop. I don't do it. I don't even try to do it. But my thinking comes to a stop, and there's an inner feeling that goes with it, and the only way I can describe it is an inner vibration, and I don't mean a physical vibration either. It's a spiritual vibration. It's a high humming. It's like when you take a pitchfork and you tap it and there's that hum. And that's the way this feels.

Something comes into my awareness the written word, the spoken word, which is the word of God. I might read it or hear it or think it or receive it within, but when it comes there is this inner, there's this moment of silence in which an inner vibration is felt. A hum, a spiritual humming. Not a noise. No, yet a hum. And I know that I must be still because there's something about this that is going to be revealed.

And so when I say to you that some of these scriptures haunt me, I mean that they set up this feeling, and I know that there's more to be revealed, and I must be still and let it come forth. And it may come forth in the next 5 minutes, 5 days, or even 5 months. I haven't had one take 5 years like Joel did when he said he sat in the airport and received the words "Beyond Words and Thoughts" and wrote it down and wrote a little paragraph and nothing else came for 10 or 12 years. I haven't had one like that. But sometimes - well, I've had many, many that come within a few days or a few minutes or a few hours.

And there's two words that do that to me, have always done that to me. I can see them, I can read them, I can hear them within, and I have that inner vibration, and I know that they are from Christ. And those two words are "*hidden manna.*" They come from the Revelation of St. John 2:17, and it goes like this:

He that hath an ear, let him hear what the Spirit saith unto the churches; To him that overcometh will I give to eat of the hidden manna.

There's a lot there. That's only half of the sentence, but in that half we have: *He that hath an ear.* That means if you're able to be still within, if you're able to listen, not with your mind, not with your physical ears, but on a higher level - if you're able to listen, you're able to be still and let it be revealed, then the Spirit says to you: *To him that overcometh*—if you will overcome I will give you—*hidden manna.*

And what is it that you are to overcome? Well, of course it's not out here, but it's within, and it's everything must be laid aside so that you can stand there as an opening, a pure opening and receive something called hidden manna.

Now, this does not have anything to do with overcoming your bad habits. I mean, maybe you made a New Year's resolution to stop smoking or to stop eating meat or to – I don't know –whatever your current beliefs are as a human. Maybe you made a New Year's resolution to stop being so critical of your family members and friends or to save money. In one way or another you made a promise to yourself to try to overcome something, and well I recently made kind of a small promise to myself that if time allowed I would walk every other day at least a mile, and I've been keeping to that, except when it's raining so hard I can't walk outside without getting soaked. And in fact today I walked for a mile and then came back home and meditated and read a little and meditated again before starting this talk.

But all those are external, and as you know by now, the entire spiritual path is internal because you live in your state of consciousness which is within. So this 'to you who overcome' means something internal.

Now there's another scripture which is Matthew 4:18, and it goes like this:

Jesus, walking by the sea of Galilee, saw two brethren, Simon called Peter, and Andrew his brother, casting a net into the sea: for they were fishers.

And he saith unto them, "Follow me, and I will make you fishers of men."

And they straightaway left their nets, and followed him.

Now, if you have an inner ear and you read this, perhaps you'll see what I see, which is that Christ walking by the sea of Galilee means on the edge of your consciousness—sitting on the well as it were, sees two brothers, Simon and Andrew. Simon called Peter and Andrew his brother. Now that's your body and your mind casting a net into the sea. You're trying with your body and you're trying with your mind to reach this Presence in your consciousness, and you're failing. Affirmations and denials, they no longer work. You're struggling with the letter and it doesn't work. But there's Christ on the edge, knocking. Says to you, *"Follow me, and I will make you fishers of men."* Or I will give you hidden manna. And in this analogy here, *they straightaway left their nets, and followed him.*

And there's a book out which Joel said in the Kailua study series not very many people bought. It was not very popular among students, and he could tell that by its lack of sales. And his book is called <u>Leave Your Nets</u>, because that's what Christ says to you. If you would overcome and receive the hidden manna, then you must leave your nets.

And your nets are nothing to do with the external. Your nets are your material sense of existence and your mental sense of existence. These must be laid down in order to receive the hidden manna, and now I will tell you what hidden manna means. It means for you to receive a new Self, a new Self, not physical, not mental, a spiritual Self, Christ. Listen to the rest of this quote in Revelation. Listen to the rest of the sentence:

He that hath an ear—can you hear me calling?—*Let him hear what the Spirit saith unto the churches;* Listen, listen. Christ within you has something to say. *To him that overcometh*—if you overcome, if you lay down your material sense of existence and your mental sense of existence, and you stand there naked—*I will give you to eat of the hidden manna.* That is, something else will begin to flow as your very Self, and *I will give you a white stone,* and in the white stone there's a new consciousness.

No longer a material sense coupled with a mental sense. No longer Simon and Andrew. No. I will give you a new consciousness, *and in the stone a new name written,* – That new name is a new nature, a new being, a new Self. I will give you a new Self *which no man knoweth saving he that receiveth it.*

No, no one with their material sense of self, their physical sense of self, or their mental sense of self can detect this invisible hidden Self. No one can detect it.

Okay, so now let's read it again and see if you can see it now what's being said in one sentence. Revelation 2:17:

He that hath an ear, let him hear what the Spirit saith unto the churches; To him that overcometh will I give to eat of the hidden manna, and will give him a white stone, and in the stone a new name written, which no man knoweth saving he that receiveth it.

And so in this book <u>Leave Your Nets</u> speaking of leaving the material sense of self—physical sense of self, and the mental sense of self which are both in the mind, in this world mind, counterfeit self—if you give up that self and you stand there willing to be silent, not knowing what's going to happen next, using no affirmations and no denials, simply saying, "Father, reveal the Self," and standing still—if you do that, you will receive the hidden Self. It will begin to flow. It will begin to take over. It will begin to <u>be you</u>.

And in this book <u>Leave Your Nets</u> by Joel there is a chapter, chapter 5 called *Hidden Manna.* And he has something to say about this hidden manna. And remember, this entire book was written so that those that are advanced past the letter and are ready to live by Spirit, by Christ, can leave their nets, can leave their humanhood and put on immortality and behold Christhood, the ascension of Christ. And so in this chapter he says:

You will not be able to enter the presence of God carrying your burdens with you. That means carrying your humanhood or your material sense or your mental sense, your affirmations, your denials. Anything by might or by power. None of that will help. *You will not come into the presence of God carrying with you any desire for God to do something, be something, or get something for you.* That's very important, because if there's a "you" going to God, that's the "you" that has to die. And die standing still. And die right there so that you may be a beholder, a witness to Christ coming out of the tomb, the hidden manna. Says Joel:

There has to be a purification of all human desires in the realization of his grace. You must consciously make the sacrifice of everything external; you must surrender the past and surrender the future. Surrender every desire for person, place, thing, circumstance, or condition—even your hope for heaven.

The presence of God is within you, and it must be consciously realized, but it will never be realized by anyone who desires God for any purpose other than the realization of God itself. Everyone who has sought God and missed the way has missed it because he has sought God for a reason: for a healing, for supply, [for a] home, [for] happiness, or for some other thing. God cannot be attained that way. God can be attained only in one way: through a complete surrender of everything. Consciously let go. "I do not want to live by bread alone. I want my life to be lived 'by every word that proceedeth out of the mouth of God.'" Then you will receive the hidden manna.

Now this hidden manna, this white stone upon which is written a new name, this Christ – all these are terms. All these are concepts in the mind, and so throw them out. You are not allowed to bring any of these concepts inside. You are not allowed now, you who have decided to really leave your nets, are no longer allowed to live by concepts. You must find this hidden manna, this new Self, and if you have learned how to practice contemplation, if you learned how to do that maybe several years ago, maybe just last year – if you learned how to contemplate until you reach the place where the mind stopped all by itself and momentarily you were silent, and into that vacuum rushed the Presence and you felt something, what you felt was just a whisper of this hidden manna.

Now the time has come for you to die. To lay down your life and to allow this hidden manna, this new stone, this new name to be revealed right here, right now. This new Self, this invisible Self, will live your life and make it its own life so that there is no longer a human being and a Christ presence, but only a Christ presence living Itself.

You said you agreed with *The New Horizon* that above this sense-life is a realm of *Spirit governed by Love, peopled with children of God*, and you said you wanted to be the child of God, that you wanted to live above this sense-life in the realm of Spirit. "My ways are not your ways," says God, and none of your ways will work now. And so leave your nets. Leave 'em, all of 'em. First here in your inner chamber. Here, right here in your inner chamber is the place to practice this principle, the principle of leave your nets. Throw them down. Let them go. Hands off! No physical self. That's a concept in the mind. Whose mind? Not this new Self, not the mind that is in this new Self. No, this is world mind. Concept is in the world mind. It's a universal concept. It belongs to no one, and so - drop it!

And what about this mind that has all these concepts, this universal mind thinking thoughts about a world, about a structure, a structural universe. This mind also belongs to no one. It belongs to no one. And so - drop it!

Now there's no physical self. There's no mental self. There's no self here. There's only a vast emptiness inside, a quietude, a silence.

Stand ye still and see and receive the hidden manna, a new Self, an invisible Self, an infinite Self. Receive ye the Holy Spirit. Not for any reason, not for any purpose. Just to rest in My Spirit. Just rest in it. You don't even have to know what it's doing. I have ways ye know not of. Rest. Behold I, your new Self. Feel your new Self. Listen, your new Self utters Itself.

You may feel this inner hum, this inner vibration. You may hear my voice say, *"It is I, be not afraid."* You may feel the Spirit moving over the face of the deep, but it is I, your new Self. Stand, stop, still.

I go before you to prepare a place for you, a consciousness for you, a body for you, a Self. Leave your nets and follow My guidance, My Spirit. I have come that you might have life, a new life, a hidden manna, a new Self, a Self that is everlasting.

Yes, to you who overcomes, to you who lays down a false sense of life, I will give you a new Self, a new consciousness, a new name. This is the initiation you waited for, you asked for, you prayed for. Now stand aside, and I will give you a new Self called Christ. And I, if I be lifted up in you, I will draw everything needed throughout eternity. This is the hidden manna, which no one knows except for you who receives your new Self.

No longer must you be concerned about a personal human self. There is none.

No, your only concern is to come here again and again to drop the nets, to turn within, to be still, be silent. No desires. Only a witness, as I, your new Self, reveal your Self to you. And I flow forth and reveal to you your new Self in hundreds, thousands, millions of ways. I am infinite. I can do this.

No, no human mind will ever understand the ways of God, and that human mind will give up and call them foolish. Foolishness! Who can receive a new self? Oh, come on! But to you who overcome in your inner chamber, in the silence, I give to eat of the hidden manna, your new Self lifted up. Now be still and feel the I.

[Silence]

And so my friends, if you do not have a copy of <u>Leave Your Nets</u> and you are serious about dying and being a witness to the birth of a new Self, your Self, the I, then it behooves you to get a copy of this book, <u>Leave Your Nets</u>, Joel S. Goldsmith. This is by Acropolis Books, and I think it's $11.95. It was $11.95. It says here: Acropolis Books in 1998, so for $12 here's a book on how you can completely leave your nets. I'd say that's a perfect price, next to nothing. I suggest you get it, but you don't read it the way you would read a novel. But before you open it, close your eyes and have a meditation and invite the Father to reveal your Self, and be still. Then open the book, begin at the first chapter, read the first paragraph slowly. See if you can see where it's telling you how to die and how to awaken to your everlasting Self, your Self. And read along until you feel this inner humming, this inner vibration. Then stop.

There's something there for you. Spirit is speaking. Look at it again. Now put it down. Now take it into meditation. Look at it a few times. I might say to myself "hidden manna." What is that? Hidden manna. Father, reveal the Self. And then I am quiet. And something will come. Oh, I can't say whether for you it'll be the still, small voice or the inner higher vibration or the movement of Spirit across the waters or just your everlasting Self rising up, ascending. I can't tell you how it will be for you, but I know that something will happen, and it will be your Self, your new Self, the hidden manna being revealed. And then you're done. You're done. Don't go back and read anymore.

And then later in another meditation try it again. And if nothing comes, and if I sat down and said, hidden manna, hidden manna, and nothing new came, then I would open the book and continue where I left off, reading the next paragraph. Very slowly, looking, after my meditation, reading and looking. Where is this telling me how to die and how to awaken? Now, here, if you do that - well, I don't see how you could get to the end of this book with all of that going on within before and after your reading. I don't see how you could get to the end of this book with all of those inner experiences of your true Self and not be another Self. I just don't see how you could do it.

So, if you don't have a copy of this book, get a copy. If you do have a copy of this book, perhaps you might approach it the way I just suggested. Because this gives the precise instructions for leaving your material sense of self, your mental sense of self, dropping those nets, coming empty-handed and standing before the very altar of God, open, receptive, and bearing witness as the light of the Father shines, revealing to you a new everlasting Self.

As this Self begins to rise, you will find it much easier when confronted with a problem to no longer take thought, but like Joel, our friend, our teacher, you will be able to turn within with no thought, and this makes no difference whether you're driving a car, swimming, watering the lawn, eating. Remember, he said sometimes it comes while eating? In the Kailua study series he said that? Your new Self will begin to express Itself without your asking, and in very strange and beautiful ways, just beautiful. You will become Christ consciousness.

People will reach out to you and before they get to the phone and before they write a letter, receive something from Christ. Because this new Self is an omnipresent Self, and as it rises higher and higher within you, you'll find that while looking at the good things, the beautiful forest as I did this morning on my walk, or the beautiful little dog who likes to follow me from down the street on my walk and stays with me the entire walk - oh, half a mile one direction and half a mile back - and then goes back home. He just decided to join me, a companion. But I know this is God. Oh sure, it appears as the forest. It appears as the dog, but something in you will reveal this new Self in whatever direction you look, because there cannot be two. There can only be one, and I within you am that One.

And so, you will find that with no effort on your part, after a time, after a while practicing this within in your inner chamber, in your consciousness, it will begin to take over. Your new Self will begin living Itself, and when you look upon the errors, you will see one Self. When you look upon the appearance of good, also errors, you will see one Self. You will see one Self. You will have that experience of Paul. In that Self *we live and move and have our being,* and that one Self in us.*"I am in the Father, and the Father in me."* Do you not know that, says the Christ? This is the truth of your new Self.

There are 12 people listening to these talks. Well now there's 14. I expect 14 people to lay down their lives and sometime in the weeks and months to follow I expect, I fully expect there to be but one Self. One Self speaking, one Self hearing, one Self living, one Self being, and die to that other self.

I want you to know that it matters to me that you come into this awareness of your Self. Though I can't do it for you, each and every one of you are lifted up in these meditations, and it is also my feeling that each and everyone are ready for this step. We may have studied only five or ten years, maybe even only two years, maybe 20, maybe 40 as in my case but, this is not our first time. We have studied before and perhaps we just weren't ready, and we turned like Lot's wife back and turned into a pillar of salt. We turned back into a human.

Now, I feel certain each and everyone is ready. Leave your nets. You that have an ear, you hear what the inner Spirit says unto you now. To you who overcomes a material sense of self, a mental sense of self and stands still, I will give you to eat of the hidden manna. I will give you a white stone, a new consciousness, and in the stone a new name. A new Self I give unto you, which no one knows about except you that receive it. Come. Eat. The table is prepared for you. For you, I give you hidden manna. A new Self, Christ.

[Silence]

CLASS 10

SPIRITUAL ALCHEMY

Bill: Good afternoon.

This is Saturday, February 9th, and this talk is directed to the more serious students. We have a handful in our group now. We have 15, and it is assumed that each of us is serious about attaining Christhood in some measure in this incarnation, in this lifespan. In this experience on earth we are serious about demonstrating the fact that we're not on earth, that we're living in spiritual consciousness in our Christhood, and to that end we have made … oh, this will be talk #10, and these talks have not been released to the public. This group of talks has not been released to the public, and so they have no idea what we're doing. Even the website, Mysticalprinciples.com does not have a link to these talks. We are the only people that have heard them, and these talks point out principles that we should be living by, not principles that we should be discussing or principles that we should be pondering, although it doesn't hurt a little bit to take it into meditation and ponder it that way, but not principles to be thinking about in the mind, but principles to be living.

These are the principles that Christ lives, and so if you would attain Christhood you must practice these principles such as *leave your nets,* which is leaving your trappings of humanhood, and such as *surrender* and surrendering to Christ consciousness. Such as *to him that hath it shall be given,* which is realizing that the only way to demonstrate your Christhood is by giving it away. So these are principles. All of these are principles, and we've had 8 principles, and 2 from older talks, so 10 principles. This is principle #10, and it's going to be called *Spiritual Alchemy*, which means *effecting a transition or a transformation through spiritual means*. Now just to refresh your memory, let's look at something from the Bible. I'll get it. I'll be right back.

And the first scripture goes like this:

And the Lord God formed man of the dust of the ground, and breathed into his nostrils the breath of life; and man became a living soul.

And the Lord God planted a garden eastward in Eden; and there he put the man whom he had formed. (Whom Lord God had formed)

And out of the ground made the Lord God to grow every tree that is pleasant to the sight, and good for food; the tree of life also in the midst of the garden, and the tree of knowledge of good and evil.

So, what we have here is someone called Lord God forming itself, and what do we know about Lord God? Lord God forming things out of dust, which is a way of saying forming things out of atoms, which is a way of saying forming things out of thought, which is a way of saying making mental images.

Lord God here is the mind, world mind! So we might as well read it how it is, which would be: And the world mind formed man of the dust of the ground, and the world mind planted a garden and brought forth the tree of knowledge of good and evil.

That's the world mind making mental images.

Images of a personal life - your life if you're living as a person right at this moment. If you're John Smith or Doris Brown, and you're thinking in terms of how much money you have in the bank and what you need to pay next week out of your funds, how much you will have left, or if you're thinking about - well, I'm approaching 60 years. I've probably got about, oh, 12 or 20 left.

Or if you're thinking about - I've been pretty nice to that person, so I've got a pretty good relationship going and if you're thinking in terms of a personal life, or making you're thinking I've been mean and I need to make an amends and say I'm sorry and get some flowers and candy and make up, **you're thinking in terms of your personal life.**

In other words, you're standing in the midst of this garden where world mind is forming out of the dust of the ground your entire existence. And it's all taking place in your mind. You're standing in the mind. Actually, it's not your real mind, but it's the world mind. It's the mind thinking about the world, the world mind. Or you might prefer, the mind about the world, or the mind about the world's business.

If you're standing in that mind and you're living that personal life, well I can tell you without a doubt I can prophecy that you're going to run out of your money, you're gonna run out of your strength, and you're going to mess up your relationships. You're going to end up bankrupt. In fact, the very world mind that forms these things out of the dust of the ground or out of atoms or out of mental images and convinces you that there's evil and good in this creation, this very world mind is going to kill you.

And that's what you have in the second chapter of Genesis.

Ah, but those of us in this group, we've decided we don't want to live in that universe. We know, we suspect, we have felt another universe, another Self, another life, or at least the possibility of another life. And so we turn to the first chapter of Genesis and the real creation, and this is the creation formed out of Consciousness, out of Christ consciousness, out of God consciousness. This is the real creation. And if you're standing in this creation, you probably should be making some talks, and I'd like to hear 'em. Because this creation was formed not by a world mind, a mind about the world, a mind concerned with the world. This creation was formed by God out of Itself. And it says:

In the beginning God created the heaven and the earth. That means God created the invisible, but also the forms as which that invisible appears.

And God said, Let there be light: and there was light. That's the very first, very first thing – *Let there be light.* And so God expressed as light as the very first and real creation, and <u>you, your identity, is in fact that light.</u>

And God called the light Day,
And the Spirit of God moved upon the face of the waters.

I love this. This is the experience that I have every time I have a successful meditation. Every single time I have a successful meditation, every single time <u>you</u> have a successful meditation, you are standing in the first day of creation. You are witnessing the real creation because there is an experience within where the Spirit of God moves upon face of the waters. It's a real experience. You become conscious of its movement. And if you stand there and don't try to do anything other than behold this creation, it will form itself as your experience, and it will appear as forms.

It will appear as companionship. It will appear as supply in every form. Not just money. Money is one of millions of forms of supply. Standing outside on a summer day and having a cloud cross in front of the sun and giving you shade while you're plowing your garden, and the shade cools you for a moment and there's a little breeze – that's supply too. The air that you breathe. Finding yourself in the right place at the right time. Trying to remember— where did I read that principle that Joel was talking about? Which book is it in, and reaching on your bookshelf and pulling down that book and opening it just anywhere and landing right on the principle you were considering. That's supply. See, we tend to think of supply as money, and that's so horrible to think of that that way.

Supply is every infinite form as which this light appears.

So, the Spirit of God moved over the face of the deep, the face of the waters. And God said let there be this and God said let there be that,

And (finally) God said, Let us make man in our image, after our likeness: and let them have dominion over (everything).

(And) so God created man in his own image, in the image of God created he him; male and female created he them.

But I think they changed that. I think it was male and female created he him.

Anyway - *And God blessed them, and said Be fruitful, and multiply and have dominion.*

Now you see what's happening here in this first real creation?

God is expressing as light, and that light is forming itself as man and every perfect thing.

The entire earth, the real earth, the plants, the animals, the stars, the rivers, the lakes, the mountains, the deserts, the snow, the rain, the sun – and that light expressed as your being is given dominion – dominion over this creation. But what does dominion mean now? Dominion doesn't mean that you move into the creation of Lord God and have dominion and start pushing things around and forcing your will, does it? No.

What does dominion mean? Dominion means God has given you the ability to enter your temple, your spiritual temple of the Most High, stand ye still and see the salvation of God.

Stand ye still and behold that perfect first creation **as it expresses.**

You are able to go within that temple, rest, and behold the Spirit moving over the face of the waters. And then with no idea whatsoever how that will form itself, you are able to get up from your meditation, do that work which is in front of you to do, and behold the light appearing as form needed in your experience or anybody's experience who turns to you.

This is called spiritual alchemy. This is so far beyond living in a world mind creation that it's called not human life anymore. It's called Christhood. And it is what you are called to do as a serious student that wishes to experience Christhood. Now in this book Leave Your Nets Joel says it like this:

Reach into (the) deep pool (within) and feel the abundance, the gentleness, and the power of (the) spirit, and let it flow; and when it flows it will come out as in a mold.

Now we can get down to brass tacks, and we can say intellectually that - well, God and the light really does not form itself into a mold. God, the light, just moves over the face of the deep and the mind interprets that as a mold, and that's fine if you want to go there, but I'm not doing that today. I'm just pointing out the difference in the two creations and the difference in where you must stand and which life you must live and I must live.

I have said I want to demonstrate Christhood now, here, this time around and stop fooling with humanhood. That means instead of standing in this personal life and using my money and my supply and my health, my companionships, and moving this around and trying to succeed and blah, blah, blah, blah, blah, and trying to turn evil into good and now I'm sick so I gotta get well, so I go to the doctors. I get that going good. Ho, hey, here comes a bill I didn't think of. Now my supply's upset. I gotta pray some more principles - blah, blah, blah, blah, blah. Trying to improve a personal life.

No. It's time we stopped that. I mean STOP IT! Who are you fooling? Stop living a human life. Quit! At least when you catch yourself, STOP IT! But it's much easier if you go to this inner temple and practice meditation several times a day. It only has to be for a minute or two, but it has to be long enough to make the contact, which means so you can stand still and see and behold the first chapter of Genesis, that spiritual creation happening live, right now. We behold the light forming itself or the light shining which later appears as form. So he says:

Reach into this deep pool and feel the abundance, the gentleness, and the power of that spirit, and let it flow; and when it flows, it will come out as in a mold. That mold may be money, home, companions, forgiveness, justice, mercy, kindness, or benevolence; but do not attempt to pour spirit into a mold, do not attempt to provide a mold in which to hold it.

Yes, the age of going within to demonstrate an automobile or a new job or a new partner or a new spouse or a new wife or a new husband or a new friend - that is over. Or even a new lung - that's over. It's over.

We go as the son of God. We go as the child of the spirit of God, and that child lives always, says Joel, and says our experience and says Christ – that child lives always as a beholder. You're beholding the spiritual creation of Genesis. You thought Genesis was way back there in history somewhere far, far back, didn't you? It's not! Genesis is taking place in your consciousness the moment you drop out of humanhood and stand ye still. Stand fast and behold. Behold, I. I come quickly. That's Genesis, and it's an experience going on now in our consciousness – those of us in this group that are reaching or resting and beholding Christ. So he says:

Go to this pool, this infinite pool of joyous substance; (and) commune; feel it as it fills your consciousness, as it circulates within your being. (And) By this I do not mean a physical or an emotional feeling (when I say feel it), he says, *but* (I mean) *an inner awareness of the divine. That is all! That is seeking the kingdom of God, and then the things,* (the so-called things) *are added.*

But remember, it's still – I'm telling you now – these are my words – it's still the kingdom of God. It's only appearing as things. You have the invisible spiritual creation, vibrant, alive. He calls it a pool. I like - the spirit moved over the face of the deep, so the face of the deep is a deep pool, I guess. But to me it feels like a deep universe. Anyway it doesn't matter what you call it. What matters is you become aware of it and its movement within you, and you can't become aware of its movement if you're thinking. **You can only become aware of your thoughts about it**, but to become aware of its movement, you must be still. And if you can't do this, then you need to go back and read things like The Art of Meditation and Practicing the Presence and get this ability to meditate.

You must have this ability to meditate. It's vital in order to demonstrate or to behold the Christ. You can't do it just closing your eyes and mumbling a few words and standing there quiet for a moment. You must have this consciousness, what he calls an inner awareness of the divine. That is seeking the kingdom of God. And then the things are added because he says *it pours itself forth, not as ephemeral nothingness or substance, but in molded form, and the mold is always fulfillment.*

When supply of whatever name or nature comes out of the depths of [that pool of that] I, that spirit, that consciousness, *out of the depths of (that) Soul, when your life is lived in that dimension of spirit, there is never just barely enough, and never too much. There is bounty, abundance, affluence, because everything comes as the gift of God, and is meant for your use.*

How can you know if you're living in this dimension? When your entire vision is on your devotion and service to God and your expectancy is of God. Not of man, but of God. And when you understand that only in his Presence is fullness, only in the presence of this movement of Spirit is fullness. Not in the presence of a person or in the presence of a bank account. Only in this presence is the fullness of life and the ability to live, move, and have your being in that inner consciousness and that inner awareness - well, that's how you know you're living in this dimension.

145

And so in this <u>Leave Your Nets</u> in the chapter *Inasmuch as Ye Have Done it Unto One of These the Least*, he tells us how to bear witness to the first creation, the real creation <u>which happens now</u>. It's a present thing! There no past in God. If God's spirit moved over the face of the deep, then God's spirit is moving over the face of the deep right now. And if you attune yourself with it within, you will behold that spiritual creation. Otherwise, if you can't do that, then you're going to have to go ahead and live your human life and have your three-score years and ten or twelve and—and die. And come back and live a human life again and experience the futility of it and turn within and say, "Oh God, isn't there an answer?" and you'll be directed at that time to the spiritual way of life and maybe you'll take it up then.

Now, which creation do you want to live in? Which creation do you want to stand in? Which creation do you want to behold? You can struggle. I've done it! You can go out and get an education. I have degrees. I know how hard it is to get them. I've done it, been there, done that, and you can apply for a position and work yourself up into management. I've done that too. And you can try to save some money and put it away for future use, and you can direct your life in that way, and gosh – there's so many things you can do now online. You can go to matchmakers.com or Christianmingle.com or whatever.com and find yourself the perfect mate that matches you perfectly, and you can go down to the local gym and you can get on an exercise program, and you can go ahead and get your body into perfect shape for your age, and the very next minute you can drop over dead and leave that all stuff unfulfilled.

That's the nature of the human world mind creation, the personal creation, personal life. That's the nature of it. It's always a matter of turning evil into good, and it's never ending! It goes on forever until it kills you. You have a brief vacation, and then you try it again. I don't know about you, but I'm a little tired. I don't want to continue to do that.

I want to see the living Christ and this perfect creation manifest itself and appear as form.

Not by telling it what I need, not by sitting down to try to demonstrate a thousand dollars, but rather sitting down with my attention completely focused on how do I experience this awareness of spirit within? And how do I rest in it with no desire of any kind, but simply an openness, a receptivity? A love really.

I can tell you there are times when I feel its movement that I can only say - I just feel within my being - I love you. I love you. It just bubbles up. I love you. And yet, I tell myself sometimes you're so silly. You know this is your true identity, so you're telling yourself that you love you? And yet, I still can't help it. And sometimes I feel the Infinite say, "I love you" back. And sometimes I see it demonstrate that love.

And so there's a love that flows back and forth, and sometimes I'm higher than that and I know there's only I, and it's a deep pool of Is'ingness, of Is'ing.

But it doesn't matter. The point is that you go within whatever level you're on and develop that ability to be still until you make contact, which is a funny way of saying until you come into the awareness and have the awareness of the living creation of Genesis happening right here, right now.

Now in his book Spiritual Interpretation of Scripture Joel Goldsmith has a couple of really beautiful things to say in his chapter near the back, which says: *The True Sense of the Universe*, which is another way of saying the true universe, because see, he lived in this spiritual creation. He didn't live in a personal human sense of life, and he tried to lay down the principles as I am doing - trying to do - lay down the principles by which you and I could attain or rest back into this same sense of universe. So in this chapter he says something that you've probably heard, but see it in a new light.

God is the divine Reality of individual being. To avail oneself of the harmonious government of this Principle, [or the forms], *it is necessary to drop all thought of human persons and conditions; lose all desire to improve humanhood.*

You see, because the real creation cannot move into that personal sense of life, into that world mind creation. It can't do it! They're never joined ever! But rather, the world mind creation is dropped, and standing in the stillness you see these new forms appearing, and they're not a part of the world mind. But he says that over here. He says:

Drop all thought of human persons and conditions; lose all desire to improve humanhood and <u>let</u> the Inner Self reveal (reveal) *in Silence the harmony, wholeness and joy of real Being.*

See, you become aware of Spirit. Now, he says:

(That which is) Soul power (or) that which we contact within ourselves results in what appears to be (forms) *health, harmony and wealth, but*—now listen—*these are not the same as that which is attained through attempts to improve (humanhood) the harmony in our affairs which results from our contact (within) with our Inner Self, (our Spirit) or Soul, is the manifestation or expression of Spirit,* (or spiritual consciousness), *Life; and (this) is the "added things" which come naturally from the realm of real substance. (Then) finite sense beholds these "added things," or spiritual reality, as material sense, or "things" and "person(s)."* Well, that's what we said before. *(But) Spiritual harmony is not attained by seeking persons, things or conditions,* we must take *no thought for these and seek(ing) only contact with the divine Reality.*

All right, so on the next page he says:

Developing a sense of receptivity; learning to silence the senses, which is the tools that world mind or mind about the world uses – *and gaining the ability to listen for "the still, small voice"* (or feel the movement of Spirit - these are just words. The experience is the same.) *this is the Way* he says. *Human thoughts—even good ones—will not help.* So all your thoughts about spiritual subjects <u>will not help</u>.

It must be the conscious awareness of the movement of Spirit or the still, small Voice, or the Presence of God. The terms he used are so unimportant. The awareness is what's the important thing—because your awareness of the movement of Spirit, of the action of Christ—that awareness is what forms itself as this new creation.

So, he says:

It is a silent state of receptivity in which the Christ or Spirit of God is manifest as our individual consciousness. It appears principally as a "feeling" of the Presence, and (it) dispels the illusion[s] of sense for oneself or another.

In other words, this movement within yourself once felt, consciously realized - the conscious awareness of it within you, melts anything that the world mind, or mind about the world is doing. It just melts it and reveals new forms in its place. So, one more time. This is like the other chapter which I love so much, *The New Horizon* in the book <u>The Infinite Way</u>, because he says here:

As soon as you have conquered the desire to heal or improve the material sense (or the world mind sense) *of existence, the spiritual or real begins to reveal itself and unfold itself to you.*

You see, you witness the birth of creation, the spiritual creation in your consciousness, and then it appears as new forms. Now listen!

Do not take lightly what I am saying. This is the Great Revelation; this knowledge will clarify for you the Master's statement, "My kingdom is not of this world"; it will reveal to you the secret of John the Revelator, who beheld the universe which is not made with hands,

149

You see? ...*but which is eternal, as Consciousness appearing; Spirit unfolding; Soul revealing.*

In other words, the spiritual creation of Genesis 1. Now, now you understand – *"My kingdom is not of this world."* Yes, yes. The spiritual creation, consciousness, the Light moving over the face of the deep, Spirit flowing appears as form, and <u>that is not</u> world mind, mental images appearing as form. One is a false sense of existence taking place only in the mind, and it's a nothingness, and it doesn't last. Very, very temporal, or temporary. But the spiritual creation keeps flowing and flowing and flowing and forming itself until your total existence is that of Christ consciousness, that of one who stands watching the Spirit form itself. Now he says to you:

The life of material man, the life of (material) tree (or) flower (or) animal (or mountain or lake or sunset), *this is not eternal Life; it is not the manifestation of the Life of God;* (It is not the manifestation of the spiritual consciousness). *It is a false, finite, mortal sense of life. (So) Do not attempt to patch (it) up (but) turn (away) from it and with your (new) consciousness discern the Life of God; "feel" through your cultivated spiritual sense (the) divine energy of Spirit; become conscious in the Silence of your Soul.* **Let** *divine harmonies appear as you disregard the evidence of sight and hearing, tasting, touching, and smelling.*

Believe me – says Joel. *Believe me –* <u>please believe me</u> *– this is the secret of secrets. This is Life eternal to know this truth. Truly Kings and Emperors would give their thrones could they but (know) this one truth,* and again, for the third time in this chapter he finishes by saying:

Only to those who have eyes to see and ears to hear can this vision become a living, vital Presence (within). Only those who have heard what is said by "the still, small voice" and seen what is visible to the "windows of the Soul" can discern "the temple not made with hands," (or) the universe of God's creating.

Now over here he said: *John the Revelator, who beheld the universe which is not made with hands, but which is eternal.* That's what we're doing as Christ. We no longer are standing in a personal sense of world mind and living that existence. We have come out, and we are coming out, and we are standing, resting beside this stream of consciousness, and we are beholding the original creation happening here, now, in this instant within. We are beholding a universe *not made with hands,* not made with world mind. Made by spiritual consciousness.

This inner vision, this spiritual consciousness, the Soul-sense, comes only in proportion (–in proportion –) *as we accept and realize this great secret:* one more time–*the life of material man, plant or animal is not the Life [of] God; it is finite sense, the manifestation of mortal, material sense.* Or world mind. *This false sense of life must be put off, disregarded, (and) unvalued, in order that* (we may stand still and) *the real Life and its forms may become evident and experienced.*

And so that's why we're calling this talk today, we're calling it *Spiritual Alchemy,* because - well - hang on a second. Let's look this up in the dictionary.

<u>Alchemy</u>: *A speculative philosophy aiming to achieve the transmutation of base metals into gold. A power or process of transforming something common into something special. An inexplicable or mysterious transmuting.*

You see – alchemy, spiritual alchemy, is taking this world mind, personal sense existence and transforming it into that spiritual creation appearing as forms. Be ye renewed, or *"Be ye transformed by the renewing of your mind."*

Be ye transformed into that first chapter of Genesis, the spiritual creation, or Christ consciousness, by stepping out of a personal sense, a world mind, mental image existence. Even if you do this only for minutes out of each hour, it will become slowly, it will transmute, transform your entire existence. And Joel says there comes an exact moment, an exact minute, an exact time when It takes over and lives Itself. Then you have attained Christhood, and Christ liveth your life.

Now, Joel attained this. I can show you in his book. It's not handy—yes it is—let's see. In his book Consciousness Transformed, which is the same thing we're talking about here, transforming consciousness from world mind to Christ consciousness. In that book he says: *It's not easy to stop seeing human beings, but I finally made it.*

He made it. **He made it.** He stepped out of the mind which sees human beings and found the inner temple not made with hands which beholds Christ everywhere, which beholds that spiritual creation. He made it. And I can hear Rumi—the mystical poet, who was Muslim and who had a love affair with God in most of his poems—I can hear Rumi saying: The two worlds have become One. I made it! He was transformed. And Paul with his declaration: Ah, now I'm no longer blind. *"I live, yet not I. Christ liveth my life."* And so he made it.

And so for those of us 15 who have gathered together for some reason we have been led to this group—I did not seek a single one, but either the person asked me if I was going to start a group or the person's name came to me as someone I should send an invitation. But I didn't think up any of them myself. Those 15 of us who are serious students who want to live as Christ consciousness must go within and become beholders of the Spirit as it moves over the face of the deep, as it moves over the waters.

And then we will behold in the minutes, hours that follow the living Spirit appearing as form, and that form always has exactly what you need because it always comes as fulfillment. And fulfillment for me might be where I am now, which is in the mountains and listening to the silent snowflakes falling.

But fulfillment for you might be sitting next to the ocean and hearing the waves. And fulfillment for someone else might be walking out into the night sky in the desert and seeing billions of stars. But it will always come as fulfillment and in an infinite yet individual way.

But it won't come if you're running your own life. It won't come if you're living a personal sense of self. It won't come if you're planning and you're plotting.

Now I'm not saying that going to school and getting an education is bad. I'm not saying that. I'm saying that if you live by this inner dimension, It will direct your paths. In all thy ways acknowledge It, and It will direct thy paths. So if you're led to move into the academic world and attain a degree, it will be for Its purpose, not yours. It will manifest. Always It.

Now I have found that I gave up seeking any kind of a relationship. I just quit seeking, and as soon as I quit seeking, I had a vision in my inner temple of Mary Magdalene, and I didn't know what that vision meant. But within days of that or weeks I met my wife, which is Madalyn, and she was named after Magdalene, and we've been together for 23 years and walking the same road. We both serve God and have God first before each other. And that's why it works so well. And it works on every level. It works emotionally, physically. It works spiritually. In every level we match. And that was only after I gave up looking and according to her, in her story she was on her knees saying: "God, I can't pick the right person, so I give up." And then we were brought together, but that was Consciousness appearing as form. That's why Joel says these are permanent then. These are not things that come and go like these mental images that world mind creates.

And so I invite you, all of you in this group, to step out of humanhood and find that inner place where you can be still enough to bear witness, to behold God's infinite spiritual creation of the first chapter of Genesis, Consciousness appearing as perfect form. And this, too, is living as Christ, and this you must do. Thank you, and I love you – and God be with you as you practice Christhood.

[Silence]

CLASS 11

ENTER THE SABBATH

Bill: Good morning.

This is February 10th, Sunday, 2013, and we are continuing our series of Uncomfortable Talks, uncomfortable to the human being, that is, because the human being must die. Yesterday we discussed the first chapter of Genesis and the beautiful experience that comes to us when we are able to stand still and behold that creation flowing out from the invisible pool of silence and forming itself, appearing as forms. We say we live in our consciousness, and we do. No illusion is ever externalized, so we either live in a human state of consciousness, which is divided in good and evil, in the belief in both of those, or we stand and behold as the Christ that expression of Christ consciousness, God consciousness flowing. And I just happened to notice in this Thunder of Silence by Joel Goldsmith, he says:

Every time that the thought comes to us, "I need this"; "I need that"; "I would like this"; "I would like that"; "I should have this"; "I should have that"; our answer must be, "Man shall not live by bread alone, by effect, by creation (that false creation) – but by (my) Spirit, the (real) creator." That must be a continuous realization.

Not continuous thought. He didn't say that, did he? Continuous realization or continuous awareness: I live by this inner Spirit, which is why we suggested that we take one or two minutes out of every hour to remember.

155

That must be a continuous realization (he says) *until we have overcome our desire for anybody or anything in the external realm. We have to lose all desire for the visible in the realization that we live not by that which is visible but by that which is invisible.*

You see, we are surrendering humanhood. We do not live by anyone or anything. We live by that invisible consciousness flowing.

And then we shall find (he says) *that the Infinite Invisible will produce in our experience the persons, things, circumstances, and conditions necessary to our daily life. In the same way, every time we are tempted to think of some power — some negative, evil, erroneous power that apparently is dominating our life, rendering it futile and fruitless and which we want destroyed — let us smile at it* (smile at it) *as we realize,* (again as we come into the conscious awareness) *"No, I have no need of any power with which to overcome this discord. There is a God, even though I do not know what God is. (And) I cannot know what God is because It is beyond the uttermost comprehension of the human mind.*

But elsewhere he says: *You can know God as an experience, not as a comprehension of the human mind.* And so you see, he suggests in this chapter called *Beyond Power* that we stop that archaic, age-old, centuries-old belief that we need a power to overcome our problems. Surely in yesterday's talk you saw that or you felt that there is no power that we need to throw at our problem. We need to realize that the problem is world mind presenting a mental image. Now, the term is not important. Again, terms are not important. What is important is that you see that there is a fabric and that all appearances of good or evil are made from this fabric and that the fabric is world thought or mental images. Now you can use the term mental images, world thought, mortal mind, hypnotism, mesmerism, illusion, this world, Maya. It does not matter what term you use. Use the term you are comfortable with because you're only using that term long enough to drop it.

You see, understanding has no meaning. It's not a matter of understanding truth. It's not a matter of understanding the world's illusion or the illusion of a world. It's not a matter of understanding that. It's a matter of seeing through that. And this you don't do with the mind. The mind, the human mind, is a tool of that very hypnotism, mental images, world mind. It's a tool of that. Just as your sense of hearing is a tool of this physical body, so is the human mind a tool of world mind, world thought, universal belief – whatever term you like.

And so it's not necessary to understand it at depth. It doesn't take a great deal of understanding. Understanding is also a part of that world mind. You see, we have to tread in a place where the mind has no existence, which is why Joel stresses again and again, or the Spirit stresses, the Christ within you stresses that this pool of silence where the mind does not function – this is where you must rest. Beside this pool, beside this deep well.

So, we who are rising in consciousness must see that there is no need for power to overcome anything at any time ever. In this realm of no power, in your ability to relax to such an extent that you—well, it's like looking at a lake, surface of a lake in the water, and there's no breeze. It's very still, and the surface is like glass and nothing is disturbing it. It's just still, just silent. No effort. It's effortless. Being, resting, is'ing. In that state of using no power, in that state where no power fills your being, in that realm of no power – God is living, being, is'ing.

And so he tells us what we learned yesterday is that in the second chapter of Genesis where we use power to overcome evil and replace it with good, that's that state of humanhood that we must rise above, rise out of, we must drop. Now I'm not saying that you need to rise out of that today and never go back, because it's not possible. You've been in there too many centuries. I'm saying and suggesting you drop it in these moments, these few moments of every hour and rest back in that pool of nothing, that pool of nothing the mind can get a hold of. That pool of silence and no power and nothingness. Out of that infinite nothingness the divine first chapter of Genesis, the perfect creation flows. And it's nothing the mind can understand, so stop trying. Your understanding is not necessary now. Understanding was something that the mind, the world mind thought it needed. But you are in a place where you are rising above that mind into a realm of no power, into a realm of peace without end, into a realm of silence.

In Joel's book <u>Beyond Words and Thoughts</u>, which is specifically how to rise into that pool of silence, he explains something in the chapter *Truth Unveiled*. It's a very beautiful chapter. It's one of my favorite chapters all time. It's right next to *The True Sense of the Universe* which we read a little from yesterday and *The New Horizon*. I believe these 3 chapters have the entire message of moving from mind to Spirit. So let's see if something in here presents itself.

First of all, yesterday we spoke of moving out of humanhood and into Christ Consciousness, and we said that Joel had made it, because he said *"I finally made it. I no longer see humans anywhere, but I behold Christ everywhere."* He says, *"I myself have beheld the incorporeal form of man dozens and dozens of times."* Now, so in moving from humanhood to Godhood or Christhood or being a beholder of Christ Consciousness forming that new creation, there's an exact time we said when the transformation takes place. Now before we read this I wanted to read this from the Kailua study series on the chapter called *No Power*, which is where the editor pulled a lot from to write that chapter in <u>The Thunder of Silence</u>. But I wanted to read this to you. It says:

Whenever truth is offered to the human mind (and we know what the human mind is), *the human mind wants to crucify that truth, because the truth demands that the human mind die.*

What does that do to you when you hear that? Your human mind must die. Doesn't it make you pause and wonder "how can I—how do I function without a human mind? Why, I've had one my entire life and maybe many centuries, most definitely many centuries. How do I function? How can I function? How do I go to work? How do I do the housework without a human mind? And I'm here to tell you that the struggle that the human mind has holding everything together in this balancing act and trying to balance plates on sticks by turning evil into good and a whole lifetime of this – that human mind really has no idea how to live without itself, does it? It can't conceive of such a thing, so it hears this truth and it says, "Oh, poppycock! How ridiculous! You're just hiding your head in the sand. What kind of philosophy is this?"

But I can tell you, and many of you know – maybe all of you know – when you step out of that mind even if only for brief moments and you find yourself in that place where God is happening, you find yourself being carried along by the rhythm of God and you find yourself in the right place at the right time, saying the right things, doing the right things, and all works perfectly and you find—well, I really can live without that mind running things. I'm not saying you'll sit in the corner and stare at a wall. On the contrary, Joel says, and I found myself, the more you live outside of that mind and live as a beholder of Christ Consciousness moving things around the busier you are. So, again, let's read it:

Whenever truth is offered to the human mind, the human mind wants to crucify that truth, because the truth demands that the human mind die. Truth demands that we die daily to our humanhood and that we be reborn of the Spirit.

And now you saw yesterday, you see reborn of the Spirit really means a whole new creation, doesn't it? Taking place now in your consciousness, in that quiet temple. That's being reborn of the Spirit. Beholding a beholder as Spirit forms Itself. So he says here:

Truth doesn't promise anybody that you can go on being a good, comfortable human being. Truth doesn't promise anybody that you can have a lot of money and a lot of fame and a lot of health and a lot of self-indulgence. Truth doesn't promise anybody a life of ease in matter.

Truth promises a terrific struggle, a struggle between the Spirit and the flesh, until the crucifixion. That is the final tearing down of humanhood, the final destruction of 'man whose breath is in his nostrils', after which comes a very barren period, a wilderness period in the tomb, a period of desolation. That's why it is called the tomb. But after that three days, there comes the resurrection. And even in the resurrection you carry around a torn body and maybe (a) torn reputation[s] too.

But forty days of that, and there comes the ascension above every claim of the human mind. You see, right at that point you rise out of the human mind and permanently dwell in your Christhood. And he says: *Then comes the pure spiritual life, in which the promises are fulfilled: 'I will never leave you nor forsake you. I will lead you beside the still waters, in green pastures. My presence will go before you to make the crooked places straight. I have never seen the righteous begging bread.' You see,* (he says) *it is in that demonstration of our Christhood that there are no problems, none whatsoever.*

All right, so he defines for us there that there's going to be a terrific struggle culminating in a crucifixion and a place of barrenness, desolation, and forty days in the wilderness and then finally an ascension. Now that sounds like one heck of a battle. That sounds like the story of Armageddon in the Revelation, doesn't it? Which is exactly how Herb interpreted it, if you remember from the Revelation series. It's an inner struggle. All right, so – but yesterday we said that there are those who have made it. Yes, the path is narrow and few there be that enter, but I truly feel all of us hearing this talk can complete this transition.

Now in this chapter *Truth Unveiled* in <u>Beyond Words and Thoughts</u> Joel talks about his completing the transition, just a little. He says:

Always, since my first spiritual experience, living in two worlds has been difficult for me – living in that higher Consciousness and then coming down to earth, going back into that Consciousness and coming back down to earth – but never was it as difficult as in 1963.

Now remember in 1964 he passed on. So, what he's saying here is what we talked about yesterday. There are two creations, two states of consciousness. One is humanhood, one is Christhood, and what he's saying here is he found that it was really difficult to go into that higher Consciousness, to stand still in that inner temple and behold the incorporeal creation, which then appeared as forms in his experience as well as to those that reached out to his consciousness. Standing there in that and then perhaps the next morning or that afternoon coming down into humanhood again. Going back and forth between the two was very difficult, but never as difficult as it was in 1963. He says:

That year marked another period of initiation for me, but, even though in 1962 I knew it was to be, I had no knowledge of its intensity, its length, or the nature of the message that would be revealed.

So he's telling you that this is an initiation. And so all of us in this class, in this group, are being initiated. We are passing through an initiation. Moving out of mind and into Spirit. Moving out of humanhood and into Christhood. The terms don't matter. It's the awareness, the inner awareness. And why you've been chosen, I do not know. I do not know why I've been chosen. I only know there's an inner burning, an inner longing, and I can't stop. I can't stop. So Joel says:

It is not unnatural, therefore, that that year should have revealed the higher unfoldment, the higher Consciousness. This you will understand as you study the work that came through during this period. (that is, in 1963) *With each successive unfoldment, something was breaking through, leading to the teaching of going beyond words, beyond thoughts, going beyond the mind.* (Here we go with that human mind has to die). *This idea you will find in all the 1963 work, revealing the nature of life as it is lived when you go beyond the mind, beyond thoughts: beyond taking thought, beyond reasoning.* (Beyond <u>power</u>!) *This is the revelation of the nature of Sabbath and of Grace.*

Now, I want to skip a little bit here over to the next page where he talks about what needs to happen.

On the spiritual path, we begin our journey by studying the truth, learning and practicing the truth. We never attain the goal (that is, Christhood) *of realization, however, until we reach beyond the mind and its knowing of the truth to our becoming Truth: "That which I am seeking, I am!"*

You cannot know truth or God with the mind. **Give up.** You're reaching the place in your journey, in your initiation, my dear friends, where the mind cannot come. And Christ Jesus says, *"Where I am going, you cannot follow Me now, but later."* That was spoken to you centuries ago – and now this is later – and now you may follow, but you cannot bring the mind.

On the Mount, in a high state of consciousness, Moses realized I AM, and thereby became I AM. Yet, there remained still a sense of Moses as is evidenced by the fact that he spoke of himself as being slow of speech.

This is Joel pointing out that Moses has this higher state of consciousness, the first chapter of Genesis, Christ awareness, and yet he drops down into a human sense of Moses and says that he is slow of speech. So there are both going on, just as there are in us. We are in an initiation as was Moses.

The realization of I AM (in Moses) *prevailed, however, and with that great illumination came such a height of consciousness that he was able to lead the Hebrews out of slavery to the Promised Land. Had Moses been able to crucify completely the mortal sense of self which still remained, he would have been able to enter the Promised*

Land, or heaven (or Christhood). *But he was bound* (for a while) *by a finite sense of himself.*

Which later he overcame. Later it was crucified because in the Mount of Transfiguration there he and Elijah met with Jesus in the invisible, and all three had overcome that. Now, says Joel in this chapter *Truth Unveiled:*

*Jesus, however, not only knew the truth but **realized** and **became** the Truth: "I am the way, the truth, and the life." Nevertheless, a sense of Jesus, the man, remained, because he said, "I can of mine own self do nothing. If I bear witness of myself, my witness is not true." This personal sense of self had to be crucified, as eventually it must be in all of us, or we will not ascend to the Promised Land, or the realization of our spiritual identity* (of our Christhood).

Jesus' realization of the need to crucify, or rise above, the seeming mortal sense of self, enabled him to make the ascension.

Now listen to this line – it's very important.

*The ascension is always the same: a rising above mind, above knowing the truth, to Truth **Itself.***

This is why I say in every meditation for it to be successful you must step out of the human mind. Bring no thoughts with you. Bring only awareness. Rest back in it. Relax. Rest. Be at peace. No power. Silence. Nothingness. Emptiness. Then into <u>that</u> vessel the Spirit moves over the face of the deep. You don't move it. You don't move. You are very still, like that lake, that crystal clear lake. No movement. And the wind of Spirit moves over the water, and there's a ripple. That ripple is the birth of the new creation, the new consciousness, and I am come that you might have life and life more abundantly. And I, the Eternal, everlasting life, am come. So says Joel:

In many classes and even in some of the Writings, I have said that I did not understand the reason for the crucifixion, why it took place or why it had to take place if it had to. It puzzled me. (and) It was not until 1963, when I myself went through the experience, (of crucifixion) *that the reason and need for the crucifixion of Christ Jesus was revealed to me. (But) Somehow* (because he didn't bring a mind with him) *Somehow, after that experience, the memory of it passed and I could not bring it to conscious recollection, (but) later the entire scene was revealed to me again when I went through the experience of ascension: rising above (the) mind (in) to Truth* (or God) *Itself.*

Now there it is in plain English, my friends. Joel made it! He rose above the mind. Remember the ascension is always the same, rising above mind into truth or God or Christ Consciousness or Genesis. And *I went through the experience of ascension* (he says), *rising above mind (in) to Truth.*

(And) This is what I saw: (says Joel) *In Jesus' statement, "He that seeth me seeth him that sent me," he revealed he had attained the goal of I AM. "'I am the way'* (I am the consciousness. I AM God.) *'I and God are one.'" And there is an experience in which he proved this: he took three disciples to what is called the Mount of Transfiguration, which again is (this) high consciousness,* (above mind) *and he revealed to them the Hebrew prophets who were supposed to be dead.*

But, to his enlightened sense, (or in that higher consciousness) *they were not dead, and he proved to his disciples that they were alive, and they were with them there in form. (And) Whether he translated them into visible form or whether he translated himself and the disciples into invisible form makes no difference because it is the same experience. He translated: he demonstrated to his disciples the truth he later proved: "I lay down my life, that I might take it again'; I can walk into (this) invisible realm and I can walk out again, I am Spirit, I am the way."*

(And) Because of Jesus' experience on the Mount of Transfiguration, I understand now that crucifixion was not necessary. Enoch was translated without knowing death; Elijah was translated without knowing death;

(and) Isaiah, also, may have been translated. Therefore, it was shown to me through Jesus' experience on the Mount of Transfiguration he could have been translated without knowing death, but he chose to accept corporeal death in order to reveal to the disciples that (even) death is not an experience, but (again) is an illusory sense (or a mental image) *(which) must be understood and seen through.*

And finally he says at the bottom of this page:

This revelation is proof of the message that there must come a rest to My people. There must come a rest from the activity of mind: taking thought fearing for our life, constantly knowing truth in order to avoid some experience.

See – that's not the way – you know truth over and over in your mind. No.

There must come a Sabbath, and in this Sabbath (now) we live by Grace.

See – not by thought taking, not by thinking of truth, but by that Grace which flows as that Spirit, that wind across the still lake.

We live by Grace, and then we do not know the truth, (now) truth reveals Itself (in) us, and we become the Truth. It is not an activity of the mind: it is Soul revealing Itself.

You see? Everything all these years has been pointing to the ascension, to rising out of humanhood and into Christhood. Everything has been telling us – Joel has been saying all this many years that we must come out of the mind permanently and live in Christ Consciousness. And he says:

This is the final tearing down of humanhood, the final destruction of 'man whose breath is in his nostrils'. (And then comes a resurrection of this spiritual creation, the Son of God, the manifestation of God, Christ. And then the) *promises are fulfilled. "I will never leave you nor forsake you."* it is in (this) *demonstration of our Christhood that there are no more problems, none whatsoever.*

Let us be still for a moment. Let us rest back in that invisible pool; deep, deep pool of Spirit.

[Silence]

Here at this point in your initiation you must leave the mind. Just drop it. It cannot help you anymore. You no longer need an understanding of truth, an understanding of God, an understanding of illusion. No understanding of principles is Spirit. The realm of the mind has been good to you perhaps. It brought you so far, but you cannot go farther with it. And so now drop the mind. Take no thought.

In this temple not made with hands, not made with mind, in this temple is your perfect Self. Spirit is its substance. Consciousness is its home. Stand still, very still. And I and the Father are One and the same. Behold, I make all things new. Behold, I come quickly. Behold spiritual creation.

In the mind you had tribulation. In the Spirit you find the Sabbath, this moment of rest. And I have been with you from the beginning; from before Abraham was, I AM. If you will stand still. If you will cease from thought, I will reveal truth here, now, flowing. And this is life eternal that you might know Me, your true Self.

On this path in this part of your initiation you will learn to rise above the human mind, which is the tool for world mind. You will learn to function by being a beholder of Grace forming Itself, and you will know truly Christ liveth my life. And to every image of the mortal mind you will know: "Be not afraid; it is I." It is I. And you will not fight, you will not use power, you will not overcome. You will see through. You will see through by standing still in no power, in silence. You will see through as My creation unfolds before you. And you will live in, through, and by Christ consciousness.

And your willingness to die, to step out of the mind is the invitation to Me, Christ, and I will take over.

My friends, this is something you cannot explain to humans even if you would like to. They have no capacity to receive it. You who have labored long and hard – let us return to this chapter *Truth Unveiled* and hear it in Joel's words, because I think they're beautiful.

When you reach that place where, instead of searching for a truth, feverishly reading or studying to latch on to some truth, (when instead of that) *you can relax and rest in the Truth – without taking thought, without (any) speaking (without any) thinking – you can be a state of awareness, and then you understand the meaning of "Man shall not live by bread alone, but by every word* (or every movement) *that proceedeth out of the mouth of God." You will then discover that every word, every feeling,* (every movement), *every emotion, every thought that comes to you from (that) deep withinness is what you now live by. (This is) The Spirit within (which) guides, directs, sustains, (and) protects. It goes before you to "make the crooked places straight."*

Our ultimate goal must be to live in, through, and as God. If we are not to do this, why did the Master teach, "Take no thought for your life,"? Life is meant to be lived by Grace, without power (of any kind). And again he says:

See what happens on the seventh day: (on the Sabbath) *"In the meanwhile his disciples prayed him, saying, Master, eat. But he said unto them, I have meat to eat that ye know not of." He was telling them not to go out (and) get meat; but to rest in the Sabbath of* **I have:** *no words, no thoughts, no might, no power.*

(You students who are going through this initiation) *You students who are ready for the Sabbath must prepare for it by learning to rest back in this realization: "(I) Let my Soul take over instead of my mind." Then every time you go within, something new and fresh will come forth.* Of course it's a new creation. Behold I make <u>all</u> things new.

In the consciousness of (this) Sabbath, (in this Christ Consciousness) *you do not have to) go out and get meat, (because) you have it.* (How do you have it?) *By your recognition that you and the Father are one.*

(Says Joel) *For six days you have labored to study and to train yourself, and those "six days," remember, are for most of you many, many years. But there (does come) a rest to* **My** *people; there comes a Sabbath; and that is when you stop all your metaphysical struggling, (and) relax,* **let** *Grace live your life.*

Those students (in this initiation) *who have been listening and studying with the inner ear* (for many years) *are now entering that period of Sabbath when they can feel* (**feel**) *within themselves: "I [don't] know any truth. I cannot live on quotations. The only truth I know is what is coming* (forth from that deep well within). *I am (now) living in (a) period of unknowing, in which every day I go within to receive the manna for that day, (I) listen for Thy voice."*

"Thy Grace is my sufficiency."

You see how beautiful this is, how beautiful. He says:

The Infinite Way takes you through the "six days" of labor— thinking and knowing truth, searching for truth, pondering truth, meditating truth—until (finally) *you go beyond the activity of the mind. Finally, you come to* (the Sabbath). *(And) Every word that flows from God into your awareness becomes the bread, the wine, the water. (the) health, (the) strength, (the) vitality, and all that is necessary for your experience.*

And so my dear, dear friends – as we walk through this initiation alone, yet not alone – I say to you that these moments of stepping out of the human mind – the world mind, the mental images of this world – and standing still in that pool; in that deep, deep universe within and beholding Spirit, the movement of Spirit across the waters – this is how you are made new. This is how you are transformed. This is how you are made a new creature. This is how you are lifted up to the place where Christ liveth your life. And this you can tell no man.

To him that overcomes this human mind, this taking thought, this thinking, Christ says, "I will give the hidden manna, and now we know what that manna is, don't we? We live by it, the invisible movement of Spirit.

To him that overcomes the mind I will give the invisible movement of Spirit, and I will give him a stone, and on the white stone a new name is written, and that name is Christhood. And no one knoweth saving he that receiveth it. No one around you will be able to tell that you have received your initiation, that you have received Christhood, that you have ascended out of the mind into Christ Consciousness, into this deep universe, into My Kingdom. But you will know that you have received it. You will know.

Isn't this wonderful? Passing - we are passing from humanhood to Christhood, from mind to Spirit, from images to the kingdom of heaven here and now. We are passing from intellect to Consciousness. We are passing from death to life. This humanhood that we thought was a life is death. Now we come into Life – Eternal life, everlasting life, Christ life, and this life will never leave you nor forsake you. And so we pass from humanhood to Christhood, right here, right now. We rest in the Sabbath. We rest on the seventh day and we behold the perfect creation unfolding before our inner eye.

[Silence]

CLASS 12

THE INNER CHRIST

Bill: Well, good morning.

This is February 24th of 2013, and the only reason I give the date is so we can listen to these talks in order. All right. The name of this talk I believe is The Inner Christ or That Inner Christ. And I'm going to share some things this morning that are my own individual spiritual experiences and not because – well, it's not something I discuss very often because somehow it cheapens it if you discuss it. But in order to bring out the principle of the Christ within I want to start by sharing an experience or two of that Christ.

So I assume as in any other talk you have had a period of silence, a period of meditation, a period of listening first before you turned on the talk. If not, you need to pause it, find your comfortable chair or sofa, sit down and have a meditation. Try to be receptive to that inner Christ. You can even invite it. "Father, Christ, you reveal yourself. I am listening. I am attentive. I am still. Let your voice instruct me. Let me feel your Presence within." Then be still until you feel that inner movement of Spirit that we've discussed in the past. And then yes, turn on the talk and listen.

And so in the year 19 – let's see if I can get this right – 1975, I had been practicing meditation for roughly two years and one evening as I sat down to meditate suddenly there was a feeling of a Presence within me and without. Within and without – those terms become kind of meaningless, but as I sat there with eyes closed after reading The Art of Meditation for a little bit I felt a Presence and a tingling on the side of the face. It's very distinct. If you've ever felt it you know what it is, and you know it's not of this world. And that touch was within and without. And with it came a sense of peace, and I knew: This is Christ. And I knew it was from another dimension.

And in the weeks and months that followed for the next couple of years I meditated quite frequently, although I wasn't sure why I was meditating at that time. I just knew that I needed – I wanted to be close to this Christ. And as time went by I had more and deeper experiences of the Christ. At one point I had the experience as I've shared in the past of closing my eyes and meditating on—well, I just said what came spontaneously, which on that morning was, "Father, lift me up into Thy Presence and let Thy Presence descend in me. Let there be no me, but only Thy Presence, and as I sat there in total receptivity, standing still, not moving – not moving my mind or my body. Just waiting. Not even waiting even—not really even waiting. Just—just resting on the sea of Spirit. Suddenly I felt that same Presence down my right arm, and I had felt it there many times, but it went then down my left leg, and pretty soon that whole half of my body was that tingling Presence, and then down my right arm and down my right leg. And instead of half of my body, my entire body was that Presence, and I knew it, and I knew I was It and It was I.

There was no me there. There was only that living, vibrating Christ, I. And then it filled the room I was in, the living room. I can still remember. All four corners from floor to ceiling, all four corners was that Presence filling the room, vibrating, vibrant, alive, and I was that Presence. But it wasn't an overpowering, dominating feeling. It was a light full of pure white energy,

Presence, Being. And then I knew it was going to go infinite. The next step was infinite from filling the body, filling the room, to filling the universe. And I knew I was going with it because oneness. And then the me came back and experienced a little fear: "What will happen to me if it goes infinite? Will I be totally extinguished?" That was the fear in a split second, and it subsided and I came back to normal. Except you can never come back to normal after an experience of that nature because now you know that the reality of you is Infinite Christ being.

And in 1978 I heard a tape called *Follow Me* by some man named Herb Fitch. I had never heard of him. I had heard tapes at tape sessions of Joel Goldsmith for quite a while. I used to go to South Pasadena and listen to those tapes. But never had I heard somebody named Herb Fitch. Who was this guy? I didn't know, but I was invited, so I sat down at this lady's home and I listened to Herb Fitch, and the tape was called *Follow Me*, and although I did not know it at the time, I know now *Follow Me* was a talk given at the 1977 Maui Sense to Soul series or seminar by Herb Fitch.

So I sat down, I closed my eyes and I listened to *Follow Me*, and I really could not believe what I was hearing. Here was another man who knew of the inner Christ, and the reason why I was so surprised is because – well, although I had read Joel's books I had never met him, and there was no man on earth that I had met up unto this point – this was six years after the spiritual experiences I had that taught me that the inner Christ is the only Christ there is. The inner Father is the only God there is. And I found no one else that knew this. Yes, I found their writings, but no human being or no man that I had ever laid eyes on knew this.

So when I heard this talk, I knew that he knew, and I determined I would go to meet him. And so I tracked down where his next seminar was. This was in '78, and the next seminar he was giving was the 1979, Avila Beach seminar, and I made it my business to find the money to get there and to go. And I even found out who was making appointments for individual appointments with Herb afterwards, and so I made an appointment for that Monday after the seminar to have an individual hour of his time. But you know now I really wanted to just look into his eyes and see if he really knew of this inner Christ.

So I hopped in my 1978 Toyota Corolla and I drove up Pacific Coast Highway 101 and I went to Avila Beach and I got my hotel room at the Motel 6. Is that what it is the inexpensive one?—because I didn't have a lot of money, and I attended the seminar.

Well, on Saturday night I had never met him before. Friday night was introductions and a good talk. It may have even started Thursday. I don't recall. I'd have to go look at the talks, but Saturday night was the talk called *Healing Outside of Time*. And it was all about stepping outside of time, and as he talked, and you can hear that talk. Just a minute—I'll see which one it is exactly. That was class 7 of the Avila Beach Beyond Time seminar, class 7, *Healing Outside of Time*. And so that's available on the website as well as *Follow Me*.

Now, I attended his seminar. I never saw him before this moment or these couple of days, and I walked in there Saturday. There was probably 200 people, maybe 150, and I found a seat and I sat down and I closed my eyes and I listened. We had the meditation before the talk, I remember, and as we were meditating, from the back of the room Herb entered through the door and walked up front and sat down, and his books were there and the microphone was there and there was a Bible there and some flowers and a glass and a pitcher of water. And he sat down and closed his eyes and I continued to meditate. Well, he started to talk, and as he talked I forgot about myself and I forgot about the room and I forgot about him, and I listened to what Christ was saying through him. Not the Christ of him. I wasn't listening to that. I was listening to the Christ within me revealing through him. I was listening to that one Christ which I had come to see is my center. And I had come to see this not by reading it in a book or somebody telling me, but by the experience that I already shared with you.

So I sat there listening and suddenly I was not there. There was none of me there. There was no room, no people. Somehow my consciousness was lifted up, way up high above this world. Joel says in *The New Horizon* that above this world is a universe of Spirit, and that's where I was lifted, and I know it. And in that universe of Spirit I felt myself one with Christ, and Christ gave me something, and I didn't know what it was. I just felt something passing from Christ to me. And yet there was no real me defined, but something was happening, and so I just sat there and watched, waited, observed.

And somewhere I heard a voice, and it was Herb's, and he said, "Now we'll take a 15-minute break or a 10-minute break and then we'll meet back here." And so at the time I was smoking still and I got up and I went outside to have a cigarette. But when I opened my eyes before I got out of my chair I looked around and I was so light, I was floating so much that I started to giggle, and then I repressed the giggle because I didn't want people to be looking at me like I was drunk or something, but I was. I was drunk on the Spirit.

And I walked outside and I looked at the ocean, the Pacific Ocean, and oh my God! I could feel myself as that entire ocean. I could feel the entire ocean in my being. I looked around the sky. I was the sky. The sky was inside of me. I turned around and looked at the buildings and the telephone wires and the asphalt, sidewalk, and the cars parked. And how strange! I felt every one of them inside of my being and my being inside of them. Nothing was dead matter. Nothing. All was alive, and I was all.

Then I turned and I looked at the other people standing. I looked at their faces. I could feel my face on theirs and their face on mine. The hard and fast lines weren't there. It was hard to tell where I left off and they began. Or where they left off and I began. There was just a feeling of oneness with every direction that I looked. I was one with all and all was within my being, and my being constituted all. And I knew again – again, there is one Christ, and that Christ is I. And so Sunday passed, Monday came, and it became time to have my individual meeting with Herb session. So I went to his hotel room and I knocked. He opened the door. I was a little bit intimidated. I didn't know what to expect.

I walked in and we sat down, and I felt an overpowering urge to say something, and so I said, "I need to tell you something, Herb." He said, "Yes?" I said, "I need to tell you, you are not my teacher. I have a teacher, and the teacher is within, and the teacher is Christ." And I remember very distinctly I didn't really know what he would say. I thought maybe he would say, "Well, if I'm not your teacher, what are you doing here?" or – I didn't know what to expect. But I had to tell him that; I couldn't keep from telling him that. "I have a teacher, and it's Christ within."

And he surprised me. He said, "Can I have your phone number?" I said yes. I didn't know what to say. I said yes, because remember, I was still feeling this oneness, not quite as intense as Saturday by Monday, but I was still feeling it. He said, "Can I have your phone number?" and I said yes. He said, "Because I'd like to give it to some students, and perhaps if they need help you'd be willing to help them." I said, "Of course." And so we shared a little more, meditated together, and that was the session.

And I drove back down south to southern California to Pasadena, my home, and after three or four more days the consciousness, that higher consciousness left and I was back to being a person, and I ran into some difficulties and some of my own character shortcomings popped up, and I felt very disappointed in myself, and I felt the urge to call Herb. So I called him up and I said, "Herb, I—I'm just not ready to help anybody. I haven't even removed the beam from my own eye." He didn't make any comment on that, but he accepted that I wasn't ready, that I felt I wasn't ready, and that was pretty much it. And I didn't think anything more about sharing or helping anybody or any of that for 30 years. And the reason is it took 30 years to discover why I never could help anybody. Only that inner Christ can.

Now I want to read you a scripture. It's from John. I love John. John 20, and it has to do with Mary standing outside the tomb after the three days. And it says:

Mary stood without at the (tomb) weeping: and as she wept, she stooped down, and looked into the (tomb),

And seeth two angels in white sitting, the one at the head, and the other at the feet, where the body of Jesus had lain.

And they (said) unto her, Woman, why weepest thou? She saith unto them, Because they have taken away my Lord, and I know not where they have laid him.

And when she had thus said, she turned herself back, and saw Jesus standing, and knew not that it was Jesus.

Jesus saith unto her, "Woman, why weepest thou? whom seekest thou?" (And) She, supposing him to be the gardener, saith unto him, Sir, if thou have borne him hence, tell me where thou hast laid him, and I will take him away.

Now you see, she's going to the tomb expecting to see Christ, isn't she? But Christ isn't there. Christ is not in that tomb. And even when she looks on Christ she doesn't see him. She thinks he's a gardener! What happens next?

(Christ says to her) "Mary." (And) She turns herself, and saith unto him, Master.

Now you see? She's looking at the tomb and expecting to find Christ buried in the tomb. Now that's what I did my entire life, particularly from the time I first picked up The Art of Meditation, which was in '72, until I had a spiritual experience in '75. I expected to find the Christ in Joel, but Christ isn't in Joel. Joel's not here. I expected the Christ to be in Jesus some 2000 years ago, but Christ isn't in Jesus. Jesus isn't here. I expected to find Christ as a presence. Well, when I was a child I expected to find God as a presence in the sky by and by.

I remember when I was six years old and I asked during Vacation Bible School —we were all working with our arts and crafts things—and I raised my hand and I said to the man, "Who is God? Where is God?" And he looked very uncomfortable. He didn't know how to answer the question, so he pointed to a picture of Jesus, and he said, "That's God." And he dropped it. Now let's go have recess. Everybody got up from the tables and ran outside hooping and hollering and taking their balls and hula hoops and whatever else they had, and the teacher went out with them. I looked at that picture of Jesus on the wall. I'm only six or seven. I walked over to that picture, and I stared and I studied and I looked, and finally I heard a voice inside said, "That's not God. That's a man." I felt a little guilty with that voice because I didn't have anybody else telling me that, but I walked outside and went and played with my friends and forgot about it.

Don't you see? Even at seven something was trying to tell me He's not in this tomb. Why are you looking in a tomb? He is not here. He has risen." And then as I got older and I read the books by Joel Goldsmith, I thought – well, Joel definitely had the Christ, but Joel's gone. I can't get—who can I find that has the Christ? And then as I began to have some experiences in 1975 I wondered—I wonder if these are real? I'm the only one that seems to be having them. Nobody else is talking about anything like this, and so when I heard that talk *Follow Me* by Herb Fitch in which he recommended finding the inner Christ, and in fact, suggested that that was the only way to freedom, salvation—ah, then I knew here is another who has the Christ. And so I went up to meet him, and yet the only thing that I could say was, "No, you're not my teacher. (chuckles) The Christ is, within."

And so all of my life Christ has been trying to tell me, "I'm not in a tomb. Stop looking there." All my life Christ has been telling me, "I am within you, and when you are still enough, when you are quiet enough, I take over."

You know, several years after that experience I had a dream. Let me see if I can find it because I think I wrote this one down. Hold on. Okay, now remember I'm sharing a <u>dream</u>. It's pointing out a principle. That's all. All right, this was in 2004, so this was after Herb had left and there [were] no other people around that I was listening to.

So in the dream there was a large audience and a spiritual teacher was up in front and I went up and gave him a ferocious hug, and while hugging him I leaned back and looked up into his eyes and I thought, "I love you so much." And he looked down at me and then looked again, a double-take, and he said, "You really have healed completely, haven't you?" Then he withdrew from my embrace, and he and several other people around the hall fell on their knees and bowed down to me, bowed down before me. But I started to object and raise up my hand, and they stopped. Then I realized – it's not me they're bowing down to. They're bowing down to the God within me, and so I relaxed and I allowed them to recognize and pay tribute and even bow down to the God Self within me. There was no feeling of ego, just observing and allowing it to happen.

You see? This dream showed me I have to reach the place where the only Christ there is anywhere is within me, and I have to allow it to live Itself and even be recognized by others. I can't allow – well, ego can work two ways. This false sense of self can puff itself up and say I'm so great, and of course we know if that's going on, Christ isn't. I haven't had a big problem with that. Sometimes yes, sometimes. My bigger problem has been with the belief that I'm no good, but that's just as much of a hindrance. Because while I'm walking around thinking I'm no good or I'm not good enough or how dare you bow down to me; don't you know I'm just a human being – there's still a self there! And that self is not Christ. And so both of those extremes have to go.

He is not here. Why are you looking at and in a tomb? And so when Mary turns around and sees the Christ she still doesn't recognize him and thinks he's a gardener until the Christ awakens her. "*Mary*." And we go through our lives thinking that Christ is up in the sky or in that temple. If I could just get to that temple in India where the meditations are so powerful. Or in that teacher. If I could just – oh, if only I had been able to have some private meditation time with Joel. Or if only I could get some meditation time with Herb or with Bill or with Virginia.

Why are you looking in these tombs? You will never find Christ there. Yet, the Christ in your own being is calling your name. Awaken! Awaken! Turn within. There you will find the living Christ, not a dead Christ from 2000 years ago or even a dead Christ from 50 years ago in Joel's Kailua classes. Stop looking in the tomb! He is not there! The living Christ is within. It's within. And the only way to experience that inner Christ is by taking the path laid down for us in those Kailua talks in those chapters called *Experience of the Christ* and *Experiencing the Christ* and *How to Pray*. Those tell us how to open the door to the inner experience.

The whole purpose for The Infinite Way and every book ever written was to lead you to your own inner Christ, but I can tell you that for a while it's kind of scary. It feels like – like Mary's experience. "Where have you taken him? You've taken away my Lord." That has to happen to you first.

First every vestige of a belief that Christ is somewhere out here has to be completely eradicated from your consciousness. And when that happens and you haven't yet experienced the inner Christ, it's—it's just like Mary. There's weeping that goes on. Oh, you've taken away the Christ, this Christ that I worshipped all these years. The Christ that walked the holy lands 2000 years ago. The Christ that came through Joel. You've taken away that Christ.

Let me tell you something. There is no external Christ. None. Zero. Nada. The living Christ sits on the well of your consciousness saying to you, "I am knocking. I am knocking. If you open, if you listen I will give you the Christ that springs up into everlasting life, that springs up into a wellspring of water. If you know who I am and you ask, if you know where I am and you ask, I will give it unto you."

And now I tell you of another dream. The only reason I'm sharing these personal experiences is that you can see in my path how I was guided to this discovery in consciousness. In this dream I was in a misty, cloudy place. A realm where there was mist rising. And in the background, in the back behind me was a big gate and someone was standing here to my left, and they said, "I'm going back," – meaning I'm going back to earth. They said, "I'm going back. I still haven't learned how to love unconditionally." And poof!—they disappeared. And I thought to myself, "I'm not going back. I don't want to go back." And then came the realization, "Well no, I haven't learned how to – no, I guess I haven't learned how to love unconditionally either." And I knew that I would be sent back. And that was the extent of the dream.

And so the dream was telling me that we need to learn how to love unconditionally, wasn't it? And that bothered me for many,

many years. How do you love unconditionally? Every time I try the ego pops up with a different disguise, and there it is dirtying up the water, muddying up the waters. Just can't love unconditionally.

Ah, but you see the experiences over the years have taught me no one, no human being can love unconditionally. **No one!** Only the Christ can love unconditionally. And so the answer to that question is: I know now. I know how to love unconditionally, and the answer is I can't. Christ and only Christ within can love unconditionally, and so as I move aside and become a beholder of Christ living Itself, then love can flow unconditionally.

And so now I know the answer. The answer is to die so that you don't have to come back and live! You can live on that eternal plane and not have to come back and prove this. And so again another experience points out that he is not in the tomb of humanhood. He is within. He is, It is, I am within. Now Joel says in The Infinite Way book in the chapter *The Christ:*

Spiritual consciousness is the release from personal effort in the realization that harmony is.

See that? It's a release from trying to be anything in the realization, the inner realization that Christ is, harmony is.

This consciousness, with its release from personal effort, is attained as we find the Christ within us (as) a present reality.

You see that? You don't experience a release from personal effort or personal sense and then have the realization. No. You can't love unconditionally. You have the inner realization of Christ as a present reality and then you're released from personal sense. See that? She could not see the Christ until the Christ Itself said, "*Mary,*" and she awakened and no longer found it necessary to look in the tomb because the Christ was right there in her consciousness. So he says:

The Christ is the activity of Truth in individual consciousness. It's not a declaration of truth it's the (reception of) Truth.

And so again and again and again we keep repeating: You have to **receive** truth in consciousness. You have to **receive** Christ. Christ has to be a living within experience, and **there's no Christ out there.** Out there is this world and everything in it and everyone in it and everyone that's ever been in it is this world, and this world is not externalized because no illusion is ever external. And so these are mental concepts. You're looking at the Christ and assuming it's the gardener! You're looking at the Christ and assuming it's your father, your friend, your spouse. You're looking at the Christ and assuming it's you, the person. And these are the tombs, and he is not here. He is risen.

However, in the real experience of the Christ in your inner meditation, when the Christ announces Itself, as Joel puts it, then – then you're released from the illusion of the tombs. So he says:

We attain an inner stillness, we become more and more receptive to Truth (or Christ) *declaring Itself within us. (And) the activity of this Truth in our consciousness is the Christ, the very presence of (Christ). Truth* (or Christ) *received and continuously entertained in our consciousness is the law unto all of our affairs. It governs, guides, leads, directs, and supports our every activity of daily existence.*

See – *"I live; yet not I, Christ liveth."* But it must be an inner Christ. No other Christ. Not the Christ of Jesus. Not the Christ of Joel. Not the Christ of Bill. Not the Christ of Herb. Not the Christ of Virginia. Not the Christ of Tony. Not the Christ of Bob. It has to be I Christ within. This one that grabbed a hold of me so strong that I was able to go up to the only person I knew with Christ and say, "You're not my teacher. Christ is my teacher within."

To many, (he says) *the word Christ persists as a more or less mysterious term, an unknown entity, something rarely if ever experienced. This, we must change if we are to benefit by the revelation of Christ Jesus (and) many others. We must experience the Christ as a permanent continuous dispensation. We must live in the constant consciously awareness of (Christ) active within. (You must) maintain always a receptive attitude within – a listening ear – and soon (you will) experience an inner awareness. (And) This is the activity of Truth in consciousness, or Christ attained.*

And so this inner awareness of this Presence within—this is Christ attained. And the inner awareness comes from a receptive attitude, and the receptive attitude comes from being still, and you become still – that comes from knowing that you are ready to go beyond the letter and have the experience.

Now, in this book <u>Leave Your Nets</u> it's all about leaving these mental images so that you may have the inner Christ experience or the experience of the inner Christ. So he says:

The greatest force, the greatest power on earth, is grace.

This is Joel's book, <u>Leave Your Nets</u>, the chapter *The New Discipleship*. See, if you have this inner experience you are part of the fellowship of the Spirit. You're not now dancing around out here quoting Scripture and talking about Christ that Joel said and Herb said and Jesus said. No. You're quietly, silently having the inner experience of the living Christ, the powerful Christ. And so Joel says:

Grace, which is the love of God for God's children, is the only real power there is, and our demonstration of it will be in proportion to the withdrawal of our dependence on and faith in man, and the establishment within ourselves of (Christ).

You see, this book is all about leaving dependence on people, places, and things and beliefs and ideas and thoughts so that you may have this inner experience of the Christ. And when you first are confronted with the—let's have it again in his words. Hang on. Okay, this is the chapter 12, *Experiencing the Christ* from the 1955 Kailua study series. In Joel's words he says:

Now, the point I'm making is this:

Now remember, the name of this chapter is *Experiencing the Christ*, and that's what we're talking about, how to experience the only living Christ. There's only one living Christ, and it is within you. No other place can you find it. Not in holy mountains, not in holy temples, but you'll have to find it within you. And he says:

The point I'm making is this: In being aware of the discords of human existence, instead of drawing on your head (for denials and affirmations, instead of drawing) *on your thinking, on your (memorized) truth, now* (from now on) *stand stock still, let the Father* (the Christ) *give you the necessary truth for the situation. Because* (that's what) *I have to do when I'm called on for help. I can't turn to a single soul or any memorized statements from my writings, if I thought they had power I'd just let them do the work. No. I never go back to draw (on) anything* (from Infinite Way) *writings or anybody else's writings (not) even from Scripture.*

There's no Christ there. Why do you keep looking there? That's a tomb. He's not here. Mary, wake up!

No. From now on when you are called upon for help, sit down in an atmosphere of expectancy. He says:

When I am asked personally for help, you all notice my attitude. It's always one of listening, (listening) *and then if I have anything to say, (I say) it. Now that is to bring you to the point of experiencing the Christ. You experience the Christ every time a discord or inharmony appears to you, and instead of you making a statement of truth or thinking a thought, you turn within and wait until (something) comes to you, doesn't have to come in words. It doesn't have to come in thoughts. Eventually you'll find that it comes in a feeling of release,* (ah, release) *and you know all is well.*

Now that's what we said before. You don't experience the release from a personal sense and then Christ experience. No! You go within, sit down, stand still from personal sense, and then the Christ releases you from personal sense. You're free from it. And that's what happened to me. I went into meditation in Herb's class there. I went into meditation. I stood still. There was still a sense of me being lifted up, but in the experience of Christ, the living Christ, I was released from personal sense, and when I walked outside there was only Christ in every direction.

Now what had changed? What we just said. Only the inner awareness, the inner awareness that saw people and places and things in all these tombs and drove all the way up to northern California to find the Christ in another man. Why, it said, "I'm right here within you, you silly, silly being. Why did you drive all the way up here? I already showed you, there's only one Christ, and it's the Christ of my consciousness.

Every Christ has to die. You remember Joel said to us over and over again: All of these synonyms for God have to die. God is love. Well, where am I in that? God is Spirit. Well, so what! All of these synonyms have to die. Every one of them. Where have you taken my Lord? There is the feeling for a while: I've got nothing now! I was relying on this belief of God. I was relying on a concept of Christ. Now you've taken that! You've taken all the people with Christ. What's left? I have nothing!

Now, yes empty-handed you can come within. Empty-handed you can stand stock still. Empty-handed you can experience the Christ and be released from personal sense. And you can do this in every meditation. So he says:

That is the experience of the Christ. That's the point I'm trying now to see if all of us can do. The method? (Don't be engaged) in any controversy with any form of error. Just Stand still. If you must think, think something that has no bearing on it.

Let's say that someone comes to you and says, "I have this cold. Will you help me?" And you close your eyes. If you've got to think—we really want to reach for the high place where we don't have to think—but if we have to think in the beginning, then we must think something like: Well, he is not here. He has risen.

See? That has no connection at all. Or, I am the Truth. But only one thought please, not a book or a paragraph. So I reach for no thought, but if you have to have a thought in the beginning to get to that place of no thought, that's fine. But get there as quick as you can. And he says:

That gives the Christ an opportunity to come to you as an experience. Later on you will follow the same method with all of the harmonies.

Why? Why would you do that do you suppose? Because the experiences of, or the pictures of inharmony, disease, death, lack, limitation – those are tombs. He is not here! Awaken! Mary awaken! I am here within. But the pictures of harmonies and beauty and color and form – all of those are also this same image, the same tombs. These are tombs also! Only the concepts of them are good tombs. Oh, now there's a good tomb! Look at that child, so full of life. Why isn't he cute! For four years old he sure is intelligent, isn't he? Why he's more intelligent than the other – wait a minute. That's a tomb!

You're looking at Christ, but saying those words and thinking those thoughts about that are—well, next to—next to useless. You won't be released from that by saying that to yourself. You cannot be released by repeating that to yourself. Well, I'm looking at an image. So? Who's saying it? **Another image**! Oh my God! How am I going to be released?

You know the way. Stand stock still. Take no thought, and I will reveal myself as a living Christ, a now Christ, an ever present right here Christ. So he says:

(And) That gives the Christ an opportunity to come to you in experience. Later on you will follow the same method with all of the harmonies. Because once you have achieved the slightest degree of success in meeting discords, the next thing that will present itself to you is the harmonies.

And so you will learn to follow this same practice when you see youth, (or) health, (or) vitality, (or) wealth. You learn to look right through it, and not rejoice in it.

Now why would you rejoice in a tomb? He is not here. He is risen.

Clear your thought in this same spiritual way, so the Christ can show you the truth.

What's it gonna show you? Well, he says:

The Christ can show you the truth about what even appears as human good.

In other words, the Christ can show you Itself, Itself as an experience. A living experience. And he gives you a statement here:

Just as you want Christ to reveal the truth about discord and inharmony, you had better want Christ to reveal the truth about a good human appearance, or it's only a question of time it's going to change to a bad human experience.

And finally at the end here he says on the last page if I can get there, he says:

The achieving of the state of consciousness (which is the inner awareness of the living Christ) *begins in this particular way, first, because the discords and inharmonies of existence are irritating and therefore (they) announce themselves more forcefully* (and you're forced to find an answer.) *And in those moments we will now train ourselves to resist temptation to deny or affirm or (even) to think thoughts, even good thoughts.* We will stand stock still and *give an opportunity for the Christ to announce Itself.*

And then you're released! The Christ announces Itself in you, in your being.

Okay? Is it clear?

Our stating truth and thinking truth does not bring it. (It doesn't bring the Christ.) *Our refraining from stating truth and thinking truth brings Christ. As long as behind it we have the inner consciousness of the correct letter of truth.*

In other words, you couldn't give this to a new student. That's why I have – well, that's why it's being given to those of us who are a little more serious. We're not looking for healing after healing after healing. We're looking for the inner experience of Christ.

Now, let's be still for a moment and see if that's it for today or if there's more.

[Pause]

Woman, whom seekest thou? Oh Lord, where have you taken my Lord? Where have you laid him? Please tell me. *He is not here: he is risen.*

I share with you those experiences that came to me over the years—several, not all by any means, but several that pointed out to me that in every way and in every area I have to experience the living Christ, and that it's no longer correct for me to look at myself and say, "Well, of myself I'm nothing. I can't do anything. I've never been any good at anything and I'm no teacher and this, that, and the other. No. That's a lie of personal sense.

When there's no personal sense, when that is standing still then the Christ announces Itself in my experience and it says, *"I am the Teacher, the only Teacher, and I am the Way. Be still. I will teach."* Then if others come and say, "Oh, I got so much out of what you have to say," I can only say "thank you" because I did too. (chuckles) I was listening to Christ as you were. And with the discords that are presented to me I'm allowed now to take no thoughts. I'm allowed now to not deny or affirm anything. I'm not allowed to do that. Those were the nets. I'm leaving those nets. I'm not allowed to go running to a teacher of 2000 years ago or a man that taught in the 40s, 50s, and 60s. I'm not allowed now to go running to a holy temple, a holy place, a holy book. Even Scriptures! I'm leaving all those nets.

All must be abandoned for My sake, says Christ. I'm not allowed to cling to anything. I'm floating here with no raft! It's very uncomfortable. You have taken my Lord! What do I do? Even the Christ that I believed in is now nothing. I realize it was only a concept. My God! I'm weeping. Where, where, oh where is my Lord?

And yet, if I will turn within, if I will be still, if I will come here often, if I will practice what I have learned and stand stock still, in the stillness Christ will announce Itself. It will set me free from personal sense, from the negative personal sense and the good personal sense. It will allow me to see through the discords to Christ as an inner experience right here, right now. It will allow me to look through the good appearances to see Christ, to experience Christ right here within, right here and now.

Christ will announce Itself and set me free, and It will do so with maybe only a word. Maybe just *"Bill."* Or maybe just *"Mary."* Or maybe just *"Brian."* Or maybe just *"Nancy."* Maybe no words at all. Maybe that inner feeling of being lifted up and the tingling sensation of being flooded with Spirit. Maybe just the inner awareness of the movement of Spirit over the face of the deep. Who knows?

Christ is infinite. Let Christ reveal Itself to you in an individual way.

You must know now that the only Christ there is is the living Christ within you, and that there's no other Christ to find. You must know now that the God of the ancients – well, it's dead. There's no life in it. It's only a story book. You must know that the God of – well, even the Father of Jesus is only a name. You must know now that the only God there is is the God within you, and that It must reveal Itself to you or you will be Godless. You must know now it is time to launch out into the deep, and now you really know what that feels like, don't you?

Launch out into the deep and cast your nets on the other side of the veil. Cast your nets within and wait and see what reveals itself. Wait! Wait! The Christ will announce Itself. *"I am here."* In some way you will know. Not because you read it or you heard it or so-and-so said it from the podium. No. You will know by a living experience the living Christ, the Infinite Christ, the Christ Omnipresence. And then let It live Itself where you are. And if people bow down to you because you've healed them, so what. Stand aside. It is Christ. It is Christ revealing Itself. You had no part in it and you know it other than a beholding consciousness, a listening consciousness, a receptive consciousness to the movement of Christ.

It's time to grow up spiritually. Stop sitting at the feet of— well, a statue, a person, or a concept. It's time to experience the living Christ and to follow It as It lives day by day your experience.

I hope it's clear. I know I talked a little long today and probably shared more stories than I should have, but I hope that it's clear to all of you that the only Christ there is is Christ within. *I* must be realized.

Thank you. Thank you.

[Silence]

CLASS 13

A NEW HEAVEN AND A NEW EARTH

Bill: Good morning.

This is March 3rd of 2013. I have much to say to you today, and so if you will, please take a moment and practice the silence and invite the Christ to speak, and you will have a definite effect on this talk. And you say, "Well how can that be? You've already given it." But that's not true, because as you attain that silence and invite the Christ to speak, it will have a definite effect on what you hear, and so you will affect this talk. And because there's no time, you haven't yet heard this talk. It's happening right now. So, if you haven't done it turn off the talk. Find a place to be still, enter the silence, and just stop and listen for the Christ.

In the garden there were two trees. The one tree was the tree of the knowledge of good and evil. But there was another tree there, and that tree was the Tree of Life, the Tree of Eternal Life. For us – for everyone – we have been eating the knowledge of the tree of good and evil for centuries; many, many centuries. But those of us in this group have been invited to a new feast, a spiritual feast in which we might eat of the Tree of Life, eternal life. A life not made with hands, eternal in the heavens.

And so the invitations have been sent, and we in this group have each received our invitation to come up higher. To come out from under the law of the tree of good and evil and come into the grace of the Tree of Life. You have your invitation; I have mine, and it is my feeling that all of us are ready. And of course that means we must find a way to go from the tree of knowledge to the Tree of Life. We must go from the letter to the Spirit, or the experience of God. We must go from the mind to the conscious awareness. We must go from a temple made with hands that is destroyed, a body of flesh, to the temple not made with hands, eternal in the heavens.

We must make this transition **this time**. We have received an invitation to the feast. We must come now. And so to this end these classes continue. And today we want to – well, I happened to glance down and see this book called <u>Consciousness Unfolding</u> by Joel, and in it one of my all-time favorite chapters, a chapter called *Peace*, and this chapter has to do with coming out of the human mind and into Christ consciousness, stepping out of humanhood and into Christhood, coming out from under the law and into Grace, coming out from the letter and into the Spirit. All the same thing. And so I thought we might touch some of the high points here. And this first sentence is so beautiful I can hardly stand it. I want to just put it on my forehead or put it on the wall, put it on the mirror. Put it everywhere. Write it on my hand. And it says:

My peace, the peace of Christ! More healings have been brought about through absolute silence than through all the arguments metaphysicians have thought up in the whole history of the world. When you are called upon for help, sit down and get at peace. Think no thoughts; just sit and wait. Wait. Be patient and wait for the peace of … Christ to descend upon you. In that moment of peace, without a word, you will witness healing.

Is that not beautiful? It's like the other statement that I love, which is: *Stand still, and in the silence you will feel the movement of Spirit over the face of the deep.* That's the same as *wait for the peace of the Christ to descend upon you.* It's the same experience. It's just colored in different words. The words that I feel are the movement of Spirit. The words that he felt were the peace to descend. It's the same thing. The point is that there's an inner experience lifting you into that Christ awareness, or lifting you into a moment in which you witness, you bear witness to the movement of Christ. Now says Joel:

The only value a treatment has is to lift us to the point in consciousness where we are ready for the Spirit to unfold.

You know, in other spiritual paths it is true that they all lead to God, but they're not all the same path. And in many paths Joel quotes in here, and I'm going to read it to you, the Hindu path, they feel that this whole world is an illusion. He makes reference to that in the book <u>A Parenthesis in Eternity</u> in the chapter *Reality and Illusion.* He makes reference to how they feel that the whole world is an illusion. It's all an illusion. So why bother! And he says:

This leads to a do-nothing attitude.

It's an illusion. Why are you bothering? Only God is. Well [he says], that may be true in the absolute, but here you have people suffering in poverty and sickness and at the same time saying it's all an illusion.

Recently there was a talk by Herb and it was put up on the website and somebody heard it that follows one of these paths, and he wrote me an E-mail saying, "Why that's absurd! This whole thing is ridiculous! Why are you bothering with any of this when it's all just an illusion? If you knew that only God was, you wouldn't even bother with healings." Now I don't think he took that tone. He was probably a lot more loving, but behind it was this belief that it's all an illusion, so why bother? Yes. In the absolute it's all an illusion. In the absolute only God is here. But what these people don't see is that no illusion is ever externalized. The illusion is not this world. Illusion is the way you see this world. All right?

There is no illusory world. You are standing in the middle of heaven. You never left the garden, but in your mind, in the human mind, you have accepted and eaten of the tree of knowledge of good and evil, and so you have—well, Lao Tzu of the Tao calls it, "You have 10,000 things—the 10,000 things, 10,000 concepts. Concepts of good and evil.

Those concepts are the illusion, not the world.

If you find a way to drop all concepts, even if only for a moment, into that vacuum rushes the very presence of God, and it reveals itself as an experience, not as a theory. As an actual awareness, a descent of My Peace. A movement of the Spirit on the waters of your consciousness. And that experience is the Christ mind, and when you see through the Christ mind you behold the temple not made with hands, eternal in the heavens, or the Tree of Life in the midst of the garden. You don't see the concepts, and so the concepts in your mind melt, and when they melt the picture out here changes. You haven't really healed anything, but on the other hand, as the concept melts it appears as healing.

And so for you, you don't have to sit by the side of the road begging for alms, full of disease, chanting over and over that only God is. For you, you are actually making a transition coming out of the human mind and the concepts of good and evil and seeing that this is a spiritual universe. **And you bring your body with you!** It is also lived in. But listen to this in Joel's words. I think he was on a roll this day when he gave this. I usually underline the important things, and this whole two pages is underlined from the same book, Consciousness Unfolding. He says:

The Hindu mystic may let his body die and may call that a spiritual demonstration insofar as "his kingdom is not of this world."

You see? The Hindu will say, "Well, so what? It's a disease. Yeah, okay. But all disease is illusion and this entire world is illusion, and in fact that body is an illusion." And so he dies.

But Jesus said, in effect: "My kingdom is not of this world, and therefore, I lift my body up to that consciousness where my kingdom is, (I lift my body up to that consciousness where my kingdom is,) and (now) I show forth my body as a spiritual body. This great truth is illumination.

You see that? If you have the book <u>Consciousness Unfolding</u>, look at the chapter towards the back called *Questions and Answers.* And on page 231 you'll find the most amazing, amazing thing, and that's what we're reading. So – *The Hindu mystic may let his body die,* but Jesus lifts his body up. Right? *This is a world of reality.* Now listen. I have all this underlined because every word is important and can be meditated on. *This is a world of reality.* **Here** (he has in italics). **Here** *is the world of reality. Right here and now is God's kingdom. This is not an illusion: This is God's kingdom.*

All right, now again I repeat.

This is the world of reality. **Here** *is the world of reality. Right here and now is God's kingdom. This is not an illusion: This is God's kingdom. (But) The way we look at it, what we see through our eyes— that is the illusion. But the world, itself, is reality. That is why we do not heal or improve it. We merely change our concept of it, because it, itself is perfect right here and now. You are the very Christ of God, the very life of God, made manifest. (But) We see you through the eyes of human concept, imperfect, but you are perfect:*

You see what he's saying there? He's saying that we are standing in the middle of My Kingdom, but we are seeing it as this world. We are standing in the middle of a temple not made with hands, eternal in the heavens, but we are seeing it as the concepts of good and evil. And so the illusion is not in My Kingdom. The illusion is in the concepts, the knowledge of good and evil through which we look and behold My Kingdom. *"For now we see through a glass, darkly; (and) later face to face."* But that later for us is now. We have come to that later. It is time to see face to face.

We have been looking through the knowledge of good and evil, through concepts. Concepts, concepts, concepts. We're given them everywhere. We're given them at school. We're given them by our parents. We're given them by our race. We're given them by the medical field. We're given them by financial wizards. We're given them by politics, politicians. We're given these concepts and all of these concepts, so many leaves on the tree of knowledge of good and evil. This is what we look through, and this knowledge of good and evil planted in the garden – what is it? Come on, let's be honest.

It's the human mind.

That is the human mind. The human mind is the knowledge, or the tree of knowledge of good and evil is the human mind. And so every time you use the human mind and see through it and live through it, you are standing in the garden eating of the knowledge of good and evil. But every time you find that moment of peace, that silence within, you are eating of the Tree of Eternal Life, which is also within. You stand in the garden either way, but on the one hand you see through all these concepts, the 10,000 things, and you don't see the garden you're standing in or you're resting in. But on the other hand, you see through the Tree of Life, that temple not made with hands. My Kingdom, eternal in the heavens.

And so Joel is right. No correction needs to happen out here. What needs to happen is a transition in here. What needs to happen is for us to melt these concepts. And he refers to this in his very first book. I read it to you before, The Infinite Way. He says in the very first chapter, chapter 1, *Putting on Immortality*, he says – well, let's read it from the beginning because it's so beautiful, and I'm sorry if you've heard it before. Get out of that mind and hear it for the first time anew.

"In the Beginning was the Word, and Word was with God, and the Word was God. And the Word was made flesh."

Which is, of course, the temple not made with hands in which you're standing.

You're standing in the Word made flesh.

"The Word was made flesh"—but it still is the Word. By being made flesh it does not change it nature, character, or substance. Cause becomes visible as effect, but the essence or substance is still the Word, or Spirit or Consciousness.

*In this wise, do we understand that there is not a spiritual universe **and** a material world, but rather what appears as our world is the Word made flesh, (or) Spirit made visible, or Consciousness expressed as idea.*

All the error that has existed down through the ages is founded on the theory or belief of two worlds, one the heavenly kingdom, or spiritual life, and the other a material world or mortal existence, each separate from the other.

You see? There's no such thing as two worlds. There's no illusory world – ever! That which is made is not made of that which does appear. There's no illusory world. There is the real world, My Kingdom, a temple not made with hands, viewed through concepts. And so he goes on to say:

*In spite of this sense of two worlds, men have always attempted to bring harmony into the discords of human existence through an attempt, by prayer, to contact this other world, or spiritual realm, and (**bring It**, bring God), bring Spirit to act upon the so-called material world.*

You see, that can't happen, can it? God is functioning now in that temple not made with hands, and you're standing there, one with God, God in expression, or the Word made flesh. But you're up here in this mind, in this tree of knowledge of good and evil and the 10,000 concepts, praying that God would please fix his perfect creation. It's a form of insanity, isn't it? It's spiritual insanity. So Joel says:

197

Let us (then) begin with the understanding that our world is not an erroneous one, but rather that the universe in which we live is the realm of reality about which we entertain a false concept. (So) *The work of bringing health and harmony into our experience is not getting rid of, or changing, a mortal material universe,* (he says) The work is in *correcting the finite concept of our existence.*

And there it is, the very first three paragraphs in the first chapter of the first book ever written of The Infinite Way. And so you see, it had been there all this time, but we had to come to the place where we were ready to come up higher, and we are ready. And so let us finish this part we were reading about the Hindu mystic in <u>Consciousness Unfolding</u>. And let's repeat it again.

This is a world of reality. Here is the world of reality. Right here and now is God's kingdom. (And you are in it!) *The way we look at it, what we see through our eyes – that is the illusion. But the world, itself, is reality. That is why we do not heal or improve it. We merely change our concept of it, because it, itself, is perfect right here and now. You are the very Christ of God, the very life of God, made manifest.* (But) *We see you through the eyes of human concept(s),* (through the 10,000 things), *imperfect, but you are perfect.*

A Hindu mystic looks at this "illusion," and closes his eyes and says, "This is not reality." (But) That is not correct. (No, not in the Christ path, not in The Infinite Way). *This that you see is not illusion: The illusion is the way you see it.* (what you're looking through). *When you see the railroad tracks that's not an illusion. (The) Illusion lies in seeing them coming together. You are not illusion. You are the presence of God, but what we are seeing with our eyes is illusion. We are seeing an illusory concept of you. So what do we have to change – you, or our concept of you?* (He asks.) *Hindu mystics say, "This world is illusion, so I will not bother to heal the body at all." But the body is not illusion. It is the temple of God, according to the teaching of Christ Jesus.*

198

Let us never forget this: This is a spiritual universe. This is the kingdom of God, and the illusion is not this world, but the universal concept of this world. The only place this concept must and can be changed is in the practitioner's thought. When the concept is healed in the practitioner's thought, the patient responds. Why? Because the practitioner's thought is the only place where he can behold an illusion.

You see that? The illusion is not externalized ever. The illusion is in the practitioner's thought, but the practitioner knows this. He doesn't try to change it out here. The practitioner knows it, so he turns within. Well, we're going to get into – the second half of this talk is going to be what we do about these concepts. He goes within. He becomes still. He takes no thought. He feels that movement. The peace of Christ descends, and the picture changes out here. But it's not really picture out here changing, is it? It's a concept melting and more of the temple not made with hands appearing.

So this Christ path is very unique, isn't it? It's unlike any other spiritual path that has ever been. All right. So he says:

We go within and ask for the spiritual kingdom, and then it appears outwardly right here and now. (But) When it does not appear, it is because your inner vision has not yet been changed.

You see, your concept has not been changed. Now listen, LISTEN! If you want to know about healing, he's giving it to you right here.

When it does not appear, it is because your inner vision has not yet been changed: the light of the Christ has not yet touched it.

You see? The peace has not yet descended. The movement has not happened. The awareness is not there. You haven't gotten the spiritual awareness of the temple not made with hands. You haven't felt its movement through your consciousness, through your being. And so therefore the concept cannot melt because you've been knowing these truths with your mind only, and the

199

mind is where the 10,000 concepts are. And do you know your concepts of truth are a part of the tree of knowledge of good and evil? Yes, they are – which is why you have to come up higher than that mind, and that's what the second part of this is going to be. So says Joel:

See the world as Spirit. (Because) Seeing it as matter is the illusion. The world is not matter. This is a spiritual universe. Sin and disease are not actualities: they are illusion or mortal concept. Once you see that, you will never again try to heal the outside, as if it were actually something you could heal.

Now do you see how the Christ consciousness is developed to the point where when you look at an appearance you know it's only a concept, and then you go within, drop all concepts, and let the Christ move? See, that's what he was trying to do for all of us in the Kailua study. He was trying to lift us up above the mind, and he waited 10 years. He said that. He waited 10 years for the students to be ready, and some of you have waited a lot longer.

All right. Now I'm going to take a moment to be still, and then we're going to go into the second half of this.

Okay. Now that we're convinced that the only illusion is the 10,000 concepts, what can we do about them? Okay, so getting back to <u>Consciousness Unfolding</u>, chapter 2 called *Peace*, we'll review it again.

Peace I leave with you, my peace I give unto you: not as the world giveth, give I unto you. Let not your heart be troubled, neither let it be afraid.

My peace, the peace of Christ! More healings have been brought about through absolute silence than through all the arguments metaphysicians have thought up in the whole history of the world.

Because the arguments of metaphysicians, the affirmations and denials, these all take place in the realm of the mind, and the mind we have determined is the 10,000 concepts. It's the 10,000 things. The mind we have determined, the human mind, is the tree of knowledge of good and evil. But absolute silence where that mind is not functioning creates a vacuum into which rushes the very presence of God, and when we feel its movement, it gives us and brings with it the awareness, the spiritual awareness of My Kingdom. And so he says:

When you are called upon for help, sit down, get at peace (or find the silence). *Think no thoughts; just sit and wait. Wait. Be patient and wait for the peace of the Christ to descend upon you.* (or for the movement of the Spirit on the waters of your consciousness) *In that moment of peace, without a word, you will witness healing.*

Now just for memory, let us look again at what he says in chapter 12 of the Kailua study series, which is called *Experiencing the Christ.*

Let me show you the principle (he says). *Every time you engage in denial or affirmation you are in the world of good or evil.*

Well now, see there it is, and I didn't even know it. I didn't even know it, but he's in total agreement that every time you engage in denial or affirmation, you are in the tree of knowledge of good and evil. So every time you go into your mind and you see a problem and you quickly think of a truth and you say something like, "There is no power in this; only God is present" —you have just entered into the knowledge of good and evil.

Let me show you the principle behind (this). (he says). *Every time you engage in denial or affirmation you are in the world of either good or evil. You are in the world of appearances or the world of the pairs of opposites, which is the human world* (or the human mind. *And so even if you change a discord into a harmony, you merely changed one human appearance for another human appearance.*

Do you see that? Now he says:

The basis of the new approach is this: No activity of thought is a healing influence.

No. No activity of thought is the Christ, is it? It's not the Tree of Life. It's not the Christ in the midst of us. No, it's the tree of knowledge of good and evil in the midst of us, which we have to melt. So the new basis is this:

No activity of thought is a healing influence. Therefore, no matter what I know with my mind, it is not going to heal anybody or help anybody or save anybody or bless anybody.

So the mind won't help. You have reached the place in your journey, my dear friends – my dear, dear friends – where the mind cannot follow. Says Christ to the mind, "*Where I go, you cannot follow.*" So says Joel:

As I observe discords and inharmonies in the world, I am not going to take thought. I am going to stop, have no opinion, no judgment. I am not going to make a statement of denial or affirmation. I am not going to let the human mind into this. I'm not going to say it is no part of God, I'm not going to say the only activity here is God. (I'm going to STOP). *I am going to put the finger on my lips.*

Also the finger on your mind. Also the finger on the knowledge of good and evil. Also the finger on the 10,000 things. I'm going to put my finger on my lips. Yes, we can fill our thought with a statement like "*Thy Grace is my sufficiency,*" but it must be *something not pertinent to what we are seeing, or observing. If it is pertinent to that, we have entered the argument. We have come into combat.* We're back in the 10,000 things, the concepts. *We are going to stand aside and not enter the human* mind. *We are going to stand aside with no judgment as to whether this is the devil or God, As if it made any difference (what* concept I have).

Now, you see? Are you beginning to see what he says we must do? We must take no thought. So says Joel:

That's why I say, don't search around in your thought for some truth that will be applicable, because you'll miss the mark. (Miss the mark means sin, right?) *The further you can get away from any statement that applies to the situation, the better you will be and your patient and your own experience.*

So Joel is trying to teach us how to see the temple not made with hands, or My Kingdom, or the garden in which we stand. He's trying to teach us to see with Christ consciousness. He's trying to teach us to come above that human mind, which is the tree of knowledge of good and evil, which is the concepts. And so says Joel:

The point I'm making is this: In being aware of the discords of human existence, instead of drawing on your head, on your thinking, on your memorizing of truth, now (I want you to) *stand stock still, and let the Father give you the truth. Because this is the way I have to do when I'm called on for help. I can't turn to anybody. I can't turn to any memorized statements from my writings* (because they don't have power).

When I'm called upon for help, I sit down in an atmosphere of expectancy, (of receptivity). *And so it is, when I am asked for help, you have all noticed my attitude. It's one of listening.*

All right?

Do not engage in controversy with any form of error. Stand still.

Now you can entertain a truth if you want to. You can entertain some truth that has nothing to do with the situation. Somebody comes to you and says, "I need help. I just lost my job." You can say, *"Man shall not live by bread alone"* or *"I am the Way"* or *"I have hidden manna"* or something that has nothing to do with that situation, but that's not the best. That's not the highest. The highest is to take no thought. That's the highest. And so we will aim for the highest. We will attempt when discord appears or just whenever we're sitting down because we want to have a meditation — maybe there's nothing appearing. Maybe everything's perfectly fine. We will reach for the highest. We will reach for no thought. We will try to obey the Master. Take no thought.

We will try to do what our good friend and guide Joel has said, and we will try and STOP and inside of ourselves consciously realize that human mind is filled with the concepts of good and evil, and seeing through it, or using it to try to remember some truth or to try to grab onto a truth like a life preserver – using the mind at all, we are still standing with the blindfold of the 10,000 concepts, the tree of knowledge of good and evil in front of our eyes. And so it will not work. <u>It won't work</u>.

We now have been called to a higher realm that is the realm of Spirit. So now when we are confronted with a problem or when there's no problem, but we're sitting down to meditate, we will come within, we will recognize and realize the human mind is the tree of good and evil, and we will drop it. We will stop. We will take no thought, and we will sit still. And as he says here:

More healings have been brought about through absolute silence than through all the arguments metaphysicians have thought up in the whole history of the world.

(And so sit down and) think no thoughts; just sit and wait. Wait. Be patient, and wait for (the Christ), the peace of Christ to descend upon you.

That's what we will do. We will wait for that movement, and if it doesn't come, like he says in the Kailua study series, we will get up, we will go about our business, and an hour later we will do the same thing.

Learn to sit down and relax, he says. Whether the case is sin, disease, death, or unemployment; whether or not it is serious, sit down and relax. Do not try to "handle" it! Do not try to "work" on it. Do not try to "treat" it. Sit back and, in silence, create a vacuum for God, for the Christ, to rush in. Sit down and relinquish the thought that the human mind is a healer: Only Christ is the healer.

We talked about that last week, how in that dream I was shown that only Christ can love unconditionally. Well, now we know here in this week that only Christ can heal.

But let's get rid of some of those concepts, shall we? The Christ doesn't really heal, since My Kingdom is perfect. But when Christ rushes in, the concepts melt and you see a little more clearly My Kingdom. And so as he told us in the very first chapter of the very first book in The Infinite Way, our job now is the melting of concepts, something that the human mind cannot do because the human mind is made of those 10,000 concepts. Only the Christ can melt the concepts. You and I must come up higher now where we can rest without taking thought and bear witness to the Christ melting those concepts, which then appears as more harmony out here. The harmony was here already. The harmony was here, but the illusion was in the concepts. So our job becomes that of melting or witnessing the Christ melting concepts. *"My peace I give unto you, not as the world giveth."*

That's our job, to sit in meditation until the Christ gives that peace which melts concepts.

The human mind is not the Christ, he says. *"My thoughts are not your thoughts."* So what good then is all this thinking we have been doing? *The truth of the matter,* says Joel, *is the human mind plays no part in any healing.* Now this is the thing I want to get across to you in the second half of this talk is that when the human mind is still, when the human mind is not functioning, when the 10,000 things have become silent, when the concepts of good and evil are stopped, then into that vacuum that you create, that's your invitation to Christ within you. That's your invitation to the Tree of Life, and it does flow into your being, into your consciousness. And when it does some concept that you may not even be aware of is melted, and more of My Kingdom is revealed in which you're standing.

And so the effort is to be effortless. The effort is to be but a witness, and you may not ever be aware what concept was melted. You may not be aware of it. And you definitely won't be aware of how it works. You won't be aware of how Christ melts the concepts. You won't. Which is why Joel says in all of his writings I have no idea how this works! I only know after the fact – hey, look, harmony's appearing, so some of the 10,000 concepts were melted. You see that? The mind plays no part in healing including understanding how it happened! The best that we can say is "I witnessed," like he says in the Kailua study series. It's like the person on the stand in a trial. They didn't play a part in it. They witnessed this happening, and the best we can do is say, "I witnessed the presence of God, and when I opened my eyes harmony, more of the Kingdom appeared."

So when we know this, then our path is not like the Hindus. We don't sit around and say, "Ah! It's all illusion. We can't do anything about it. No. We recognize – no, the only illusion is in the concepts, and this I can do something about. This I can be still, knowing I can do nothing about except be still and witness. Create such a state of peace, such a state of receptivity, such a state of listening, such a vacuum, that into that nothing the Spirit of God flows and the concepts are melted. This I can do. It's called the practice of meditation, and it's called The Infinite Way.

"If your consciousness is imbued with this silence, with this peace, then it is imbued with Christ power. Healing takes place through the consciousness of the practitioner. The state of your consciousness determines the healing of those that come to you. Not that the healing is yours. No, the healing is the presence of God, the Spirit of God appearing as your consciousness."

So do you see what we're doing, what we're about? You have been called to a new feast, feast of the Tree of Life in your midst.

We must know the nature of God and we must experience, (in italics, he says) experience God. We should not go on the next ten years as we have been doing up until now, just talking about God. The time has now come when we must experience God. Do not pass lightly over this part of the teaching, because it is the most important part of all. We (you and I, my friends) must see God while we are yet in the flesh, here and now. We must experience God through our periods of silence, our periods of peace.

Now, in talking of the 10,000 things, he says:

(Do), *you see the danger of believing that your affirmation or denial is necessary, or that you have to think some kind of a thought (or think some truth?) What if you were in a position where you could not think?*

How would you heal without a mind? (he asks elsewhere).

That statement, that question haunted me. How would you heal without a mind? And the answer: Without a mind is the only way that healing can happen. You see, the Christ mind is your awareness of the movement of Christ. Only Christ can be aware of Christ. So if you are so still that you become aware of the movement of Christ, you are the Christ mind at that moment, and that mind melts concepts and reveals Itself, Its harmony, Its temple not made with hands, the Tree of Life in your midst. And so the answer is: How would you heal without a mind? By bearing witness.

"*It may be true that you could never get away from the presence of God, as the Hindus also believe, but you do not benefit by it simply by knowing that. You benefit only in the degree that peace descends upon you with no thought.*"

See where we differ in this path? That is why on this path we practice healing, though now we know it's not really practicing healing, is it? What we practice is meditation. What we practice is stepping out of—well stopping the tree of knowledge of good and evil. Stopping it long enough for the descent of the Spirit or the peace or the movement of Spirit. And then bearing witness to its movement, to its peace, to the Tree of Life in our midst. And then watching, waiting, beholding as I make all things new. So says Joel:

If we could have (total) silence for the space of half an hour, true silence, we would find ourselves in heaven.

We would find ourselves where we already are, but we would be conscious of it, because the 10,000 things—that veil would be lowered—and we would see not through a glass darkly, but face to face.

Silence is God in action.

You know, there was an old—in centuries past there was a mystic that said God abhors a vacuum, can't abide a vacuum anywhere. All you have to do is become empty of self—that's the 10,000 things, the human mind—and automatically you're full of God. And so says Joel in his words:

Silence is God in action.

But silence—understand silence now is just not this (pause for a few seconds). That's not silence. That's quiet. Silence is when you actually inside your being step out of the human mind, and it's a state of no thought, a state of no effort, a state of no fighting, a state of no resistance. A state of peace, a state of stillness, a state of silent awareness, a state of witnessing, a state of just is'ing, being. No effort.

Christ told me in my dream I was flapping my arms rising up above humanity, the sea of humanity, and I looked down and I started to sink, and I knew that I had to flap my arms to get back up there a little higher, and suddenly this quiet, little gentle voice in my being said, "You don't have to work that hard." And as soon as I heard the words my complete being relaxed on that sea of Christ, and suddenly—whoosh! I was lifted up, up, up, way up.

See? You can't with the human mind flap your arms and rise out of the human mind. No. You simply rest back on this sea of Spirit. Feeling its movement, It lifts you out of the tree of knowledge. It melts the concepts.

You don't know how! I don't know how it lifted me. I just know that when I gave myself to it completely, totally, complete abandon, rested back with the allness of my being instantly— whoosh! Christ lifted, and I was lifted way, way up. So he says:

*When a problem confronts you, whether it's your own or another's, (please) sit down, find that silence and let, (**let**) the solution appear.*

You see? Our path is a path of peace really. Let that peace permeate your whole being, and when you have accomplished that, sit with a listening attitude and watch the light dispel the darkness. Christ will lift you up, my friends. You are a witness, watching that state of peace do the healing. Be a beholder. How many times has he told us that? Only now, only to this day have you and I finally come to understand. Be a beholder of the activity of Christ. Watch it work in you, through you, and ultimately as your consciousness. And he says:

No mortal, (no) human being, can see God or know God. Only the Son of God, the Christ consciousness of you can witness and behold the presence of God.

So that is why when you are not in the 10,000 things – that is, in the human mind, in the concepts of good and evil – when you are still, when you are silent, when you're resting on that sea of Spirit and you suddenly become aware of the presence of God, you feel it, feel its movement. You feel that peace descend upon you. You feel the movement of the Spirit over the water of your consciousness. You witness the movement of Christ. When you do that, when you have that Christ awareness, you are standing in your Christ Self. You are the Christ, because only the Christ can witness that. And so you have left humanhood for that moment and you are standing.

Now that was John's vision of the Christ, his vision of heaven while he was on this earth. He was right here. He was walking, talking, moving among people. He saw what no human brain or human eye can see. He saw the temple not made with hands, the spiritual universe, the spiritual body. That is what you—you, my friends will behold when instead of using any thoughts you become a state of silence, a state of peace. When you have felt that divine reality, then you have seen the temple not made with hands, the body which is life eternal. And Joel told us in the Hawaii Hotel talks at the end of one of the chapters, he says:

It's not easy to stop seeing human beings or the concepts or the belief in good and evil (or the 10,000 things). *It's not easy to stop seeing human beings,* (says Joel), *but I finally made it.*

Which is his way of saying he, too, saw the temple not made with hands in which he was standing and saw it with eyes open. He says on the next page:

The human mind is always offended at truth because it's a reversal of everything the human mind knows. (Yes, it's a melting of all the concepts). *Imagine saying to the human mind when it is still and doing nothing, great and wondrous works and healings can be accomplished!*

And yet, that is what we are saying.

You, my friends, there are 18 of you – you have reached the place where you will be a witness of silence, peace, Spirit doing its work. There is a Spirit in man which can lift him up and guide him, and it will. It will, but the secret is – the peace that passes understanding. You see? You can't understand that peace. You can never understand how it works.

How? How does this peace flood my being and melt concepts and suddenly I become aware of harmony in which I was standing, but I didn't know it. We call that a healing. How does that happen? Just what does it do? We do not know. The mind cannot know. It will never know, but when you're standing in your Christ awareness you can behold it. So he says:

Beginning today, at this very moment, remember: your consciousness does the work for your family, your business, your home, your body. It is not some far-off God.

We said that last year—I mean, last week—seems like a year sometimes, doesn't it? We said that last week. The only God, the only Christ there is is this movement within you when mind stops. And so It is what does the work.

It is your own individual consciousness when it is imbued with silence and peace. All you have to do, and all you will ever be called upon to do, is to achieve that sense of (My) peace (or that sense of silence).

There is one thing you must practice and achieve, and that is a state of peace within your consciousness, coupled with the realization that it is your own consciousness which is the healing Christ.

In other words – well, he says on the next page:

All that the Christ consciousness is, is your individual consciousness when you no longer fear, hate or love error (or the 10,000 things or the 10,000 concepts).

You see what we're doing? You see what the transformation is? See what the transition is? We are transitioning out of the tree of knowledge of good and evil, or the human mind and its concepts. We are transitioning out of illusion, as the illusion is only in the concepts. We are knowing that I never was this concept. You're not this concept. Everything that I knew about you in these concepts is just concepts, and it's a lie and it's the father of lies.

Now we are transitioning out of the human mind. We are transitioning into a state of receptivity, silent awareness, witnessing the movement of Christ, the movement of Spirit on the face of the deep, the descent of the Holy Ghost, the descent of Spirit, the descent of My peace. When we witness that, we are standing in the Christ mind.

We are the living Christ, and that my dear friends is the only Christ there is, the only God, and that melts the false – the seemingly false – and reveals Its presence within and without as the only presence, and you open your eyes and *"Behold, I make all things new,"* and we see a new heaven and a new earth and a new Jerusalem descending. We see it. We actually see it. It's a real experience, and we behold the revelation that My Kingdom is here and now. And what a joy it is.

And my love flows to you hearing these words, and thank you so much for your help today uplifting my consciousness. I have been blessed immensely, and I'm sure that you have too.

"My Peace I give unto you: not as the world giveth, giveth I unto you."

Blessings.

[Silence]

CLASS 14

THE GREAT SECRET

Bill: Good morning.

This is March 17, 2013. I know my voice sounds a little strange, and that's because in the last week or so I've been bombarded with reminders of allergy season, and I was so busy I didn't sit down and do anything about it, so here I am with a perfect demonstration of allergies. But I'm not taking it too serious and hopefully you won't either.

Well, it's been a couple weeks. Nothing really hit me last week, so I took it as a feeling that I should just take the day off. I don't mean the day off from meditating, but the day off from talking. And this morning I picked up a book I haven't looked at in a long time called The Joel S. Goldsmith Reader. It says a selection from the writings of America's most renowned teacher and spiritual healer. And I happened to have a bookmark in there, and I wondered what I had bookmarked. And I picked it up and opened it up to the place, and it's a subsection called *Spiritual Consciousness Reveals Reality*, and the interesting thing is it sort of picks up right where we left off two weeks ago. It says:

You may wonder then, why there are such things as rotting trees or erupting volcanoes. Are they, also, of the essence of God? No, they represent our concept of that which actually is there.

And so there you see it and there you hear it. We are looking at our concept of God and calling it a rotting tree or an erupting volcano or an earthquake or allergy season.

In the kingdom of God, there is never a rotting tree, nor are there any destructive or disruptive forces operative. The German mystic, Jacob Boehme, saw through the trees and through the grass to reality. To all mystics, it is as though the world opens up and they see the world as God made it.

What does that mean *"the world opens up"?* It means that when you have the spiritual sense of existence, the world opens up. He explained it in his chapter *The New Horizon.* There he says what Jacob Boehme experienced. Here he tells us what he experienced and what he experiences. He says:

In this moment of uplifted consciousness, we are able, even though faintly, to see ourselves free of material, mortal, human, and legal laws. He says: *The fetters of finite existence fall away.*

The "wider, grander view" is coming into focus. The freedom of divine being is becoming apparent.

The experience at first is like watching the world disappear over a horizon and drop down from before us. There is no attachment to this world, no desire to hold onto it – probably because to a great extent the experience does not come until a great measure of our desire for the things of "this world" has been overcome. At first we cannot speak of it. There is a sense of "'Touch me not; for I am not yet ascended' – I am still between the two worlds; do not touch me or make me speak of it because it may drag me back. Let me be free to rise; [and] then, when I am completely free of the mesmerism and its pictures, I will tell you of many things which eyes have not seen nor ears heard."

And so he speaks of watching the world disappear over horizon and drop down from before us. In other words, like Jacob Boehme he says: *To all mystics, it is as though the world opens up and they see the world as God made it.*

214

God is the underlying substance and reality of all form, but what we see, hear, taste, touch, and smell is the product of the human mind, or mortal mind or material, finite sense. The sum total of human beings in the world, under what is termed material law— medical, theological, or economic law—has set up this finite sense of the universe which they see, hear, taste, touch, or smell.

Nothing is what it appears to be.

All right. If you have been wanting a healing, if you have been wrestling with a physical problem or a financial problem or a problem with relationships or any other kind of problem and you have been wanting a healing, today we are going to explain exactly why the healing has not come. And so if you will pay attention and take it serious, you will find your answer. And so he says:

All of us can look at the same object, and every one of us might see it differently. Why? Because each one of us interprets it in the light of the education, environment, and background of his individual experience. To understand that what we see represents only our concept of that which is actually there is very important, because on this point we make or we lose our healing consciousness.

Now hold on there, hold on. What did he just say? *To understand that what we see* hear, taste, touch, or smell *represents only a concept* in the human mind about *that which is actually there is important, because on that point we make or we lose our healing consciousness.*

So there's your first hint. We're gonna be specific later.

God created all that was created, and all that He created is good. Therefore, this whole world, whether seen as human beings, animals, or plants, is (really) God manifest. But when we see it, we do not see God manifest. We see only our finite concept of it.

So where are we seeing that concept? Out here? No. We're seeing a concept in the mind, aren't we? And we're turning to God and we're saying, "Now how can I know these principles so that this concept will be healed?" Though we're not saying it that way, because then it would probably alert us to what we're doing. No. What we say is, "Well, what principle can I practice so that my body is healed? What principle can I practice so my supply will improve?" Is that not true? And your body and your supply and your relationships—these are concepts in the mind. And so you're entertaining God, but you're unaware of it because you see through a glass darkly. You're looking at God, which needs no healing, and you're seeing concepts, which need healing. Pretty strange, huh?

This is vitally important (he says), *because it is on this premise that all spiritual healing is based.*

On what premise? On the premise that was in the line before that:

This whole world is God manifest, but when we see it, we do not see it as it is: We see only our finite concept of it. [So understanding that we see only our concept of the reality] *This is vitally important because it is on this premise that all spiritual healing is based, and a lack of recognition of this point accounts for ninety-five percent of the failure in spiritual healing.*

So if you are experiencing failure in spiritual healing it's just not happening for you it is because—well, there's a ninety-five percent chance that you do not really understand:

(A) You live and move and have your being in God. You don't have the conscious awareness of that, only the intellectual understanding of it, or

(B) You don't see that you're living, seeing, hearing, tasting, touching, smelling a concept, which is a blinder, which is a veil before your eyes, blocking out the awareness of God. And so you're living in concepts in the mind. But you don't see that clearly. You understand it perhaps intellectually, but you haven't gone down to the depths enough to see through the concept to the underlying reality. Something more is needed than just a human understanding of this.

So he says:

Many metaphysicians are trying to heal the physical body, and it cannot be healed.

I want you to know I'm feeling and sensing this underlying Presence right here, right now, my friends. Let us continue.

Many metaphysicians are trying to heal the physical body, and it cannot be healed, because there is nothing a metaphysician can do to a physical body, but when he changes his concept of the body, the body responds to the higher concept. Then the patient says, "I have been healed!" He has not been healed: He was perfect in the beginning. What was wrong was not in the body, but in his false concept of himself and of his body.

If you can grasp this idea, it may save you from making the fatal mistake of trying to heal somebody or somebody's body.

All right. I'm gonna read back over here the beginning of this chapter where he says:

The German mystic, Jacob Boehme, saw through the trees and through the grass to reality. To all mystics, it is as though the world opens up and they see the world as God made it.

And you know how I have shared with you the fact that in many meditations as well in the class that I attended with Herb Fitch, *Healing Outside of Time,* I saw God inside of everyone and everything, and everyone and everything inside of God. The two were one. My Kingdom and this world were one. I was aware of the concepts, the facade, the cover – but also felt I – well, I saw through to the underlying reality just as he says. Just as Jacob Boehme said. The world opens up and they see the world as God made it, and that's what I saw. I beheld the temple not made with hands. And this is what we must see, "feel," (quotes around feel – f-e-e-l) that means sense with spiritual discernment—we must "feel" this underlying reality. And so for Joel he says:

When I see your body through spiritual sense, (that's in his meditations) *I behold you as God made you, and (then) you declare that you have been healed. God's creation is intact; it is perfect and harmonious, and that perfect and harmonious creation is right here and now. But this cannot be seen with the physical eyes. It can be discerned only through spiritual vision, spiritual sense, through spiritual consciousness, or what is called Christ-consciousness.*

All right. So what have we learned here so far with just a page and a quarter? We have learned that ninety-five percent of the problems in spiritual healing come from not being able to stand on the premise that God is all and what I am looking at with the mind is concepts in the mind. Not being able to go into that deeply to where I drop those concepts, spiritual sense rises and reveals – It reveals Itself, the temple not made with hands. And so there's the answer to why spiritual healing hasn't occurred. And so he cautions.

Do not try to reform the outer picture. When you meet with thievery, drunkenness, or any form of degradation, do not look at it, look through it. Do not look with the eyes. Close the eyes or at least turn away. Look through that individual, behold through your spiritual sense the reality of his being, and you will bring about what the world calls healing.

It's always the same, isn't it? We could make probably a hundred million talks looking at this from all the facets of a diamond, and we would see the same thing every time. *"Not by might, not by power,"* but by spiritual sense. So let us continue, because we're going to go into that a little deeper. All right.

Look through the individual, behold with your spiritual sense the reality of his being, and you will bring about what the world calls healing. With your inner, God-given, spiritual sense.

Ah – a *God-given, spiritual sense* – not an intellect, not a mind understanding, because now that's a spiritual concept. Right? It's a spiritual concept. Now we have a concept of spiritual being, but we still have no awareness of it. We have no consciousness of it. We have no *feel* of it. Without the feel of it, the understanding is what? Yes, you all get an "A" today. It's the letter, the letter, and the letter does what? The letter kills. That is why up here he says don't make the fatal mistake. *If you can grasp this idea, it may save you from making the fatal mistake.* Why is it fatal? Because the letter kills.

He is so tricky with his sentences, the Spirit working through him. But when you study these things, it comes to you. So:

With your inner, God-given, spiritual sense, look into the heart of every man and see Christ, and there you will find the most wonderful healing force there is in the world. Then let your feeling [of the Christ] guide you. Get a sense, or a feeling, of the Christ sitting right there in the center of individual being, and when you reach that Christ you will have an instantaneous healing.

Now he did not say get a sense of the Christ in his individual being or your individual being. No. He said *get a sense of the Christ sitting right there at the center of individual being,* one individual being, and so in your meditation you and I must get a sense of Christ as individual being. Not 200 million individual beings – one individual being. There's one Son. So all the work is within you. You don't deal with somebody out there. Joel says take nobody in your meditation. Do not take the person into your meditation. Do not take the problem into your meditation, because if you do that you're still trying to fix, trying to heal, trying to improve humanhood, and that means that you're experiencing that ninety-five percent of the problem is you haven't grasped the premise that these are concepts going on inside of you, being presented inside of you by the mind. You must see through these concepts to one Christ individual being, and then sense it. Feel it. Get a feel of it, of its movement, of its Beingness, of its Isness. So he said all takes place within One, and that One is the I of you. So he says:

To bring about a healing of sin or disease, do not be concerned about a human being or (a human) body. (But) Become silent within your being: Feel (__feel__) the presence of God, the presence of Good, the divine or (the) inner Sense, (capital S, inner Sense) and then you will not be tempted to think of any one person.

No. Don't think of a person. Think of an individual infinite being called Christ. In fact, don't think at all. Get a sense of that infinite individual being called Christ. So he says:

It is not necessary to think of the name of the person or his form, or his disease. The all-knowing Intelligence knows (all about that, so) therefore when you feel a sense of Soul, (a sense of Christ here and now) you will have witnessed a healing.

And down at the bottom of this page in real tiny writing it says: *For a more complete explanation of this point, see the chapter on "The True Sense of the Universe" in (the book) Spiritual Interpretation of Scripture* which was published in 1947 for the first time, so the same year as the book The Infinite Way. Very strange that in 1947 Joel presented the fact that you have to go beyond the letter to an actual awareness, and nobody caught it, and so nine or ten years later – almost ten years later, because he first started talking about it in 1945, so that in 1955 he had the Kailua study series where he came right out and said we're going to do this now together, and then he went around and told the other students the same thing.

But we're here in 2013, and I have to ask you: How many people do you know even in The Infinite Way that have the conscious awareness rather than the intellectual understanding?

In other words, how many people have the spiritual sense that's operating them rather than an intellectual understanding of the principles?

Not very many. Can you count 'em on one hand? So, the path is narrow and few there be that enter.

All right. So I went over here to *The True Sense of the Universe* because I already love this chapter in order to see a greater explanation of what he's talking about. And remember, the basic premise of that two pages we just read are – what? You're standing in the middle of God, but you're appearing mind looking at concepts. If you find the way through silence, through standing still, through meditation, then the world will drop away. Spiritual sense will take over and reveal Itself, and you will say, "Wow, I'm living and having my being in God," and you agree with the New Testament and the author of that statement. Or like John you might say, "Wow, now I see the temple not made with hands, eternal in the heavens," and that temple is one infinite individual being. And as you rest in that awareness, whatever it was that was plaguing you is dissolved.

The concept is dissolved and more of reality out here appears, or whoever reached out to that consciousness and is standing in the consciousness with you, Oneness reveals that where they are also this Presence is, and we call that healing.

All right, so *The True Sense of the Universe*. This is a powerful, powerful chapter. If you don't have it, get the book <u>Spiritual Interpretation of Scripture</u>. This chapter more than any other in this book is the secret, and he says it. He says he's gonna tell you the secret. Okay –

The beliefs we entertain about the body constitute our sense of body. (Right? Beliefs we entertain about the body constitute our concept of the body.] *The truth about body is something entirely different from your concept of it. The body itself is perfect.*

It is as immortal and eternal as God, Soul, which is the substance and Principle of the body.

Now you can look in the mirror and you and I would have to agree—uh—I'm sorry, this body is not perfect! (chuckles) It is beginning to show age at 60 years. Umm – what is he talking about? Well, he tells you.

Your body seen through the universal material beliefs (which is what's going on as concepts in the mind), *was born, matures, ages and dies.* (However), *this very body when correctly known, or spiritually discerned, is the very appearing of Soul substance, Spirit-substance, eternal being. It is neither functional nor organic. What appears to us as functions and organs are our false finite concepts of the activity of consciousness appearing as spiritual body or spiritual formation.*

So my friends you're walking around—I'm walking around—we're looking at Consciousness appearing, Spirit appearing, spiritual form, an eternal body not made with hands, one individual being, Christ. <u>But we don't even see it</u>. We see the concepts, the universal material concepts handed down from one generation to the next to the next. And if we don't see that clearly, Joel says we're going to be attempting to heal something. We're going to be attempting to heal one of these concepts, to improve it. In other words, we're going to be attempting to add God to our humanhood, <u>and it can't be</u> <u>done</u>.

I want to take you through this chapter if you've never heard it because it's fabulous.

As long as we entertain a material concept of body, we will have concern for it, we will cater to it, find in it both pain and pleasure. As we continue to lift our concept of body until we gain the realization of what our body really is, then we will find less and less of pain or pleasure in it until we arrive at that state of consciousness where we realize the body as an impersonal vehicle or mode of expression.

Think about that. We said in our last talk that, or we read that the Hindu mystics look and say, "Well, this is all illusion out here, so why bother. I mean it's just karmic law that I'm paying and paying the price and when I pay it long enough it'll stop. It's an illusion, so I just accept it." But Joel told us that Christ Jesus lifted that concept to a spiritual awareness of body, and then it was healed. Right? And that's the difference.

So here he says: *we arrive at the state of consciousness where we realize the body as an impersonal vehicle.* An impersonal vehicle.

What does that mean? This is one of those uncomfortable things we don't want to see or hear. Yet we say, "Oh, I want healing, and I want the healing Christ consciousness. Oh, but don't tell me that!" And what is that that I'm referring to right here? The body as it really is is an impersonal vehicle. In other words, it doesn't belong to you, the person. It can't belong to you. It's your belief that you have a personal body that's killing you. (laughs) Literally. (laughs) You have no personal body.

And you know, he talks in the books and he talks on tapes and we listen and we read. Okay, yeah, it's not my supply, it's God's supply. Well okay, yeah it's not my health, it's God's health. But here he speaks plainly. <u>You have no personal body</u>. The belief in a personal body is what's killing you, because if you have a belief in a personal body, the person can die.

But here he's trying to say: Lift it up higher. Lift it up. Contemplate, meditate. What is this impersonal body that belongs to infinite individual being? What is this one Christ body? Oh God, give me a conscious awareness of impersonal body, and when you have the conscious awareness or the feel of impersonal body, then you will know in an instant where we started, which is: It is as immortal and eternal as God, and it is perfect. You see?

It all comes down to that conscious awareness of, and so he says:

Every suggestion of discomfort or inharmony coming from the body must be met instantly with the understanding of the true nature of body as spiritual.

But you can't do this in the mind! You see? You can't overthrow a concept with a newer concept. I'm gonna overthrow a material concept by repeating all day long "the body is spiritual, the body is spiritual, the body is spiritual. It's immortal. It's eternal." Okay? That's not what he means when he says you must meet it instantly. Probably he should have used a different word than understanding.

He should have said it must be met instantly with the <u>awareness</u> of the true body. See? That's spiritual. Now that would have put us in a different direction. Ah! Okay, so I can't do this on a mental level. No. Not by might, not by physical might can you wrestle and make God appear. Nor by power, not by mental power. Not by mental argument. Not by mental affirmations. Not by understanding. Not by a new spiritual concept—that won't work. No but by my Spirit. We have to go beyond the letter. Something has to happen inside of our consciousness, and that something has to be the awareness. And so he says:

Only as we understand that errors of sense exist merely as suggestion and false sense, can we find freedom from the pains and pleasures of the body. We are never correcting the body, its so-called organs or functions. We are correcting the false concept or sense of body.

You see? It's not about getting God to improve this concept. It's not about trying to make this concept into a spiritual concept. It's about dropping all concepts, standing there still until the inner awareness comes. **It comes**—you don't make it happen, and when it comes it lifts you out of the concept, and you have a glimpse of reality. Well, there's a feeling, he says, that the world drops away, but this can't happen, he says, in <u>The Infinite Way</u> – it can't happen while you're trying to improve it. But he says it probably won't happen because it does not come until a great measure of our desire for the things of this world has been overcome.

You see, he's not talking about whether you have to stop wanting money and you have to stop wanting fame and you have to stop wanting power and you have to stop wanting companionship. That's not what he means. He means you have to stop believing that you can improve the concept. You have to step <u>out</u> of the concept. You can't do that if you haven't grasped the premise that you're already standing in God. You can't do that if you haven't grasped the premise that what you see, hear, taste, touch, and smell is only a concept. So you have to go inside of your being. You have to read, you have to listen, but mostly importantly you have to meditate until you have the experience of stepping outside of concept and having a glimpse of reality or spiritual discernment. Then, then you open your eyes—wow! Hey, my throat is getting better. Hey, it's disappearing. Wow! Then you come to see *"My kingdom is not of this world."*

Now we can change that. My Kingdom—let's change that into: My Christ Self or infinite individual being is not of these concepts. All right? God is not of these concepts. That's what it means: *"My kingdom is not of this world."* We already said no illusion is ever externalized, so this world must be this series of universal concepts. So My Kingdom, My Presence is not of these concepts. My Being is not of these concepts. My realm is not of these concepts.

No. because above these concepts is a spiritual realm, *governed by Love, peopled with children of God*, and so my kingdom is not of these concepts. There is nothing of God or reality in the world we see, hear, taste, touch, or smell. And he says in the other book, The Joel Goldsmith Reader, ninety-five percent of the problems is not being to grasp the premise.

He doesn't mean not being able to understand it, that's easy. But can you sit down and see through the concepts and stand still until spiritual awareness comes? Until it dawns, like the rising of the sun at dawn. Can you have that inner experience? Well, he says:

The failure of religion in this age is due to (not being able to have that experience). *Theology is attempting to spiritualize a mortal concept called **man**. (And) this man and his universe is no part of God.*

Why? Because my Being is not of this concept.

You have no personal self! Uh oh! And that's the big one, isn't it? There's no person here either. Now if that doesn't bring thinking to a standstill, I don't know what will. There is no personal self.

Joel told me, "You haven't got one!" I asked him in a dream – what about this and that? And he looked at me and he said, "You haven't got one," meaning you haven't got a personal self. (chuckles) Why am I working so hard then? Then he says that's ninety-five percent of the problem. Not that you're chasing after riches out here, but that you still believe there's a personal self. You still believe in these concepts, and it's killing you, and it will kill you. Ah, but not if you rise out of this concept, stand in the awareness of My Kingdom, My Self, infinite individual Christ being. Then you have stepped into your eternal Self, and the more time spent in it, the more it will become your permanent dwelling place. So he says:

This man and his universe is no part of God, because God or His kingdom is not of this world. [Or this concept or this man or this person.] *Be assured that if God were in this scene there would be no wars, accidents, diseases or deaths.*

That's right, but you can't pull God into this scene either, not by might nor by power.

God, the infinite Power of good, is able to maintain harmoniously and eternally Its own creation.

In "My kingdom," the realm of Spirit and Truth, there are no errors, no defeats, (no deaths).

(So) Prayers uttered for the purpose of healing, improving or aiding the people or conditions of (this) universe, reach no farther than one's own belief.

God is the divine Reality of individual being.

Now again, he doesn't say of individual <u>beings</u>. He said *the divine Reality of individual being.* And so in his awareness, in his moment of silence when he looked through the concepts, he became aware of infinite individual being – Joel did, or he wouldn't say it.

To avail yourself of the harmonious government of this Principle, it is necessary to drop all thought of human persons and human conditions; you must lose all desire to improve humanhood.

And then when you've lost all desire – there's two parts to this. He's told us over and over and over and over and over and over and over, over the years: You're not going to do good spiritual work if you don't have the awareness of the nature of error. You can't just go around with the nature of God and affirm it all the time. Well, you can, but you'll die in poverty.

You must have both of them to have a complete demonstration, and here he is saying it again back in 1947.

It is necessary to drop all thought of human persons and conditions; lose all desire to improve humanhood.

And then you don't have that ninety-five percent of the problem. If you really grasp that these are concepts in here and there's nothing to do out there and there's nothing to do with these concepts except to drop them and stand there very still and wait upon the Lord – if you understand that and you do that, then he says:

Let the Inner Self reveal in Silence the harmony, wholeness and joy of real Being.

Not of real <u>beings</u> – real Being. One.

So, is he lying? Is he making it up? Am I making it up? Is Jacob making it up? Or is there a way to see – okay, this is a concept. There's no personal self that needs healing, and this concept's in the mind, and now whose mind is it in? Is it in my mind? Wait minute! There's no personal self here either. Well now I can dispense with both of them. Drop 'em both. Drop all personal sense of self. Now God, reveal Your Kingdom. Thy Kingdom come in consciousness, in awareness, Thy Presence. Let me feel Thou, or let me feel the One Self. And stand still. And there's a way to have the inner experience, *the Inner Self reveal in silence the harmony, wholeness and joy of real Being.*

There's a way to see the world drop down from before you. There's a way to see through the world to My Kingdom. There's a way to see through the appearance to God inside of everyone and everything, the one Infinite Presence. Because if it were not so, I would have told you. Yes, it is a narrow path, but it is the Way, the Infinite Way. So, I want to get to the real secret here. We're coming up on the real secret, and Joel is very, very serious about it, and this was in '47.

Spiritual good is not composed of more or better material conditions. No amount of increased physical health or wealth can testify to the reign of Spirit. We rise above sense evidence to find the realm of the real.

See? We're getting down to the nitty gritty, huh? It's about two sentences. Actually, it's one sentence. *"My kingdom is not of this world."* And there you go. So he says:

Soul power or that which we contact within ourselves -- results in what appears to be health (and) harmony and wealth, but these are not the same as that which is attained through attempts (by might or by power). *The harmony in our affairs which results from our contact with our Inner Self, or Soul, is the manifestation or expression of Spirit,* (It's consciousness appearing) *and it is the "added things" which come naturally from the realm of real substance.*

You see? It's consciousness appearing.

(And) Finite sense beholds consciousness appearing or spiritual reality, as the objectified material universe or "things" and "persons". Spiritual harmony is not attained by seeking persons, things or conditions.

No, because then you really don't have the understanding of the nature of concepts or error, do you? But if you drop that, if you stop that, if you have risen above the need to fix any of these concepts and you see it clearly for what it is **a nothingness**, an impersonal nothingness—ah, then you're able to stand still and stop fighting, stop resisting. You realize—ah I don't have to work on that and Spirit, **Christ announces and reveals Itself.**

By *taking no thought for these and seeking only contact with the divine Reality of you.* (Spiritual harmony appears).

Humans cannot put on or wear the robe of Christ. The human mind cannot be spiritualized it must be "put off." (And a personal sense of self must be "put off.") *Developing a sense of receptivity; learning to silence the senses gain the ability to listen for "the still, small voice", this is the Way. Human thoughts even good ones cannot help.*

So in treatment to close the eyes and declare truths, or make affirmations and denials, this is not the way of Spirit. (No, this is the way of letter.) *Be silent – hold a listening attitude, be receptive, be still and* **let.**

Now this is the second time he said *let,* or third, and it's always in italics.

Be still and let the presence and power of God be made manifest through Silence, this is the Way. (The Infinite Way.)

It is a silent state of Receptivity in which Christ or Spirit or God is manifest as individual consciousness. It appears principally as a (quote) *"feeling"* (unquote, he says) *of the Presence, and this feeling dispels the illusion of sense.* (or it melts concepts)

Okay? Now, let's get down to the nitty gritty. And here it is: *I want you all to understand the great secret of the universe.*

And remember, if you have this great secret of the universe you won't suffer from ninety-five percent of the reason for failure in healing. So you might want to really, really listen. Listen within your being. Not listen with the mind. Listen with spiritual discernment.

I want you all to understand this great secret of the universe. Had the ancients known it, our modern living would be in a paradise.

If we learn it now we can help to usher in a new Millennium. (Or a new heaven and a new earth, new Jerusalem). *The few who have known this secret in the past could not teach it;*

This has got to be an experience, doesn't it? You must have some sort of experience.

It would appear that only a very few had the spiritual capacity to grasp it. Some few understood it intellectually, but rarely was it understood in its spiritual significance.

So here is the secret which will do away ninety-five percent of failure in healing. Here's the secret which will allow you to see through concepts and have that spiritual awareness reveal itself.

I am not a dreamer of idle dreams, (he says), *but I have a vision of eternal Life. I would not have you sitting on a cloud or anchored with your feet on the ground. My idea and my ideal is that you be rooted and grounded in Truth;* (in the letter) *(but) that you be fed with spiritual meat and you drink waters from the wellsprings of eternal Spirit and Soul.*

(And so) **The secret**, *that which has been so rarely understood is that spiritual meat and spiritual water and the secret is this: The life which you behold in man, tree animal* (mountain, sun, moon, personal sense of self, personal sense of lover, personal sense of friend, personal sense of student, personal sense of teacher), *that life is not a manifestation of God, and therefore is not immortal, eternal or spiritual. The life of material man or flower is mortal sense.* (It's a concept, a universal series of concepts which dance through our minds most of the time); *it is a false sense of Life* (capital L Life) *which is real.* It's a false concept about infinite Christ being.

The understanding of this truth. (Deeply when you see through it, when you have the experience of seeing through it. Not the intellectual understanding. Oh yeah, I can see how that is. Uh-huh. No. (chuckles) That won't do. The depth of awareness that sees through the concept to the underlying reality of the Isness of God—**That Experience!**) *will enable you to look away from the objects of sense; it will enable you to refrain from attempting to heal, correct or reform the mortal sense of existence.*

And what does he say elsewhere? We read it. When that has been overcome, then ninety-five percent of the problem is gone. Now you only have to stand there until spiritual discernment reveals God in your midst, I in the midst of you.

As soon as you have conquered the desire to heal or improve the material sense of existence, the spiritual or real begins to unfold and reveal itself to you.

Bang! There is the secret of living, of life.

As soon as you conquer the desire to heal or improve the material sense of existence, it means you've seen through the concept. You've allowed 'em to drop away inside your being. Then the spiritual Self, *the spiritual or real begins to unfold and reveal itself to you.* You don't do anything to make it happen. You can't make it reveal itself, but once you've fulfilled the condition, the great secret, then it reveals itself. And he says:

Do not take lightly what I am saying. This is the Great Revelation; this knowledge will clarify for you the Master's statement, "My kingdom is not of this world"; it will reveal to you the secret of John who beheld the universe not made with hands, but which is eternal, as Consciousness appearing; Spirit unfolding; Soul revealing itself.

And then down here in another paragraph he repeats it in case you missed it.

The life of material man, the life of tree, the flower, the animal, this is not Life eternal; it is not the manifestation of Life which is God; it is a false, finite, mortal sense of existence. Do not attempt to patch it up but turn from it and (now with spiritual discernment) *discern the Life which is God; "**feel**"* (with quotes, "feel") *through your cultivated spiritual sense this divine energy of Spirit; become conscious in the Silence of your Soul.*

And here it is again – one more time – in italics:

***Let** the divine harmonies appear as you disregard the evidence of sight and hearing, tasting, touching and smelling.*

Believe me (please, he says, believe me) *this is the secret of secrets. This is Life eternal to know this.*

Yes, why? Because in order to know this, the personal sense of self has to be dropped and you have to be standing in your Christ Self or your eternal Life, the temple not made with hands, eternal. And finally, he's gonna repeat one more time.

Only to those who have eyes to see and ears to hear can this vision become a living, vital Presence. Only those who have heard what is said by "the still, small voice" and seen what is visible to the "windows of the Soul" can discern "the temple not made with hands" or the universe of God's creating (right here and now).

This inner vision, this spiritual consciousness, this Soul-sense, comes only in proportion as we accept and realize the great secret: the life of material man, plant or animal is not the eternal Life of God; it is finite sense, the manifestation of mortal, material sense. This false sense of life must be put off, disregarded, un-valued, (**dropped** —and then standing in that stillness, in the silence) *the real Life and its formations become evident and experienced* (as your infinite, immortal being).

Now, is that not a powerful, powerful chapter? If you see it as I do, if you feel it as I do, then you know that this is—this is just awesome! Just, just—it is the secret! And so there's two parts, isn't there? The conscious awareness that these concepts, these universal concepts of a personal self are nothing and let them drop. No more desire, no more attempts to heal or improve. We just let them drop. We cast our nets on the other side. We launch out into the deep. We <u>let</u> spiritual consciousness appear. We <u>let</u> God reveal Itself. We <u>let</u> the Father reveal My Kingdom here in our midst. We <u>let</u> spiritual discernment reveal infinite individual being. And we rest in it. And we say, "Thank you, Father. Thank you. Thank you for revealing yourself. Thank you." This concept that I started an hour ago, this concept of a person with allergies is gone. It's gone, and now there's only your Presence. Now there is only your Self, and Father, fulfill Thyself. And we rest. We rest back. God is.

Thank you my friends for listening, for always bringing your consciousness to this work and blessings, blessings, blessings.

[Silence]

CLASS 15

CRUCIFIXION

Bill: Good afternoon.

This is Sunday, May 5th, or Cinco de Mayo as it is called where I grew up in Southern California. We have just completed, most of us, perhaps all of us, listening to Herb Fitch's series of talks from the 1990 Chicago Healing seminar and before that the Preparation talks and before that the talks I made called The Uncomfortable Talks, and this talk today might be another one of those Uncomfortable Talks. Because today we're going to take the veil off. We're going to remove the veil today, now – and as you know, Jesus was crucified for removing that veil because he made himself "equal with God." So be still, be receptive. Listen to your own indwelling Presence and let the veil be lifted from before your eyes.

I am going to guess that everyone listening to this talk knows what the veil is. It's had many names. Some have called it the glass darkly. That would be a dark veil, wouldn't it? Some have called it illusion, Satan, Maya, hypnotism, duality, universal belief in good and evil, the belief in two powers, or sense perception, or personal sense. We've all read where Joel talks about the need to surrender, come up over personal sense, and that the personal sense of existence will bar one from the kingdom of heaven. And we see that, we read it. Perhaps we understand it intellectually, and then we put down the book, eject the tape, turn off the CD, click off the MP3 player, and we get up and we go about our business as a person. And maybe we remember once a day to think about God or read about God or hear about God. Maybe we even become still as a person and attempt to meditate on God. And yet the veil is not lifted. Still we continue in a sense of me and God.

You can see that this thing called personal sense is – well, it doesn't want to move, does it? Yet that's the very veil that covers a realization of God. Surely you know now, because I know I've pointed it out, what realization is. Or maybe you only know what realization is not, which is also helpful. A realization of God is not when you sit down and think and ponder God's magnificence. When you sit down and envision in your mind, infinite, an infinite being, an infinite Presence. When you sit down and ponder the glory of infinite love, an endless sea of love. You contemplate these things in your mind, and yet there's still a you contemplating a being. There's still two, and if there's two, the veil has not lifted.

It's very stubborn, this sense perception. It does not go back just 40 or 50 years. It goes back 40 or 50 centuries at least. Do you remember when you were a child and perhaps you had a pet and that pet died? If you were unfortunate, it ran out under a car and was killed. Or perhaps it just lived out its years and at 17 or 18 it passed away. I remember as a child a neighbor poisoning one of our animals and so it died. Do you remember praying to God up in the sky somewhere it would take care of your little pet? I do. I always had a belief in God and I prayed, "Take care of Fluffy." And you know – there is no such God. I was praying to a belief. Not only that, I wasn't even praying to my own belief. I was praying to a universal belief. There's no such God up in the sky. None whatsoever. Yet many of us prayed to just that belief, didn't we?

And you remember going to church if you did? I remember being sent to Vacation Bible School because my mother was working and there was no one to watch us, so she thought that

that would be a good place to keep us busy while she worked until she got off and could come pick us up. So off we went to Vacation Bible School even though my mother was an atheist she said, and there was no dad around, so she sent us to Vacation Bible School and there we learned to color and work with crafts and sing songs and go on field trips and be taught about a man named Jesus. And I remember saying to the – well, it was the middle of the day, late morning, and we were working on crafts of some sort. Think we were gluing tongue depressors together making little cabins out of 'em or something, or maybe making crosses and decorating the crosses – something like that. And there was a man up front and I raised my hand and he called on me and I said, "Where is God?" or "Who is God?" – something like that. I remember he looked kind of frustrated with me like he didn't want that kind of a question coming from a six-year-old, seven-year-old, and so he said, "That's God," and he pointed to a picture of Jesus up on the wall, and that's the one with him looking sideways and the long, curly hair and the light glow around his head. I think that really that's a picture of King James, but anyway he pointed to that picture and he said, "There's Jesus and uh, I mean there's God, that's God." He seemed kind of short.

Anyway, soon after that he announced a recess and everybody got up and ran outside to play and his aides and himself went outside to watch the children, but I remained behind and no one was looking and I walked up over to that picture of Jesus and I looked for God and I looked and I looked. I could not find him and suddenly this inner voice said, "That's not God, that's a man." I heard it as plain as that. "That's not God, that's a man." And I stopped looking and I went outside to play and I forgot the whole experience. I never thought about it again until 30 years later.

So some people have the concept of God as Jesus, the man that walked around 2000 some-odd years ago and taught. They have the concept that he is half man and half God, the only son of God, the only begotten son of God. God in human flesh. And so they pray to Jesus. And I had a particularly desperate time in my life when I was—oh, 18, 19 – I think it was 19. Everything in my life was falling apart. My wife wanted nothing to do with me. We'd only been married two years. I lost my job and was fired. They said I had an attitude that the world owed me a living, and I hated my guts and I was contemplating suicide, how I might exit this world, which I hated. Hated the world and everyone in it, but more than anything else, I hated myself and I wished that I was dead. And I remember praying, but feeling nothing. No return, nothing.

I wasn't even sure if there was a God. I started to think people are fooling themselves. Maybe Mother's right. Maybe there is no God. People are just calling it God and it's really them. And yet, I wanted – I wanted there to be a God. I really wanted there to be a God, something that I could turn to other than myself. Oh, how I hated myself! And one particularly lonely night I walked in front of a stained glass window on the side of a church and I looked up there, and there was a picture of Jesus and he had a lamb or – yeah, he had a lamb in his arm. He was holding a lamb, and I looked at that picture and I prayed to the picture, "Oh, please help me. Show me how to live. I'll do anything."

And I waited, and I felt nothing, absolutely nothing. Because you see, that's not God. That's a concept. It's a picture of a concept of a man that supposedly lived 2000 years ago that was the only son of God. And that concept, the Christian concept, didn't work. I prayed to it and nothing happened. And I suppose if something had happened and a cloud had opened and I would have heard a voice at that point, you might be finding me on a John Hagee program or – uh, ah yes, Pat Robertson. (chuckles) I looked it up. Pat Robertson. I'd probably teamed up with him or with John Hagee down in Texas or something because I would have been

237

a Christian if I prayed to Jesus and the sky opened and I heard a voice say, "Follow me." But that didn't happen.

But you know, at the same time that I was going through that I was going to a little room in the back of I think it was the Green Hotel in south Pasadena and I was listening one night a week to tapes of Joel Goldsmith. And I was really out of place because I was 19 years old and there's all these old fogies in there, people in their 50s, 60s, and 70s – and me, 19. I never did fit in real well with people my age. I think I got here as a senior citizen. But anyway, I was listening to Joel Goldsmith and I couldn't make it work. I understood – I had a really good intellectual understanding of the principles, but I couldn't *feel* any of it.

And so I prayed to that stained glass picture of Jesus and nothing happened, because there is no such God. I'm not saying there's no such entity, being, as Jesus. Please don't hear that, because I'm not. I love Jesus Christ. I really do, and I have felt his presence many times during my life, but that night I didn't. And that night the prayer did not work because that's not God. That's a man. That's a man with a consciousness of God. And so it didn't work for me. That did not remove the veil. And even if it had, if I had had an experience I would still have me and Jesus. I would still have two.

And so onward I went until finally in a few months after that I found myself on my front porch steps at two in the morning or three in the morning and I cried out and I said, "God, Jesus, Buddha, Christ, Cosmic Consciousness – anything, anywhere – I'll do anything if you show me how to live." And inside myself a stone had been pushed away because inside myself I had become teachable. I had most of the prayers in the Bible memorized and yet I became teachable in that early morning. I was willing to do anything if I could just know God aright. And it didn't come right away. No, it didn't come right away. And yet there was a strange freedom because I was no longer trying to pretend. Now I could do like Joel recommended and I could ask inside, "Father, God reveal yourself." And my total being became that prayer: "Father, reveal yourself."

And one night a few weeks or a month or two later I was sitting in my living room. I had just finished reading something in The Art of Meditation. I closed the book and I put it down, I closed my eyes, and suddenly there was a Presence there with me, and that's the only way I can describe it. There was a Presence. And there was a touch on the side of my face, a tingling feeling as if – as if entering my being, within and yet without, all around and yet touching my face. Very strange.

And with it came a sense of peace and I knew it was – it was Father revealing Itself. And I rested and relaxed in that Presence. And I can tell you from that moment, which was 1973, until this moment, and it's 2013 – so what does that make that? How many years is that? That's exactly 40 years, isn't it? Forty years, and I've never, ever, ever been without that Presence. Oh, I don't mean it's there all the time during the day and night every single day and night. That's not what I mean. I mean it's there at some time during the day and night. And sometimes it takes over and is running everything. At other times it lingers in the background, but that Presence, that Omnipresence, the conscious awareness of Omnipresence has never left my being.

Yet as I sat in that chair there was me and there was the Presence, still a state of duality. Still the veil was not lifted entirely. And perhaps all of you have had your own experience. Have you? Have you had the experience of feeling in your meditation the Presence? Have you felt what I have called the Spirit moving over the face of the deep within your being? Have you been consciously aware of invisible Self? Have you heard a still, small voice? Have you felt lifted up by a divine light? Have you felt – well, here's what Joel says. Joel says:

*My sense of God is that of an indescribable Presence and feeling.
I do not know God except through feeling. I feel the Presence all
through me, through my chest, through my fingertips. No matter
what the external circumstances are, even when at times they might
seem discordant, I am always conscious of this Presence, a sensing, a
feeling, an awareness.*

And he comes closest to describing what I experience, because
I also call it a Presence, or the Presence, or just It or I. At any rate, it
is something that I feel. I feel its movement through my being, and
I can't describe that any better than he could. What did he mean
when he said he feels that Presence moving through his chest? I do
not know. I do not know. I've asked him, but he's never shown me.
What do I mean when I say to you I feel the movement of Spirit
over the face of the deep? I feel it move across the waters of my
inner consciousness. You—you don't know, and I can't describe it.
But I know that's what it is when I feel its movement.

So perhaps you've had your own experience as light. Maybe
you felt flooded with divine love or perhaps resting back on a sea
of Spirit or floating on a cloud of unknowing. However you have
experienced the Presence, you surely must have by now, if you are
one of the 19 or 20 people listening to these Uncomfortable Talks,
surely you must have felt the Presence somewhere, sometime.

And you've prayed to this Presence, haven't you? I know you
have because I have. And perhaps it did not respond. Maybe there
was no response because you located that Presence that you felt
somewhere out there. Maybe you located that Presence in the
deity of Jesus the Christ. Maybe you located that Presence in
Siddhartha, in Buddha. Maybe you've located that Presence in
Krishna or maybe even Moses, Elijah, Joel Goldsmith, Herb Fitch.
Maybe you've located that Presence in Bill Skiles. And if you have
and you've prayed to it, I am sure you've had no response because
you still have me and that Presence.

And that my dear friends is the veil. That's the veil. Now how do you have the veil removed? Well, over here there's a chapter in <u>Beyond Words and Thoughts</u> called *Truth Unveiled,* and in it we are given a few hints. Listen.

On the Mount, in a high state of consciousness, Moses realized I AM, and thereby became I AM. Yet, there remained a sense of Moses as is evidenced by the fact that he spoke of himself as being slow of speech. (And so he still had the I AM Presence and Moses, did he not?)

Jesus, however, not only knew the truth but <u>realized</u> and <u>became</u> the Truth: "I am the way, the truth, and the life." (Or I am the Presence.) *Nevertheless, a sense of Jesus, the man, remained, because he said, "I can of mine own self do nothing. If I bear witness of myself, my witness is not true." This personal sense of self had to be crucified, as it must be in all of us, or we will not* (have the veil lifted).

Jesus' realization of the need to crucify, or rise above, the mortal sense of self, enabled him to make the ascension. (Now here's the biggest clue I have ever found). *The ascension is always the same: a rising above **mind**, above knowing the truth, to Truth <u>Itself</u>.*

And so the veil is the mind that knows the truth. The veil is the mind that knows God in the sky. The veil is the mind that knows God in a man, in Jesus. The veil is the mind that knows God as a Presence somewhere, here today, not here tomorrow, back again the next day. The veil is the mind that knows. Yet, how many times have we been told the natural mind receiveth not God, for God is known only through spiritual discernment. And so the veil is the mind that knows. This is the veil. This is the glass darkly.

Anything you can know with the mind, any truth you know with the mind, any truth you have ever known with the mind is the veil.

Now says Joel:

In many classes and even in some of the Writings, I have said I did not understand the reason for the crucifixion of Jesus: why it took place or why it took place if it had to. It puzzled me, and I, I frankly admitted this (says Joel). *It was not until the year 1963, when I myself went through the experience of crucifixion, that the reason and the need for the crucifixion of Christ Jesus was revealed to me.*

Now here's a man, Joel, who flatly declares right here in black and white plainly for all time that inside of his being the mind that knows, was crucified. He went through the experience, and he says:

After the experience, the memory of it passed from me, and I could not bring it to conscious recollection, until later the entire scene was revealed to me when I went through the experience of ascension: that of rising above the mind (that knows) *to* (the experience of) *Truth Itself.*

Now what was the ascension again? The ascension is always the same: rising above mind, above knowing the truth to Truth Itself. And so if you would have the veil lifted today, then today must be your crucifixion. Today must be the day in which you go beyond a mind knowing God to God. Are you ready? Are you willing? Are you able? Be still. Close your eyes.

A couple of years ago I introduced to you once it was shown to me the 1955 Kailua study series. In that I said close your eyes. Now close 'em. In that study, the Kailua study series, we were given the talk *Experience the Christ* and *Experiencing the Christ*, and in those talks we were taught how to pray and how to go beyond knowing the truth to Truth Itself. We were given a method. We were told that when a problem was presented to us that we were to know no truth with the mind. We were simply to close our eyes, refuse to respond with any truth whatsoever and simply to stand stock still. You remember?

In this which Spirit gave us through Joel it was hoped that we would discover each of us what that inner feeling is when Christ, when the Spirit of the living God moves over the face of the deep and announces Itself. And if you have had that inner experience, then you already know what that inner feeling of the Presence is, and so the veil is becoming thinner and thinner. And yet, it has not lifted because there's still a you sitting there feeling the Presence. And yet, you cannot go beyond the veil until you've had the experience promised in the 1955 Kailua study series. You must have that experience first, which is why it was presented to you first so that you would have ample time to practice until the experience of the Presence of the living Spirit filled your being.

Now there is another step, the next step, the uncomfortable step. Joel hinted at it in that same Kailua study series when he said: Eventually, and he did it very quick at the end of the talk, just a paragraph or two at the most. He said, *"eventually you'll have to learn to do this also with the good things, not just with the problems."* In other words, when you're looking at a sunset, when you're looking at your spouse, your granddaughter, your grandson, your grandma, when you're looking at a promotion, when you're looking at a seminar, a spiritual seminar, when you're looking at a beautiful lake – you're to do the same thing. Close your mind. Close it to those concepts, the same as you would for a problem and simply turn within and open your spiritual discernment and wait. Stand stock still.

You are now to experience the crucifixion so that the veil will be lifted so that you may also experience the ascension on a permanent basis. But first the crucifixion. First you must become the living demonstration of someone who no longer knows any truth. You must become the living embodiment of one who rises over knowing anything with the mind. You must become a complete and total nothing, a state of receptivity, an utter and complete silence, a window to the Soul. And in the crucifixion of the mind I reveals Itself.

I cannot tell you ahead of time what the crucifixion will be to you, but I can tell you what it felt—what the experience was when I had it. Suddenly the Presence was there. I felt it, and I was realizing, resting in "I am in the Father and the Father in me, and I am One." And the Presence spread throughout my body. I felt it. I felt that tingling Presence as my Presence. I and the Presence were one. And suddenly it filled the room I was in, and I and the Presence, that tingling light being was the only being, and I Am That. And suddenly it filled the house, and I knew I Am That, and I am infinite, and I knew conscious awareness was about to go infinite. And I, that infinite being, I Am. And there was no more me. There was infinite I, One. One being, one presence, one light, one life, one Self. Infinite eternal God. And there was a sense of be still and know I am God.

And this is an experience, and how your experience, what your experience is when the veil is lifted and there's no more me and God, but only God, I can't tell you what it will be. I can only tell you that it must be, and for this cause came ye into the world, that you might know God, whom to know aright is eternal life. And when the veil is lifted you will know "I am God, and beside Me there is no other, and I am Infinite, and I am Eternal, and I am beyond the beyond, and I am Omnipresence Itself." And there you will find in that 'now' the mind, the little tiny mind that thought it knew something, is crucified. It's gone, and the infinite Mind which was in Christ Jesus, the Omniscience Itself, is flowing. And you will discover that you live and move and have your being in this infinite consciousness.

And as we learned in the Healing Talks, any problem presented to consciousness—there's no one to heal. How can there be someone to heal when I am Omnipresence? No. When someone calls or writes or asks for help, this is a concept presented to consciousness. You are to know no truth. You are to be still and behold truth knowing you. And as the crucifixion becomes complete, any good that is presented, as soon as you recognize it's good being presented, you do the same thing. You stand still. You know nothing. You listen, and the Spirit makes intercession. Consciousness reveals Itself.

You have no more healing work. You have only to listen and behold consciousness revealing Itself. And as you crucify in each meditation the mind, then consciousness reveals its infinite nature, its infinite being always expressed as I AM. And it takes you and it dissolves you and it reveals I in the midst of thee am the only and the one Presence.

Joel describes this in this chapter *Truth Unveiled* as the Sabbath. See if you – well, see if you can feel this.

There must come a rest from the activity of the mind: taking thought for our life, fearing for our life, constantly knowing truth. There must come a Sabbath, and in this Sabbath here we live by Grace, because then we do not know (any more) truth (now) Truth reveals Itself and we become the Truth (living Itself). *It is not an activity of the mind: it is Soul revealing Itself.*

And finally over here he says:

As you have learned to work hard and long with the principles of The Infinite Way, (now, in this crucifixion) *you must learn to stop doing this* (you must), *say to yourself, "Let me not trust in the mind. Let me relax in God."*

And again he says:

You students who are ready for the Sabbath (that is, ready for the crucifixion and the ascension,) *you must learn to rest back in the realization: "Let my Soul take over (not the) mind."*

For six days (he says) *you have labored to study and train yourself, and those "six days," are for most of you many, many years. But there*

comes a rest; (there comes the seventh day) *there comes the Sabbath;
and that is when you stop metaphysical struggling* (you stop), *relax,
and let Grace* (let Consciousness) *live* (Itself).

And so The Infinite Way is designed, was designed to take
us through the letter to the Spirit, to take us through the six days
of labor to the seventh day, the Sabbath. To take us from the law
of the mind to the Grace of God. To take us from knowing the
truth to being the truth. To take us from the outside God and the
concepts of God and the various myriad beliefs of Gods through
the crucifixion, rising above knowing the truth, rising above the
mind to an awareness of infinite spiritual being to the I that I am.

And consequently he tried to show us by putting that ascension
and the experience of this ascension as the last chapter in his book
The Infinite Way. After the chapter *The New Horizon* comes the
chapter *The New Jerusalem,* and do you remember where we are
told in Revelation that I saw a new Jerusalem coming down from
heaven. Now the new Jerusalem is the new dispensation that
comes out of the Consciousness which is in heaven. When the
crucifixion is really complete and you have risen above a mind
that knows anything, then Consciousness lives itself, reveals itself,
expresses itself as the new Jerusalem, a new heaven, a new earth, a
new Self, an infinite Self, I.

And so having experienced it, he gives us this:

"The FORMER THINGS have passed away," and *"all things
are become new. Whereas I was blind, now I see,"* and not *"through
a glass, darkly,"* but *"face to face."* (Yes, the veil has been lifted.)
*Yes, even in my flesh, I have seen God. The hills have rolled away,
and there is no more horizon, but the light of heaven makes all things
plain.*

*Long have I sought thee, O Jerusalem, but only now have my
pilgrim feet touched the soil of heaven. The waste places are no more.
Fertile lands are before me, the like of which I have never dreamed.*

Oh, truly "There shall be no night there." The glory of it shines as the noonday sun, and there is no need of light for God is the light thereof.

I sit down to rest. In the shade of the trees, I rest and I find my peace in Thee. Within Thy grace is peace, O Lord. In the world I was weary – in Thee I have found rest.

In the dense forest of words I was lost; in the <u>letter</u> *of truth was tiredness and fear, but in Thy Spirit only is shade and water and rest.*

How far have I wandered (from Thee) from Thy Spirit, O Tender One and True, how far, how far! How deeply lost in the maze of words, words, words! But now am I returned, and in Thy Spirit shall I ever find my life, my peace, my strength. Thy Spirit is the bread of life, finding which I shall never hunger. Thy Spirit is a wellspring of water, and drinking it I shall never thirst."

And see, Spirit is Thy Consciousness, Thy being, Thy Spirit which is the I of me, the I of you, the infinite I.

"As a weary wanderer I have sought Thee, and now my weariness is gone. Thy Spirit has formed a tent for me, and in its cool shade I linger and peace fills my Soul. Thy presence has filled me with peace. Thy love has placed before me a feast of Spirit. Yea, Thy Spirit is my resting place, an oasis in the desert of the letter of truth.

In Thee will I hide from the noise of the world of argument; in Thy consciousness (see – Thy consciousness above the mind) *...in Thy consciousness find surcease from the noisomeness of men's tongues. They divide Thy garment, O Lord of Peace, they quarrel over Thy word – yea, until it becomes words and no longer Word.*

As a beggar have I sought the new heaven and the new earth, and Thou hast made me heir of all.

How shall I stand before Thee but in silence? How shall I honor Thee but in the meditation of mine heart?

Praise and thanksgiving Thou seekest not, but the understanding heart Thou receivest.

I will keep silent before Thee. My Soul and my Spirit and my silence shall be Thy dwelling place. (Again, my silence from that mind *shall be Thy dwelling place.*) *Thy Spirit shall fill my meditation, and it shall make me and preserve me whole. O Thou Tender One and True – I am home in Thee.*"

And so do you see how he waxed poetic when he experienced the ascension and the stillness and the peace and the oneness of I? And finally we have John describing the same experience as he witnessed it. This is John, chapter 1 of course.

"*In the beginning was the Word, and the Word was with God, and the Word was God.*"

And now you see the Word to John is: Above the mind that knows anything is the Word which reveals Itself in a moment of silence. And so he says:

"*In the beginning was the Word,*
And the Word was with God, And the Word was God.
The same was in the beginning with God.
All things were made by him;
And without him was not any thing made that was made.
In him was life; and the life was the light of men.
He came unto his own, and his own received him not.
But for you, my dear friends, you will receive him.
And as many as received him, to them gives he the power to become the sons of God, even to them that believe on him."

And so if you will step into this crucifixion willingly, knowing that it will hurt. Mind does not want to be crucified, but if you will step into the crucifixion, go through it, stand ye still, then you will have the power. You will become an expression of God, God Itself expressing.

(You will be) "*born, not of blood, nor of the will of the flesh, nor of the will of man, but of God. And the Word will be made flesh, and dwell among us, and we will behold the glory, as of the only begotten of the Father, full of grace and truth.*"

And do you see John is describing the same experience, the experience of crucifixion, which he also went through, he and

Joel, and the experience of the ascension. Now do you see why these talks are so uncomfortable? Because inevitably this is the path which Christ Jesus laid before us so that we may follow. Pick up our cross and follow and be crucified and rise again and experience a new Self, an infinite Self, an eternal Self. One divine, infinite, spiritual omnipresent Self as an experience, as a reality. Not something you can describe. Not something the mind can discuss. Something spiritually discerned.

So I invite you all, and we're going to close with one more time realizing this:

"Jesus' (the Christ's) realization of the need to crucify, or rise above, the mortal sense of self, (the mortal mind which knows truth) enabled him to make the ascension. The ascension is always the same: a rising above mind, above knowing the truth, to Truth Itself."

This journey is really an Infinite Way. This journey leads you out of mortality, out of a mind that can know mortality, into an eternal everywhere Self. And there is but one Self, and I, the I of you, am That.

You can do this. I know. I will help you. I will give you life eternal. I am the resurrection. Be still and know I am God.

[Silence]

CLASS 16

ALL THAT I HAVE IS THINE

Bill: Soul to soul, Spirit to spirit. Blessings.

Well, good morning everyone. This is Sunday May 12th, Mother's Day 2013, and this talk today is about living our Christhood. You remember Jesus said, *"Who is my mother? Who is my brother? Those that do the will of my Father in heaven."* And so those that do the will of my Father in heaven are Christ, are demonstrating their Christhood. Only Christ can do the will of the Father in heaven. There comes a point in our spiritual growth where we have to ask ourselves are we practicing these principles – are we still practicing these principles for the good that I might receive? Am I still looking for some personal good such as health or such as companionship or supply? Do I not believe that all the things, all these things are added unto me when I seek first how to demonstrate Christhood? Are these just pretty, poetic words, or is there a principle here?

There is a principle here, and the principle is: *To him that hath it shall be given, and to him that hath not shall be taken away even that which he has.*

That principle puzzled me for a long time until I began to live and demonstrate the principles of Christhood, even in a little measure. Then I began to understand that principle.

Now my observation over the years is that people have – some people have a difficulty with supply. They always seem to be limited. There's not much supply coming in and not much going out, and they're having a problem in that area. Other people demonstrate supply quite beautifully, but there's a problem with health, with life, with living, and they're limited in that area and they have problems. They don't know how to solve them. And some people demonstrate health and life and living perfectly fine, but they're alone and they have a problem finding the right companion. They have a problem with companionship. They may say to the person experiencing lack and limitation, "I don't understand this – supply is so easy to demonstrate." And the one experiencing lack and limitation may feel, "Why are you alone? I mean God is everywhere. How can you not be a companion to God?"

And so each of us has the area where we need to practice these principles perhaps a little more diligently than our neighbor. Yet all of us will come to the place where we can practice that principle and demonstrate that we *have*, that we really are the Christ.

I'm gonna talk about myself today, but only so that I can point out the principle and how it is that I practice it, not so that you can think there's anything great about me, because there isn't. I can tell you without hesitation that of myself I can do nothing. This I know. However, I also know that with Christ all things are possible. *I can do all things through Christ which strengtheneth me.* I know that too. And if I did not admit that to you I would be a liar. So please take this talk today in your good graces and not think that I'm trying to brag or anything, 'cause I'm not. But it is important to understand the principle.

Now we say that we want to live as Christ and we're ready to give up our humanhood. And yet we turn around and we look at my bank account, my companions, and my health. Now there can be no such thing in the kingdom of heaven. Incidentally, the kingdom of heaven is not some place you're gonna go to, not even some place you're going to attain. The kingdom of heaven is here and now. You're standing in the middle of it. The only thing that's preventing you from seeing it, from feeling it, from the conscious awareness of it, is this personal sense of life, a life in which you have my finances, my companions, and my health. That's the very thing that must be seen through in order to demonstrate your Christhood, in order to demonstrate that you have. And we don't want to give it up. I know I certainly didn't. It had to be practically ripped from my hands.

Once upon a time, maybe 40 (47 now) years ago, I was married, happily married I thought, although that was a lie because we were having problems and I was just denying them, and one day I came home and she said, "I'm leaving. I've met this other fellow, John, and I'm moving in with him." And she took our 1-year-old son and she moved in with him. The next day I came home from work and I was just dashed to pieces. I looked through the house and the baby's room was empty. There was nothing but blue walls, not even a crib, and I looked in our room and all her things were missing. There was a big, gigantic, king-sized bed and nothing there but my pillows and bedspread. And even in the kitchen things that she liked were missing, and there was no note or anything. Just like that (fingers snap) she was gone.

And so my world fell to pieces, and I didn't know what to do. And I felt like, well, it must be my fault. I had a spiritual adviser at the time and his name was Don and he had given me a copy of The Art of Meditation and I had been reading it for about a year or year and a half. I was trying to practice the principles, but I wasn't getting anywhere. I was praying to God to show me how to love, and he was about to do just that, and boy I didn't—once that prayer was answered I was sorry I ever prayed it for quite a while.

And so I went over to Don's house and I said, "What do I do? I can't take it, these thoughts. I see her with other guys and these thoughts, they just drive me crazy." And he said to me something that you don't hear very often. He said, "You know, most people would get out of this problem by transferring their love to another woman. But (he said) if you did that, in a very short time you'd be just as dependent on the next one, because you see, you're not hurting from love. You're hurting from dependency. You need her."

"Well, what do I do about that? How do I get over that"?

"Well, (he said) I don't know. You're going to have to find a way to transfer your feelings to God." He said, "You're going to have to transfer that love you feel or felt for her over to God."

"Well, I can't how do I do that? I can't see God. How do I do that? I can't hold God at night."

"Well, (he said) I have a feeling there's something for you in that book, The Art of Meditation, but I can't tell you what it is. You have to find it for yourself."

And so I went home and I had two principles. One was that I going to have to find a way to let go of her, and two, I was going to have to find a way to transfer my feelings to God. And I had asked him, I said, "What do I do when these thoughts come of her with these other guys?" He said, "You live by yourself, so just talk out loud and say 'hey, I've given that problem to God. It's not mine. I'm not working on the problem. The problems – the answer's not in the problem'." And so I took that too. Took that home and I fell apart. I was not able to do it. Here's what happened.

I became so depressed. I don't know if you've ever been that depressed, depressed where it's hard to move your body. I would get up in the morning and the first thing of course I would see is that she was not there. The bed was empty. Go in and have my coffee. Couldn't eat. Dragged myself down. Get on the bus. Go to work. I worked in a factory. Pushed—you ever been that depressed that you have to push your body around? I pushed my body around all day. I went through the motions, and then at night I'd walk down the driveway to the back house where we had lived, opened the door, searched the house. Nobody was there, just me. I plopped down on the couch and cried my eyes out. And then I got mad at God. I'd yell at God. "I asked you to teach me how to love and you take away the only person I love. What are you doing?" And then I'd get down on the floor and beg him for help. "Please take this pain away."

Oh, I was crazy. Probably certifiably so. I'm sure they would have said, "oh, nervous breakdown" and given me some medication if there had been a doctor present. Finally, I turned to <u>The Art of Meditation</u>. I remembered that Don said there was something for me in there. And so I opened the book just anywhere and I came upon *"For Love is of God"* and I thought, well, that may have something to do with this. Maybe there's a principle in here I can use. And I got down to this part here where it says:

The essential ingredient of all satisfactory relationships is love. Our love for God is made manifest in our love for man.

And remember, he told me to transfer my feelings, my love, to God. And so I'm looking and I'm reading as if my life depends on it, because it did. And I'm reading where, how do I love God? And here it says:

Our love for God is made manifest in our love for man. We are not only one with God, but we are one with the children of God: with our families and relatives; with our church members; with our business associates; with our friends. When we recognize God as our neighbor, we become members of the household of God, saints in the spiritual kingdom: there is a complete surrender of self into the infinite Sea of Spirit. The good of God flows to us through all who become part of our universe. (And) To those who live in communion with God, serving God through their fellow man, the promise is literally kept: All that I have is thine.

No longer is there a need or a desire for any person or any thing.
Hmm. I wasn't feeling that way. Boy, I needed her. Maybe there's something to this.

Every thing and every person become part of our being. What we surrender, we have; what we hold in the grasp of possession, we lose. Every thing we release, we draw to us; every thing we loose, we have; every thing we set free, we bind to us forever. "Loose him and let him go." Let everyone be loosed in Christ. We trust everyone to the God of his own being. We do not hold anyone in bondage to a debt of love, hate, fear, or doubt. We do not demand even love from anyone. (Aah) *We agree that no man owes us anything. Only when we do not feel a debt of obligation and only when we hold no one in a debt of obligation to us, are we free, and do we set our world free.*

And those two paragraphs my dear friends completely changed my existence because I put down the book and I made the decision I was going to follow those principles. I was going to love God by loving God's creation, for God and his creation are one. And I was going to surrender, let go of having to have her or anyone. And I did that. The next morning I woke up and my head started out, "Oh, she's with these" and I spoke out loud and I said, "Hey, take that out of here. That's not my problem." And then I turned to God and I said, "God, I love you. What do you want to do today?"

And I realized that if I had a new sweetheart I would call her up and say, "What do you want to do?" And if she said, "Let's go to the beach," we'd go. That's the way it is when you're in love. What does she want? You give it to her. And I thought now I'm gonna do that same thing with God. And I said, "God, what do you want to do today?" And I waited. I got quiet and no answer came. So I said, "Okay God. Here's what I'm gonna do. I'm gonna do the dishes there and vacuum the floor, and if you need something, let me know and we'll do it."

And so I went over and I started doing the dishes and I remembered Brother Lawrence. He said he practiced the presence while doing the dishes. And so I did the dish and I said, "Here God. This one's for you," and I did the very best I could on that dish, and I said, "Look God. It's so shiny I can see myself in it." I put it in the drainer on the – what is that called? I put it on the drainer there on the counter next to the sink and then I did the next dish and the next dish, and I did 'em all for God, talking to God the whole time. And then I went and I got the vacuum cleaner and I vacuumed the floor for God. I did the very best I could just for God, talking to God the whole time. "Oh, look at that. I can get in the corner there."

And then I put that away and I sat down in my chair. I read a little from <u>The Art of Meditation</u>. The phone rang and on the other end of the phone was Ray and he said, "Can I come over and talk?" And I said, "Yeah, come on over." Said he had a problem. And so I couldn't really talk out loud to God while Ray was there, so I had to go within myself, and within myself I said, "Father, how may I best be of service? Please use me." And outside I said, "Hi Ray. Come on in. Would you like cup of coffee?" He said, "Yeah," so I made him a coffee and inside myself I said, "Father, you say whatever he needs to hear." And outside I said, "So tell me, Ray. What's going on?"

You see? I was praying without ceasing, and I was concentrating on God, not Ray. And I looked through Ray to God, and an amazing thing happened. Ray was expecting me to have all these problems and instead he brought his problems. His problems came to the surface and he spoke them and they dissolved. The answer was revealed right there between us and he went away and he said, "Wow, thank you!" And I said, "Don't thank me, thank God." And off he went.

I had a plant in the living room there. It was a wandering jew and it never got any sun and I talked to the plant and I looked through the plant to God and I would get up in the morning, say "Hi Father. How are you?" And I'd water the plant. "Are you thirsty"? And then I had a cat, a black cat named Sufi, and Sufi would come in and I would say, "Hi Father. Are you hungry?" I'd give Sufi some food. And I looked through the cat to God. And I started to look through everything.

Remember? Joel said in the book serving God through his fellow man, the promise is literally kept. All that I, God have, is thine, and I started serving God through my fellow man. I went to spiritual meetings at a church and I stayed on ready in case anybody needed to talk or wanted to talk so that I could share. And strange things started to happen, very strange things. Things I've never forgotten to this day. What kind of strange things? Well, one, I went to a restaurant I used to like. I ordered a hamburger and fries and a cup of coffee and the coffee came and it was hot and there was some ice in my water, so I took the spoon and got the ice out, a little bit of ice and put it in my coffee and cooled it down and I was able to drink it. And the waitress from way across the hall there, the restaurant, way across the restaurant suddenly appeared beside my table with a cup full of ice. She said, "I saw you putting ice in your coffee. I thought you might like a –"

"Oh yes, I do." And I thanked her and inside myself I thanked God. "Thank you, Father." The plant in my living room that never got any sunshine, the wandering jew, it grew like crazy, the recognition of God where the plant appeared. The cat would come walking out of the kitchen. I'd be reading <u>The Art of Meditation</u> or <u>Practicing the Presence</u> and I could see it out of the corner of my eye. I'd say, "Just a minute, Father" and it would sit there like a dog and I'd reach the end of the chapter and I'd say, "okay" and it would run over and jump up in my lap. Now if you have cats or have had them you know they don't respond that way. They ignore you.

This is one of the strangest things that ever happened. I was sitting there trying to read one of these spiritual books one day and a fly was flying around the room and it landed on my forehead and I swatted it away and it landed on my arm. It landed on the book, it landed on my nose. It was bothering me and so I started to get up and get the fly swatter and I stopped in my tracks and I said, "Now wait a minute, now wait a minute. God's inside of everyone and everything. Right?" So I stuck out my hand and I said, "I'm only here to serve, so come on over here and land in my hand here and I'll put you outside." And I looked and the fly made a couple more circles around the room and it came over, landed dead in the center of the palm of my hand which I had open and I got up from the couch and it never moved!

This busy fly that was buzzing and buzzing and flying around and lighting on my forehead and arms and nose and book – it did not move! It stayed in the center of my palm, and I got up and I walked over to the door, and there was a door and a screen door. So with my right hand I opened the door and I still had my palm there and the fly was still there. He didn't move. That's not possible! You know that's not possible. I opened the door and I opened the screen. I stuck my hand out and I said, "There you go, Father." And off he flew.

I was beginning to practice the principle: To him that hath, it shall be given. I was spending my days and nights serving God through – well, loving God through loving God's creation or God as his creation, and these strange and wonderful things were happening.

Another week or two passed. I was sitting there in a meditation and I realized, "Oh my goodness. I don't have to have her in order to love her. I don't have to have anybody. And yet I love the whole creation." I realized that what I had started out practicing and pretending halfway had come true and I fell in love with God inside God's entire creation.

Strange things were happening, and I went to this man Don who told me to look for a chapter in The Art of Meditation. I said, "Don, this is – why its fabulous. I'm free. I no longer have to have her. I have discovered God is inside of everyone and everything and I love God more than life itself. And he said, "That's fabulous." He said, "I'm giving a talk down here at this church Wednesday night. Will you come down and give one with me?" I said, "Why certainly." Because why? Because it was put in front of me to do and I was serving God through serving the creation. I was practicing the principle: I have love and I can give it.

And so Wednesday night came and I talked for about 15 minutes and then we had a coffee break and some doughnuts and whatnot and then we went back to the main speaker, which was Don. He was to speak for 45 minutes to an hour, and he got up and he talked for about 5 minutes on certain spiritual principles he'd discovered in his life and then he looked down at the podium and he dropped over dead. At least he dropped his body right there and entered the invisible and never came back.

Now, I don't know if you know the significance of this, but while the room was breaking into pandemonium and calling "call 911" and all that, I went around the corner where nobody could see me. I sat down, closed my eyes, and had a meditation because I knew God was inside of everyone and everything, and the voice said to me as clear as anything, *"Behold, I shall make all things new."* And indeed, that voice has taken me from that little corner of that room to around the world and in many dimensions. But the point is of this whole story is I learned by being a companion to a plant, to a cat, even to a fly. By being a companion to God I demonstrated companionship with the Infinite, with Omnipresence from then until now.

One evening before this experience of going to the meeting and talking with Don I was sitting by myself reading The Art of

Meditation and I put it down and I got quiet and I meditated. And suddenly there were no more thoughts. There was just a little period, a few seconds of silence, and at the same time I felt this Presence, this Presence right there in my room, and it touched me on the side of the face, a very tender, loving touch. And with that – well, it was a tingling feeling in my face – in it, on it, around it, through it, a Presence which I saw as my Father, as Christ, as the Isness of God. And with it came a sense of peace and from that moment until now I have never, ever, ever been alone.

And you see, I demonstrated the principle of Christhood. To him that hath, it shall be given. I am a companion and the Comforter is my companion, and all that the Father has is mine. And the Comforter has never left me. Omnipresence is mine from that time until now and forever throughout infinite and eternity. I will never be alone again. I demonstrated my Christhood, that I have perfect omnipresent companionship.

You see that? I demonstrated it by giving it away. And so you don't demonstrate companionship by practicing principles until you get a companion. Yes, I have a wife. It's been 23 years, 24 years, (30 years now) and we are completely in love with each other. I love her. She knows she's second to God in my life, and I know I'm second to God in her life. We put God first, and the funny thing is that it includes her, it includes me because God is inside of everyone and everything.

So, that's not to say how great I am because I almost died having to learn that principle. And you see, when Don introduced me to God, his mission was done. He left. He left, and he passed the torch to me, and now I have it and hopefully I'm introducing you to God, the God of your being.

So that's companionship. That's how Christ lives companionship—by *being* a companion. By pouring out love, by serving God through God's creation. Now that's how Christhood practices companionship, and it's never alone because all that the Father has is mine.

And what about supply? As long as you're thinking in terms of I need to demonstrate money; I don't have enough of it. Well, you're lost. It's not gonna work or it's not gonna work very long. Again, companionship is not something you get. You know now from the story that I just gave it's something you give, you pour it out from within you. And so if you're going to demonstrate your Christhood the principle must be the same with supply. It must be something you pour out from within your Christhood from the center of your being.

So now how do you pour out supply, especially when you don't have any?

Well, that's a mistake. There's never a time when Christ does not have supply. "*Son all that I have is thine.*" All that God has. What does God have? Does God have money? Now, really seriously. Does God have money? No, because God is an invisible spiritual Presence. God doesn't have money. What is supply? If supply is not money, what is supply?

Joel always tells us the story about the oranges, and he talks about the oranges on the tree and when the oranges are used up and given away or thrown away, in one way or another an invisible substance begins to form itself as the oranges. You remember that from the book The Infinite Way in the chapter called *Supply*? And he says in the Kailua study series that evidently very few people have hooked that up, that principle up with themselves. And you know it because they're not demonstrating supply! They're still calling him. "Oh, please help me. I have a problem with supply." It's because they're thinking of supply as money, finances, stocks, bonds, income, and that's not supply at all. Then what is supply?

I discovered it like this. I discovered it in this, pretty near the same experience I just shared with you, that by pouring out love, life gave me love back. That waitress seeing across that restaurant came and gave me love in the form of service to me. That was the love that I had poured out. It comes back heaped up, pressed down, and running over. Christ Jesus did not lie. That principle is correct. To him that hath, it shall be given.

And Joel points out that there are many ways to prove that you have. How do you prove that you have supply? Well, how did I prove that I had love? By giving it away. Right? Right! How do I prove I have money? Let's take money. How do I prove that I have money, that I own it, that it's mine. I prove it by giving it away. Now remember, I'm telling you this principle not so that you will think how great I am. Please! Don't go there. But so that you can see how to live it, how to live your Christhood.

Now last month we gave away over a thousand dollars. We don't give that much every month, but we give something every month, and last month it just happened to be over a thousand dollars. It was the right thing to do. It seemed indicated, and I can tell you that the more that you pour out, the more comes back. But if you do it for that reason, if you start taking inventory like an accountant and keeping track – well, let's see now. I gave away two hundred dollars, so some thirty, some hundred – I should get back at least, you know, six hundred dollars. Just don't go there! Just don't do that. Okay? It's all and – it's all and nothing. It's a thousand to nothing.

Our job is to live our Christhood and not worry about how life will give – reflect that back to us. We can know that it'll be heaped up, pressed down, and running over and that will be filled with joy, and that's all we need to know. And so last month we gave away over a thousand dollars to different places, and we can sit back and rest and know that the universe is going to pour that back somehow. I don't know how. I know it's already started because several people have also given to us online as well as in other ways. Finding gifts in the post office box.

Now that's one way. You can pour out money, and Joel says you can even do that even if you do not seem to have enough. You can pour that out in little ways and see what happens. Do you remember he discussed so beautifully how in the early days he would charge for his practice. Somebody would call or write or cable and say please help me, and he would help them, and then he would send out a bill for twenty dollars or twenty-five or whatever he was charging. And the people were having problems and they couldn't seem to pay him. You remember what happened? I remember it.

He said he was taking a walk one evening and he didn't have the money for a bus or a cab, so he was walking. And on the walk suddenly he had a realization: I Am That I Am. Only it was no longer just words; it was a realization, and he realized I am supply. Oh, I. Yes. That substance at the center of my being that in a tree forms oranges in me can form money. It can form housing. It can form cars. It can form clothes. It can form a body. It can form a companion. Yes, I am supply.

Now, if I am supply, then why do I have to look for it out here?

And immediately he made the decision he was no longer gonna send out any bills ever again. And people continued to call and ask for help and he continued to meditate for them, but he no longer sent out bills. And within a day or two somebody, he saw somebody in an elevator and they said, "Oh, hey Joel. I owe you two hundred bucks. Here." You see, by pouring out, by demonstrating his Christhood by pouring out service and money, he stopped looking for a return and just rested in his Christhood, and the universe started pouring back, heaped up, pressed down, and running over.

And I know whether—I don't know if you realize this—but I paid attention really close, anybody that's living these principles I look at them almost under a microscope to see what they're doing.

263

And Joel Goldsmith gave away eighty percent of his income. Eighty, eight—O percent he gave away to spiritual foundations, to universities and to higher education, different programs. He gave it away, eighty percent, and the twenty percent that he kept was more than enough to take care of him and let him live in the beautiful islands of Hawaii and travel the world.

So he demonstrated Christhood. And you have to start somewhere, so you give what you have to give. To him that hath, it shall be given, and that's where I started. How do you prove that you have something, that you own it? The only way you can prove that you have it, that you own it, is to give it away. If I say I have this - we're still talking of money here - if I say I own these five dollar bills right here, this five dollar bill, but I'm clutching it to myself – well, I don't really own it. It kind of owns me. But if I have the ability to give it away here – yeah, sure, take it – without any thought of return, just pouring out the same way,.I would pour out love or service – then I prove that I own it. If I own it I can do what I want to with it including give it away. You see that?

So in relationship to supply – and now supply is that spiritual substance. Do you understand that? That spiritual substance at the center of your being which you have to find a way to let that imprisoned splendor escape. You have to find a way to share that substance in acts of kindness, especially acts of kindness where you don't get found out; they're anonymous. In flowing out your funds, your gifts of money, your gifts of clothes. In service. In time. In prayers when you pray for others. In love when you love God inside of his creation. This is the way you live your Christhood and prove that you *have*. You *have* companionship, and you *are* a companion. You *have* supply, and you can pour out things and service and money and love, and you prove that you have. To him that hath, it shall be given.

Now prove that you have it by giving it away.

Does that clear that up some? It may not change the picture out here in a day or two, but consistently practicing Christhood, the universe will reflect back to you Christhood and will reflect back to you all that I have is thine. Because the principle is: To those who serve God through their fellow man, the promise is literally kept. *Son all that I have is thine.*

Now what about health? What about life? That confused me for a long time. I could see how I could pour out love and the universe would give me love. I could see how I could pour out supply in things and money and service, and the universe would give back supply. But I could not see how do you pour out health so that the universe would give you back health or life? How do you do that? And it puzzled me, and I looked at it and looked at it, and I finally came to see.

Well, this morning I went on a walk. Now I'm – in a few months – well, I'm headed towards sixty, and I took a walk this morning and I walked for about a mile. And here in the mountains it's not a flat walk. You go up some really steep hills and down and up and down and around. It's the mountains. And when I take my walk in the morning there's a dog – you know this thing about companionship? Even the animals start to come to you because they recognize Christ. And there's this dog that lives down the street and he sees me come out my front door and here he comes barreling up the street, just dying to be with me. (chuckles) His name is Rocket I found out, and so Rocket is rocketing up the street, and he's about ten years old, and he comes rocketing up the street and wagging his tail and next to me. He's like part wolf, so he's really furry, and I pet him and I say, "Oh hi. Are you gonna join me on my walk?" And off we go and we walk for about a mile and we come back and then he slowly walks back home and I come in my house.

Okay, well when I share that walk with him and I pet him I am pouring out energy. Am I not? I'm pouring out life. I'm pouring out health. Now what about when you guys call or send me an E-mail and say, "Would you pray for me? I'm having this problem." And I sit down and recognize that there's no such problem and no such life. That right where you are, God is, and God is the life. God is the substance. God is the health. God is the only being, and all that God has is you. Am I not pouring out life and health? Yes, I am. I'm pouring out a realization of health, realization of life.

Now, again please don't think I'm trying to brag. I'm not. I'm showing you how the principle works. I am involved in many places. I'm involved in a twelve-step organization and I work with people that are abusing drugs and alcohol and want to stop. And I work with those people because I myself had a problem forty-one years ago, forty-two years ago, and what freed me from it was spiritual principles. And so I work with these people to teach them to help them to learn these spiritual principles that they themselves might find the same freedom in God or freedom in Christ or freedom in whatever higher power they choose.

Now in addition to that you know that I work with the principles of The Infinite Way and teaching some of those principles and sharing some of those principles with whomever will desire to download these talks. And you know that I have practiced taking the old Herb Fitch talks from reel to reel, putting them on the computer, cleaning them up some, converting them into MP3's and sometimes typing them out and editing them and making sure they match the talks into an e-book, and I even took the twenty-five tapes of *The Revelation of St. John* and turned them into a hard copy which was put into print as a two-volume set of books. And so in that way I'm pouring out the message of The Infinite Way to the universe.

You know also that my wife and I have special needs foster children, and these foster children have been severely abused and they don't always come to us in the greatest shape. Often they're very, very angry, and we have had little children that are violent, and we had one little boy that every night at six o'clock he would say, "I'm gonna get a hickory stick and beat your ass." Little six-year-old. He was about three feet tall, and he was just spouting out what he had heard. And we had another child that would mark her room or some room the way a cat will mark it instead of using the bathroom like the rest of us. And we had one girl whose arm was severely burned because her father was teaching her a lesson and held it in the fire. And we had another girl who watched her father murder her mother while she hid under the bed. And we had another boy who had to wear eight sets of clothing, one on top of the other, to bed at night, and so I guess you can imagine what happened to him at night.

And so the point is that we get these children and they're very angry, very hurt, and we work with them for a few years. And with these principles, these spiritual principles, looking through all that muck to the Christ at the center of their being, it doesn't mean that we permit them to do these things. We tell them that these behaviors are unacceptable, and we teach them, we help them learn other and more appropriate behaviors, and they turn into sometimes very fine human beings, and even better than that, sometimes they begin to grasp these spiritual principles. The point is, they heal, and we've proved it over and over again. Often we get them with as many as nine medications, and usually when they leave here they're on nothing.

So the point is, we work with these troubled children and we have for twenty-odd years. In fact, two more children and we'll be on our one-hundredth child (121 now). And so, you can see – can you not see that the principle to him that hath, it shall be given, that I'm living that principle, and that that is living Christhood. Pouring out in the twelve-step program, pouring out in The Infinite Way, pouring out with these children, pouring out in the neighborhood. This is pouring out life and health and love and service. This is standing a little to one side instead of being selfish and self-centered, and allowing Christ to be demonstrated.

In the silence, when I become silent, I have a period every day most days if I can remember, I have a period where I just get quiet and let the Christ pour through. I just feel that presence and I let it flow to whomsoever it will in a service to mankind. And so my life is filled with companionship, it's filled with supply, and it's filled with life, with health. But why? Have I sought these? Have I prayed for these? No. Oh no. No.

This presence, this presence within, this substance at the center of being, this wonderful, beautiful Christ flows out, forms itself in acts of kindness, in acts of service, in acts of love. Sometimes in acts of responsibility, but it flows out.

It pours itself out, and because it does I am standing in the center of Christ consciously aware of It forming itself, and I know that I will never be alone, and I know that all that the Father hath is mine, and I know that my life, God life, Christ life, is eternal and will never die. And so I am consciously aware of Christhood living itself, practicing itself. I am standing, living, being the principle: to him that hath, it shall be given. Heaped up, pressed down, and running over.

Now do you see that it's time for us to stop thinking in terms of my supply, my companionship, my health, my life? Do you see it's – it's time to surrender all that? Just throw it away. Just let it go, I mean. Let it go. Bring your attention into the answer. Remember? Joel told us how many times that the answer's not in the problem. Do not meet a problem on the level of the problem, and the problem is a personal sense of existence, and the answer's not there! That has to die! So let it go. The answer has to be in the answer: To him that hath, it shall be given.

But it can't be a principle you know with the mind. It has to be a principle you live or you allow to live you. You must be the Christ now pouring out from the center of your being all that the Father hath. We say that we are ready to die and be reborn. Well, this is the way it works. You die to a personal sense of self and you are reborn as Christ living Itself, pouring forth that which the Father has, which is infinity. Yes, to him that hath, it shall be given, but you must prove that you have by giving it away.

Now, there's not one of you hearing this that cannot begin to pour. It does not mean that you have to pour with things. You can pour with service and love too, which will eventually spread over into things and into funds. But eventually you must be the Christ that pours out in all of your affairs. You can't be the Christ in part of your affairs and human in the other part. I remember when I was working in a factory I used to stay over and work just a little bit longer, and I had already clocked out. I did it just as a service to the company. See, there's a lot of ways to pour, a lot of ways. And I guarantee you, it returns heaped up, pressed down, and running over.

You stand in an infinite kingdom. You stand in an infinity of supply. You stand in the ever-present, omnipresent companion. This is Christhood. This is why you are here. If enough of us will do this we shall demonstrate Christhood around the earth, around the world. And anyone, anywhere reaching out will touch Christ, and the torch will be passed, and our light will light their light until the universe is transformed from earth to Christ.

How about you join me? How about you decide now to step out of humanhood and begin demonstrating Christhood? How about you go within and discover that substance at the center and let it pour out itself. You will be amazed. You will be astounded.

You will find amazing, wonderful things happening. You'll find yourself – well, you will discover the temple not made with hands, the temple that will stand eternal in the heavens, and it will be your resting place. It will be your being.

Now let us be still for a moment while we see if there's anything else left to pour out.

Yes, there's one other area I forgot to tell you about. It may be important, and that is about four or five years ago I discovered that I could do something else besides go down and buy another copy of Windows. I have nothing against Windows except that I discovered that there were several organizations working on something called Linux, which is open source software.

Now what's open source software? Well, that's – you can take the software that they wrote, which is an operating system like Windows, and you can change it. You can package it, put your own name on it, sell it. You can do anything you want to. You can share it with anybody. It's absolutely free, completely free a hundred percent. And I like that. And the people that were writing this software were people like me who had some knowledge of computer science and were able to program in the language of C or C++ or machine language or assembly language. They were able to program and so they wrote these programs and they gave 'em away to humanity, and I like that. I like that principle. Something about that sounded really good to me.

So I investigated and I put Linux on my computer and I love it. I absolutely love it. I'm using Linux (L-i-n-u-x) Linux Mint, Linux Mint 13 (19 now) interestingly enough called Maya, which we know is illusion. (chuckles) So I'm using an illusion on my computer and I love it. I just absolutely love it. And I investigated it and got into it and discovered some useful things and I went on the web and I found different Linux websites and I shared things and wrote some tutorials and in that way was able to give back to the Linux community worldwide, and I donated some money to different Linux operating systems like Mint and Ubuntu and Solus operating system and Descent operating system and Debian and things like that.

So in that way I was able to pour into the computer communities which had already given me so much. And sometimes those gifts are anonymous. I just go online there and I find their website and I donate using Paypal and they don't know my name because it comes to them under Mystical Principles and so I'm able to do that anonymous. Now I'm telling you there's only nineteen of you, eighteen of you and hopefully you'll keep it a secret and the only purpose of it is to show you that this principle can be practiced anywhere in the world. To him that hath, it shall be given. And so I gave away to these different operating system websites because they're doing really good work and they're giving it away to the world. You see?

So there's lots of ways to give. Lots of ways to practice this principle, and I live by this principle. To him that hath, it shall be given. And interestingly enough, I didn't really know until making this talk today that I am practicing Christhood, and I'm sure glad because it really has come back heaped up, pressed down, and running over. Anyway, that's the principle today. To him that hath, it shall be given. You must die to a personal sense of companionship, to a personal sense of supply, and to a personal sense of life and health. You must demonstrate Christhood, and the sooner the better. You can't live as a human. Remember? You can't pull God into a human sense of existence says Joel. And he's right. God will only express as Christhood.

And so you either stand on the principle to him that hath, and you begin proving you hath by practicing and demonstrating Christhood, or you stay in humanhood and prove that you have not, because to him that hath not shall be taken away even that which he hath because he thinks that's all he has. All right? All right.

So now all of you need to demonstrate Christhood by pouring out from that substance at the center of your being, pouring out love, pouring out service, pouring out substance, pouring out supply, pouring out life, pouring out health, pouring out prayer. I expect that of all of you. I expect that you really do want to live as Christ. And so who is my mother? Who is my brother? Those that pour out their Christhood, and so in that sense I would say to you Happy Mother's Day.

Blessings.

[Silence]

CLASS 17

BEHOLD I MAKE ALL THINGS NEW

Bill: Good afternoon.

This is Sunday May 19, 2013. In this morning's meditation there was one thing that came to me: Thy kingdom come. Just three words, but the more I turned it around and rested and looked, the more I wondered how many people know what that means. Oh, we hear the Lord's Prayer said all the time; maybe we say it all the time. Thy kingdom come, thy will be done on earth as is it is in heaven. Right? Or in earth as it is in heaven. We say the words all the time, but what does – what are we asking for? What are we saying when we say "thy kingdom come"?

In the first place, does God have a kingdom some place where he's a king and there's all these servants wandering about? Or does kingdom mean consciousness? Does kingdom mean spirit? Spirit and consciousness are the same thing, you know. When John says *"I was in the Spirit on the Lord's day"* in Revelation he means he was in that high consciousness. So, God is a spirit says our dear friend, Yeshua. God is a spirit. Don't you know God is a spirit and you must worship him in spirit. God and consciousness are one, and you must be one with that consciousness.

And so thy kingdom come means that higher consciousness, spiritual consciousness, Christ consciousness come. Manifest. Be.

Is. And so we're asking for that higher consciousness, but we're living in a physical realm. Oh, Joel tells us over and over you can't add God to your humanhood. And here I am, a little human being, praying up there to God somewhere, "Please give me your kingdom. Let it come."

Oh, in metaphysics we thought that meant let us have harmony of purse, pocketbook, wallet. Let us have harmony of health, body, mind. Let us have harmony of relationships, of friendships, of companionship. Right? Thy kingdom come. Now, however, we are more advanced on this path and we have a little bit different meaning to that. If you haven't done that, if you haven't done so, take that into meditation.

Thy kingdom come. What does that mean?

I noticed, or I was led to this chapter, these one, two, three, four, five pages called *The New Horizon*, because the new horizon is—well, thy kingdom. Joel has experienced that kingdom. And he says:

Above this sense-life, there is a universe of Spirit governed by Love, peopled with children of God living in the household or temple of Truth. (And) This world is real and permanent: Its substance is eternal Consciousness. In it there is no awareness of discords or even temporary material good.

So we know from that, from his little hint there, that when we say 'thy kingdom come' we are talking about an invisible spiritual universe. We're asking for an invisible spiritual consciousness to come. And what happens when we experience that? Well, he tells us that too.

(When thy kingdom comes) *The experience at first is like watching the world* (this whole world) *disappear over a horizon and drop down from before us. There is no attachment to the world [anymore], no desire to hold onto it.*

Are you experiencing that? Have you experienced that? Have you experienced thy kingdom come, thy kingdom coming? Have you experienced thy kingdom, this invisible spiritual realm, invisible spiritual consciousness? Do you think you can pull that invisible spiritual consciousness into this world? He tells you right here:

The experience does not come until a great measure of our desire for the things of "this world" has been overcome.

So you cannot experience this spiritual realm, which is permanent. Cannot experience '*the water that I shall give him*', which is life everlasting. You cannot experience spiritual being, invisible spiritual being – your invisible spiritual being – until you have no more desire for this world. And so you can't enter this higher realm, this realm of *Spirit governed by Love, peopled with children of God*. You cannot meet these people and experience the spiritual realm until the desire for this world has been overcome.

So those who are living the metaphysics of the message and trying to demonstrate a heart, a liver, lungs, a companion, or financial harmony – they're not ready for this higher consciousness, are they? And Joel tells us that. They're not ready for *The New Jerusalem*, which is the following chapter in this book. That state of consciousness we talked about where you enter the Sabbath. They're not ready for that, are they? No, they're still demonstrating things. They're still having rounds of demonstrating things in this world. Yet, he says you can't have it until you overcome that.

And is that not what Christ means when Christ says specifically to us, "*He that overcomes will I give to eat of the hidden manna*"? The hidden manna is again in an invisible realm. There's an invisible realm *closer than breathing, nearer than hands and feet*. It's in your very midst, right here, just less than a breath away. Yet you have no contact with it if you're trying to pull it into this realm.

And when you do have contact with it, Joel says:

At first you cannot speak of it. There is a feeling of "'Touch me not; I have not yet ascended' – I am still between the two worlds;"

275

And the two worlds are this world, this heaven, this earth, these concepts of heaven and earth – and the invisible spiritual realm, which is right here and now in your midst. Again, he says:

The more fascinated we are with conditions of human good and the greater our desire for even the good things the more intense is the illusion. Think neither on the discords nor the harmonies of this world.

Because both of them keep you chained to the old earth and the old heaven. They keep you chained to the mind, which is trying to demonstrate things. The ascension, we understand, is always, always rising above mind. Remember that from <u>Beyond Words and Thoughts</u>? Here he says:

The ascension is understood now as rising above the conditions and experiences of "this world," (and we look into the invisible) and we behold "many mansions" prepared for us in spiritual Consciousness – in the awareness of (the invisible).

And finally he says:

Let us not judge our good (by the senses). No good thing is withheld from us as we look (above the senses), above the physical evidence to the great Invisible (realm). Look up, look up! The kingdom is at hand!

And the kingdom at hand is this Great Invisible realm. So he recommends that you look up into that Great Invisible realm.

So when you pray "thy kingdom come" it's enough to stop there and rest and let thy kingdom, that new consciousness, that new heaven, new earth come.

Let that new consciousness manifest and form itself. You have no idea what that new earth is going to look like.

It's your necessity to continually form pictures and concepts in the mind into which you want to pour that invisible, that Great Invisible realm, that's keeping you from attaining it.

Thy kingdom come – and stop! Thy kingdom come – and behold.

Since Joel was at that place where he had attained that consciousness and could go in and out at will, he was at the same state of consciousness as our friend, John. Now listen to John as he explains thy kingdom. This is Revelation 21, and he says:

"And I saw a new heaven and a new earth: for the first heaven and the first earth were passed away; and there was no more sea."

Now the sea is that level of consciousness known as material consciousness. And here he says he stood in silence and saw a new heaven and a new earth. He saw that invisible spiritual realm form itself as something new, something new, even a new self. And the old had passed away, and there was no more material consciousness. You see? This is exactly the same as Joel saying this world drops down from before us and we rest in that spiritual consciousness. This is the same.

"And I John saw the holy city, new Jerusalem, coming down from God out of heaven, prepared as a bride adorned for her husband."

New Jerusalem, we learned, is that state of consciousness in which you rest back and are carried, carried by Christ consciousness. I've experienced it in thousands of meditations and sometimes with eyes wide open driving or talking or walking or shopping.

"And I heard a great voice out of heaven saying,"

Now he looked into the invisible and he beheld spiritual consciousness forming itself, and he heard a voice saying:

"Behold, the tabernacle of God is with men."

Yes, in your very midst, I am.

"And he will dwell with them, and they shall be his people, and God himself shall be with them, and be their God."

Now that's the experience: *Touch me not, for I have not yet ascended.* I am still between the old heaven and the old earth and the new heaven and the new earth. I'm still between them. I cannot yet discuss it, but I am watching. I am waiting upon the Lord.

"And God shall wipe away all tears from their eyes; and there shall be no more death."

No, because when the Infinite Invisible forms itself as your being, who is there to die? When the Great Invisible, when you look up and rest back and behold the Spirit move over the face of the deep and form itself as a new heaven, a new earth, a new self as you, your being – there is then no one to die.

"and there shall be no more death, neither sorrow, nor crying, neither shall there be any more pain: for the former things (humanhood) *has passed away."*

"And he that sat upon the throne said,"

This is Christ consciousness – he's still listening. First he watched, now he's listening.

"And he that sat upon the throne said, Behold, I make all things new."

And that includes you. You want to be born again, then let the human die. Yes, pray. Thy kingdom come. Realize you're asking for the Great Invisible to form itself where you stand and to stand there as your being.

"Behold, I make all things new. And he said unto me, Write; for these words are true and faithful."

"And he said unto me, It is done."

What is done? The Great Invisible has formed itself. God is on earth.

Immanuel is appearing. Christ is born.

"It is done. I am Alpha and Omega, the beginning and the end. I will give unto you that is athirst of the fountain of the water of life freely."

"He that overcomes shall inherit all things; and I will be his God, and he shall be my son."

And what did we hear? To them gives he power to become the sons of God. You, my friends, my brothers, my sisters – we are one in Christ, and we have received the Word from the Great Invisible, and we have the power to lay down our human sense of life, and we have no more desire for the things of this world. If they come, they come. If they don't, they don't. What is that to thee?

Now we have one desire, to watch this world, this physical sense of self, fall down over the horizon and rest back on an infinite sea of Spirit and stand so still without thought here in the silence: *"Behold, I make all things new."* Including you, for I become you. For I now am the only presence. Here above the mind, here in the silence, in the resting Sabbath, I overcome the world and I reveal the kingdom formed from a new heaven as a new earth, as a new self, as a new life, as a new beginning, as a new kingdom, as a spiritual realm formed.

You heard long ago that you must live by every word that proceedeth out of the mouth of God, and now you know what that means. Yes, thy kingdom come. Look up! Look up! Let the Great Invisible form itself. And here's how Joel said it:

Look up! Look above the physical evidence to the Great Invisible. The kingdom of heaven is at hand!

(I, the Great Invisible spiritual consciousness, Christ in your midst) *I am breaking the sense of limitation for you as an evidence of My presence and My influence* (right here in your midst). *I, the I of you, am in the midst of you revealing the harmony and infinity of the spiritual (realm). I, the I of you, never a personal sense of "I", never a person but the I of you, am ever with you. Look up* (to the Great Invisible).

Those were the words that came to Joel on a red scroll with gold lettering in Old English lettering. You remember? And though it appeared in a dream, when he opened his eyes it was still hanging above his bed. And so this comes from the Great Invisible right out there hanging above his bed. The Great Invisible formed itself as the chapter *The New Horizon*, which means the new consciousness, the new heaven, the new earth, the new kingdom.

Dying to all of this is overcoming. Being born again is coming into the conscious awareness, seeing the new heaven and the new earth and hearing the voice that says, "*Behold, I make all things new.*" And I am your God and you are my son because you have died out of the world. You have ascended. You are no longer standing between the two worlds. You are resting, a witness to the kingdom really coming, really manifesting, really appearing.

So let us be this stillness. Joel says, "let my silence be Thy abiding place," in the chapter *The New Jerusalem*. This is inviting the Great Invisible. This is saying thy kingdom come. Have no idea whatsoever, no outline, no plan. "*I stand at the door, and knock.*" Look up! Look up above the sense mind. Have no images. Just look. Just listen.

"*Behold,* [I make all things, including you] *I make all things new.*" In this silence, in this stillness, be a beholder. How many times has Joel told us that? Be a beholder. It was the whole purpose of <u>The Contemplative Life</u> book. Be a beholder. Watch as the Great Invisible forms itself, lives itself right here, right now, and Christ appears on earth.

When Christ Jesus made his ascension he was still on earth, for he said, "*I have overcome the world.*" And there was no crucifixion. He had already made his ascension. He walked out and he walked back in. He walked into the invisible and he walked back out. This is how he was able to disappear in the midst of a crowd and reappear outside the temple.

You can do the same thing. If it is I, then be not afraid. I will never leave you because <u>I am you</u>, and this must be a conscious awareness. This must be your consciousness, Christ appearing, and you must have the power to lay down this sense of life and pick it up again. You must have the ability to walk in the invisible realm and back out, for all that I have is thine, and I demonstrated this as Christ Jesus, and I will demonstrate this as Christ You, as Christ I.

You are on earth to overcome that old earth. You are here to no longer be here. You are in passing time to stand still in the now. Behold, I, the Great Invisible, manifest my kingdom. Now when you hear that prayer, now when you say that prayer, you know what you're asking for. You have the spiritual maturity to know: Thy kingdom come. Let the Word manifest. Let the Christ liveth itself. Let God be in his son and his son in God, and let there be one, and let there be light, and let there be a new heaven and a new earth.

It is said that there shall be no night there and the light will shine forever, meaning there shall be no personal sense of self, no personal sense of life. No concepts. No mental images, but only the light of I. Every day you must have, we must have a period, and I must have a period of meditation, a period of silence, a period of stillness, a moment of nothingness in which I rest, I behold thy kingdom come, and I witness God Itself made manifest. And I behold the Spirit moving over the face of the deep.

Yes, the experience that Moses had he expressed in these words. This is him beholding, as you will, the Great Invisible manifesting itself, and this is how he saw it:

"The earth was without form, and void; and darkness was upon the face of the deep."

He's just resting in the silence, and there's nothingness.

"And the Spirit of God moved upon the face of the waters."

He felt it. And then he heard the voice, just like John.

"And God said, Let there be light: and there was light.

And God saw the light, that it was good: and God divided the light from the darkness."

These are two states of consciousness. This is the old heaven, the old earth – an earth formed out of images in the mind – and the new heaven and the new earth – the Spirit of God forming itself.

"*And God said, Let us make man in our image, [and] after our likeness: and let them have dominion.*

So God created man in his <u>*own*</u> *image, in the image of God created he him; male and female created he them.*"

I think that was changed. I think it said originally "male and female created he him."

"*And God blessed them, and God said unto them, Be fruitful, and multiply,*

And God saw every thing that he had made, and, behold, <u>*it was*</u> *very good.*"

And then on the seventh day he rested from all his work. Remember? So Moses sees the Great Invisible Spirit, spiritual consciousness forming itself, and he explains it as God creating, manifesting its own image. And so this is the new heaven. This is God creating its own image, that image you.

This is the experience, this first chapter of Genesis. This is the realm where spiritual consciousness forms itself. This is why you are here, that you might behold, that you might bear witness to the Great Invisible spiritual Christ Consciousness forming itself. That you might bear witness to God's Word going forth and taking form. That you might be one of those that stand so still that you behold a new heaven and a new earth coming down from God. That you might drink of these everlasting waters, that you might experience your Eternal Self.

God expressing itself is your Eternal Self.

That you might experience the infinite, eternal, invisible I and watch as it lives itself. For this cause came ye into the world that you might have life and life everlasting.

And again, as Joel stood there in silence, these words came forth from within, and we hear him say:

How shall I stand before Thee but in silence? How shall I honor Thee but in the meditation of mine heart?

Praise and thanksgiving Thou seekest not, (ah) *but the understanding heart,* [the beholder] *Thou receivest.*

I will keep silent before Thee. My Soul and my Spirit and my silence shall be Thy dwelling place. (Which is exactly the same as, "Oh Father, thy kingdom come.")

Thy Spirit shall fill my meditation, and it shall make me and preserve me whole. O Thou Tender One and True – I am home in Thee.

And so Joel has discovered a home above this sense-life, a realm of Spirit, the kingdom of heaven. A new heaven and a new earth, Christ consciousness, the fountain of everlasting waters, the image and likeness of God. I in your midst am come. Be still and know, and let us rest in that I.

This I comes as a thief in the night. Into your silence the Spirit flows. It comes as a thief in the night. You – you are just still. You are staring into the Great Invisible, and I come as a thief in the night. And I come that you might have this new life everlasting. I am the life. I stand in the midst of you now, closer than your very breathing. Look up to the Great Invisible. Look up! The kingdom you have asked for is at hand right here in your midst.

And have I been so long a time with you, and you have not known me? You may know me now as you utter the words: Thy kingdom come. Rest back and receive that eternal kingdom. Be a beholder as Christ manifests, as the new kingdom comes, as the New Jerusalem, the new city, the new consciousness forms itself. And behold, all things are new.

Have one meditation, at least one, more if you feel led, in which you have nothing to heal, nothing to prove, nothing to demonstrate. Only standing still looking into the Great Invisible that you might catch a glimpse of the Spirit moving over the face of the deep, that you may hear the voice say unto you: Stand ye still. I have come whose right it is, and I am the life. I am that truth. I am the Way. Look unto me. Look! Look up! The kingdom comes in silence.

As this Invisible, this Great Invisible, forms itself and makes all things new, just be a beholder. Just stand still in receptivity. Just know I can do all things and behold, I am your inheritance. Your everlasting life is I.

And after these periods of silence just open your eyes, do whatever is at hand to do, and in a way ye know not of this Great Invisible will appear as harmony of being, harmony of life, harmony of purpose.

I tell you, you are so blessed to be at this banquet, at this supper of Spirit. Many, many kings would give up their entire kingdom for this real spiritual kingdom, and it is yours because you laid down your personal sense.

Now, listen to this one last time, because this is Joel explaining the experience of receiving divine Sonship, this new spiritual kingdom. He's explaining it in Spiritual Interpretation of Scripture in the chapter *True Sense of the Universe,* and he says it's a secret. He says it's a secret.

(And) The secret - which has been so rarely understood - That secret is how you make your ascension: *is spiritual meat and drink; and the secret is this:*

Remember over here – we just read it in The Infinite Way – you must overcome the desire for things of this world and then you may have the spiritual realm. You must overcome this world, and so he says it here again. This was his experience.

The life which you behold in man, tree, animal is not the Life of God;

And so stop trying to pull God into this realm, this material realm.

The life of material man or flower is mortal sense. It is a false sense of the Life which is real.

Yes, this world is false images about the Invisible, the Great Invisible. This is mind manifested, but now we are ready for the Great Invisible to manifest, the new kingdom, the new earth. So he says:

The understanding of this truth will enable you to look away from sense objects; it will enable you to refrain from attempting to heal, correct or reform the mortal sense of existence; and as soon as you have conquered the desire to heal or improve the material sense of existence, (as soon as you have conquered that, you have let it go, you are standing now in silence, then) *the spiritual or real begins to unfold and reveal itself to you.*

You see that? Do you see that? Ascension's always the same. Coming up over the mind and its images and its desires to change, improve, or heal, and resting in the spiritual Invisible, the great spiritual realm and beholding the Word made flesh.

He says:

You cannot behold or experience eternal Life and its harmonies while accepting the evidence of the senses.

Do not take lightly what I am saying (he says). *This is the Great Revelation; this knowledge will clarify for you the Master's statement, "My kingdom is not of this world";* (Yes, it will clarify that. Now you know my kingdom, and when you pray 'thy kingdom come' you're asking for the Great Invisible to manifest itself as life, and you are willing to drop all personal sense of life and all of its attachments. (He says;) *It will reveal to you the secret of John the Revelator, who beheld the universe which is not made with hands, but which is eternal, as Consciousness appearing; Spirit unfolding; Soul revealing itself.*

You see that? Do you see that?

Believe me (he says:) *This is the secret of secrets.*

This is Life eternal to know this truth. (And) Truly Kings and Emperors would give their thrones could they but learn this one truth …

The life of material man, (this is the one truth: The life of material man) *the life of tree, flower, animal, this is not Life eternal; Do not attempt to patch it up, rather turn (away) from it and with enlightened consciousness* (in the silence) *discern the Life which is God; "feel" through your cultivated spiritual sense (the) divine energy of Spirit;*

Which is the same as watching the Spirit move over the face of the deep. It's the same as watching the new heaven and the new earth come down, the New Jerusalem come down out of heaven. It's the same as watching the fountain spring up into life everlasting. It is the same!

Feel through your cultivated spiritual sense the divine energy of Spirit; become **consciously aware** *in the Silence of your Soul. Let the divine harmonies appear (***let*** the divine harmonies appear) as you disregard the evidence of sight and hearing, (and) tasting, (and) touching and smelling.*

That which is real and eternal is not seen or touched, it is spiritually discerned. It is realized only by the intuitive or inner consciousness. Reality (this Great Invisible) *is perceived by the Soul (sense), by your inner vision.*

Only to those who have eyes to see and ears to hear (which is you, my dear friends) *can this vision become a living, vital Presence. Only those who have heard what is said by "the still, small voice" and seen what is visible to the "windows of the Soul" can discern that "temple not made with hands" or the universe of God's creating* (or the Great Invisible manifesting itself).

The false sense of life must be put off, disregarded, un-valued, in order that the real Life (the Great Invisible) *and its formations may become evident and experienced.*

So there it is yet again another way, and now you know, don't you? Yes, you do! You know as well as you know your own sense of existence: When you pray, thy kingdom come, what you are asking for is that I manifest My Kingdom, My Presence, My Self. That the I of you out-picture itself.

Again, there are five or six billion people on earth and only a handful ever learns in any given age that there is an ascension out of the sense realm into the Great Invisible realm of Spirit, and that here Christ Jesus flows and here stands Joel, for he said to those that know the secret, I will never leave the earth, but I will be available in the Great Invisible. And here stands Moses and Elijah and here, if you step into this Great Invisible and rest back and behold, you may meet up with Elijah, Jesus, Paul, Joel, John, with Krishna, with Moses, with Abraham, with Shankara, with Buddha. But more importantly than all of that, you may just witness I in the midst of you manifesting.

Look up! Look up! For the kingdom is at hand, and I in the midst of thee am the Way. And I shall surely meet you there in the invisible.

Thank you. Many blessings and Thy kingdom come.

[Silence]

CLASS 18

CONSCIOUS UNION
WITH GOD

Bill: Good morning.

This is Sunday June 2, 2013. In today's meditation the subject came up and the experience came up: Conscious union with God. There's even a book out, one of The Infinite Way books, called Conscious Union with God. Do you know what that experience is? Because it's the whole purpose of all of the thousands of miles, all the lectures and classes and meditations that Joel put forth for you, so that you might have the experience known as conscious union with God.

Have you had that experience after these many years of study? Do you know what it is to feel consciously one with God? Are you consciously aware of God and you being one?

I think it's abundantly clear now that the purpose of prayer is to have an inner experience of the living Presence of your own true identity of God within, and feeling the movement of that Presence as your inner being is conscious union with God. You're consciously aware of oneness.

The infinite invisible, inner spiritual kingdom, inner spiritual omnipresence flowing into manifestation appearing as form as your outer life and having the conscious awareness of that experience, really the conscious awareness of Genesis in you. This is conscious union with God, and this is what we've been discussing.

For many years we practiced knowing these truths mentally, perhaps repeating them to ourselves with our eyes closed, maybe remembering them and reciting them to ourselves many times throughout the day. And all of that was good and necessary because it took us out of the mind that plots and plans and schemes into a state of receptivity, and if we persisted in that state of receptivity, then we began to experience – and here I'm going to say realization instead of real-i-zation because someone pointed that out to me, and I looked it up, and they were right, so I will try to remember realization even though I like real-i-zation.

Okay, so all of these experiences, this receptivity, gets us to a point of realization of oneness, conscious union with God. Now if we never practiced the presence, which is what we were told to do in the book with the same name – if we never practiced remembering God when we took a bite to eat or remembering God when we woke up in the morning or remembering God when we walked out the front door, remembering God throughout the day and night – if we never practice that, then we've left out a critical part disciplining ourselves to remember God, to almost pray without ceasing. And that's a mental exercise. Yes, indeed it is. But that's a critical part of our first steps toward conscious union with God and living a life consciously at one with God.

And if we never practiced meditation in the morning, in the afternoon, in the evening, and at night – if we never practiced listening, being receptive, not asking for anything, but just simply knowing the truth mentally and then resting for a few—well, for 30 seconds or a minute or two—if we haven't practiced that which we were taught in the Kailua study series: How to go from the letter to Spirit or how to go from the mind to listening, to receptivity – then we've left out that critical part.

Can you see how the steps were designed to lead us from a person with a human mind to an inner experience of consciously being one or conscious union with that Divine Presence living itself as us? So if you've left out a critical part, then you have no choice. You need to go back and do it. Go back and begin to practice the presence throughout your day and night, or go back and begin to practice meditation, real meditation. Not a lot of speaking, but only reminding yourself of truth enough so that you calm yourself and can get out of that mind which thinks truth, because it's only in the practice of those two – practicing the presence and adding meditation – that you come to a place of being still enough and receptive enough and taking no thoughts enough to hear the still, small voice or to feel the movement of Spirit or to experience God's grace pouring through you as you. And this, of course, is what we all want.

The Infinite Way is designed to take you by the hand and lead you into a new consciousness, and attaining that new consciousness or experiencing that new consciousness – a consciousness not made by hands, a consciousness eternal in the heavens – you no longer need The Infinite Way because The Infinite Way becomes your consciousness. It always was your consciousness, but you become aware of it. You have the conscious awareness of Consciousness living itself.

So, that's the whole purpose of The Infinite Way, to lead you to a point where Consciousness lives as you. God lives itself as you.

Now this does not mean that you become an automaton or a robot. It means that—well, in the beginning you start to have the inner experience of consciously being one, feeling the movement. And every time that you feel its movement and every time that the voice utters itself and every time that an impartation comes to you from the Great Invisible and not from the mind, there is a change out here. Consciousness forms itself, and it always forms itself as fulfillment, peace, and joy.

And so you know if you are really experiencing conscious union with God by the fruits. It's not a big mystery. You just have to look and see. Are you finding yourself in the right place at the right time without consciously thinking about it? Is harmony governing your affairs? Are you beginning to experience a straightening out of your concept of supply where things come into your life that you haven't prayed for or thought about? Are you experiencing peaceful relations with the people you come in contact with in your consciousness? What is happening? Is there harmony in your affairs? Is your daily living experience becoming smoother, which means less and less physical difficulties to try and overcome?

The fruits are that invisible Presence, conscious union with it, and resting in it and feeling its movement and hearing its voice. The fruits are it forms itself, and you don't know what form it's going to take.

I remember one time I called Herb Fitch and I said, "Herb, I don't understand. I keep meditating on love, and I think that God's going to show me how to love or appear as love, and instead I'm getting more and more dollar bills. Now what is this? (chuckles) I remember he said, "I think you're looking at this a little wrong." He said, "You have no right to draw an outline on how this is supposed to manifest. You can't sit down and try to funnel God into this or that or the other. You simply rest back and let God live itself." And he said, "Besides, the dollars bills are given to you so you don't have to worry about that. You don't have to work on that, and that frees you up to pour out and love other people, so you see that love was manifesting."

So we have no right to have a personal sense in the driver's seat, and that includes in our meditations. We have no right to be living a personal life, and we have no right to be meditating for some personal reason even though we think we know what we need or what the person coming to us needs. Because we don't. We don't have any right idea.

Now I know this gets difficult when family member calls you and says, "Will you pray for me? I just lost my job." And of course you become—if you're practiced and you've been practicing this for a while you are able to say "yes, I will help you" and hang up the phone and become still without seeking anything and rest back and feel the Presence. But if you open your eyes after that meditation and look around to see what new job opportunity or how supply is going to come to this person, then you are praying amiss.

This is called praying amiss. You have a funnel. You have a mold and you want God to fill it. God doesn't work that way. There's this thing called Omniscience, and it functions in a million different points at the same time, and so it knows how to form itself and what is needed. You don't have to direct it.

And we've all had examples of that in our own lives, praying and praying for something that we are positive that we need and it never manifests and instead this other thing opens up and in the end we find out that was what we needed, not what we thought. So this is part of emptying out of the human mind.

You know, for centuries we have had a physical body which works for so long and if it's sick it doesn't work so good and later on it slows down and can't do things it used to do, and we've had a mind, a human mind, and that too is only good for so long. Sometimes in our youth we have obsessions of the mind driving us to do this or that or the other and later we might have senility. We might have Alzheimer's. We might have dementia and the mind begins to deteriorate. We can't remember things the way we used to. Sometimes it's so bad we don't even recognize our loved ones we've been with for 50 years, 60 years, 70 years. And then we die and we come back and we try it again. Now that's living in a human mind, and we all know how to do that, and we all know where that takes us. Eventually it kills us. It's a strange thing, but the mind that wants to be in charge all those years eventually kills itself.

Now if we're fortunate we come across a spiritual path which reveals that there's another mind. Could be called the Buddha mind, could be called the Tao. It could be called the mind which was in Christ Jesus. It could be called simply Omniscience. Could be called Is, which is the same as Tao, the Tao. So we are fortunate when we learn there's another mind and this mind when we rest back and listen to it, it flows freely and it forms itself and begins to appear as a life out here, and it's your life, it's you. This invisible – this Great Invisible, Spiritual substance, Omniscience – forms itself in a moment ye think not. And if you are still and not thinking, not choosing words, not choosing the thoughts to think, simply looking, resting, being consciously aware, you experience It. You have conscious union with It. It moves through you. You and It are one, and then you simply watch in awe as it manifests itself, forms itself as your outer experience day after day after day. And then you are consciously aware to the point where you can say with Paul, *"I live; yet not I, Christ liveth (my life)."* Christ liveth its life.

And it's not a thing where you're bragging and it's not a thing you have really attained. It is a conscious union you have become aware of. It is a new mind. It is the mind which was in Christ Jesus which is now beginning to function where before you only had a human mind. And now this mind which was in Christ Jesus is your mind. It's functioning as your life. It is you. And now you have a temple *"not made with hands, eternal in the heavens."* Once this mind begins functioning you *"I will never leave thee or nor forsake thee."* Lo, I am with thee always forever and ever and ever. For infinity you now have the Comforter, your very own inner spiritual consciousness in which you can rest and be a beholder as it lives itself. It's wonderful and it's full of wonder.

More and more says Joel in <u>The Contemplative Life</u>, we must live life as a beholder. See, we didn't really know what that means the way we know now. More and more. Over and over he says to us we will begin our meditation by recognizing there's no patient out there. It's a mental concept in this human mind, and so we step out of that mind. We have nothing to do with it. We do not meet anything on that level. We drop it.

Ah, but now we're stuck with us, the personal practitioner, personal Infinite Way student, and God. And now he says we have to get rid of the person. We do that by realizing the mind, the human mind, is a series of universal beliefs, and so we're not going to hang onto it. We're not going to function through it. For just right now we're going to be still. We're going to rest back in the Great Invisible, and we don't know what that is. We have no definition. We can't draw pictures of it. We just know that it is. *"It is I; be not afraid."* And we rest.

And the words aren't important. We may say, "Oh Father, fulfill Thyself" and rest. We may say, "Christ liveth" and rest. We may say "Grace" and rest. But the point is we rest back, listen, are receptive to I, the Infinite. (silent pause). *"Be not afraid; it is I,* and *"I am the Way." "Behold, I make all things new."* I, (silent pause) and we rest in the silence, for now we know the silence is not <u>not thinking</u>. The silence is not <u>no thought</u>. We have learned the secret of secrets.

The silence is <u>no self</u>. *"I am the Way."*

[Silent pause]

Many are called; few are chosen. If you feel this inner Self, this inner I, you feel it – I feel its movement. If you feel its movement, if you hear its voice, if you receive an impartation, a feeling of I, the Invisible, then you are chosen. This is the chosen people of God. This is the chosen who will receive and be led into the New Jerusalem, the new city, the new consciousness. Conscious union with God, the Source. Says Joel in the book, <u>The Infinite Way</u>, you must come to the realization that you are Source. You are Cause and not effect. Conscious union with Cause, with Source, with God. This I is what I am. I am Cause. Behold, I make all things the new city, the new consciousness.

And this awareness of Self, of I, of God – this is your new consciousness for eternity. A hundred years from now I will be your consciousness, and you will have conscious union with I. Five hundred years, five thousand years – I, I. And I was with thee before Abraham, and I am with thee now in this moment. Feel me, and I will always be with thee. For I am the conscious union with I.

And so in our inner meditation we have conscious union with God, the center of our being, and rest there with no plans, ideas, thoughts, but most importantly no self. And behold, I form Myself as your self, the only Self, one.

Yes, it was a long journey for many of us coming to The Infinite Way expecting trinkets; little healings. But this was just a trick of your Self to lead you back to your Self in which you would receive the ultimate gift – God Itself as your very being – and conscious awareness of this, of I.

Now listen. This, my friends, is from the book <u>The Altitude of Prayer</u> by Joel. And in the very first chapter he points out this:

Those of us on the spiritual path are building a temple, the temple of our consciousness. As human beings, we were born into a three-dimensional consciousness (a three-dimensional consciousness) *with our only faculties and capacities the five physical senses and the power of (thought or) reason. All of this applies to the human world.* (Ah, but now <u>this</u> sentence:) *None of it applies in any way to (My kingdom).*

Something else is needed, isn't it? Another faculty, another mind, another Self – a Christ Self.

So he says:

(This is) why a person can pray and pray, rarely receiving an answer. (And it is because) *No prayer that is uttered through the mind ever reaches the kingdom of God.*

Now you must know this. You must really if necessary put it on a 3x5 card and put it on the wall next to where you meditate or use it as a bookmarker so you see it first thing.

No prayer uttered through the mind ever reaches God.

And so all these mental exercises – this is why you haven't received answered prayer. It's backwards, which is what the mind always is. It interprets everything backwards, and the mind thinks that if it prays, thinks these spiritual thoughts up to God, they'll reach God and God will respond. But what is it he said here?

Rarely receiving an answer to (that) prayer. (Because) No prayer uttered through the mind ever reaches God.

Well, if we're going to experience answered prayer we're going to have to use another faculty, and we're going to have to understand that prayer is not what the mind utters. Prayer is what the Spirit within you utters. Prayer is what comes to you out of the mind which was in Christ Jesus. Prayer is the experience that comes to you, the movement that comes to you, the impartation that comes to you, the feeling that comes to you, the awareness that comes to you, the consciousness, the conscious union with – this is prayer. And it's a movement in your Soul, not in your mind. And this prayer uttered within you is answered because it forms itself as your experience, and anything else is not prayer.

So he says:

Spiritual impartations (and that's the real prayer) *begin to come to an individual when his Soul-faculties have been opened.*

All right. What does that mean? That means when you have discovered silence, then prayer can happen to you. Your Soul can pray and then manifest itself. The center, the Source, God will utter itself. In other words, only God within you can pray. The human mind cannot pray. Only the mind which was in Christ Jesus uttering itself is prayer, and this is experienced when you know that silence is no self but God.

And on the very next page, page 7, he says:

The moment that we receive an impartation from within, whether it is only a feeling or whether it thunders in the silence or comes as a very gentle whisper, we can be assured that some part of this earth is beginning to dissolve, some problem is going to yield, some discord or inharmony is going to be removed from our experience. (And) In its place will come some grace from My kingdom. (But always remember), "My kingdom is not of this world." (And so) The blessing that we receive is always the blessing of "My kingdom," a spiritual blessing.

The blessing that you receive is the conscious union with God, conscious feeling, conscious awareness of the kingdom within. That's the spiritual blessing. And he says:

We have no way at all of knowing what form it will take (on earth). One thing is certain, however: it will (always) come as the gift of God.

Now that's part of the fun. I mean when I was a child part of the fun was not knowing what presents I would open on Christmas morning, and part of the fun of resting back and allowing God to manifest itself, part of the joy is seeing the beauties that it manifests as, that it forms itself as. Things we had no idea that we needed, yet things that we love. And above all, we love the Source out of which they came. That's the first thing. Thou shalt love the Lord thy God with all thy might, heart, and soul, and so we love the Source more than anything at all. But there's nothing wrong with loving also that which the Source appears as, knowing that if it's appearing out here, it's temporary.

So part of the fun is not having a plan and seeing It manifest Itself. Father, glorify Thyself, and then watch what wonders it performs. Now we read in our scripture:

"My peace I give unto you: not as the world giveth, give I unto you."

And so we know that the peace that the world gives is either from matter and from having enough matter that we think we're okay, or from mind, from thinking we know what things we need and know what we're going to do. That's the human way. But My peace has nothing to do with any of those, and so says Joel:

"My peace" is something the human mind cannot grasp.

Again, the human mind is pretty much worthless when it comes to prayer and understanding things of the spiritual realm or the spiritual kingdom or the spiritual Self. And so it will not help you and it can't even understand My peace. So the human mind is not going to help us, and that self must be surrendered to find the real silence, and in the real silence the movement of Christ reveals itself first as an inner movement, voice, experience, awareness, union, and then as that consciousness formed.

(And) Every individual (he says) *will find (it) taking the form necessary to his experience at the moment.*

And that's the beauty of it. So what are we doing? What is this all about? We are building a temple, a consciousness not made by body, not made by human mind, not made by thoughts. We are building a temple not made with hands. A temple invisible, a consciousness of the Infinite Invisible. A conscious awareness of the living Spirit, conscious union with Christ which will never leave us nor forsake us. Eternal in the heavens.

If you understood the gift of God, says Jesus Christ at the well, and who it is that's talking to you, you would have asked me and I would have given you living waters that spring up into life everlasting. This source is your Self, and it will form itself more and more and more as your experience until the two become one and the inner and the outer are one, and you are the living conscious union with God, and this will be your everlasting life. For eternity this will be your awareness.

Thus you understand to know God aright is conscious union for eternity.

Now let us be still for a moment. Let us drop any urgency or sense of needing something out here for ourselves or any other self. These are mental images. Let us drop them. Here in the inner temple I would know thee, God, and so I will be still. I will be silent. I will be no self, just beholding. Christ liveth. God is, and I am the Way. Be still. Be still. I am God.

[Long Silent Pause]

Have I been so long a time with you and you have not experienced conscious union? Now it's time. You have been chosen. Be still and know I am God. And I will never leave thee now, for I am thee, and in the next plane and the next plane and the next plane, I am God, your center. And in this life and in any other life, in this form and in any other form – male, female, or some form on some other planet – you will always have me as your center, I the living Christ. And I have come that you might have life, real life manifested abundantly.

Feel me now. I am here. The consciousness is formed. The outer experience is formed, cut out of the consciousness without hands. The stone is cut out of the mountain without hands. The outer experience is formed by Infinite Consciousness with no help. Simply be still and experience the grace of conscious union with I.

[Silent pause]

Thank you very much for being with me in this consciousness today. Let us all stand still and behold the glory of God. Let us watch. Let us be beholders as the Father glorifies Itself, as Consciousness forms Itself.

Infinite Invisible, pure spiritual Consciousness forms Itself eternally, infinitely one.

[Silence]

299

CLASS 19

ONE IMMORTAL SELF

Bill: Good morning.

This is Sunday June 9th about 11:48 a.m. And today's talk is on the principle of immortality revealed. Do you know immortality? Do you know the immortality of God? Do you know your immortality? Do you know that there is a part of you, the greater part which is invisible, immortal, and eternal? Do you know your own immortality?

The reason why I ask is because I've been looking at this book by Joel called The Altitude of Prayer, and this book I first received maybe 40 years ago or more, and at the time I believe I wasn't quite ready for it. I needed really to be sticking with Practicing the Presence and The Art of Meditation and perhaps Living the Infinite Way. But this book has some very deep moments in it or it's changed over the years since I last opened it. Well one thing for sure, my consciousness has changed and I see things in it that I never saw before. Deep, deep things. Deep principles. And there is a chapter here, chapter 4, which is called *This is Immortality*, and in it is revealed the necessity, the absolute necessity for you to find your own immortality right here and right now. And this chapter begins like this. It says:

Life, real life, is lived in consciousness; it is lived in the secret place within ourselves.

Now this is assuming many things in this first sentence. It's assuming that you have found your inner Self. It assumes that you've found this thing called consciousness, the secret place of the Most High, and that you have found a way to dwell there and live there and live and move and have your being there even while right here on earth. *This is life eternal, that they might know thee, the only true God, and Christ, whom thou hast sent.*

Why is it life eternal if you know the true God and Christ, the emanation of that God? Why is that life eternal? How does knowing God and the Christ of God translate into eternal Life for you? Do you know? Do you have the answer? Oh – no, not an intellectual reply. No. I mean are you living that life eternal? Have you gone within and discovered the God referred to? Have you discovered the Christ referred to? And have you discovered your own eternal life? If you have, then I guess you're just listening to this because it's nice to hear someone that also knows. If you haven't, well – Joel has a word for you. And he starts by saying:

We have circumscribed life by giving our attention to the baubles of life: to our work, our profession, our home, our family.

So right here he calls home and family and work baubles, trinkets, toys really. He gets to the point two paragraphs later when he says:

The human life we (are living) is nothing but a dream.

And so the answer to the question is, why should we know God aright and why is that life eternal? The answer to that question is because when we know God aright we find our own immortality. We find our own immortal life, and this human life, this dream, this series of mental images passing in time appearing as a human life, this we begin to see as a dream and we begin to see through it to the underlying immortality, the underlying immortal life that we are.

On the next page he says:

The purpose of life on earth is to bring forth (God's life, His image and likeness), His nature, His character, His qualities and His quantities.

Yes, the purpose of life is to go within, find that immortality. Recognize, realize God, Christ, immortal Self, and then bear witness as it expresses Itself. This then is not a human life, is it? This then is the son of God appearing. This then is Christ made manifest. And just to bring the idea home, on the next page Joel says:

Some of the first fruits of prayer are health, a greater sense of abundance, happier human relationships. (But) These are not the end and aim of prayer.

What is the end and aim of prayer? Now remember, remember now – we have learned together prayer is not what you say, not what the human thinks, not any truth known in the mind. Prayer is that which is uttered within our consciousness. That which the Spirit speaks. That's prayer – what God speaks, manifests. And so in that light, he is saying some of the first fruits of hearing that voice are health, abundance, and happier human relationships, but these are not the end and aim of listening to that voice.

The end and aim of prayer is that we discover our eternal life, the life that was lived before birth, the life that will be lived after the grave, we can encompass right here on earth the totality of spiritual existence, a divine and immortal existence.

And so you see we come to The Infinite Way and we have a problem of some sort and we learn that we can pray aright and that when God speaks the problem dissolves, the earth melts, the stone is cut out of the mountain without hands, and wow – we have a decent income maybe for the first time ever. Hey, these human relationships are harmonious and I'm not working on them. Wow, my health improved. We think we've found land of milk and honey, but we're still living as human beings and something happens, and it pushes us and pushes us and we come to see finally that those are the added things. The real aim and end of prayer is that we discover our immortal life, that we discover God, the only true God, and Christ, the manifestation of God, which is our immortality. And so you must have an experience of a life before birth, and you must have an experience of a life after the grave – right here on earth, he says. Right here, right now, in your meditation and sometimes with eyes open, you must experience an immortal Self that lives now before Abraham, now. That lives now after the end of the world, right now. Before birth and after the grave there is a life, an immortal life, and you must find this life within you. That's the real aim of prayer and meditation. So he says:

There is a you that I have met within myself; there is a you that I love to be with. This is the you that God made in His own image and likeness, a you that existed before you were born.

So says Joel, he knows how to go within and live with this immortal Self, which he has discovered is the Self of him and also the Self of you and the Self of you and the Self of you. The one immortal Self. How many Gods are there? One. How many Christs? There is one. One God, one manifestation. So how many sons? One Son. So how many lives? One life. How many immortalities? One immortality. One immortal Self. If you discover within you that one immortal Self, your Self, you must know it's also my Self and Joel's Self and Herb's Self and Jesus' Self. It is the one Self of all.

This is life eternal, to know the one Self. But it must be an experience. It must be an inner experience, not a mental ideal, not a mental idea, not a mental concept, not a mental thought, not of the mind. It must be an experience, an inner experience of the Soul.

When your Soul is receptive, Spirit Itself manifests, and we call that Christ, the expression of God. And this is life eternal, that you may know God and that Christ as your eternal, immortal Self, as the immortal Self of all. And Joel tells you what it's like to experience it. He shares his experience, because on the next page he says:

Having been lifted up to the point where my heavenly Father could impart truth (to me), I then beheld you as you are, because I first beheld myself. I saw myself in the image and likeness of God; I saw myself as spiritual being existing before my birth and still alive after my death, still living after my death. Because I saw that, I saw your identity. It was only then that I began to love people.

Before that, what was he loving? Let's go back and look. It's important that you swallow this.

The human life that we live is nothing but a dream.

Our home, our family are baubles.

(It was only after being lifted up and beholding immortality) *that I began to love people,* (or the Immortal appearing as people).

There are many people in my life that tell me, that speak those words "I love you," and sometimes it occurs to me they don't. They don't even know me. Here I am, immortal Self in the secret place of the Most High. I am me and I am thee. Ah, but when someone in this consciousness speaks those words "I love you" with the recognition of that immortal Self at the center of all being, then I am lifted up. I am lifted up because I, if I am lifted up through recognition and I look at you that way, I draw you unto me, unto the same place where I am, and that is why when someone is looking at me that way, and they may not even speak a word, but in their presence I feel lifted up. I'm sure you have met people that way.

I never had the joy of being in Joel's presence on earth. Well, it's possible we passed, because he lived in San Gabriel when I was a small child, so it's possible we passed on the street or he nodded to me in a grocery store or smiled at me. That's entirely possible, but I have no recollection of it. So for all intents and purposes I've never been in his presence on earth. I've been in his presence on the inner planes, but not here on earth.

But there are those. I was in Herb's presence in that Avila Beach seminar, and wow, was I lifted up in the experience I've shared over and over. I definitely felt the one immortal Self in me, in thee, in all. And there are others, you just love to be in their presence, don't you? There's a man named Alan Marsh. Last I checked he was in New Mexico, and we did a class together, and being in his presence is wonderful. You just feel lifted up, and I observed everybody and their relationship to him, and I even had a couple of people tell me that he was their special friend, and so the feeling around him was one of being accepted and loved because he recognizes the Christ of them. I know he does, because I've talked with him.

And so in some people's presence you just feel lifted up, and that's because they are recognizing the Christ. They are recognizing God. They are recognizing the one immortal Self. They're not being fooled by the dream. They're not seeing you as a human being.

Why do you think we're told over and over and over throughout the books that one of the most important principles is impersonalization? Because when you impersonalize, when you look at a person and you say, "well, this evil is no part of them. These are mental images projected by world thought," and when you look at that same person and say, "This love, this wisdom pouring out of them – this is not of them. This is that one Divine Self." When you do that, when you impersonalize them, you lift them out of personal sense. You lift them up into immortality, even if it's only them feeling, "I don't know why I feel so good in your presence." You're still lifting them up, and one day they will catch it too. And so says Joel:

That part of me which is visible was born into the belief of two powers, will pass out of it, and will reincarnate, unless (and this is a big unless, so I circled it in my book – unless) *during this lifetime* (here on earth) *I come into the realization of my true identity. Then I will not have to reincarnate.*

I'll read it again because it's very important, and that's why we started off this talk – Why is it important to know your immortality, to experience it – not believe in it. You may believe in immortality and have no experience of it at all. You must **experience** it. That's why Joel is always talking about the Experience – capital E, Experience. If you will contemplate, if you will add that to being with others on the spiritual path and add in meditation, then you will have the experience, and that's what he always says. Leading to the experience, coming to the experience, the Christ experience, the God experience, experiencing immortality here and now. It's important because then you will not have to reincarnate. And so again, listen:

That part of me which is visible was born into the belief of two (two) *powers,* (two selves, two lives). (That self) *will pass out of it, and will reincarnate, unless during this lifetime I come into the realization of my true identity* (of my immortality). *Then I will not have to reincarnate.*

That make-believe life (the dream) *will keep on making believe over and over again, until there is a "dying daily" leading to the final death of personal sense.*

You see? And this is life eternal, that we might die to this personal sense and come into a feeling of our own immortal Self. And then he spells it out here. He says:

Someday each one of you will have to realize what I am saying to you: I am I. I am that I AM, I always have been, and I always will be.

You see that? We're here on earth not for all these baubles. We're not here to improve our work lives. We're not here to improve our home lives or even our family lives. We're not here to improve our health, our wealth. Those are things that just come as we give up seeking for them. We are here to delve deep down within us and have the inner realization of immortal Self. We are here to know through experience resting in the secret place of God. Resting in the secret place where Christ is manifesting. We are here to rest in the secret place of immortal Self, to feel it, to observe it, to behold it, to bear witness to it as it manifests itself. This is life eternal.

When you know that Self as an experience, you no longer have to reincarnate. There is no break in consciousness. You no longer have the experience of dying to a personal life and having a sort of amnesia, being born again to a brand new personal life and not remembering anything that ever came before, and going through another personal life and coming to the bitter end and crying as you leave behind your loved ones and passing out of this picture and being cleaned up and being born again into another life and not remembering those lives and thinking it's brand new and fresh and having the motivation to amass a large amount of money and succeeding in that and coming to see that it amounts to nothing. You see how fruitless that is? That thing called reincarnation? Buddha called it the wheel 'cause you're going round and round and round – you're not getting anywhere. That's the cycle, the "Wheel of Life" he called it.

We want to get off that wheel. When we get off that wheel, well, this is life eternal to know Thee, the one immortal Self, your Self. To have that inner experience of that Self and to see that it is the Self of all. Then you step off the wheel, come right off that wheel. Now there's no break in consciousness. You may take a form after that. You may still appear here on earth, but it is because you have a mission like Joel had – to awaken, to help serve mankind, to help serve all those who still think that they're persons and people. To help lift all into the one Self that they are, that I AM. But there won't be any break in consciousness. You'll remember what you were before. You'll know what you are now and you'll remember what you are yet to be, the one immortal Self. You will know your eternal Self from before Abraham. You will know it even after the end of this world. This is life eternal. So says Joel:

Dying does not ensure (your) immortality.

No, he says elsewhere immortality is not this human sense of life going on and on and returning again and again. Immortality is something else, something different, he says, in the Kailua study series. Here he says:

Immortality is an activity of truth in your consciousness and can be experienced while you are on earth.

So the goal of prayer – remember, the name of this book is The Altitude of Prayer – the goal of prayer is to experience your own immortality, and that's why we started with the question: Have you experienced your own immortality, your own immortal Self? If you haven't, I suggest you – well, he has a suggestion here, doesn't he? Yes, right here. He says:

Do not wait for immortality to come at some later time. If you are not experiencing it (now, then) *retire into a meditation in which you realize the omnipresence of the life of God as your life.*

He means really look at the omnipresence of God. See it, feel it as behind you, as the life that is you.

(And) If you do not succeed today or tonight (keep practicing). He says: *Continue doing this whether it takes a day, a week, a month, or a year. Continue until the "still small voice"(within you) says, "I will never leave you nor forsake you, for I am come that you might have life eternal." Then you will be living your immortality* (or immortality will be living you)."

And so if you haven't experienced this yet, the suggestion is to continue to meditate. Ask, ask: "Father, lift me up. Let me feel my own immortal Self, the Self that you gave me before the world was." See? That's what Christ Jesus was saying. *"Glorify me with the glory (that) I had with you before the world was."* So, if he can ask, why can't you? You can. "Lift me up, Father. Reveal immortal Self, the one immortal Self."

Joel's always telling us over and over: You must close your eyes and you must say, "I don't know what God is. God, reveal Yourself." That's the same thing as saying, "God, reveal My Self or God, reveal the Self, the one Self, immortal Self." And he says you must persist in this even if it takes a day, a week, a month, or a year, or in some cases several years.

I know some of you have been studying for several years and until you came to the Kailua study series it had become a mental exercise, and hopefully now you've all learned to stand still and listen. Stand still and <u>be</u> receptivity. Stand still and bear witness. Stand still and behold: I reveal your immortal Self, for I am that Self. Hopefully we've been through that in the Kailua study series, and now we're ready if it takes a day, a week, a month, or a year, or several to wait upon the Lord.

You must have this inner spiritual experience and through the inner Christ of you, through knowing God as the Christ of you, be lifted up into spiritually discerning the one immortal Self. This then is life eternal, when you know the Self, and it puts an end to a break in consciousness. It puts an end to reincarnation. It puts an end to a personal sense of self as the only self and reveals that there is behind you your own infinite eternal immortality. Joel says:

We do not deny the fact that eventually there is a transition from the human plane. No, we don't deny that.

(But) Why not begin to understand it. (he says); *As merely a change of locale, a change from one state of form of life to another?*

Yes, why not? Why not understand that? And says he:

Always under the government of God. Neither life nor death can separate us from the government of God, from the love, the care, and the life of God. Once we have that awareness (as an **experience**), *death* (then) *has no sting, and when the sting is gone out of death, death itself becomes impossible.*

Do you not see that this is life eternal, to know Thee, the true God, and Christ, the manifestation, the one immortal Self? This is life eternal because it takes the sting out of death. When you're not standing in a personal sense of self, when you're standing in an immortal sense of self or a sense of immortal Self, then you see – there's no break in consciousness, there's no death ever again.

I lay down this body that I may pick it up again. I lay down this personal sense of self that I may pick it up again. I now am I, and I walk out and I walk in freely. If I have a mission, I walk in. When I am done, I walk out.

You see, you're free from the law, from the wheel of life, from karma. If there's no human to sow, if there's only Spirit, then you can only reap life everlasting. It's right there in scriptures. Search the scriptures, for in them you think you have life eternal, and you do if you put those scriptures to work. So says Joel:

Some day you will have an experience [an inner experience] *and learn that you are I, that your Self cannot be confined in time or in space, but that you exist beyond time and beyond space.*

This is the experience that I had in Avila Beach.

Then (he says) *you will know the secret of preexistence. You will know that "before Abraham was, I am,"*

And that is immortality

That's his chapter called "*This is Immortality*," or those are excerpts from this chapter. And you know now why he is always saying that you must practice that exercise, his famous exercise where you look down at your feet and you ask yourself, "Am I in these feet, or are these feet mine?" And that you take your time with it and move slowly. "No, I'm not in these feet. These feet are mine. I can use them to stand. I can kick. I can jump. I can walk. I can run. I can skip. I can do leg bends. I can swim. What about these ankles? Are they mine, or am I in them? What about these legs? Am I in them?"

You see? You move on up until you've completed your search throughout the body and eventually he says you come to the realization that I am not in this body. This body is mine. This body is an instrument for my use here on earth. Okay? What he's trying to do is give you the inner experience of your immortal Self, and some people can practice that exercise until they come to the conclusion I am not in this body, and then they can stand still, and there will be an inner movement, an inner shift, an inner feeling, a still small voice, an inner realization that I am I, and that's why he suggests that exercise, because it worked for him.

Now, it doesn't matter what exercise you use. It doesn't matter if you don't even use any words, although sometimes words in the beginning of our meditation can help us escape those words and come to a place of stillness, come to the secret place of the Most High, and so if that works, do that. But some day, he says, you must have the experience of your own immortal I, your immortal Self, the one Self.

Now, you may have experienced this Self in the past. I know many people who have had one experience. Sometimes they weren't even trying for it; it just happened, and they call that a spiritual experience, and they can't really say why it happened. But they never had that experience again. Does that mean that that person who lives out their entire life as a human being, because they've had that one experience will not reincarnate? No. No, it doesn't, because they have not experienced a change of consciousness.

The transformation must start with that experience, but that experience must come again and again.

Remember from Joel's writings where he says I myself have witnessed immortality, the incorporeal Self, thousands and thousands of times. Now that means he's had thousands of meditations in which he's experienced that Self. And I submit to you, if you really delve into his writings he never healed a person – ever. Anybody that turned to him, he dismissed it knowing it to be a universal belief in two. He dropped it, and then he went within and he dropped a human sense of self until there was only the one immortal Self, and in that Self he rested. He rested as if on a sea of Spirit. He felt it, he said, as clouds behind his shoulders. I feel it as a movement, but the point is, he rested. Thousands of times he did that, recognizing the only true God and Christ, the one immortal Self, and in resting there the person called back and said, "Thank you. I've been healed." And he had no idea how they were healed. He admits it freely. He did not know how to heal. He did and does, however, know how to rest back in that Presence. And our training all through these years has been to lead us to the same secret place of the Most High.

And I hope that each of you sees the necessity to attain that consciousness, or that mind which was also in Christ Jesus, so that you become Christ Barbara or you become Christ Peter or you become Christ Paul or you become Christ Mary or you become Christ Robin, and you do that when your consciousness becomes the living awareness of the one immortal Self almost continuously with eyes closed or with eyes open. Then as a continuing consciousness, as a continuing awareness, you will not reincarnate, and if you ever come back, it will be to help lift the rest of us, and for that I say "thank you."

All right. I'm going to be still for a moment and rest back in that immortal Self without words, without thoughts – just I.

(Silent pause)

And this is life eternal, that they might know Me, the only true God within, and Christ, my manifestation. *Behold, I make all things new.* I reveal the one immortal Self. Rest. There remaineth a rest to you who know Me. This is life eternal. This is immortality. This is the I.

My friends, please join me in the fellowship of the Spirit. John said, *"I was in the Spirit on the Lord's day."* He means he was in the conscious awareness, feeling the one immortal Self. I invite you to join us, us that know how to rest back in that consciousness. We are the vanguard. We are those individuals who have come here to earth to do this at this time right here and right now. We are creating the consciousness which will save all mankind.

We who attain this, we who have conscious awareness of the one immortal Self, we are lifting up the consciousness of all of the entire world so that future generations will not have to struggle as we did, but they will be born into this consciousness. It means the moment they become aware of themselves at five or six or seven, they will also be aware of the one immortal Self expressing individually as them, and then we shall see heaven and earth have become one. We shall see truly there's no death there. There's no darkness. There's no crying. There's one immortal Self individualized infinitely, and this will be heaven. Heaven and earth shall be one. The new heaven, the new earth, the new Jerusalem, the new consciousness. I stand revealed, one immortal Self.

And the last thing I want to bring up is when you're in this consciousness, in this secret place of the Most High, in the awareness of the one immortal Self – here are all those who are of like mind. Here you find your friends such as Joel, Herb, Jesus, Shankara, Buddha. Here you find Krishna and all those who have gone before you and have attained this consciousness are still in this consciousness, and when you dwell in it, when you rest in it, you commune with them. And should you need a message from one of them, they will contact you. You will hear them. My sheep hear my voice, and they follow me.

Remember, Joel said to those that know this one eternal Life, I will never be dead. I will always be walking among them in their consciousness. Yes, you can have direct teaching from Joel. It has happened to me, but only when I dwelt in this one immortal Self.

Blessings to you who sell all that you have, your entire personal sense of self. All of the baubles of work and home and family. Sell them all. Come within and you will find the hidden treasure, the hidden manna, the life source flowing freely. Yes, there is a river and it flows constantly and it flows up into life everlasting, into eternal Life.

This is life eternal, to know Thee, the only true God, and Christ, whom Thou hast sent. The one incorporeal, invisible, immortal Self. I am come.

[Silence]

CLASS 20

TIME SHALL BE NO MORE

Bill: Good morning. Its nice to commune with you again.

Last week we spoke of coming into the conscious realization of your true identity. We spoke of "This is life eternal to know thee the only true God and Christ whom thou has sent" and we discussed and touched on what is life eternal? And it is to be standing in your true Self. Your eternal Self. And so when our good friend suggests the topic of "Stepping outside of time," these two are one. Standing in your eternal Self and stepping outside of time are one. In the first place you cannot step outside of time because there isn't any. You are not standing inside of time. Time is an illusion.

And so like Joel described in his book <u>The Art of Spiritual Healing</u> you cannot get rid of a white poodle, there isn't any. You cannot step out of - outside of time, there isn't any, you're not standing inside of time. And because all illusions or rather no illusion is ever externalized then all illusions are in the mind. And so you do not have time. You have the mental image of time. You have the mental concept of time or we who are living in a sense of time – time is not out here, no illusion is out here - you remember you're standing in the Kingdom but unaware of it because of the mental concept of passing time. And so its impossible to step outside of time. But, however you may learn to step outside of the mind and then for you "time shall be no more."

We know from experience hopefully that when we step outside of the mind in our meditation and we rest back in the silence we experience eternal life. We experience the infinite invisible and its movement - we feel it, or we feel I or we feel the infinite Self, the One. And in that experience the mind is still. Its not functioning. Its silent. And in the silence, in the Spirit you dwell in the now. You have stepped outside of the mind. Which is the only - well its the location of the concept of passing time. If you've experienced that then you know when you're in that state, time is no more, it does not exist for you.

I remember Don telling me in 1973, he said jokingly, "eventually you'll discover there is no time. And then you will find that you have all the time in the world to complete this journey because there is not time." And we, he and I discussed what Joel was talking about when he said often in meditation, in his meditations, he would be still for 30 seconds and it felt like an hour passed, or he would be in the silence for an hour and it felt like five minutes passed. That's the experience of stepping out of time sense and into eternity. And I will tell you of some experiences I have had and do have but first I want to look at the principle as its been hinted at.

Probably the one that is quoted most often is from Revelation and its an angel speaking to John and to shorten it somewhat it goes like this;

"And the angel which I saw stand upon the sea," of course the sea is Consciousness *"...and upon the earth,"* and of course the earth would be the time sense or material sense or personal sense. *"...and the angel which I saw stand upon the sea and upon the earth lifted up his hand to heaven and swore by him that liveth forever and ever who created heaven and earth that there should be time no longer. But in the days of the voice of the seventh angel when he shall begin to sound the mystery of God should be finished as he hath declared to*

his servants the prophets." And so the angel standing upon the sea and the earth swears by him that liveth forever and ever that there should be time no longer and that the mystery of God should be finished.

Now what is that mystery of God? That leads us over here where we read from the Kailua Study Series. *"And without controversy great is the mystery of Godliness. God was manifest in the flesh, justified in the Spirit, seen of angels, preached unto the gentiles, believed on in the world, received up into glory. The mystery of Godliness is God was manifest in the flesh,"* or as Joel says here, *"I appear as body."*

So the mystery of Godliness is what John told us, *"And the Word was made flesh and dwelt among us, and we beheld his glory, the glory as of the only begotten of the Father full of Grace and Truth."* And so in Revelation the Angel is saying, *"And the Angel which I saw stand upon the sea and upon the earth lifted up his hand to heaven and swore by him that liveth forever and ever..."* which is the one eternal self, *"...that there should be time no longer and that the mystery of God should be finished."* In other words the Word was made flesh and dwelt among us.

Do you see how this all ties together, this is one transition in Consciousness. The transition whereby that time sense is no longer creating its image and likeness. But the eternal Word, the eternal Godliness, the eternal mystery, the eternal I, the eternal Self, the eternal invisible - infinite invisible manifests. Thats the transition to live in the Consciousness where you bear witness to that experience.

Now Herb says in his Avila Beach seminar "Beyond Time" eventually you're going to have to face this because its going to be scripturally authorized and authenticated, you're going to have to see that our world does not contain time but time contains our world. You see the difference? If you think theres a world out here and passing time out here you still haven't located the illusion where it is, *"no illusion is ever externalized."* And so he says here in these talks, our world is in time and my Kingdom is not of this world in time and therefore the Kingdom is placed outside of time and that's why we haven't discovered it.

Now says Jesus in John 18, *"Now is my Kingdom is not from hence,"* I always assumed that hence meant here in this place, in this time but when you assume that then it has the wrong meaning because then you would say, "Well my Kingdom is not form here its from later on down the road in the future, right? Some other time, some other time." But that's not what it means. I looked up hence in some of the older dictionaries and it means: From away. In other words when Christ Jesus says, *"Get thee hence Satan,"* he means get thee from here away, away. And so when he says, "Now is my Kingdom not from here and away," he is saying, "Now is my Kingdom right here and right now." And in the chapter The New Horizon, Joel so eloquently read on those letters suspended from the ceiling, "Look up, look up the Kingdom of heaven is at hand." He says, "we're not tied by visible concepts of time or space." No in this new Consciousness when this transition takes place whether its momentarily in a meditation or whether its a permanent change of Consciousness, in this new Consciousness the Angel is right "Time shall be no more." In this new Consciousness right here, right now is my Kingdom. Not from away. Oh how we missed what was right here in the midst of us because we stood in the consciousness of time. And so no you cannot step outside of time, you must step outside of the sense of time - the mind, the mind. The letter kills, the Spirit gives eternal life.

Do you see that it is a transition within? There's nothing to overcome out here. There's nothing to step out of out here. There's an inner transition from sense to Soul and in the book <u>The Thunder of Silence</u> in the very first chapter Joel says to born of the

Spirit means to be reborn through a transition of Consciousness and this can occur right here on earth. There will always be the opportunity to make this transition because in the Kingdom of God there is no time. Well that's pretty plain and he doesn't say it because he read it somewhere, he says it from the experience of standing in the timeless eternity.

"If you can be fooled into believing that something's taking place in time then you're not standing in your eternal life. You're standing in a mind which has a sense of time and a world inside of that sense of time turning."

But Joel tells us in the Wisdoms of the Infinite Way in the very last Wisdom.

"If it takes place in time and space do not accept it at its appearance value search deeper in the realm of the Soul."

Again he's telling us to move from sense to Soul and that we must make this transition. And now I'm going to tell you - well let us be silent for a moment before we continue, I'll just let this run for a moment.

Father thy Grace is now.

[Brief Silence]

I guess everyone hearing this talk has heard the description of the experience that I had while I was in this class that Herb gave called "Healing Outside of Time" on a Saturday night. If you can't remember you can go and read it in several places - I think its even on the website under Herb's talks, but anyway it was quite powerful it lifted me right out of the conscious awareness of time and I stood in eternity and beheld - I couldn't say it any better than John when he says, "We beheld His Glory the Glory as of the only begotten of the Father full of Grace and Truth," and that's exactly what it felt like, exactly what it looked like. Only it wasn't his it was 'I' the 'I' of me and the 'I' of everyone.

And shortly after coming home, returning to the mainland from my visit to Herb over in Hawaii after having attended the seminar a few months before, I was in normal everyday Consciousness. I was on the job I was working as a substance abuse counselor and my shift was over and I climber into my car and started it and headed up the road to my house. Now my town was one town over and I had to drive surface streets to get there. There was no highway I just had to drive the streets. And this particular street that I was on was a four lane divided by a center island, if you have any towns like that you know what that looks like. Theres two lanes on your side then there's an island with bushes or trees or sometimes lights and on the other side there's traffic coming the other way on two lanes and then there's, because its city more than town there is office buildings and businesses along each side. And there's a light, a signal, yellow green and red every so often, maybe every mile.

So I'm driving up this road, this street and I come to an intersection and the light's green I have the right of way and I start through the intersection and theres a lady standing on the curb and she's calling to her dog. Interestingly enough a white poodle (chuckles) and that dog is trotting across the street and right in front of me there's no way I'm going to miss this dog. I can see the horror on her face. I can see the dog under my - the front of my car, I'm slamming on the brakes and at the same time I'm slamming on the brakes I stood totally still inside myself, it wasn't something I planned or accomplished it was a reaction. I stood still. I may have blinked for a moment I don't know.

But I'm heading straight up and I'm going to run over this dog. And there's no way to prevent it. And as I'm standing still with my foot on the brakes and everything is slowing down, suddenly I was on the other side of the island! I was on the other side of the island and my car was still going forward and I was facing oncoming cars and there was a driveway to my left and I just eased on into that driveway and the cars coming toward me passed until there was no more cars and I backed out, backed out of the driveway and drove the direction of the traffic, made a U-turn and headed up the same street I was going originally and I looked over to my right and there was the lady and her dog and everybody was okay.

And that experience - well you have to live through it to know what it feels like but one moment I was there and one moment I was here. The dog was not hit. I don't know to this day how it happened. I did not turn the wheel. I did not drive over the center island. The lady must have seen from her point of view it must have looked totally normal because nobody gathered 'round or nobody had expressions of - nobody made exclamations or had excited expressions on their faces, everything looked normal. And so I headed on the road, on the street until I got to my house and put the car away and didn't give it another thought, well I did give it another thought later in meditation but you know what I mean I went on with my day.

So, I am convinced having lived through it that for that moment not only was I outside of time but in some way I was outside of space. And standing in the stillness there was no accident. There was only now, and in the now everything was in its rightful place. And so that was an inner experience but it also governed the experience out here. The Word was made flesh. That experience of standing still in the now and I beheld His Glory full of Grace and Truth as it manifested. As it took form right where passing time appeared to be. Appeared to be happening - the dog was trotting, the lady was experiencing fear, the traffic was moving and I was moving. Right where all that passing time appeared to be, which was in the mind, when one second of stillness occurred time was no more and space was no more.

Now I have a wife whom I love very very much and she is somewhat more traditional than I am when it comes to Spiritual matters. And often when we go on a trip and we're running behind, we're late, for instance we have to be at a meeting in Waynesville which is an hour and fifteen minutes from here, and we've left and we only have an hour, something happened to make us late. We get into the car and she often grasps my hand and says something like, "Father put us on your time. We know that in you everything is perfect," or something like that, and then she smiles and I smile and I start the car and we go down the road.

Now I have had this experience dozens and dozens of times, where I'll start out on the journey, I don't drive fast. I don't drive any faster than the speed limit. I know it takes an hour and fifteen minutes. There's no way that that little prayer can make any difference and when I get to the town I'm going to and to the store I'm going to, I turn off the car I look at my watch, I'm at the meeting where I'm supposed to be and I'm fifteen minutes early. Now I have seen this happen so many times that I don't even give it another thought anymore. I almost come to expect it.

What am I saying to you? Am I saying her little prayer is changing time somehow? No I am not, if you're hearing that then you still have time located out here. I am saying that her little prayer releases us from the time sense and we dwell in the now, we dwell in the now. And in the now time is not passing. And in the now she's right. In the now is God's perfect timing and in the now you're right where you're supposed to be.

And so I am submitting you to this - submitting this to you. We must make a transition in Consciousness, we cannot step out of time because there isn't any. Its like saying how do we step out of this world? We can't there isn't any. The culprit, the fabric, the author, the father of time is the universal belief. This is located, this is speaking, appearing in the mind. And you can step outside of the time sense. Out of the mind. Out of the mind that has a sense of time. Out of the mind that has a sense of person. Out of the mind that has a material sense. You can step outside of that.

And our work becomes living, standing outside of that time sense, that mind. First in meditation. Then with eyes open and finally forever.

Well at first we must have the very first experience, and I told you mine and there has been many others which I won't go into now. And I told you my first experience and that was the experience I had at this seminar "Healing Outside of Time" the Saturday night class. That was my very first experience. That was kind of a - well I was rocketed into a fourth dimension of existence right here right now. In the midst. Not from hence but the Kingdom at hand and I was shown the Consciousness that I was to have. The Consciousness that I would have after the transition is made within. And its wonderful, its beautiful and I have that Consciousness now in meditation often. And sometimes like when I'm driving up the road without even trying - what is it Joel says? It begins to take over, yes that's becoming my experience.

Alright so, we cannot step outside of time but we can step outside of the mind which sees time and which sees space. And we start with our very first experience probably while in meditation. In that timeless eternity the silence, what Joel called the womb of creation the Spirit moves over the face of the deep and we behold his glory made manifest, the Word made flesh. Eternity, infinite eternity formed. And if we aren't resting in that Silence, then we're beholding mind and the concept of passing time and the world in that concept. The are the two states of Consciousness and we are moving from one to the other - from sense to Soul.

Okay let us be still and see if we can at least touch that eternal Self, and pull back within yourself not from away but here now at the center of your being and just be still, be still.

[Brief Silence]

Here within, the other evening I had a meditation, and in it it seemed I pulled up above the earth and so come with me now. Pull yourself up above the earth - you've seen the picture from satellites, you know what it looks like from space and you're looking down upon the earth from the moon and it is surrounded by the milky way. And there are millions and millions of stars but you're concerned with the earth and the earth's out there and in the distance, the sun, and the sun is shining and the earth, the earth is turning but for right now you're not on the earth - you're not on the earth you're just watching and it occurs to me that time is not passing. Here now, looking just looking, the earth turns but here from this vantage point in space up above the earth time is not passing. The sun is shining forever the earth is turning but there are no days here, there are no nights here. There's simply a galaxy and the planets are turning, do you see that? There are no days and no nights there's only now.

And if you pull out farther then you're not even in the milky way galaxy you are simply in space and there are an infinite number of galaxies and it is now and it is here in your Consciousness because Consciousness is what I am. Consciousness is what you are. And Consciousness beholds infinite galaxies, infinite planets, no days, no nights, no passing time just infinity. One infinite universe. But there are other universes. There are theories of parallel universes. And so if this is an infinite universe and there are other universes how many universes are there? There must be an infinite number of universes. And all within Consciousness because Consciousness contains it all. There is one infinite Consciousness without beginning without end. No time, no passing time just infinite Consciousness **ising**. Way way back before Abraham was I Am, Consciousness Is. Way back before the world was, the glory I had with thee before the world was I have now for time is not passing. All the way past the end I shall be with thee always even past the end of the world and so past the end of this world concept, I Am. Before the beginning I Am, Consciousness Is. After the end I Am, Consciousness Is. There is no passing time I embrace all of that. Before the beginning after the end Consciousness Is Now - Now. And so I Consciousness reveal time is not passing. Now I Am.

And there are other dimensions. "For I knew a man," says Paul, "In the seventh heaven," there must be at least seven heavens. This heaven of now. This heaven which is at hand. This heaven which is not from away, but right here right now, Consciousness, infinite eternal. This Consciousness has seven levels and you move from level to level, until the final level of Christ Consciousness in which you know that you are the Word, now. But God is beyond any levels and beyond the beyond and so Consciousness, the I, "I Am beyond all Galaxies, beyond all universes, before the beginning after the end. I Am in all dimensions and beyond all dimensions. I AM Consciousness. I Am that I Am. Now. Here. This is your eternal infinite Consciousness. This is what I Am. Stand still and behold the glory of Consciousness expressing, Consciousness being, Consciousness ising. Consciousness, I Am the way. Consciousness, I Am the Truth. Consciousness, I Am your Being. You Self infinite invisible eternal. Beyond the beyond. Rest in this sea. And behold I make all things new. Just rest in the eternal isness of now, Consciousness.

[Brief Silence]

Here in this Consciousness you hear what Christ has always said, "I have overcome the world. Be not afraid it is I, Consciousness. Consciousness is what I Am."

Rest here often and let Consciousness live itself, express itself. You cannot step out of time. You can step out of the mind and rest in Consciousness and be consciously aware of Consciousness. The infinite eternal now. Then it lives itself and you go along as a beholder, Consciousness lives you. And passing time - well what is that to thee?

The Word is made flesh, and dwells among us, we behold his glory. The glory as of the only begotten of the Father full of Grace and Truth. Now is my Kingdom. Now. And here in this Consciousness time shall be no more. Let this timeless eternal Consciousness lead into your everyday experience. Let it bring about the transformation from the sense of passing time to the eternal now, to the eternal Is. Let it transform you. You cannot transform yourself. You cannot decide, "I'm going to be Christ." But you can come within, stand still and receive ye the Holy Spirit.

I can tell you this, the more you come here within to this eternal Womb and rest in it and lose yourself in the eternal Self the more you will begin to have these rather strange experiences that you cannot repeat to other people because no one will believe you and if they did believe you no one would understand. Some of these things you cannot speak to anyone. There are experiences that I have had that I cannot tell you about - not yet anyway. And even Jesus Christ said the same, "I have many things to tell you but you're not ready. You cannot bear them." There are some things I know from the past when I have brought them up even with people supposedly on the Spiritual path and argument starts and then of course I have to agree with my adversary quickly and realize uh oh I was supposed to keep my finger on the lips and I'm sorry I will do better.

There are some things cannot be repeated yet. Oh I'm sure when we're standing in that Consciousness and one of us faces another we can share all these things. But when you're standing in that Consciousness - well I've said it before - you're standing in that Consciousness in your meditation and you walk down to sit on the bus bench and some of it still lingers and you're still in it - you're in the Spirit, the isness of eternal now, eternal now Consciousness and someone sitting next to you says, "What time is it?" you look at your watch and you say, "It's three minutes to one," and they say, "Thank you." and you realize, "I'm standing in a completely different universe. I really am standing in the Kingdom of here and now." And you wonder to yourself sometimes, "What would he think if he only knew, what would she think?" but you know better than to say anything. Then of course you catch yourself right there and say, "Wait a minute now I'm judging again." and I'm slowly seeping back into time sense and personal sense - uh oh (chuckles) and you get back to work. You pull yourself back in. Eventually, we won't seep back into everyday mortal consciousness.

That's the point. Eventually we will complete the transition right here, right now. And stand in this Consciousness of timeless eternity of a timeless eternal self with no break and that's the point of "To know thee aright is life eternal." And Christ which is the manifestation of thee or the movement of thee. Standing in the stillness of the eternal Womb is where it starts. But seeing the movement the Word made flesh - that completes the demonstration.

Joel told us over and over and over "One demonstration, demonstrate God," and that's what he meant. Demonstrate the eternal infinite invisible Consciousness right here, right now. And you will experience creation of a new heaven and a new earth. You will experience creation in your Consciousness just as if you were standing in the first chapter of Genesis. Time will be no more but the Word will breathe out and creation unfold before your eye. And how do you describe that? You can't.

Well I don't know if I helped in any way with the original question of expanding upon the idea of stepping outside of time, I don't know if I have done that or not today but I can tell you this, there's no time out there to step out of. Time is another concept of the mind and in that time the world is passing. In that time concept the world is passing. And so again, the answer is turning within. Stepping outside of that mind. And finding that you're no longer passing in time. You are standing in the eternal Self, the infinite Self, the I Am Consciousness.

Blessings, blessings in the now.

CLASS 21

ASCENSION INTO THE SOUL REALM

PART I

Bill: Good morning.

This is June 30th about 11:30, 2013, and I had an idea for a talk today and was going to cover some of the principles of spiritual healing, because it seems that nobody likes to practice or study the nature of error and practice impersonalization and nothingization. It seems they'd rather just concentrate on the beauty of God. The problem is that according to Joel if you don't have the other half, you won't experience the full realization. But I was told "no" and directed to cover the Introduction in this book called <u>Man Was Not Born to Cry</u> by Joel Goldsmith, and the Introduction is called *Awake*. So that's what we're gonna do, because I do what I'm directed. And let us have a moment of silence, a few moments if possible. Enter into a state of receptivity to your Soul and to the Soul realm, because that's what we're going to be talking about. Let's take that moment now.

[Brief pause]

329

How many of you I wonder are familiar with the Soul realm? I noticed the other day because I was reading, studying, taking one sentence at a time from *The New Horizon*, that chapter in <u>The Infinite Way</u>, and I noticed that – well, I'll read it to you and tell you what I noticed. It says:

The first glimpse into the heaven of here and now is the beginning of the ascension for us. This ascension is understood now as a rising above the conditions and experiences of "this world," and we behold the "many mansions" prepared for us in spiritual Consciousness—in the awareness of Reality.

Well, that all sounds logical. If you remember in <u>Beyond Words and Thoughts</u>, Joel told us the ascension is always the same, rising above the mind. Rising above the mind. And he hints in many of these books and in many of his talks, he hints at the fact that the world mind – well, in fact, I'll give you one right now. Hang on. Let me get it. It's in <u>The Art of Spiritual Healing</u>. Let me get that and I'll have it. In this chapter *What Did Hinder You* he says:

For years after I learned to recognize all forms of sin, disease, lack, limitation, (and) depression are hypnotism, the puzzle was to discover how to break that hypnotism.

It was then that I discovered the scriptural passage "the stone was cut out of the mountain without hands." The weapon against error – our offense and defense – is something that is neither physical nor mental (not by might nor by power) *no action, no words, no thoughts – only the awareness of God.*

Now pay attention to that word "awareness."

As you carry this out in practice, watching the stone being formed in and of your consciousness while you stand to one side as a witness or a beholder, eventually a state of peace will come. (And) you will catch a glimpse of God as Is not a power, just God is. All problems fade out in proportion as you develop this ability to be quiet, to be silent, to behold, and to witness divine harmony unfold.

And finally, the point that I was getting to:

When the human mind is not functioning,

This is the principle behind the process.

When the human mind is not functioning, there is no more hypnotism. When you are not thinking thoughts or words, when you are in a stillness, the human mind is stopped – the hypnotism is gone. (And) When you experience this, you will feel something which transcends the human dimension.

Now listen.

When the human mind is not functioning, there is no more hypnotism. The human mind is stopped – the hypnotism is gone.

Well then the hypnotism **is** the human mind! Right? Right!

And so he says in Beyond Words and Thoughts, that:

The ascension into the kingdom of heaven here and now, or into the realm of Soul, is always the same: rising above the human mind.

Do you see? So now going back to The Infinite Way, reading what we just read, he says:

The first glimpse into the heaven of here and now. Or into the Soul realm, into your very Soul, into God, because God and your Soul are one.

The first glimpse into the heaven of here and now is the beginning of the ascension for (you) we behold "many mansions" prepared for us in the awareness of Reality.

So in The Art of Spiritual Healing he says that the whole principle is rising above the mind into an awareness of something not human. And in The Infinite Way, in *The New Horizon* he says that the awareness of the Soul-realm is the first glimpse into heaven, and that takes place in the awareness of Reality. So what are we saying? We're saying that the entire spiritual path is nothing more than an inner transformation from mind to Soul. From the mind – the sense-mind, the three-dimensional world that is in the mind – to the realm of Soul where your incorporeal Self is, and so that's where the spiritual path takes place. There's no path out here. It's a transformation. *"be ye transformed by the renewing of your mind"* And trading that human mind for the mind which was in Christ Jesus, you are transformed. All of this is pointing out that it's an inner realization of oneness, so you're rising in awareness.

Now getting back to what I was directed. This book, <u>Man Was Not Born to Cry</u>, before the first chapter is an Introduction, and he titled it *Awake*. So we'll look at some points in this which should suggest to you that you're making a transformation within. You're not going anywhere. The kingdom of heaven is not a place. The kingdom of heaven is at hand right now, closer than breathing. But your unawareness of it keeps you in the human mind, which is a human sense of existence, or the universal dream. You step out of that sometimes in meditation into an awareness of the Soul-realm and you're making a transition from that human mind. You are ascending up into Soul awareness, and that takes place when you step out of that human mind within yourself. All right. *Awake:*

When you first come to (the) spiritual study, it is only because some circumstance or condition of your life is in need of adjustment.

Yes, most of us found this because we were unsatisfied. There was a lack or a limitation of some sort which pushed us and drove us to find an answer. In my case I couldn't find it in organized religion. I tried, but I couldn't make it. I sat there and I became angry at the preachers and I wanted to tell them to stop scaring people, and so I just could never be comfortable and find it there. But it pushes us on until we begin to look for a spiritual answer. If we are inclined towards metaphysics, perhaps you started the same way I did with Emmet Fox or Walter C. Lanyon or some of the other metaphysical people. Perhaps some Unity writings, Charles and Myrtle Fillmore, if that's their names – I can't remember it's been so long. But at any rate, you started with some metaphysics. Maybe you went right into Christian Science. Eventually, however, the mental approach seemed to not be quite enough, and we were driven, and eventually maybe we all found <u>The Infinite Way</u> and Joel's writings or Herb's talks, and so here we are. He says:

During your spiritual study, you found some degree of improvement taking place in your life, but I can assure you, you never will find all that you are seeking humanly, because it does not lie within the nature of a spiritual teaching to give you all the human good things you think you would like. In some avenues of your life, you will experience improved health, increased supply, and other forms of human happiness, but you will not find the completeness you expected. (Because) About the time you actually realize that it never is going to happen (for you), you will likewise perceive the reason, which is that you have been praying amiss. You have been trying to patch up or improve this human existence, and that is not the function of any spiritual message.

It is very clear from the message of every mystic the object of the spiritual path is that we may "die" to the human experience and be "reborn" of the Spirit (or of the Soul realm). We learn that the spiritual kingdom is not of "this world," even a healthy, wealthy, (or) wise world.

On the mystical path, you learn that the goal of life is not the metaphysical goal of better health, (or) a beautiful home, (or an) expensive automobile, (or) a satisfying companion the goal is releasing the Soul from the tomb of human existence, (and) more especially (from) the tomb of the human mind.

So there you have it. We came to metaphysics. We practiced the principles. We saw improvement in our life and yet, we went on and something happened or the principles seemed to stop working. We searched deeper and we find out that it never was about improving the human scene. The spiritual path is not there so you can have better companionship, a larger home, an increased supply, or better health. The spiritual path is there so that you can die to wanting any of these, so that you can die out of the human mind and the dream universe of two and begin to launch out into the deep into the Soul realm and let down your nets there.

Of course, you'll find that Omnipresence, omnipresent Soul includes in it everything you need. Not necessarily everything the mind wants, but everything you need is provided abundantly with 12 baskets full to share – but that only when you are no longer seeking that. So we find ourselves finally ready to practice what the Master told us: Seek ye first the kingdom or the Soul realm, and maybe we are all standing there in this class, ready at last to seek the Soul realm, to seek to ascend into that Soul realm, which is not a place or even a kingdom or a realm, but an awareness in Reality.

And so we are trading thoughts for awareness. We are trading mind for Soul.

We are trading the letter for Spirit. And so he says:

Every human being is in prison, the prison of the mind and the body, and during the normal human lifetime of an individual, he never gets outside of that prison.

All right.

There are some, however—explorers, artists, adventurers—who do try to widen their horizons physically, mentally, and artistically, but only occasionally have there been one or two or three who wanted to explore the realm of the Soul.

The realm of the Soul is God awareness, or awareness of God, for God and the Soul are one.

Think of that word "Soul" for a moment (he says;) *and see how little you know about it, and remember the rest of the world knows (even) less than you do, because you have discovered a great deal about it in the writings* (and in the recordings). *The knowledge of the Soul, the life of the Soul, the wider horizon (of the Soul) is the greatest experience that can come to any individual.*

The Soul is imprisoned in the tomb that we call human experience, the tomb of the mind and (the) body, and if we are to experience the Soul, we have to break through the limitations of body and mind. (And) This, the Master called taking no thought for our life, but seeking the kingdom of God, the realm of God, the Soul.

And there he just slips it in there so quietly you – you almost don't notice. He says:

This, the Master called taking no thought, but seeking the kingdom (or) the realm of God, the Soul. (God, the Soul).

So if you're wondering where God is, you have no more need to wonder, because he spells it out right there – God, the Soul. God and the Soul are One. Your Soul is God. God **is** your Soul. And if the – as we know, the mind and the body are concepts, the dream images, the dream world, the dream mind – then when you take no thought you, your reality, your Soul, your God Self – begins to make itself aware, begins to express in your awareness. You become aware of the I of you, and that's the whole point of this.

So, let us look at this because I'm sure that most of us pass this by also. This is from the Hotel Wellington, and Joel wrote it. It's a copy of what he wrote by hand on June 13th of 1960 at 7:00 p.m. Well, that was just a little while ago, but the same month we're in now, only it was what – 53 years ago, something like that? Was it 53? Sixty plus 53 – is that 2013? Yes, it is. Okay. So it's 53 years ago he sat in a hotel in early evening in England, or no – where is this? New York! Hotel Wellington, New York. And he wrote this. This was just before he was giving a class. Very important, and so I'll read it to you.

At first he put: *There are two secrets the world does not know,* but then he overwrote that. He wrote on top of that: *There are four secrets the world does not know,* and when you read this he actually has one, two, three, four, five secrets the world does not know. So we'll read what he wrote here. *There are four secrets the world does not know.* The reason why I'm reading this to you is because it explains the need to ascend into that Soul realm and the method to do so, and most people don't want to do this. As I said at the beginning, we don't want to study the nature of error even if we're told that that's the way to ascend! But we are very plainly!

Remember in the Kailua study series, chapter eight, which explains the secret of healing or the nature of error. He says at the end of that chapter, the end of that talk — *You can throw out every other talk, every other chapter, and just stick to this one, and when you learn the principles you will have the secret of how to ascend,* [or in his case, how to heal — in the case of that chapter, how to heal]. The ascension out of humanhood and into the Soul realm is the same as the secret to healing. They are one. And this will explain that. So:

There are four secrets that the world does not know.

1. All evil has its rise in the universal belief in two powers, this belief operating as a universal, mental malpractice. This we sum up as the activity of the carnal mind or mortal mind, originally called devil or Satan.

Now that's the first secret. What is it, first secret? Everything you see that appears evil and everything you see that appears good in the human scene is a universal mental malpractice. What does that mean? What does that mean to you — universal mental malpractice? Because he says you must understand this in order to ascend into the Soul realm. Well, to me it means there's a universal dream, and that wherever you find yourself in this universe, that dream is pumping mental malpractice out. In other words, images, beliefs, concepts — always the belief in two powers, the belief in two. In the Kailua study series he says two selves, two universes, two activities, two beings, two minds. Always two.

And so it's a universal mental malpractice always going on like a television station being broadcast constantly, and if you are in the human mind – what did he say in <u>The Art of Spiritual Healing</u> just now – that **is** the hypnotism. And so if you are just in a human mind and a human body walking around and occasionally you have a moment of prayer, then you go back to being a human mind and a human body, then you are, well – you're hypnotized, aren't you? You're in the control of mortal mind or carnal mind. So that's the first thing to understand if you want to be free. If you want to enter the Soul realm, the first thing is: *All evil has its rise in the universal belief in two powers, this belief operating as a universal mental malpractice. This we sum up as the activity of carnal or mortal mind, originally called devil or Satan.* Because it's a temptation for you to believe you're human. That your name is Mary or Bill or Tim or Jack or Susan or Martha or Betty, and it's not – or Laurie. That's not your name. It's the name given to this mental image, this mental malpractice, this universal belief in a separate self, or a personal sense of self. That's the name given to the dream person. But you want to ascend and feel and know your own omnipresence, your own Soul. So he says that's the first thing. That's the first secret.

2. *The second secret is that this mental malpractice has no power in and of itself beyond that of tempter, but it operates as power where not known and understood.*

Now that's the second secret. This mental malpractice pumping itself into your mind has no power behind it other than being a temptation for you to accept, but it looks, it smells, it tastes, it touches like power when you are not aware, when you are asleep. Hence, the name of the chapter *Awake.* You see that? It operates as power. Elsewhere he said that he used to say that the belief in two powers – this carnal mind, this mortal mind – was without power. But he said that's an incomplete statement.

337

He said, "I should have said it's without power in the conscious awareness or in the presence of Christ." And so when you have the awareness of your Soul – you're standing in that awareness – then, then, and then only is this mental malpractice – does it have no power. Only when you're standing in that awareness. If you're in the human mind, as we read in The Art of Spiritual Healing, then it operates as power, but it's a little worse than that. Listen as he continues:

3. The third secret: *Furthermore, the human scene, good or evil, is the product of this universal malpractice or carnal mind.*

And so whether you're looking out there and seeing your beautiful sunset or your cute little grandchild or your beautiful spouse or whether you're looking and seeing a burglar or diseased tree in your yard or the corpse of a dog that was run over in the street or whether you're seeing cancer eat away at your body – both of those are made from the same fabric. Remember he says in the Kailua study series: It's vital that you see that this is a fabric and don't treat the disease, but treat the overall fabric. It's because he's trying to get you to awaken. So number three is the human scene, good or evil, is the product of this mental malpractice which is being pumped into your human mind. We're like the walking dead, aren't we, listening to this and responding like a puppet on a string? Doesn't that make you uncomfortable? It makes me uncomfortable.

When I hear that and I see that I want to awaken. So let's read number three. *Furthermore, the human scene, good or evil, is the product of this universal malpractice or carnal mind* (and he has this underlined) *and has no contact with God and is not under the law of God.*

All right. Why do bad things happen to good people? That should answer it right there. I studied so hard. I know this stuff backwards and forwards. You can give me a written test. I will pass it – a 100, 99 at the worst – but I will pass it 100. Give me that written test. I know these answers! Yes, you know these answers, but do you have an awareness of Soul? Are you ascending out of the mind that knows these answers into an awareness of Soul? Because if you aren't, then your existence and your life has no contact with God and is not under the law of God. Ouch! Wow, who wants to hear that! I call these talks uncomfortable for a reason.

4. And number four: *Harmony of a permanent nature* (now listen to this, because he says), *can only be attained...* (and that means there's one way) *Harmony of a permanent nature can only be attained as the spiritual Self is realized through impersonalization and nothingizing. Impersonalizing and nothingizing of the carnal mind.* (I'm gonna read that again because I tripped over that). *Harmony of a permanent nature can only be attained as the spiritual Self is realized through impersonalization and nothingizing of the carnal mind.*

That's what he wrote. What does that mean? Why did I bring that up at all? Because he says harmony of being can only be attained as your spiritual Self or your Soul is realized or you become aware of your Soul or the Soul realm through impersonalization and nothingizing of the carnal mind. You see now why it's so important? He says in the Kailua study series in that chapter: [The Healing Principle], If you only know the beauty and joy and the experience of mystics of oneness with God, communing with God, but you don't know the second half, then you will have very limited experiences of harmony. You may have communion with God in your meditation and come out of it and then experience lack and limitation. Why? Because you're in the dream of two because you believe that inside yourself you can commune with a presence and then when you open your eyes you're back to this human life. You believe in two, the dream of two.

So that is why he says the way that you come into an awareness of the Soul realm is through impersonalizing and nothingizing. So there's two parts. He always says he starts his meditations with God and he recognizes his oneness with God, and then he goes into that part of the meditation where he realizes the appearance, good or evil, is nothing – has no power and no life and no law. He said that dozens of times, hundreds of times, maybe thousands. And then he rests. He rests in the Word and he waits in silence until he feels that movement – or expressed another way – until he comes into the awareness of Soul. Because in the awareness of Soul, then the mental malpractice is nothing. It's dissolved. The light shines and the darkness disappears. Nobody knows where the darkness goes because the darkness is not a thing. It's a no-thing. But when the light shines in the awareness of the Soul, in that inner quickening movement, ascension above the mind, then the duality disappears. It dissolves.

5. But wait! There's still a fifth secret. *Then there is another unknown that is responsible for world discord. The secret of harmony is not in using power, but in refraining from the use of power since Omnipotence recognizes no power to overcome or destroy. The recognition of nonpower establishes harmony in the human scene.*

Which is the whole purpose of the meditation, because when you come to the awareness of Soul and you have that inner release, then—well, you've recognized the nonpower of your Soul. Again, he said here: *The first glimpse into the heaven here and now is the beginning of the ascension and we behold "many mansions"* (or many levels) *in the awareness of Reality* (or the Soul).

Now, I'm going to explain that release one time and then we'll get back to the chapter called *Awake*. Now he says here: [Art of Spiritual Healing]

When you really begin to comprehend in healing you are not dealing with people, when you learn to eliminate them and their

340

claims from your thought and in every instance deal with the root of the problem, which is the carnal mind, the arm of flesh, or any word you choose so long as it means nothingness, you will find how quickly you will be able to become consciously aware of your Soul, the Presence within you. This Presence cannot be felt until you are free of the barrier, and the barrier is the belief in two, in two powers or in something apart from God.

Now, the minute you have made the carnal mind a nothingness, no power, you no longer have two powers and you can do just what it says in Scripture: You can rest in his word. You can rest in this word waiting for the Spirit of the Lord God to be upon you, (which is a fancy way of saying waiting for the awareness of Soul), *and when it comes, it breaks the hypnotism.*

You see that? Once more:

If with every claim that comes to you you can set aside any thought of the person, his name or the claim and go back to some word or term which to you represents nothingness – not something to fight or even rise above – but something that's just nothingness so that you have only one power, then you can sit in meditation and you will feel the descent of the Holy Ghost, which means the awareness – you'll have the awareness of Soul. *You will feel the peace that passes understanding. You will feel a divine Presence and a release from fear or discord.* And again, *the principle behind this process is that inasmuch as the activity of the human mind is the substance of hypnotism, when the human mind is not functioning, there's no more hypnotism. When you experience this you will feel something which transcends the human dimension.*

Do we see? It all is one big circle, isn't it? He spent all these words to tell you you need to go from the mind and thinking thoughts, which is twoness, into an awareness of Soul and its many mansions, which is oneness. So getting back to this chapter *Awake,* and this may end up being two talks. We'll see. He says – and this is important. I want to read this too.

Some become so frightened at the first glimpse of the Soul realm that they never go that way again.

And I can tell you that I had an experience that was frightening to the human mind, and in that experience I was almost completely dissolved. There was just a tiny little piece way back there saying, "I'm afraid," and then the experience diminished. So he says:

Some become so frightened at the first glimpse of the Soul realm that (they never want to go that way again, or) they never go that way again. God is light, and to come face to face with that light is more blinding in its intensity than to look directly into the hot sun. So, if it has been frightening, it takes an adventurous spirit to make more than one attempt. It is not that God is frightening, but that the human senses are frightened by the unknown. (And actually) Actually there is nothing to fear.

And so I felt in that one intense meditation I had in Florida that I was going to be completely dissolved and dispersed somewhere in the Infinite, but the fear itself made the experience diminish and subside. Now he says here: *It takes an adventurous spirit to make more than one attempt*, and trust me, I have been launching out into the deep over and over and over for some almost – well, for 41 years [Now 48 years]. All right. So now do we see what we're saying? All of this – it's taken 40 minutes to simply prepare you for what we're going to talk about, and that is that it's absolutely necessary to die out of humanhood, out of the human sense of existence, out of the human mind, in order to begin to have these glimpses or this awareness of the Soul realm, of your Soul, of God, because God is your Soul. I am that I Am. I am your Soul. And in order to have glimpses, in order to begin the ascension into the Soul realm, it's necessary to impersonalize this mental malpractice pumping into you as a human life and nothingize it by realizing in the presence of Soul it's dissolved. Okay?

As a rule (he says), *progress on the spiritual path is so gradual that the entire way is a joy. Here and there, there will be experiences that are momentarily frightening because you had perhaps expected something different. For example, you may have thought that every day would be a joyous experience, whereas* (are you listening, my friends? – whereas) *those periods are few,* (and so there are few periods of joyous experience) *and the periods of barrenness and emptiness and the feeling that you are separated from God are many.*

Well, I'm sure glad to read that! (chuckles)

Actually, these (periods of barrenness) *are more necessary to your spiritual unfoldment than sitting on "cloud nine," because without that complete barrenness you are a vessel already full, and nothing new can enter.* (You must) *You have to lose your concepts of God and what you expect of God.*

I wish I could use a title for a book Santa Claus God because that is what the majority of the concepts of God are. Be assured no one can enter the realm of the Soul with such a God in mind.

Yes, you have to leave all of the mental concepts to have a glimpse of the Soul realm. You cannot have a concept of God. You cannot have a synonym. Any concept in the mind on which you rely will keep you tethered to the mind, the very thing you have to ascend out of in order to rise into the Soul realm. Now just in case you forgot – well, I'll think we'll start the second talk there. So we'll finish this here.

The reason why this is an uncomfortable talk is because we are saying that you have to lose every concept you have or have had of God. Even the concept of omnipresence. Even the concept of spirit. The concept of infinite invisible. Anything to which you can get a mental picture of or mental idea. All of that has to go. You have to face entering the Soul realm with no idea at all about what you'll find. **None.** You must be completely dead in order to be born, and this takes place in a moment ye think not, because all these concepts are thoughts in that mind.

Hence, the reason for Joel's insistence that meditation is the way. Meditation is the way. Meditation is the way. We hear that over and over, and we think that if we become quiet and we rehash and rehearse some truths in our mind that we're meditating. Well, we're not. We might be contemplating mentally. It might be a form of contemplation or contemplative meditation, but it's not enough. It's won't produce any harmony, but it may calm us down. It may calm us down. It may slow the mind down, which is what he says in The Art of Meditation, and eventually thought will come to a stop. Now is when real meditation can take place, that of being a complete empty vessel. That means none of the human is there. There's no one home.

There's a vast empty nothingness and personal sense doesn't want to go there. It does not want to die even for these few moments in meditation. You've noticed it yourself if you see how you're as quiet as you can be and these thoughts go marching on. Remember, he says we do not fight these thoughts. That won't help us. That'll tether us to the mind, tie us to the mind, bind us. No, we have to learn to contemplate long enough to become quiet, to become still. To be that empty vessel waiting upon the Lord.

You cannot lift yourself into the Soul realm, but you can prepare yourself by your being with others on the spiritual path, by your reading inspirational literature which lifts you into periods of quiet and calmness, and by listening to a talk or a tape or a class. These are the ways that you become still, but they're not enough. No. You must launch out into that deep, empty, infinite ocean of nothingness, not knowing what you'll find, and allow It, your Soul, God Itself to reveal Itself.

This is meditation, and in the presence of Soul awareness, the good and the evil of appearances in the mind dissolve. Or put it this way – in your awareness of Soul, mind is dissolved. In the shining of the light, the darkness disappears. It's all one, and it is all leading to that transformation from human to Soul.

Once you learn to—well, I believe we'll leave that for talk number two. This is talk one, the first half of the Introduction, *Awake,* from the book <u>Man Was Not Born to Cry</u>. Perhaps we are centered inside ourselves now and calm enough and quiet enough to have a meditation before part two. So I suggest you have that period of silence now inside of yourself and invite the Soul to speak. Invite the Soul to reveal Itself. Invite the Soul to take over, he says in the <u>Beyond Words and Thoughts</u>. Invite the Soul to take over.

And let us be still now for a moment.

[Silent pause]

Okay. We will wrap this up by reading this. I want you to understand this clearly, so we'll wrap this up, this first part, by reading this one more time from the Hotel Wellington in New York by Joel, five secrets.

1. *All evil has its rise in the universal belief in two powers. This belief operating as a universal mental malpractice. This we sum up as the activity of the carnal or mortal mind originally called devil or Satan.*

2. *This malpractice has no power in and of itself beyond that of tempter, but operates as power where not known or understood.*

3. *Furthermore, the human scene, good or evil, is the product of this universal malpractice or carnal mind and has no contact with God and is not under the law of God.*

4. *Harmony of a permanent nature can only be attained as the spiritual Self or Soul realm is realized through impersonalization and nothingizing of the carnal mind.*

5. *There is another unknown that is responsible for world discord. The secret of harmony is not in using power, but in*

refraining from the use of power since omnipotence recognizes no power to overcome or destroy. The recognition of nonpower establishes harmony in the human scene.

All right. Take a walk. Have a stretch. Take a break. Have a silence, and we'll meet you back here for part two. And as always, thank you.

[Silence]

CLASS 22

ASCENSION INTO THE SOUL REALM

PART II

Bill: Well, welcome back.

This would be Part II of the Introduction from <u>Man Was Not Born to Cry</u> by Joel Goldsmith, which he entitled or titled *Awake,* as in *"Awake thou that sleepest."*

We were talking about the ascension, always the ascension, ascending up over the mind into the Soul realm, which the Soul realm has many mansions in awareness of reality, and so the many mansions are not a kingdom up in the sky by and by. They're not even another dimension here. The kingdom is the realm of Soul, and the many mansions take place, or the many levels, are the levels of awareness. And so your transformation from mind to awareness is the difference between this world and the kingdom of heaven here and now.

In the old days, in the days of King James when the King James Bible was written they used terms such as kingdom. But I looked in some—I think it was Strong's concordance, and the word originally meant "realm," and realm, of course is, now we know, awareness. So it all takes place in your inner awareness. There you come up over the mind and seeing things through the mind darkly into awareness—pure awareness— which of course is the first chapter of Genesis. Pure awareness of Soul or God.

Now what can you expect to see? Well, it's different for everyone. No two people see the same thing, but we are given some hints in the chapter *The New Horizon* because *The New Horizon* now you know is the Soul realm. And so he says:

The sense which presents pictures of discord and inharmony, disease and death, (and also all the good that you behold) *is the universal mesmerism which produces the entire dream of human existence.*

See, there it is again, mental malpractice or universal mesmerism. The word's are not important. He says, you can use whatever words you like. Hold on a minute. I wrote some down here the other day or actually quite a while ago. Let's see where I keep notes in my little journal here. I was looking at this one day and in April of 1998 I wrote:

A belief in two powers, universal belief, world mind, carnal mind, a glass darkly, appearance, illusion, a false image, Maya, hypnotism, mesmerism, personal sense, material sense, this world, or concepts or universal dream world.

So there are many terms. There are many words used to describe it. Maya is of course from Buddha and his describing illusion. And remember, it's not out here! Illusion – no illusion is ever externalized. And so the illusion you are looking at if you're calling it illusion is mortal mind. It's a series of beliefs or thoughts in the mind. Therefore says Christ: *"Take no thought."* Stop that! **STOP!** And in the silence behold, I am God. I, your Soul, and you have a glimpse of the kingdom here and now, or the Soul realm or awareness of Soul.

So the sense which presents all these pictures is a *universal mesmerism which produces the entire dream of human existence,* and so look at that backwards, and human existence is a dream. All of it. And therefore he says:

It must be understood there is no more reality to harmonious human existence than to discordant world conditions. It must be realized that the entire human scene is mesmeric suggestion, and we must rise above the desire for even good human conditions.

This is why he says over and over we must come to the place where we're no longer trying to establish harmony in the human scene, because if we succeeded we would have a happy dream, a happy dream world, and we don't want a happy dream because then we still die in humanhood and have to come back and try to find the Soul realm again. No. Therefore he says:

Understand fully that suggestion, (or beliefs) or hypnotism is the substance, or fabric, (there's that word, fabric) *of the whole mortal universe and human conditions good and evil are dream pictures having no reality or permanence.*

And when you get to that place it's really uncomfortable, especially if you haven't found the Soul realm, because on the one hand you're standing there – it's very uncomfortable. You're looking, you're saying: "Okay, okay. The good and evil of this experience here of this human, of me – this is a dream world. It has no reality. It's hypnotism, the entire mortal universe, and it has no contact with God."

Well, that's pretty scary! God's not in the human scene, Joel says, and we ignore it and go on thinking with our prayer and meditation we can bring him there. But no, he says here at the Hotel Wellington:

Has no contact with God. The human scene, good or evil, is a product of universe malpractice, carnal mind, mortal mind, and has no contact with God and is not under the law of God, and that is something you must know and know at depth.

That's half of the equation, the other half being the awareness of Soul.

So he says *understand fully that the fabric of the whole mortal universe is suggestion, belief, or hypnotism.*

And more than that, more than just understanding:

Be willing, (willing) *for the harmonious as well as the inharmonious conditions of mortal existence to disappear from your experience in order that reality may be known and enjoyed and lived.*

Or in order that the Soul realm or the kingdom, the awareness in Reality may be known and enjoyed and lived. So to ascend you might as well take *The New Horizon* in The Infinite Way and take this entire first paragraph and understand that this is the first half, or rather, this is half of the equation. Doesn't matter if it's the first or the second half. It's half of the equation, and all of this must be true in your experience. You must be living this and understanding this fully in order for you to launch out into the deep. Be willing for the good as well as the evil to disappear from your experience in order to launch out into the Soul realm.

So on the one hand you're standing there and you recognize all of this is a dream taking place within, not without, and has no reality, no permanence, and no contact with God and no law to support it. It's impersonal, being pumped into the mind by this universal mental malpractice and it has no power. It's nothing, nothing behind it.

So on the one hand you're knowing that, but you haven't yet experienced the Soul realm.

You haven't ascended out of it. You're still standing in it. And then someone says launch out into the Soul realm, but don't bring any of those concepts with you. Don't bring any concepts – not of God, not of Spirit, not of Soul, not of Christ, not of love, not of the kingdom of heaven, not of the Soul realm. Bring no concepts with you. And oh, by the way, don't bring that self either. Step out of that. Stand there. Stand there knowing that it is a nothingness, and be empty – listen. Listen for the still small voice. Wait upon the movement. Wait for Soul to reveal Itself, and know not what that experience is going to be. Have no idea whatsoever. Totally empty, a nothingness, waiting for the movement of the hand of God. And there you stand. It's very uncomfortable at first, but it becomes – well, it becomes quite wonderful.

And now he's going to give you some clues here. He's going to describe his experience of the Soul realm, of the Soul, of God.

Above the sense-life, there is a universe of Spirit (or realm of Soul) *governed by Love, peopled* (or populated) *with children of God living in the household or temple of Truth. This world* (this universe, this realm) *is real and permanent: Its substance is eternal Consciousness. In it there is no awareness of discords or even of temporary material good.*

So in the Soul realm you will find a universe of Spirit governed by Love, and the fabric of it is eternal Consciousness. You will have no awareness of good or evil, just eternal Consciousness is'ing.

The first glimpse...

And there we go with glimpse again. Ah, now here he spells it out.

The first glimpse of Reality—of the Soul-realm—comes with the recognition and realization of the fact all temporal conditions and experiences are products of self-hypnotism. With that realization that the entire human scene—good as well as evil—is illusion, comes the first glimpse and taste of the world of God's creation and of the sons of God who inhabit (the Soul realm or) *the spiritual kingdom.*

Okay. So he says here the first glimpse of the Soul realm comes with the recognition and realization all temporal conditions are products of hypnotism. What did he say here at the Hotel Wellington? Now remember, this <u>Infinite Way</u> *New Horizon* was written in the 40's or 50's. Right? And now here we are 1960 at the Hotel Wellington and he's saying the same thing. Here are the four or five secrets you must know to find the Soul realm. Here in *The New Horizon* he says:

The first glimpse of the Soul-realm comes with the recognition and realization all temporal conditions and experiences are self-hypnotism. (It comes) *With the realization that the entire human scene – good (and) evil – is illusion.*

And here at the Hotel Wellington he writes down: *Harmony of a permanent nature can only be attained* – in other words, the Soul realm *can only be attained as you come into the awareness of it through impersonalization and nothingizing of this mental malpractice*, or carnal mind, or this world, or the dream universe, or mortal existence, or humanhood.

See, he's saying the same thing, and people do not want to hear about the nature of error, and yet it is through this realization that all temporal conditions are hypnotism and that the entire human scene, good and evil, is illusion – it's through that realization that you get your first glimpse of the Soul realm, and so you must have both parts! You must have the inner deep realization that – well, there's no more reality to harmonious human existence than to the discord or discordant human conditions. You must have that at depth. Then you can let it go. Stop trying to improve it, patch it up. Then you can recognize it for its nothingness, universal mental malpractice being pumped into the human mind, but nothing is standing behind it. No God is behind it, so it's nothingness. But it acts as if it's a power, he says, until it's realized and understood and seen through, and the way you see through it is in ceasing from taking thought, as he said in <u>The Art of Spiritual Healing</u>. Take no thought. Rest in the Word, and it doesn't matter what that word is – whatever word you came to in your contemplation.

God is. I am. It is. I rest here. I take no thought, not might nor by power, but by the Soul. And then rest in that capital W-o-r-d, Word. Not the words you just said to yourself, but the Word, the original Logos. *"The Word was God,"* and *"the Word was made flesh."* So you rest in the Word, that Word, the original I within.

And then you catch a glimpse of the Soul realm and you find out that there's a universe of Spirit, a realm of Soul governed by Love, and there's beings in it. These beings are children of God, and this realm is real and permanent. Its substance is Consciousness, eternal Consciousness, and in that realm there's no awareness of duality. There's only awareness of the Soul.

(So) With the realization that the entire human scene – good as well as evil – is illusion, (comes) the first glimpse and taste of the Soul realm (or of) God's creation and of the sons of God who inhabit (this) spiritual creation.

So in this first glimpse attained by impersonalizing and nothingizing the dream world and dream mind out of which it came or comes, in the standing still from that, recognizing both sides to it, good and evil, are illusion in the mind, hence ascending up over the mind in the realm of the Soul where you feel its movement even as I do right now, here you become aware of the Soul realm, the Soul of you, God of you, God as you, and you rest. And you rest. And the light is shining and it dissolves these mental projections.

Now, (he says) in this moment of uplifted consciousness, we are able, even though faintly, (at first) to see ourselves free of material, mortal, human, and legal laws. We behold ourselves separate and apart from the bondage of sense, and in a measure we glimpse (there's that word again) *(glimpse) the unlimited boundaries of eternal Life and of infinite Consciousness. The fetters of finite existence begin to fall away.*

See, we're having an awakening, aren't we?

The experience at first is like watching the world disappear over a horizon and drop down from before us. There is no attachment to (it), no desire to hold onto it – probably because to a great extent this experience does not come until a great measure of our desire for the things of "this world" has been overcome.

You see how you have to come to the place where he's starting this chapter *Awake* in knowing that this is not about patching up the human scene. He says elsewhere that he had a hard time explaining to the students that it's not a matter of bringing God down to the human scene, but in rising above the human scene to the realm of Soul.

At first we cannot speak of it. There is a sense of "'Touch me not; for I have not yet ascended."

I want you to understand when you first have this glimpse, if you haven't had it, it is so—well, earth shattering, so startling, so wonderful that you will know intuitively you cannot speak of it. You just cannot. So there is a sense of *"Touch me not, for I have not yet ascended."* No, I'm not up here permanently. I'm still traveling back and forth. I ascend up into the Soul realm and I come back down to human thinking, and I ascend back up and I come back down. But eventually, eventually the ascension will be a permanent transformation.

So he says one more time – he wants you to know this. Remember now:

This is the secret that the world does not know, which is that harmony of a permanent nature can only be attained as the spiritual Self or the Soul realm is realized through impersonalization and nothingizing of the carnal mind or mental malpractice and then a launching out into the deep in silence.

So he says:

A universal illusion binds you to earth. Realize this, understand this, because only through this understanding (that's half of the equation) *can we begin to lessen its hold upon us. The more fascinated we are with conditions of human good the greater our desire for even the good things, the more intense is the illusion.*

And so if you're still practicing principles to heal that cold of yours or to increase your harmony at work or to increase your supply, if you're still trying to demonstrate anything other than death of the human and ascending into the Soul realm, then you are – well, more intense is the illusion.

(However) In proportion as our thought dwells on God, on the things of the Spirit, the greater freedom from limitation we are gaining.

This should not be "thought" here; this should be "awareness" – in proportion as our awareness is on God. So he says:

(Don't think.) *Think neither on the discords nor on the harmonies.*

That's it. Don't think on either one, because then you're thinking – well, then you're in the human mind!

Let us not fear the evil nor love the good of human existence. In proportion as we accomplish this, the mesmeric influence (lessens).

And we are lifted. We catch a glimpse – well, here it is:

The first glimpse into the heaven of here and now is the beginning of the ascension. This ascension is understood as rising above the conditions and experiences of "this world," (or the dream mind) and we behold "many mansions" prepared for us in spiritual Consciousness – in the awareness of the Soul realm.

So, the many mansions are in your awareness of the Soul realm. And finally:

No good thing is withheld from us as we look above the physical evidence (or the mind) to the great Invisible (to the Soul realm). Look up, look up! The kingdom of heaven (the Soul realm) is at hand!

And finally:

The I of you – am ever with you. (So) Look up.

All right. So that is *The New Horizon* where he explains the Soul realm and gives you some hints about what you might experience.

Now getting back to our original halfway point in this Introduction from the book <u>Man Was Not Born to Cry</u> called *Awake*, remember he says:

355

I wish I could use as a title for a book Santa Claus God because that is what the majority of the concepts of God are. Be assured that no one can enter the realm of the Soul with any such God in mind. You have to leave behind all that you have heretofore expected.

All right? So, he says:

You long to tell your companions what you are thinking and what you are doing (on the spiritual path) *and you want to share your joys and your successes. (But) That cannot be done on this path because those who have not been there can have no way of being able to share them. Only rarely do you find a companion with whom you can share, and even then you discover that there are some things that must remain forever hidden.*

Do you not understand that if you tried to explain to someone—well he—he was sneaky. He wrote it in the chapter *The New Horizon* very briefly, just in one or two or three paragraphs that above this sense-life is the Soul realm and here's what you'll find. But he couldn't go out and explain that to people, talk to every day people as he's riding in an airplane to South Africa and finds himself next to a person on the airplane. Could he start talking about that? No. He said he never talked about spiritual matters. Like everybody else he talked about the weather and whatever the current politics were probably. Whatever topic the person brought up. Always with his finger on his lips because no one would understand that.

I can't go tell somebody what it felt like when I was dissolving right there – sitting in my meditation I was dissolving and becoming infinite. I felt my presence everywhere throughout the house in every room and every room inside of me, and we were one and I was about to go infinite. I can't explain that. Who can explain that? How does that feel? They think maybe you are fooling yourself.

So he says:

Does this not account for the Master's loneliness during his three-year ministry? When he wanted to reveal some of the secrets of the (Soul realm or the) fourth-dimensional life, he could take only three of his disciples with him. All twelve could never have been prepared to see that the men who lived five hundred years before the time of the Master were not only living then, but were standing right there with them sharing with them their wisdom. He never told that to the twelve disciples – only to three – and I am sure there were some secrets he did not tell even the three. This is that "aloneness" that comes in this life when we find that we can share our accomplishments and attainments with only a very few.

And that again is something that makes people very uncomfortable. It makes some very uncomfortable because who wants to live in this inner ecstasy and not be able to tell a single person? It really is sometimes quite lonely, and yet it's not alone because the presence of God is right there with you. Your own Soul, the Soul realm is right there at hand. You may go in and come out and find pasture. Yet we long to have another person to look at eye to eye and say this is the experience and it's so wonderful and hear them say, "Yes, I know!" I was told by my very first teacher that, years ago, centuries ago, you might go your whole entire life and only see one other person at some point that had this awareness. And he said now we're spoiled if we go a year or two and we meet somebody. We think that's not enough, and perhaps he was right.

So I'm talking to about twenty of you (200 now in 2020) and I hope you are not afraid of aloneness.

The moment you enter the higher consciousness, (or the Soul realm) your vision expands and you can see events of the present, the past, and the future. It is like standing on an eleventh floor balcony where you can see for miles in all directions, whereas the man on the street is aware only of that which is taking place right before his eyes.

And again, that adds to the aloneness because if you can see – or let us put it this way. When you are in the Soul realm and you see all of this, all the good and the bad, are a part of this mental malpractice being projected into the mind, how can you then stand up and fight for a cause, any cause? I don't care how beautiful it is. Are you not patching a human dream world? Now I'm not saying that you should go live on the side of a mountain in a cave somewhere and become an ascetic, but on the other hand – well, like Joel he says he believes that these principles need to be practiced right in the midst of wherever you find yourself and that he finds joy in meeting others on this path, and you can't do that when you're sitting in a cave.

But do you not see that it sort of drains from you all of these causes you were ready to pick up and battle for? You see the futility of it? You're standing on the eleventh floor looking out. You can see all the way to the coast and maybe beyond partway to the ocean. But the man on the street, he just sees the stores across the street and the cars coming down the street and the people. Perhaps the clouds overhead and the trees. And you can't talk about it. It becomes lonely at times, and so many people cannot endure that aloneness. It's too uncomfortable and they go back. They choose perhaps unconsciously to remain a human being – not quite ready to launch out into the deep, the unknown, Infinite Eternal.

Man was not meant to cry, and all his tears are shed only because of a sense of limitation. Every tear you shed is proof of some form of limitation being experienced in your life. Man was not born to cry!

The more you search around in your body and in your mind, the more imprisoned you will become. Do not think for a moment that you are free of the body or the mind. Rather you must understand through your study, you are breaking out of the body and the mind into the realm of the Soul. When you reach that (Soul) Realm, and even as you approach it, the mind and the body will be discovered to be more receptive to God-government and require less and less of human attention.

Eventually you will be released from this imprisonment by an act of grace.

Something will happen to you.

Again, what is he saying? He's saying that this will be a permanent transformation. Remember he told us one of his secrets at the Hotel Wellington that he realized that the human scene has no contact with God. Yet in the final secret he says harmony in the human scene does come when we reach the realm of the Soul through impersonalizing and nothingizing. It all fits together perfectly. So this is the same as seek the Soul realm and harmony will be revealed. Why? Because as the light touches the darkness, the darkness disappears and more of the Soul realm is revealed – only the mind interprets that as harmony.

So eventually something will happen in you, an act of grace in which the Soul realm becomes the governing factor to you. The Soul realm manifests itself. Now you're no longer living, watching the human mind manifest its good and its evil – sometimes good, but mostly evil – as a human existence, a dream world. Now you're not living in that sense of me. Now you're standing aside and watching the Soul realm manifest itself as the son of God. Divine Love forming Itself. And eventually this becomes a permanent transformation. You become not a human, but you become Christ, which is the activity of God on earth, or the activity of God appearing. And it becomes a permanent dispensation.

All right. So he says:

Eventually you're released from this imprisonment by an act of grace. Something will happen to you.

In the <u>Beyond Words and Thoughts</u> chapter, The Unveiling, *(Truth Unveiled)* he says, eventually, the Soul takes over. It lives you. That's what we're doing. We're making a transformation within and we're standing – well, we're making the ascension over the mind and the human dream experience into the Soul realm and the living Christ experience. We've had this opportunity presented to us many, many, many times. Now I believe that we're ready. I believe we're really ready to do this, to have this experience.

With (all) these efforts you prepare yourself for (that) act of grace which will eventually set you free. You can see why angels are pictured with wings, and the reason (that) I speak of "soaring thoughts," "mountaintop experiences," or "lofty heights of consciousness." (Because) When the Soul is released, it flies upward, not in time and space, but in consciousness.

Again, the realms of Soul, the many mansions are in awareness of Reality, and the Soul flies upward in consciousness. It's all taking place in your consciousness – moving out of the mind into the Soul.

It is no longer anchored to the ground or entombed in a body and a mind: it is a soaring awareness, a soaring faculty.

When a person experiences physical death, it is mistakenly thought that his Soul leaves (his) body, but that's a mistaken sense of an actual truth. (And the truth is) *As you "die daily"* (which is what we're talking about) *to the mental and physical sense of life, then the Soul is released and flies upward.* (All right?) *It becomes alive because of your "death" of the false sense of self. In that day you are released from the tomb of body and mind, and then the Soul is free.*

Thus the Soul realm becomes your permanent dwelling place whether walking, talking, eating, sleeping.

You are the Soul that lives. But first you must know the you that is that Soul, and then you must begin to explore, search, and seek until you find Me, until you find your Self (your Soul), the real you. That is the you that God sent forth to live God's life on earth, the you that was never born, the you that will never die, the you that for a moment is entombed in a "parenthesis," and struggling to break out.

And here he repeats his exercise.

If you search your body from your toes to the top of your head trying to locate where you are, you will discover you do not exist anywhere between the head and the toes. You cannot find your Self in any part of the body, and this should give you your first clue "If I am not in this body, where am I?" (And so) the search for the man of God's creation begins. (And) The great adventure has begun!

So the search for the man of God's creation begins. That which is made is not made of that which doth appear, and that includes you. You are not made of that which doth appear. That which doth appear is a mental malpractice, universal, pumping into everyone's mind. But that is not you, and as you let it go and become willing to let it go – bad and good – be willing, he says – you must be willing to let 'em both go and stop trying to patch it up. Then you can drop it and stand still, and in the stillness ascend into the Soul realm. All right.

You will be able to see God has planted the fullness of himself in you (and) nothing can be added to you and nothing can be taken from you, you really (do) live in your Self-completeness in God (in your Soul, in the Soul realm). You will then never seek outside yourself, but you will be free to share twelve baskets full every hour of the day without any thought. Then you will be living a life of joy, heaven on earth, but not until you see Me as I AM – see your Self as it is, not locked up in a body (no), incorporeal, spiritual, omnipresent, free.

(And) Then you will know why is it written (in the Song Celestial by Krishna):

"Weapons reach not the Life; Flame burns it not, water cannot overwhelm," for you are I, made of the very nature of God— indestructible, indivisible, inseparable from God. Neither life nor death can separate you from life, God, love, fulfillment!

And that's the Introduction by Joel written in June – well, written on June 30th, which is today, only 1963, and so he wrote that exactly 50 years ago today. Isn't that interesting? I had no idea. He invites you in that Introduction to leave behind the limited human sense of self, that universal mental malpractice pumped into the human mind. He invites you to drop it, to see its nothingness. Make no attempt to patch it up, change it, or improve it. Just drop it. Do not bring it with you. He invites you to leave behind all your concepts. Leave them on the shore. Leave them. Loose them and let them go. He invites you to step into the boat, the boat of Is. Launch out into the deep, into the center of the Soul realm within you. Let your Soul reveal itself. Be still and know. Launch out into the deep and stand still. Invite the Soul to reveal itself to take over.

No concepts. No self. No ideas. Just an empty vessel floating, listening, waiting upon the Lord.

[Silent pause]

And says Joel:

The day will come when this will be your permanent dwelling place and the Soul will take over. And then Grace lives your life. You are no longer under the law of mental malpractice. You are free. No more evil. No more good. Just God, Soul manifest, Is'ing the harmony of being. Your incorporeal, spiritual Self, your eternal infinite Life living itself as itself as Soul.

Thank you, Joel. We accept the invitation. We take your invitation and we launch out into the deep. We recognize our place in infinity. We recognize we are in the middle an ascension, a transformation from humanhood to Christhood. We do not know what that is as an experience, but we are ready. We launch out. We act on the invitation. *Act as though I am, and I will be, saith the Lord.* And this act is an inner act, letting go, launching out, and resting on an infinite sea of Spirit.

Thank you, Father. God Is. I am Soul.

Please, my friends, take a moment. Drop me a private E-mail or public – it doesn't matter. Tell me if you are enjoying these uncomfortable talks. If it's helping, I would like to know.

In 1959 Joel became aware that he wasn't aware that the students weren't getting the principles of impersonalization and nothingization. They were not understanding the nature of error and so he devoted the entire – or he was <u>instructed</u> to devote the entire year of 1959 to teaching those principles so the students would have a firm grasp on that half of the equation, because until then all they knew was contemplating God and how beautiful God was and they were missing the other part.

Now here we are fifty years after his writing that Introduction called *Awake*, fifty years to the day, and <u>I'm</u> wondering if you're getting these principles I'm spending time pouring out. Now if you are or you aren't, I would still spend time pouring out because that's what's happening to me. I can't stop it. But I would still like to know if you're getting, if you're benefiting. If you're finding these talks helpful, I'd like to know because sometimes I make a talk or two or three and time goes on and I hear from one or two people, and I know hundreds are hearing them when I put them on the website, and yet no one is saying anything. And so it would be helpful to me if I could get a feeling of whether or not you're getting something from these talks. Okay?

So I look to hear from you and if you have questions – oh, by all means write! Please write! I have to give it away. I have to share, and so if you have questions, I can share and maybe lift your burden, make it easier. Or if you have things to share that are beautiful, I'd like to hear that too. Okay?

This then brings to a close Part II of the Introduction *Awake* from the book <u>Man Was Not Born to Cry</u>, and as always I wish to say thank you very, very much, and I love you.

[Silence]

MY KINGDOM IS NOT OF THIS WORLD

Bill: Good morning.

This is Sunday August 4, 2013. You know, it never ceases to amaze me, but every time I pick up this little black book called The Infinite Way, I find something new, and this morning was no different. In the very first chapter called *Putting on Immortality* is probably the answer to every problem we've ever had. And so I thought maybe a review is in order. And so let's look at it together, shall we? It starts with a quote from the Bible:

"In the beginning was the Word, and the Word was with God, and the Word was God. And the Word was made flesh."

"The Word was made flesh" but it still is the Word. By being made flesh it does not change its nature, character, or substance. Cause becomes visible as effect, but the essence or substance is still the Word, Spirit or Consciousness.

In this way we understand that there is not a spiritual universe <u>and</u> a material world, but rather what appears as our world is the Word made flesh, or Spirit made visible, or Consciousness expressed as idea.

And so there you have it. There is not a spiritual universe and a material world.

Now we reviewed and looked at the chapter *The New Horizon* several times; many, many times, and in it he says that:

Above this sense-life is a universe of Spirit governed by Love.

And that can give you the feeling that there's two universes, a spiritual universe above this one or behind this one or however you want to say it. But still we can come away with a misperception, a misconception that there's two universes. Yet right here in the very beginning before we even start our study in this book he spells it out plainly.

We understand there is not a spiritual universe <u>and</u> a material world.

Well then, what does that mean in relation to our trying to get a healing of our body? What does that mean when we try to go to God and get a healing of our finances, of our relationships? What does that mean when we try to pull God into this world or practice spiritual principles upon this world? Somehow pull that spiritual influence into my every day life.

Seems like that would be a total waste of time, doesn't it? And yet that's exactly what we do for years and years. Clearly he says:

All the error that has existed down through the ages is founded on the theory or belief of two worlds, one the heavenly kingdom, or spiritual life, and the other a material world or mortal existence, each separate from the other.

Now that is <u>all</u> the error is founded on that belief, and so if in any way we find ourselves in our prayer and meditation attempting to contact that inner realm to produce a change out here in this realm, in this world, then we are operating in error.

In spite of the sense of two worlds, men have always attempted to bring harmony into the discords of human existence through an attempt, by prayer, to contact this other world, or spiritual realm, and to bring Spirit, or God, to act upon the so-called material existence.

And that's completely wrong. So he says:

365

Let us (And *us* is italicized. It means all of us in The Infinite Way.) *Let us then begin with the understanding that our world is not an erroneous one,* (I can't tell you the number of E-mails that start out by saying, "I understand that the world is an illusion." Right here he says), (We must) *begin with the understanding that our world is* (not an illusion), *not an erroneous one.*

Well, let's read the whole paragraph.

Let us then begin with the understanding that our world is not an erroneous one, but rather that the universe in which we live is the realm of reality about which man entertains a false concept. The work of bringing health and harmony into our experience is not, then, getting rid of, or even changing, a material (mortal) universe, but (in) correcting the finite concept of our existence.

All right. Clearly, very plainly he spells out you are standing in Reality, the realm of Reality. Now remember over in *The New Horizon* he says:

Above the sense-life is a universe of Spirit.

So you could have just as well said behind or below or next to or beyond – not necessarily above in the sense of you look up and see the sky up there. More in the sense of when you ascend up over the mind you see clearly. You don't see through the concepts in the mind – that sort of above.

So plainly he says here we must begin with the understanding that we are standing in the spiritual realm. Right? Is this not what this means? We live in the realm of Reality, but we entertain a false concept? So the work, our work then is not to try to get spiritual principles to act upon these false concepts because it's never going to happen. Joel in his Wisdom said plainly:

I have told you the <u>real</u> secret of life: God is not with mortals. Take it from there.

And so if you can see it, hear it, taste it, touch it, or smell it—God's not with it.

If you can see it, hear it, taste it, touch it, or smell it – those are concepts, sense perceptions, concepts. Your sense perceptions turned into concepts in the mind, and that's what you're dealing with – concepts in the mind. Standing in the spiritual realm, standing in the realm of Reality, but not seeing any of it. Praying for some outside force to come in and change these concepts, only we don't even see them as concepts. We see them as my leg, my finances, my relationship, my friendship, my spouse, my partner, my job.

All right. Let's continue.

(When we seek for truth we start out our search) *with a problem – perhaps with many problems. (And) The first years of our search are devoted to overcoming discords and healing disease through prayer to some higher Power or to the application of spiritual laws or truth to these mortal conditions. The day arrives, however, when we discover that the application of truth to human problems does not "work" or does not work as it once did.*

All right. And if you find yourself there that's a good place to be! It means you're ready. Remember over here in *The New Horizon* where he says:

Be willing for the harmonious as well as the inharmonious conditions of mortal existence to disappear from your experience in order that reality may be known and enjoyed and lived.

So we must be willing for **all** of these concepts to disappear out of our experience, and that means a healthy leg or a sick leg. That means abundant finances or lacking finances. That means harmonious human relationships or discordant human relationships. Be willing for the pairs of opposites to disappear in order that you may enjoy the realm of oneness in which you stand. We can see this is an internal work, which is why he says:

The work of bringing health and harmony into our experience is not getting rid of, or changing, a material universe, but correcting (or dissolving) *the finite concept of our existence.*

So he says:

Eventually we are led to the great revelation that mortals only put on immortality as mortality disappears – they do not add immortal spiritual harmony to human conditions. God does not create, nor does He control material affairs. "The natural man receiveth not the things of the Spirit of God: they are spiritually discerned."

So he asks you a question. Remember this is the very first chapter! Seems pretty advanced now, doesn't it? He asks us a question:

Are we seeking "the things of the Spirit of God" for some human purpose, or are we really endeavoring to "put off" the mortal in order that we may behold the harmony of the spiritual realm?

And there you have it right there. That's the inner work that we should be doing. Are we seeking the Spirit of God and trying to get God to – and trying to apply God to our sore foot or to our bad finances or to our unhealthy relationships or to our miserable job? Are we seeking to apply spiritual principles to bring about a change in those things? Well if we are, then we're not putting off, attempting to put off mortality. We're not willing that the good and the bad images be removed, concepts be dissolved so that we may behold the spiritual Real. No, we're still clinging to them and thinking somehow we can have our cake and eat it too! I can hang onto this mortal existence and I can apply God to it. But that's what we did in the very early days, according to Joel, and now we should be at a point where that's no longer working. We should be at a point where we're ready for these difficult talks. So he says:

While we strive and struggle and contend with the so-called powers of this world, (and we fight and combat) *sickness and sin or lack.*

While we're doing that – we're fighting these things or maybe just trying to apply spiritual principles to them, well – the whole time while we're doing that.

Spiritual sense reveals that "My kingdom is not of this world."

Now again, that has been misunderstood. *"My kingdom is not of this world"* does not mean that there's two worlds, a kingdom and a this world. This world was a name given to sense perceptions formed into mental concepts. There is no "this world!" It was never made. **It was not made!** In the beginning God breathed into existence the Word, which then appeared as flesh. It formed Itself, and so you're standing in a divine kingdom, in a heavenly realm, completely and totally unaware of it. You have no awareness of it because you're entertaining these concepts, walking around in the mind all the time.

And so our work as he says – well, what do you do about these concepts? Are you able to heal yourself? Are you able to break these concepts, what he calls elsewhere "breaking the hypnotism?" If you are, then you don't need to ever read anything again. You don't need to listen to any talks and you should probably be teaching because there are others that would really love to know how you break the hypnotism. Now if our job is to dissolve these concepts so that we may open our eyes and behold the Reality – the realm of Reality – you have to ask yourself, "How do I break these concepts? Why they seem to run me." Well, we're going to explain exactly how to do that.

Only as we transcend the desire to improve our humanhood do we understand this vital statement.

What vital statement? That *"My kingdom is not of this world,"* or you might say, the realm of Reality has nothing to do with these concepts of human life.

When we leave the realm of human betterment, we catch the first glimpse of the meaning of "I have overcome the world."

Now you see how exactly that ties into *The New Horizon?* Look! Listen!

When we leave the realm of human betterment, we catch the first glimpse.

And over here he says in *The New Horizon:*

The first glimpse of Reality – of the Soul-realm – comes with the recognition and realization of the fact all temporal conditions and experiences are products of self-hypnotism. With the realization that the entire human scene – its good as well as its evil – is illusion, comes the first glimpse and taste of the world of God's creation and of the sons of God who inhabit (that) spiritual kingdom.

All right. Our work is what? Is it practicing spiritual principles to improve humanhood? No. Every time you catch yourself practicing spiritual principles so that you might have a little more supply or a little better health or more harmonious relationships – you need to stop right there because probably it isn't working. That's what we did in the past when we were in the metaphysical part. Now we're moving into the mystical part where we should be willing to put off mortality, where we should be willing for the harmonious as well as the inharmonious conditions of humanhood to disappear. Both! All! So he says:

We have not overcome the world while we are seeking to have (less of the world's troubles or) *less of the world's pains and more of the world's pleasures and profits.* And (if we are still doing that) *if we are not overcoming the sense of struggle over worldly affairs,* (well, then we cannot enter the realm of the Real or) *the realm of (heaven or) heavenly affairs.*

And then he quotes this – he says:

"Love not the world, neither the things that are in the world. If any man love the world, the love of the Father is not in him." (And he asks) *Does this sound as if we were becoming ascetic?*

I mean doesn't that sound like we're supposed to leave the world and go live in a cave somewhere? Yet now we know that this is an inside job, don't we? Has nothing to do with any changes.

Has nothing to do with whether you eat meat or you don't eat meat, whether you pray in a church with your hat on or your shoes off, whether you wear a veil or nothing, whether you bow to the east or the west, whether you light incense. None of those things have anything to do with it! And that's what he's going to say:

Do we appear now to be desiring a life apart from normal successful walks of life? Do not be deceived. (No.) *Spiritual sense does not remove us from our normal surroundings, (and it does not) deprive us of the love and companionship necessary to a full life. It places it on a higher level where it is no longer at the mercy of chance or change or loss, and where the spiritual value of the so-called human scene is made manifest.*

So you see, you don't have to go anywhere. You don't have to move to India or Mecca. You don't have to go anywhere – Jerusalem. No, not lo here or lo there. The kingdom and the realization of the kingdom takes place within you. That's where the concepts are broken, are melted, are dissolved so that you may see the realm of the Real in which you're standing. So that you may have glimpses of the Word made flesh.

So to continue:

When (you're) confronted with any problem, instead of laboring for an improved human picture turn from the picture and realize the presence of (a) divine Spirit in you.

Now, this does not mean – now listen – that you turn from these concepts in the mind to other concepts in the mind and start repeating in your mind, "Oh, this is not true. This is an illusion. Only God is here, only God is here, only God is here – because then are you dissolving these concepts? No, you're taking and forming new concepts, spiritual concepts, and putting them on top of these other concepts.

It's still all taking place in the mind, and he told us truth cannot be known with the mind. That's the starting place in the Kailua study. Truth cannot be known with the mind. So, it's something else then, isn't it? When he says – see, he's very tricky here. It takes sometimes years to figure out what it means. And he says here:

The work of bringing health and harmony into our experience is not getting rid of, or changing the mortal material universe, but correcting the finite concept of our existence.

Yes, but how do you break the finite concepts so that you may see Infinite Being? Let me know how you bring that about in the mind.

Well, you can't.

So to continue:

Turn from the picture (he says) *and realize the presence of divine Spirit.*

Now this "realize" means be still until you come into the awareness, the actual feel of infinite Spirit because—*this Spirit dissolves the human seeming and reveals spiritual harmony.* So there you go. Your mind can't do it. Your body can't do it. *"Not by might, nor by power, but by my Spirit."* Only Spirit can dissolve these human concepts and reveal spiritual harmony.

Though to sight this harmony will appear as improved human health or wealth.

Yes, when you have the awareness of Reality, the concepts dissolve and you see more of Reality. Of course, the mind translates that as prosperity or health or harmony.

When Jesus fed the multitude, it was his spiritual consciousness of abundance that appeared.

See, it was the consciousness of abundance.

When he healed the sick, it was his feeling of the Presence.

So up here we have the consciousness or the conscious awareness of infinite abundance and down here we have a feeling of the divine Presence which appears as health and strength and harmony.

So he says:

We are living in a spiritual universe, but the finite sense has set a picture before us of limitation. While thought is on the picture(s) before us (that which is called "this world") *we are engaged in the constant effort to improve or change* [well, what– concepts?] *As soon as we lift our vision and take thought off what we shall eat or drink or wear, we begin to behold spiritual reality which appears to us as improved belief, but which is really more-appearing of reality. This more-appearing reality brings with it joys untold here and now.*

All right. So our work is an internal work. First the recognition that we are living in a series of universal concepts in the mind and recognizing at least intellectually at first that we're standing in the realm of Reality. We're standing in our true identity. We're standing in infinite being. Standing in the kingdom of heaven, but entertaining these concepts. So now we know that the work is going within and finding a way to have these concepts broken or have them dissolved. And he spells it out so beautifully in The Art of Spiritual Healing that it just ties in here perfectly. If you want to awaken, this is the way. This is The Infinite Way.

In spiritual healing, whether the claim is named Jones, Brown, or Smith (no matter what the concept); *whether the claim is named cancer, (tuberculosis), or polio; whether the claim is called unemployment, depression, or unhappy relationships; do not be tricked into treating persons or conditions.*

Because those are concepts and you're trying to improve concepts. No. What do you do? How do you get these concepts dissolved? That's the question!

Leave them alone get back to (a) substance-less substance to which you can give any name you like.

All right. So if you look at these and you go, "Wait a minute! Wait a minute! These are concepts, mental concepts, universal concepts," or you can call them universal belief or carnal mind. You can call them hypnotism, mesmerism. He says:

*It can be anything as long as you interpret it as meaning (nothing)
nothingness – having no substance, no law, and no cause.*

So if you come up with—okay, these are universal concepts
about the kingdom. This concept says it's female and it's 35. This
concept says it's male and it's 90, almost dead. This concept says
it's dying. This concept says it's being born. This concept says
it's abundant. This concept says it's lacking. This concept says
it's harmonious. This concept says it's limited. You see? If you
like concepts, then you can see that they're universal concepts,
universal beliefs, nothingness—then that'll be what you do. You
don't try to practice spiritual principles to improve these concepts.
You come within—well, here. He'll explain it right here.

*It can be anything as long as you interpret it as meaning
nothingness.*

When you really (really) *begin to comprehend that in healing you
are not dealing with people as people, when you learn to eliminate
them and their claims from your thought, and in every instance
deal with the root of the problem* (which is concepts) *carnal mind,
nothingness – then you will find how quickly you will be able to
become consciously aware of a spiritual Presence within you. This
Presence cannot be felt until you are free of the barrier: (And) The
barrier is the belief in two powers;* (or a concept of two powers) *the
barrier is the belief in something apart from God.*

You can choose the word temptation if you like that too.

*The minute you have made it a nothingness, you no longer have
two powers and (then) you can do just what it says in Scripture, rest
in His word. You can rest in this Word, waiting* [**waiting**] *for the
Spirit of the Lord God to be upon you; and when it comes* [**it breaks
the concepts**], *it breaks the hypnotism.*

The Spirit does, not your mind and not your memory of truth.
Not your reciting truth. Not your spiritual concepts. None of that.
You have to get <u>out</u> of those concepts. The work that we have

to do is turn within, recognize these are concepts, nothingness. Drop them. Stop playing with them or trying to improve them. Just stand stock still. Remember that from the Kailua study series? Stand stock still and wait. He told us that. Remember? Do that twelve times a day. Wait and sooner or later you will feel an inner movement.

He says here, and this is probably the most important paragraph I have ever read:

For years after I had learned to recognize all forms of sin, disease, lack, limitation, and depression are hypnotism, the puzzle was to discover how to break the hypnotism.

It was then that I discovered the scriptural passage "the stone was cut out of the mountain without hands." Our weapon against error (or against concepts – the weapon that will break them) *our offense and defense is something that is neither physical, mental, no action, no words, no thoughts—only the awareness of God.*

You see, your awareness – awareness dissolves mind or concepts. It doesn't dissolve mind – it dissolves mental concepts in the mind. So standing in spiritual awareness dissolves mental concepts and then you become aware of, more aware of reality appearing of the spiritual realm in which you are standing. Again he says:

As you carry this out in practice, watching the stone being formed of your consciousness while you stand to one side as a witness or a beholder, eventually a state of peace will come. Then you will catch a glimpse [there's that word again – a glimpse] *of God as Is – not a power over anything, just God is. You begin to understand no power does anything to anyone, and you become a beholder as reality begins to appear. All problems (will) fade out in proportion as you develop this ability to be quiet, and to behold, to witness divine harmony unfold.*

Now, one last piece here from – well, that is by the way, that's the chapter *What Did Hinder You?* from <u>The Art of Spiritual Healing</u>. One last piece from here. He says:

The principle behind this process, (If you need a principle, here's the principle). *The principle is; Inasmuch as the activity of human mind is the substance of hypnotism.*

Okay, did you catch that? That's just as plain as you can make it anywhere. The activity of the human mind, the thoughts of the human mind are the activity of hypnotism. Yes, because they're concepts!

We are going to learn to live outside of the activity of the human mind. We are going to live in spiritual awareness.

(So) *The principle behind the process is; Inasmuch as the activity of the human mind is the substance and the activity of hypnotism, when the human mind is not functioning, there is no more hypnotism. When you are not thinking thoughts or words, when you are in a stillness, the human mind is stopped – the hypnotism is gone. When you experience this, you will feel something which transcends the human dimension.*

So he warns you –

Do not battle forms of error. Do not try to lop off rheumatism or (tuberculosis) or cancer. Do not try to lop off old age. Do not try to change the appearance world.

Do not try to apply spiritual principles to bring about a change!

Get back, get back (inside yourself)*!*

If, with every claim that comes to you, you can set aside any thought of the person (or the condition) *and go back to some word or term to you which means nothingness, so that you have only one power – then you can sit in meditation and you will feel the descent of the Holy Spirit; you will feel the peace (which) passes understanding; you will feel a divine Presence* (and this will release you from the concepts).

Now is that not plain? Do we not see our work? Do we see what work we're involved in? How we're putting off mortality and putting on immortality and in the process we catch glimpses of the realm of Reality?

So to continue with *Putting on Immortality*, he says:

How often do we go on the rocks! How frequently we attempt to understand spiritual wisdom with human intellect! This leads to mental indigestion we are attempting to digest spiritual food with our educated mentality. It will not work.

Now what that means to me is – well, I have three degrees. I have one in computers, one in business management, and one in counseling/psychology. Now with all of that educated mentality, I cannot melt a single concept because what I really have is three degrees in material concepts! (chuckles) Right? And all of my great thinking, my best thinking is the problem. We just read that. Human thought is the activity of hypnotism. Ouch!! Wow, this is a little bit deeper than I thought, huh? I have to be willing for all of my human concepts, good and bad, to be dissolved so that my immortal Self may stand there in its purity.

Truth (he says) *is not a reasoning process.*

That's why when you go within and you say these truths to yourself mentally and you repeat them, nothing happens because knowing this truth is not the same as having the spiritual awareness. Spiritual awareness is a coming up over knowing the truth to being the truth. Remember? The ascension is always the same he says in *Truth Unveiled* in <u>Beyond Words and Thoughts</u>, that of coming up over the mind from knowing the truth to being the truth. Awareness of I is quite different than talking about the presence of God.

So our educated mentality will not help us! So in his words:

Truth is not a reasoning process; therefore, it must be spiritually discerned. Truth does not appeal to our reason, and when it appears to do so, we must search deeply to see if it really is truth. Be suspicious of a truth that seems reasonable.

And so if you were to tell a person or even if you think about it with your educated mentality – all right – I'm standing in a spiritual realm and I can't see it, hear it, taste it, touch it, or smell it. I'm completely blind to it. All I am doing is living up here in the mind in a series of universal concepts, universal beliefs, and I never get outside of it for my entire lifespan.

But if I will go within, transcend that, come up over that or step out of that or be still about that, eventually if I practice like he tells me in the Kailua study series twelve times a day, waiting, eventually I will feel the movement. I will feel the descent of the Holy Spirit, the movement of Spirit across the face of the deep. I will feel the breath. I will hear the Word. Something will happen. There will be a movement, and when that happens the concepts will be dissolved and I will get glimpses of the realm of Reality of God Is'ing, of I.

Now does that sound very reasonable? And when I have those glimpses something out here will fall away – a pain, a limitation, a lack, a disharmony will be dissolved. And that's all there is to it! Ta da!! Now you tell that to someone at Yale or Harvard – not to – I'm not putting down higher education because I have it myself and I have benefited from it. I am saying put this in front of educated mentality of any university – Oxford, any university – and see if they can believe this or accept this. Why, they'll laugh you to scorn!

That's what they did to Jesus. She's not dead, she's sleeping, and they laughed him to scorn. Well eventually he had to put them out of the room and then what happened? His awareness of reality – it manifested and it dissolved the concepts of death, and there it was, eternal Life appeared. Eternal Life was there before, but he was the only one that could see it.

Now says Joel:

Jesus, walking on the water, feeding the multitudes with a few loaves and fishes, healing the sick and raising the dead – does that sound reasonable to you? (chuckles, yeah, oh yeah!) *If the principle underlying these experiences was understood through reason, all the churches would be teaching them. But this principle is apparent only to spiritual sense.*

You see? This principle is apparent only in your silence when you feel that movement and the awareness comes to you. That's the only way to be aware, and that's the only way concepts will be broken or that's the only way to break the hypnotism. What was possible to Christ consciousness then is possible to that same consciousness now.

So he says:

Instead of trying to make Spirit operate upon our human bodies and material affairs, let us learn to disregard these pictures (these concepts) *and keep our vision on things above.*

That does not mean mentally affirm or make affirmations. That means step out of that mind and be fed from within.

When we "come down to earth again," we shall find the discords and limitations (have disappeared) *and more of reality (is) appearing.*

All right.

To receive the word of God (or the awareness which breaks concepts) *or spiritual sense,* (he says) *we need to feel rather than reason. This is referred to as receiving the word "in the heart." We understand that neither seeing, hearing, tasting, touching, (or) smelling will reveal spiritual truth or its harmonies;*

No, they won't. That won't dissolve the concepts. We've tried that.

Therefore it must come through a different faculty, the intuitive faculty which acts through feeling, (through spiritual feeling). *Heretofore, we have sat down to pray or to meditate and immediately a stream of words and thought[s] started to flow. Perhaps we began to affirm truth and deny error. You can see that this is in the realm of the human mind.*

Yes, this is adding – trying to add spiritual concepts to our human concepts. Trying to add God to our humanhood, and it does not work. And in the very first chapter in the very first book, the very first principle he ever revealed to us is exactly the same as what was in the Kailua study series. We must come up over that mind filled with universal concepts and in the silence, in the non-activity of that mind, Spirit reveals the realm of the Real, and that awareness, every glimpse of that realm, melts some concepts.

In cultivating our spiritual sense we become receptive to (that) which (comes) to us from within. We become hearers of the Word not speakers. We become so attuned to Spirit that we feel the divine harmony of being; we feel the actual presence of God. Having transcended the five physical senses (and the concepts which are derived from them)*, our intuitive faculty is alert, receptive and responsive to the things of the Spirit, and we begin our new existence as a result of this spiritual rebirth.*

Now see how he just slides things in there. I mean, listen to that half a sentence:

We begin our 'new existence' as a result of this spiritual rebirth.

He's telling you right there that the way to be born again of the Spirit is to be born again by stepping out of these universal concepts and allowing that Spirit to motivate, to move, to function through us, as us. That awareness to descend, to flow. Use whatever words you like. It means that Spirit is living us; no longer a mortal, but an immortal is living us. And he tells us right here – this is the rebirth. This is it! This is the thing itself. How, how Nicodemus says. How do I get born again, and Jesus pretty much tells him you can't understand. I can't explain it to you. You don't have the spiritual discernment. And Joel says to us – look, this is going to take spiritual discernment. You can't do this with your body. You can't do this with your mind. In fact, **you can't do this!** It has to **happen** to you when you stand stock still.

So, he says:

Heretofore, we have been concerned with the letter of truth, (but) now only with the Spirit.

You see, right from the start he was trying to tell us the difference, and I thought that it took all the way until 1955 before he revealed the principle in the Kailua study series. It turns out in the very first chapter in 1947 he said, "Here it is, folks! Do this." People read it and they didn't get it. They read it and they thought they still needed to make affirmations and denials.

We are not so concerned now with what is truth as with feeling truth.

You see? You don't want any new concepts. You don't want spiritual concepts. You don't want an understanding of what truth is so you can go write a book. That won't break the concept or the hypnotism or bring about what appears as a healing. No.

This is accomplished in proportion as we give less thought to the letter and more receptivity to the feel. This word "feel" refers to awareness, consciousness, or sense of truth.

You see? You see, he said it right from the beginning. You need to have awareness of truth. Awareness dissolves thought. How do you break these concepts? Now this is the whole work again, remember, right from the very beginning of this chapter. It looks like it's one, two, three, four, five – the fifth paragraph in the very first book:

The work of bringing health and harmony (in) our experience is not getting rid of, or changing, a material universe, but correcting the finite concept.

And replacing it, replacing the finite concept with awareness of being.

So says he:

Spiritual healing is the natural result of a divinely illumined consciousness.

We misunderstand immortality (he says) *when we think of it as the immortality of the human personality, or personal sense.*

Yes, that's not rebirth into an eternal life, and that's again – see, we thought from the very beginning we did not understand what Joel had experienced. He experienced a transformation. He transitioned out of humanhood into Christhood, and he was trying to explain to us how he did it and how we could go and do likewise. But we came from a completely human point of view and thought – well, okay – I guess he's – he's teaching me spiritual principles so I can fix my human problems, or he's telling me how I – meaning me, the person – can come into my eternal life.

Well, me the person has no eternal life! There is no me the person eternal life. These are part of these universal concepts. Me the person is a universal concept, a series of universal concepts.

You see? That's why these are The Uncomfortable Talks. We're coming face to face with the truth. Me the person is a series of universal concepts, and that is not eternal. That needs to die and die as soon as possible, and when that dies, even if just for a moment it dies in meditation and I find I am not in that – I am standing still and beholding – I'm witnessing – then this movement of Spirit reveals an infinite being right here, right now, and I am one with it, and it is one with me, and I am in it and it is in me, and it is the I that I am. That is the eternal Life. That is the immortal.

And so he says:

Immortality is attained in proportion as personal sense is overcome, whether here or hereafter. As we put off the (person or the) *personal ego and attain the consciousness* (or the awareness) *of real Self - the Reality of us, divine Consciousness - (then) we attain immortality. And that can be achieved here and now.*

You see? From the very, very first chapter he told us what we're going to have to do. We're going to have to die to awaken. He says:

The desire to perpetuate our false sense of body and wealth ensnares us (unto) death, or mortality.

Now remember in *The New Horizon* where he says that we have to be willing for both the good and the evil to fall away to come into our spiritual awareness of the spiritual realm, of the realm where the sons of God are governed by Love? And he tells us that doesn't happen, that can't happen until a large measure of our desire for things of the world has fallen away. Remember? Hold on. We'll find it exactly instead of me trying to paraphrase. Okay. He's talking about glimpsing the realm of the Real.

The experience at first is like watching the world disappear over a horizon and drop down from before us. There is no attachment to this world, no desire to hold onto it – probably because to a great extent the experience does not come until a great measure of our desire for the things of "this world" has been overcome.

All right? So back here in *Putting on Immortality* when he says:

The desire to perpetuate our false sense of body and wealth ensnares us into death, or mortality.

He's saying if you are standing in those universal series of beliefs or concepts called your human life and the human lives you see around you, if you're standing in that – well, then you're going to have to die and you're going to have to experience death again and again and again. But if you're standing in the awareness of the real, of the realm of Reality, if you're standing in your spiritual identity and not entertaining these thoughts but receiving impartations from within – then you're standing in your eternal Life and you never have to experience death again. Never! So – but that won't come until you're willing to let go of the concepts of good and evil both. That won't come until you're really willing to put off mortality and put on immortality, and now you know what that means to put off mortality and put on immortality, and now you know what it means when he says:

God is not with mortals. Take it from there.

I have told you the real secret of life: God is not with mortals.

And he did! That's the real secret of life! Every time he sat down to have a meditation and somebody called for a healing, he disregarded the person and the condition entirely. Saw them as concepts and dropped it and stopped taking thought. Stood stock still. Felt the descent of the Holy Spirit. Felt the movement of Christ and knew that it had been met. The concept in him was dissolved, and then when he opened his eyes again he saw more of Reality appearing. He did what he suggested we do. It's not like it's just a theory or a belief. He lived it, and he's saying that we can too.

And he says:

The first step in the attainment of immortality is living out from the center of our being, as in the idea of unfoldment from within, rather than accretion: It is giving rather than getting; being rather than attaining.

And he says:

It is not a simple matter (to do this) to show forth joy and peace of immortality, because to those intent on preserving their (humanhood) *immortality would appear to be extinction. (But that's not the case). It is the eternal preservation of all that is real, fine, noble, harmonious, gracious, unselfish, and peaceful. It is reality brought to light in place of the illusion of sense* (or concepts). *It's being in the world but not of it.*

So that is the principle – that chapter is the principle: My kingdom is not of this world. And now you know my kingdom is not a place, and this world is not a world. My kingdom is an infinite awareness, and this world is a series of mental concepts, and my kingdom is Consciousness, and this world is mind, human mind. And my true identity is this spiritual kingdom, this spiritual being, spiritual awareness, spiritual consciousness, and I am that. And me, the human – well – was not made.

Yes, *"In the beginning was the Word. And the Word was made flesh,"* and it's still the Word today and you live in the Word and by the Word, and the Word is you, and the Word is I, and there is one Word, and I am That. And there are seven billion me's, seven billion humans, and billions that lived before and billions that will live after this, and yet not one of them was made by God. God has one son, and that son is not of me. Not of the little me.

And so if you've reached a place where these uncomfortable talks are resonating with you or at least part of them are resonating with you, then perhaps you are ready to lay down your human life, your human sense of life, or your sense of human life, and pick up immortality; *henceforth know we no man after the flesh* means now don't see him as a human. Don't see her as a human. Don't see that as an animal. Don't see that as a plant. But stop. Stop. Turn within, as Joel says. Let that go. No person, no condition. It's a series of universal concepts, nothingness.

Now, now Father, reveal the Self, the one Self, the being, the kingdom and stand stock still. And says Joel, if you do this, if you will do this, then the reality of her, of him, of it will be revealed in you. You will have an experience called immaculate conception. The immortal of it, of him, of her – the immortal standing there will be revealed. You will come into the awareness of it.

This is the experience known as the Sabbath where we take no thought, no affirmations, no denials. Let go of the concepts and stand still and wait, and the Spirit moves across the water. It really does. It really does reveal – well, you really do have a glimpse of Reality. And the glimpses come closer and closer together and sometimes you begin to have them with eyes open.

You might be driving a car and suddenly a glimpse of the Real comes upon you. You have opened your consciousness. You have opened the door. You have invited with your inner movement – you have invited Christ to come in and sup with you. *"I stand at the door, and knock,"* and now you have opened it and it comes. And you might be driving down the road and suddenly you have a glimpse of the real. It doesn't affect your driving. You continue on while at the same time inside yourself seeing more of Reality. You might be sitting at work, working on something diligently and suddenly there's that movement within. You feel the Spirit come upon you.

Says John: *"I was in the Spirit on the Lord's day."* You find yourself in the Spirit as an awareness flows into you. Concepts fall away. It happens. It's automatic. The minute you feel it, the second – the nanosecond that you feel that Spirit flowing in, you stop. You stand still. You can't do anything else and awareness comes. It all happens in a matter of seconds. Those standing around you on the job won't even be aware of what happened, which is why we can say that you're standing two feet apart, but in two entirely different universes.

You are standing in the awareness of the kingdom. They're standing in the kingdom, too, but entertaining concepts. And as I say, they come closer together, closer and closer until they begin happening without your – well, without your trying to make them happen. They just come upon you. And according to Joel – it hasn't happened to me entirely yet, but according to Joel eventually It takes over and lives your life completely all the time constantly, and I find that that happens to me maybe an hour at a time, maybe a couple hours, but I still come back to these concepts. And so I'm practicing like you, putting off mortality and putting on immortality, and I'm experiencing it closer and closer together and I'm experiencing it coming upon me while I'm going about my day-to-day affairs. And so I am thoroughly convinced that it will take over and be a constant conscious awareness of the living Reality and I am inviting you to join me.

Now let us be still for a moment.

[Silent pause]

And to sum up one more time: My kingdom is not of these concepts called this world. My kingdom is some other substance, comes from another Source. Not from the mind but from Consciousness. My Kingdom is the Word made flesh and that happens in a moment you think not. You can be consciously beholding that Word becoming flesh. You can behold God itself appearing and *"Behold, I make all things new."* You can be a witness to that newness, to a new heaven and a new earth.

All this Joel told us in the very first chapter in the very first book where he put down what he was experiencing and how we may go and do likewise.

Thank you. Godspeed on your rebirth and blessings, too many to encompass.

[Silence]

CLASS 24

SPIRITUAL RESURRECTION

Bill: Good morning or maybe good afternoon.

This is Sunday August 18th, about 12:30. I was delayed in getting started today because I was drawn to a chapter in this book called <u>Consciousness Transformed</u>, and it is from the 1963-1964 Hawaii Hotel talks by Joel S. Goldsmith. These were the last talks that he ever gave – some of the last talks that he ever gave. There [were] a few more, but not many, because the last talk in this book took place on May 10th of 1964, and I think it was less than a month later he made his transition.

This book is – if you've never seen it – it was out of print for a while, and I'm happy to see that there are some versions available again, but it was out of print for a while and you couldn't get it. It's really thick. It is probably – well, it's like an old family Bible it's so thick. Let's see just out of curiosity. It is 611 pages, so that's pretty thick and the writing's not real big either – 611 pages! It starts on the week of – let me find it – January 20th of 1963 and it runs to May 10th of 1964, and so this was the year as you recall that Joel said he was going through another initiation. He was taking the message out of the letter into the Spirit, or out of metaphysics into mysticism. He was lifting the message and trying to lift the students. [These are] also the talks from which came the book

Beyond Words and Thoughts which was published four years after his transition.

All right, so we have the book called Consciousness Transformed, the 1963-64 Hawaii Hotel talks. He canceled all his reservations to give classes because as he said he was going through an initiation. If you look in Beyond Words and Thoughts in that chapter *Truth Unveiled* he says in there that he was going through an initiation the entire year and that he went through the crucifixion and the resurrection, and that was taken from this book, because I found parts of that chapter in the chapter in here. The book Beyond Words and Thoughts was edited by Lorraine Sinkler and she changed it around to how she felt best. The reason why I like Consciousness Transformed, this thick book, is because it is the talks as he gave them and pretty much they are transcribed. So anyway, this was the last year that he was on earth in a form that you could see with your material eye, and these were the last talks he gave. He didn't travel anywhere. He stayed at home in the Hawaii Hotel. He gave these talks once a week, sometimes twice a week, sometimes twice a month.

All right, now I don't know if we've done this chapter or not. I have it marked, but it's really quite beautiful. It's called *Hidden Manna* and it was August 24th. And I don't know the place right now, but later in this book or later in his talks or in some other book he says – yeah, I'm sure it's in this book – he says that the talks from August on are some of the deepest that were ever given, and this is August 24th. It's on page 327, so we're more than halfway through, and this one's called *Hidden Manna – The Real Infinite Way*. And so there's a real Infinite Way and an unreal Infinite Way. There has to be to designate the real Infinite Way. Now of course the real Infinite Way and the Hidden Manna is the Spirit and he is attempting to lift us out of the letter into the

Spirit, the real Infinite Way, the Hidden Manna. So let's look at a little bit of it, August 24, 1963, Honolulu, Hawaii:

Good afternoon. It is very noticeable that far too many students do not know what makes The Infinite Way, or why there is an Infinite Way message. If our students knew the answer, their progress would be very rapid; but, because they do not catch this major point, they struggle for years not knowing where they are going or why. That which started me on the spiritual path and which ultimately led to The Infinite Way, was the realization that there is no God in the human world or in any religious teaching as such. There is no God answering the prayers of people. For this reason, and for this reason only, there can be a world filled with all the things you can think of which constitute horrible world conditions. (Now) *None of this would be* (there) *if there were a God in the world. In the presence of light there is no darkness. You cannot have the presence of Christ and have sin, death, lack or man's inhumanity to man.*

So what did he say? He said the students in The Infinite Way suffer and struggle for years and years because they do not know where they are going. He said there's a major principle or a major point, rather, and that point is: *there is no God in the human world* (and) *no God answering prayers of people.* And furthermore he says:

Eventually it was revealed to me, you cannot reach God through (your) *mind, and that is why prayers are worthless except as one's blind faith might make of them a little power – just as it is possible to give a little sugar pill and stop pain.*

All right, that's on the very first – well, the first and second paragraph of the very first page of this chapter. The *Hidden Manna - The Real Infinite Way* is something that cannot be reached with the mind. And so if you think you know what The Infinite Way is you're already misled, aren't you? You cannot know The Infinite Way with your mind. So he says it is a major point and if you don't catch it you'll struggle for years and years, and the major point is there is no God in the human world. There is no God answering prayers of people and you cannot reach God through your mind. Well, that about sums it up, doesn't it? That's the long, drawn-out version of Paul's statement: *"the natural man receiveth not the things of God: neither can he know them, (for) they are spiritually discerned."* And that's Paul saying you must come up higher than the mind.

Remember when I gave those classes out in California I asked the audience how would you heal if you could not use the mind, and I sent them home to look at that. And I submit it again to you. There's no God in the human world. Okay, if you have your eyes closed, open your eyes, look around. You see this human world, this material world. You're sitting in a material house. You're sitting in a material body. There's a material wall over there, a material window perhaps, material ceiling, material floor. There's no God in this world, and – and if you, as Mary Jones or John Smith, pray to God to bring God into this world, well – your prayers aren't answered.

And so now what can you do? Well, you can sit down and you can think about God and all these truths that you've memorized over the years, but you cannot reach God through your mind. Now what? You're kind of in a big mess here. There must be something else, something different, something you've never had before, something called an experience, a God experience. And so he says:

In this realization you must remember that (it) makes any religion or any religious teaching nothing more or less than a philosophy.

Yes, it's very nice to sit around and philosophize about The Infinite Way and its principles. Maybe you've had that experience after going and listening to a tape and you perhaps go out for coffee or out for tea and you're talking with your friends about it and you discuss the principles. It's all very intellectual, isn't it?

But with that capacity and those traits you cannot reach God, and there's no God in that gathering.

(We must have) *something that brings the actual presence and power of God into concrete manifestation, and it is for this reason that we say The Infinite Way is not so much a teaching as an* <u>experience</u>.

There are spiritual principles, but these do not constitute The Infinite Way.

And so if you say – well, I've learned that God is omnipresent and the material world is an impersonal image and has no power – those are principles, and principles we found in The Infinite Way, are they not? Yet here he states clearly these *spiritual principles do not constitute The Infinite Way.* Well, what then – what?

(Well), These are (only) stepping stones over which you walk. You have not reached the goal of The Infinite Way until you have the actual realized presence of God or (realized) activity of the Christ.

And again, in my words: If you are outside of that intellectual mind and you're knowing, or you're unknowing – you're not knowing anything. You're just at rest like a piece of ice floating in the water, you're just resting on a sea of Spirit. If you're resting there and you feel Spirit moving, you feel its movement over the face of the deep, that's an experience. That's an inner experience, an experience in your consciousness. Or as he puts it over here in the chapter *The New Horizon*, he puts it this way. He says:

The first glimpse into the heaven of here and now (or the first God experience) *is the beginning of the ascension. (And) The ascension is understood as a rising above conditions and experiences of "this world,"* (And so when we sit and we rest and we behold this movement, in his words he says:) *we behold the "many mansions" prepared for us in spiritual Consciousness – (or in our) awareness of Reality.*

And so as you sit there and you become consciously aware of the movement of Spirit in your consciousness, as your consciousness, in that awareness are many mansions because in the awareness are many mansions in the awareness of Reality. That's the way he put it. So there are mansions. There are levels. There are states of consciousness. There are degrees in this awareness of Reality, and there are different ways.

For you it might come as a still small voice that says, "I am here." For me it may come as a conscious awareness of that movement of the Isness of God is'ing, moving, flowing, the rhythm of Spirit. For someone else it may come as an intuitive feeling (which says) – go pick up that book, look at page 37. It's just a feeling and you go do it and you see exactly what you are experiencing in your consciousness at that moment. For someone else it may be just a tingling feeling on their skin. For someone else it may be an ocean of bliss, just an ocean of bliss and you're floating in it and there's nothing to do and nothing to know. There's just that ocean of bliss and I Am That, but these are all mansions in the awareness of Reality. And that's the way Joel puts it. It's quite beautiful I think, I feel. So he says:

(The spiritual principles that you know with the mind) *do not constitute The Infinite Way. You have not reached the goal of The Infinite Way until you have the actual realized presence of God or activity of Christ* (or activity of the Spirit). *It is for this reason we cannot have outlined or formalized prayers or treatments. They are of no value (unless they) quiet you.*

But quieting you is only so you can prepare for this real experience or the hidden manna, the real Infinite Way.

Therefore, the teaching of The Infinite Way is valueless, (just as valueless) *as any other teaching if it does not result in the actual experience of the presence of God, the feel of the presence within you. You can study the Bible and quote it and fall right into (a) ditch, if it does not elevate you in consciousness to where the actual meeting with God takes place.*

Right? See how he's telling the students that are here and they're recording it and they're going to turn it into the book Beyond Words and Thoughts and perhaps some other books?

He's leading them to that state where they become a nothing, and in the nothing they behold the everything. It's really quite fantastic. In your nothingness, you are everything. So he says:

No human being knows how to heal.

By human being he's meaning that one that's taking thought, the one that's sitting in the chair in the room with the material walls. These are all concepts. Take a look again if you haven't lately at the chapter, and maybe we'll do that next week or soon, the chapter in The Thunder of Silence – what's the name of it where he talks about baggage? (*This is spiritual universe*) Remember he lost his baggage in the airport and then he prayed and meditated and he couldn't find it no matter what he did and then he finally realized – wait a minute! This is spiritual universe and here I am looking for material baggage. How silly is that! And he dropped the whole idea and then the baggage showed up! So this human being that would try to pray to God to produce baggage or some sort of healing, that's the human being that must die because he just said it over here in the first couple lines: *There is no God in the human world* (and) *no God answering prayers* and God cannot be reached with that human mind.

So: *No human being knows how to heal. No human being has the power to heal. No human being knows or receives the "Things of God." Therefore, there can be no healing or real spiritual teaching until you are spiritually endowed, until the presence announces itself.*

Let's put this another way. The human being that knows all these statements of truth and thinks he can grab a hold of one and throw it at the material problem and change it, this human being must die. In your inner temple this human being must die. And so as you go into, move into your inner temple, so that you may have, not an understanding of truth, but an experience of the movement of the Isness, the human being must die. And Joel calls that the Sabbath, when you reach that place where the human being 'takes no thought.' Then you're resting as a piece of ice in the water. You're resting and in your awareness of Reality you behold the movement of Spirit, the Isness of I. You feel it flowing. It just flows. You rest. You have nothing to tell it. You're not there. Just its movement now. Only the movement of Spirit. That movement of Spirit is the resurrection. The human has died and the movement, the Isness of I, is revealed right here, right now. This is the resurrection. Remember?

"Oh Jesus, if you would have been here my brother Lazarus would have lived!" " Did I not tell you he would live again in the resurrection?" "Oh, I know he will in the last day."

And so, see, this person is seeing the resurrection as happening somewhere down there in the future on the last day somewhere. The body will come out of the grave and float up into heaven in the sky or something. This is the concept, and what does he do? Does he have pity on this person because they're grieving their dead brother? Oh, oh – that's okay. Oh no! No, no. He takes the opportunity to awaken them. *I am the resurrection!*

Wow, that person must have stumbled as they were walking along. What? Yes, I, I. When you die within and you feel this movement of Spirit and you come into the conscious awareness of I and its movement, its flowing, its rhythm, the Isness of God, the Isness of Is, I am resurrected. This <u>is</u> the resurrection into consciousness of I, or I consciousness, or I awareness. And this resurrection takes place here and now in your inner temple as the human dies.

Therefore, there can be no healing (says Joel) *or real spiritual teaching until you are spiritually endowed, until the Presence announces itself. Then you can sit back as a beholder and watch your life change. As you watch your life change you can say: "I did not do that." When you reach this place, you are then functioning in The Infinite Way. (And) Now The Infinite Way becomes alive whereas before it was just a preparation.*

People keep asking (me), "Why was this innocent child murdered why was my dog run over when they did nothing wrong?" The world does not know the answer, but as students you should know there is no God in the human world.

That was the very first principle that sent Joel onto his spiritual path when he recognized there is no God in the human world, and then the search began. Well, how do you find one? Is there a God? Where is it and how do you experience it? And as he discovered it after years of practicing and seeing its movement over and over again which appeared as need fulfilled, then he came and he taught it. He shared what he did. And even then the students couldn't get it! They had this intellectually. "Oh, I understand the principles. I can take a test and pass 100%." Yes, yes, you do understand the principles, but that was supposed to be a preparation and you stayed there for years and years and years.

Now says Joel, take the next step. Take the next step and die. Die to all of that. Die to everything you thought you knew. Die to your human beliefs. Die to that form of prayer. How would you reach God if you could not use the mind or any words or any thoughts? That's all he's asking you to do – just die to all of that. So he says:

Anything can and will happen until the child or the dog or the business or the profession or anything else is brought into the presence of one who is spiritually endowed.

Why? Why? Why? Because I, if I be lifted up – if you experience that inner resurrection, look out with the eyes of I – you behold I everywhere and in the presence of that conscious awareness, I is lifted up. The I that beholds is lifted up where it beholds.

Then (he says, when that happens) *you can trust your child or your dog or your business or your profession because now the grace of God is operating them. It is the spirit of God itself. Until this is understood, The Infinite Way can mean nothing to you except another teaching or something nice to read or listen to, (the tapes, but) that is not its intent. The intent of this message is that every student shall reach that place in consciousness where the Spirit of God is upon them and they can say,* (Ah) *"I live; yet not I,* (Christ really is living me)", *"Whereas I was blind, I see." And they can sit back and say, "I can fulfill all obligations,"* not because they're doing it but because they are being guided, strengthened, and wisdomed from within.

The principles of The Infinite Way, as they have been given to me, will definitely change your consciousness so that spiritual endowment can take place (or so spiritual resurrection within can take place).

So he says:

Let me explain: The moment you learn that God or Spirit is the only power and the only law, and you accept this even intellectually, you (may be able to) *meet a claim of bad weather. Or, when you are faced with the threat of an atomic bomb you can say: "If it is true that Spirit is the only power, I do not have to worry." Or, in the case of a disease such as flu epidemic:* (you can say) *"What is that to me, since the spirit of God is the only power." However, if you persist in working with the principle of one power, eventually it will leave the mind and go down into the heart. When that takes place, then you can say,* (Ah) *"Now I see."*

What he's saying here is we all started and prepared for the inner resurrection by knowing these principles intellectually, but the time comes when you must step out of that—well, it's just like Peter stepping out of the boat and onto the water when Jesus Christ says come and stretches out his hand. And what happens to Peter? He starts to think. "Wait! This can't—wait my body!

And he starts to sink until the Christ catches him, and now he's walking on the water.

This water is the consciousness, the consciousness in which you rest. This boat that brought you across so far, this was the intellectual knowing. This was the mind, but now you must step out of the mind and Christ says, "Come," and can you and will you do it? Can you really abandon all that's on that ship? Everything on that ship that you've clung to all these years, was safety. Why, it kept you from drowning, didn't it?

And yet, and yet you know you feel something within you says there's more. There's something deeper. There's another Self. There's another level, another consciousness, another I, and it's calling, "Come," and you see it, you feel it calling. You hear it in these messages week after week. Come, come. Let go of the mind. Step out of it. Step onto the sea of consciousness, and I will catch you. But only you can step out. Nobody could push Peter out. Nobody could help him or convince him. He had to take the step. You have to take the step. You have to die and step out on the water of Spirit. So says Joel down here:

This is the function of The Infinite Way: to bring you to the place where you live by God, (or by Spirit or) by the presence of God, not by statements of truth. The one demonstration you can make (now) in The Infinite Way is the demonstration of the presence of God – that moment when you feel (God is here) *"God is on the field." Then you are living by grace.*

Then you will realize: "Thy grace is my sufficiency in all things." Not the quotation, but the actual realized grace (the actual felt) *Presence is my sufficiency, and there is always a sufficient* (amount of presence or) *grace to meet the needs of this moment.*

(See), everyone wants God ten years from now (he says) *but, just as nature provides enough air in your lungs for this second, so God is sufficient grace for this second. There is no future heaven; there is no*

heavenly heaven; this moment is the only heaven there is, (says Joel). *The only heaven there is, is living in this moment, because only in this moment do you have the grace to provide you with spiritual bread, spiritual meat, spiritual wine, even spiritual resurrection.*

Okay? All right? Says Joel:

(Now) *If you witness Infinite Way students going on year in and year out and not receiving any fruitage or grace,* (not showing forth any grace), *you can know they are just **reading with the mind and remaining there.** That* will never reach *God.* Yes, *We are to live with a passage of truth until it becomes our own.*

But once you have the inner experience, he says:

(You can) *put away all the books and all the tapes.* (Yes) *Through the books and the tapes we present truth and, if you could take one statement of truth and demonstrate it, then the books and the tapes would have fulfilled their purpose.*

So he says:

We started out today with a reminder that there is no God in the human scene and there is no way to reach God with the (human) mind, and that harmony (only) begins to come (in) your experience as you attain the actual realized presence of Spirit (or) God. (Yes, it's true) *In many metaphysical approaches you hear it said that evil is not power (and) there is no evil or error* (error) *is not real or evil is not of God; but in The Infinite Way you must get out of that habit, because it is a habit which leaves you in the very error which you (are) denying. There is error, there is evil, and that is why we are searching for God. Had there been no evils in the days of the Master, there would have been no Master on earth because there would have been no need for one.*

That is not a true statement, all those metaphysical statements.

*The true statement should be this: "Temporal power is not power in the (**realized**) presence of Spirit," which means that evil or error of any nature is not power in the presence of the realized presence of God.*

You see the difference? Now listen to me. Please listen to me! These experiences that you have, or let's say that you decided to take this seriously and you practiced what we are talking about this morning – stepping out of the boat onto the water and just resting, just free resting back and let the water move you wherever it will. And you witness the movement of Spirit. You feel its inner energy pulsating, flowing through your being, as your being. And you see the Isness of I and there's nothing to think and nothing to know. And then you open your eyes and you recognize it's ten to ten and at eleven o'clock you have an appointment with someone, perhaps at the dentist's office. Maybe you decided to go shopping at that time. Maybe you have to take your car in for repairs. Maybe you have an appointment at the library where you're meeting a friend. The point is that you step out of that meditation and you're operating as a human being and you're moving about in a human world and you're doing that with a human mind.

Now Joel says in this very chapter or the next one – I read both of them this morning, so I'm not sure. He says this experience that you had in meditation must be repeated—are you ready—twenty to thirty times a day. (chuckles saying wow) Wow! It doesn't leave much time for anything else, does it? And he says that it must be repeated because we lose that consciousness and we drift back down into a state of humanhood, into the mind again. It's like resting back in that water and then opening our eyes and climbing back into the boat. And now we're back into a boat on rocky water. And so it must be renewed he says, renewed several times a day.

Now you don't have to sit down in a formal meditation to do this. True, if this was the very first time you had this experience you're going to have to do that, but once you've had this experience dozens of times – what does he tell us? You can do it with just a blink of the eyes, and it's true. It may not be a fast blink. It may be a slow one, but you can get to that awareness simply by closing the eyes for a moment. Or if necessary, if you're in a fast-paced job you can disappear into the bathroom for a moment. You know, there are dozens of ways to renew this. And he says, "Now listen, this is the part I wanted you to know:

If you renew this dozens of times a day every day, the day comes where this spiritual resurrection has happened within you on a permanent basis and you can't lose it. You don't go in and out and in and out anymore, It takes over your experience; this inner Spirit, this infinite Spirit, this infinite sea of bliss. The movement of the Spirit over the face of the deep, the spiritual resurrection. This awareness of reality becomes your permanent dwelling place. This mansion is now what you move into and live in, and it lives you. And you still function. You still go to work if you have a job. You still pay your taxes. You still drive your car. You still shop for groceries. You still wash in the bathtub or shower. But you are always in this higher consciousness because you have been lifted. No, not you the person. I speak now to the I of you because the I of you has been lifted into awareness of Itself.

And so that is the Hidden Manna of The Infinite Way.

(Now) *Whatever temporal power is tempting you, you must bring the actual presence of God into the situation, whether you are so close to it that blinking your eyes does it, or whether you are so far away that you have to sit for days and nights until the Spirit breaks through* (or until you feel that inner movement). *If you are expecting any help until this* (inner experience) *happens, you are going to be sadly mistaken. Nothing happens to the errors that come into your experience until you have attained the realization of the presence of God —* but then (when you dwell in that consciousness) *temporal power is dissolved (just) as darkness is dissolved in the presence of Light.*

See, if you get up in the middle of the night, perhaps you go into the bathroom, you flick on the light. That was pitch black.

401

Here it's pitch black. I'm not in any city. I'm in the Appalachian Mountains. There's no light here. If you go outside you can't see your hand in front of your face, and I like it that way. I don't like all the lights and noise and activities, sounds that I heard growing up in Los Angeles. So you go into the bathroom, it's pitch black, you can't even see your hand. You turn on the light and now you have a room. You have yourself. You have a million things right there that you couldn't see before. What power did that light use over that darkness? Was there some sort of pushing or shoving or forcing? No. When the light came on, the darkness disappeared. It was as natural as the next breath you take.

And so the Light of your inner being, the movement within you dissolves the concept or the image just as the Light dissolves the darkness. There's no force. Not by might nor by power, but by the resurrected Spirit within you. And so you don't direct it, you don't pray for it. After a while you don't even think about it. It's just as normal as that Light dissolving the darkness. Something comes before you. You see how silly it is. You don't even work on it. You're in that higher state of consciousness and it goes around you. I don't know how that works, but it does. It goes around you. It's dissolved. In some way or another it changes. You don't even know how. You didn't try to do anything. You're just observing. You're just sitting in a state of observation. *More and more,* says Joel, *we must become the beholder.* And so you're sitting, you're resting in that Sabbath consciousness. You're in that spiritual resurrection and the I is functioning and you behold as it moves itself.

This should give you such an understanding of the nature of the 'The Infinite Way' that you will not rest or rely on any statements. Instead, you will know that they are to remind you to go within and bring forth the (real) Presence. You must actually experience God, then that invisible goes before you to make the crooked places straight.

You see that? So he says:

*The question is asked, "What is truth?" I will tell you no one
in the history of the world has ever known what truth is because
it is infinite. (so) it would be a horrible thing to say, "The Infinite
Way is truth." (Because) Truth must continue revealing itself one
hundred years from now, (and) not the same truth of the Bible or (the)
Christian Science or Infinite Way.*

*When you are dealing with your daily experience, you are
opening yourself to an inflow of truth, but be careful do not depend
on yesterday's manna. Go within for inspiration of the moment – for
this moment's manna – and then the Spirit of God does the work.
A statement of truth is not God. A statement of truth is a reminder
which sends you back inside* (so you can die! Only he says:) *sends
you back inside for further impartations.* (Yes, so that you can die
and receive the Spirit.)

Jesus was crucified and the disciples were afraid and they
were up in the inner chamber, upstairs in the inner chamber,
which means they were in this meditation in the silence, and in
that silence Christ appeared in their midst. It just appeared. They
felt that movement, and what was its first words? *"Receive ye the
Holy Spirit."* And this is what Joel has been saying and this is
what The Infinite Way has been saying. This is what Christ, your
inner Christ, the Spirit within you has been saying to your outer
awareness all these years that you have studied the letter.

Oh please! Put down the letter and now *"Receive ye the
Holy Spirit."* And it is being said to all of you right now, this
moment. *"Receive ye the Holy Spirit."* If you will live constantly
and consciously aware that there is sufficiency of grace for this
moment and that I have hidden manna and then go within to feel
that flow, you will be living by it.

*Be sure you never (ever) forget the function of The Infinite Way
is to reveal to you - you do have an inner grace, an inner hidden
manna, a "meat the world knows not of."* (And you must) *Go within*

for the flow; then go about your business and, whatever your need is, the solution will appear in its own way. This (is what) has carried me from the (very) beginning of my work. Once touched by the spirit, I knew there was something within me (and) that (it) did the work. (And) Everything necessary to my experience always appeared, even in time to correct my mistakes. You cannot avoid making a mistake (once in a while) *but even if you do, this inner manna corrects it.*

(Oh) It is really very sad if an Infinite Way student does not catch this point, that there <u>is</u> an inner grace, "a meat the world knows not of," a hidden manna.

I imagine he was sad, or no, that's not said correctly. I imagine he saw the – what word – ridiculousness, the pity of it – that so many people were coming to hear the message and he was repeating over and over and the Christ through him was saying: Here – *"Receive ye the Holy Spirit."* And they were saying, "Hey Joel, I've memorized the entire first chapter of <u>The Infinite Way</u> or I've memorized *New Horizon.* Now I imagine that was a little bit like the Christ. *"Oh Jerusalem, Jerusalem how often,"* I would give you this whole thing and *"ye would not."* He must have felt some of that, and surely some of us feel that sometimes. And yet, and yet every knee will bend, so sooner or later everyone, **everyone**, will come back home within to that Spirit.

Can you not see the sin of having anyone set up as a savior, whether it is Buddha or Jesus or (whether it is Joel or Herb or whether it is Bill or whether it is Alan or whether it is Tony or Bob)? *Can you not see the sin of believing that anyone of us is different from another, except in (our) degree of realization? (Yes) There should be spiritual leaders, because in their presence temporal power does not operate. (And) They can help in the overcoming of discords but only to a certain point, because "If I go not away, the Comforter will not come."*

You see, even Jesus had students that wanted Jesus to do it for them and he said, "Oh, I have to go away in order that you may go within and have this inner experience of the movement of Spirit," and they did up in that upper temple. From Christ they received within the Holy Spirit. So he was right.

No matter how advanced we become, there are times when problems can become so hypnotic that we ourselves may not be able to bring release and so we turn to each other. The Master was not ashamed to say, "Stay awake and pray with me," so there should be no hesitancy in turning to each other for help. I have no hesitancy whatsoever to do this when I need it, and I receive the help.

And so Joel is saying that we are turning to that inner Spirit and when we are so hypnotized with the problem that we cannot seem to make that contact, then we reach out for that Spirit in someone else, knowing all the while it's the same Spirit, and then when we are released from that hypnotism and it's broken – ah – we're back in our right mind, the mind which was in Christ Jesus which feels this inner movement – then all is well again.

The students who have been with us here all year know that this has been a difficult year for me in which I have been going through a period of inner initiation waiting for a message. (He says) *We made no tapes this year except four teaching tapes, which were made in the actual teaching of those who were here for instruction. We made no other tapes because I recognized that the message which has been coming through each week was a "leading up" message, (and) not a fulfilled message.*

During the last two or three weeks it all came to a head, and then it became clear that we are entering the consciousness that does not need words or thoughts. We can sit down to meditate and realize: "The kingdom of God is closer than breathing. (All I have to do is) tune in and listen. I need no words I need no thoughts. I need only receptivity and, when the Word of God comes, the earth of error melts."

In The Infinite Way our dependency is on a hidden manna, a "meat the world knows not of," a Presence you cannot define. You do not have blind faith – you go within and bring forth Spirit. Then forever after, you can say: "I live; yet not I, but (this) Christ liveth in me." (But) Because of the mesmerism of the world, you must go within twenty to thirty times a day. In other words you must get back inside where you (can know), "I have hidden manna" – and then let it out.

You don't push it out or know it out (chuckles). You rest and behold and It flows.

(And) It will not be long (now) until someone will say to you, "What is it you have?", "Can you help me?" No, it will not be long (now). Only a few are ready, because of previous incarnations, to catch this in a year or two. (And so) I can be very patient because I know that human wisdom cannot be replaced by (this) spiritual (resurrection) until onion skin after onion skin has been peeled away and they become transparencies. I can be patient with them until they have reached that place where self-preservation is no longer the first law and (their) first need. I know it takes patience on my part and I always hope (that) they will have the courage to persist.

And I have the hope that you here listening to this have the courage to persist. I know this is not comfortable. That's why these are called The Uncomfortable Talks. I know they are not comfortable because I am asking you to die to everything you knew or have known and step out on the water not knowing at all what will happen. I'm asking you to go within yourself in that inner temple in the upper chamber, invite the Christ, and then stand stock still until It says or It indicates or the experience happens that you receive the Holy Spirit, the Infinite Being, the Isness of God, the movement of Spirit.

Miracles do happen, some far greater than you would believe if you heard (about) them. (But) They are not due to a "miracle man" they are due to consciousness and receptivity. Not even Jesus could perform miracles unless he was approached with receptivity. It really makes no difference what degree of spiritual height I attain, it can only affect you by the measure of your receptivity. That is why no practitioner can ever guarantee the measure of your healing or how long it will take, because it depends on your receptivity.

All right, so, receptive to what? Receptive to the message? No-o-o! Receptive to what? Receptive to receiving the Spirit within or the movement or the conscious awareness. Receptive to spiritual resurrection. And let's see:

We have arrived at a place in our work now where, if any of you are satisfied with anything less than the (actual) *experience of God (within, then) you are satisfied with too little. (From now on) Nothing should satisfy you but the experience itself, and you can accomplish that by turning within. It will come, and, when it comes, it must be renewed. Because of the hypnotism of the world* (I am telling you) *it must be renewed.*

And that is the chapter *Hidden Manna - The Real Infinite Way.* And you can see, I hope, that you're invited to the real resurrection, the resurrection within you of this Infinite Spirit, Infinite Being, Infinite Is, Infinite I Am. But these are terms now, so throw them away. They're part of the boat. You're stepping out of the boat of the human mind. The human mind has no contact with God and can never, <u>ever</u>, <u>ever</u> know God, and so it must be released. It doesn't mean you're not going to pick it up and use it to balance your checkbook. It means to know God you're not gonna use it! To know God aright is life eternal. To know God with the mind is another set of concepts.

All right, so let us be still for a moment.

[Silent pause]

And Christ invites you to the inner Spiritual Resurrection. I am the resurrection, that I within you, that Spirit within you, that movement. And again, I just love this in The Infinite Way in *The New Horizon:*

407

The first glimpse (of that Holy Spirit, the first glimpse of the movement of Spirit or) *the heaven of here and now is the beginning of the ascension for us.*

And what is the ascension? Ah! The ascension is above humanhood, above words, above thoughts, above the human mind. And here above that, here in the stillness, in the silent inner tomb where the human has died, right in this tomb where there's nothing, nothingness, here in this tomb the I, the Spirit is resurrected. Right here flows the everything, the infinite everything. Out of the nothing flows the everything.

And so:

This ascension is understood now as a rising above the conditions and experiences of "this world," (or those which are in the mind) *and (now) we behold "many mansions" prepared for us in spiritual Consciousness – in the awareness of Reality.*

And so when Jesus Christ or Christ appearing as Jesus said, *"I go to prepare a place for you,"* here is the place he prepared, this mansion in which you live and move and have your being when this human has died and Spiritual Resurrection of I, of Christ, of Is, takes place. Here in your awareness of Reality is the mansion of the risen Christ. It's the mansion of the risen Spirit, and this place is for you. It was prepared for you. It's taken you 2,000 years to come to the place of readiness to step out of that boat and onto the water, grasping nothing, but you are ready.

I remember in 1972 Don said to me, "You will reach the place on your path where you come to the edge of a cliff and you stand there not knowing how you will continue, and the inner voice will say, 'Walk!' and you will step into nothingness. But (he said) be happy because the Everlasting arms will catch you."

And now my dear friends whom I may never meet in person and yet whom I feel in consciousness, let us step off that cliff. Let us step out of the boat and onto the water. Let us enter that inner tomb and rise into the upper chamber and die completely. Stand stock still and witness something called Spirit as It moves Itself...and...

"Behold, **I** make all things new."

[Silence]

CLASS 25

FROM LAW TO GRACE

Bill: Good morning.

This is Sunday August 25th of 2013, about eleven o'clock, and I have here in my hands Joel's book The Thunder of Silence. In the beginning of this book he states clearly that – I think it's in the Introduction – that he doesn't expect anyone to understand this book for years to come, and I suspect he was right yet once again. This book deals specifically with making the transition from one who is under the law, under the tyrannical dictatorship of the law, to that place where you're at peace and you're under the grace of God. So in short, he tells us how to come out from under the letter into the Spirit, and that's the whole intent and purpose of this book. To ascend up over the mind, and you can hear it. You can hear it in such phrases as this in the chapter *Henceforth Know We No Man After the Flesh*:

To heal, it is necessary to transcend thought. Even though a meditation begins as a contemplation, it must, before the healing is accomplished, rise into the higher realm of silent awareness.

And we can see that he's trying to lead us students from the mind which knows truth to a state of silent awareness in which we bear witness that I am the truth. And I feel it's necessary to review this other part too. Let me find it and I'll be right back. This is from Galatians, and it says:

"For it is written, that Abraham had two sons, the one by a bondmaid, the other by a freewoman.

But he who was of the bondwoman was born after the flesh; but he of the freewoman was by promise.

Which things are an allegory: for these are the two covenants; the one from mount Sinai, which gendereth to bondage, which is Agar.

But Jerusalem which is above is free, which is the mother of us all."

Can you not see in this clear statement that these things are an allegory, the two covenants? One from mount Sinai, which is the law, and one which is Jerusalem, which is above and is by promise.

"And I John saw (a) new Jerusalem, coming down out of heaven,"

Well now, that's a promise, and that new Jerusalem is this new state of consciousness. If you've been following along and listening to the Herb Fitch talks on the Catalina Island series, then you know he's been speaking to us of Noah and the Ark being this new state of consciousness, which of course rides upon the sea. It's safe, whereas material law and everything that is material is covered by the sea. Always and always and always the path as Christ Jesus set it forth for us is this very same path that he took, that being crucifying of material sense, rising above mortal mind and resting in a state of *"It is finished,"* a silent awareness.

So now today we are looking at the chapter, chapter IX, *This is a Spiritual Universe*, because last week we said we might look at it this week. And if you don't have the book, <u>The Thunder of Silence</u>, I will read you a little bit about the story here so that you can follow along when we talk of the principles later on. Joel says:

Several years ago when I was on my way to South Africa, I stopped off for a day in the Belgian Congo, and after the man in charge of the bookings and his assistant had taken care of my tickets, made whatever examinations were necessary, and weighed my luggage, I called a little native boy to carry my three bags out to the plane which I was boarding for Johannesburg. This was such a small air station that I could see the boy as he walked out of the gate onto the field with one large piece of baggage in each hand and a small piece under his arm. A few minutes later he returned without any baggage and I said to him questioningly, "O.K.?" to which he replied, "O.K."

When I arrived in Johannesburg the next morning, there was only the one tiny little piece of baggage waiting for me, and the other two large pieces were missing. Immediately, the personnel of this tremendously big and active airport at Johannesburg began searching for my baggage, but they did not find it in the enclosure nor was it with the crew's baggage; and furthermore when they sent someone to search the plane, there was no baggage there, either. The person in charge of the airline said that he would immediately contact the station in the Belgian Congo and would soon have an answer for me, so there was nothing for me to do but go to my hotel.

The Infinite Way students in Johannesburg had arranged for me to visit Krueger National Park, so after buying some necessary clothing, we started out on a three-day trek through this fabulous wild-animal preserve with the full expectation of picking up my baggage when we returned. But upon our return no baggage had yet been found. The only explanation the airline had to offer was that somebody must have stolen it, and that that somebody must have been the little native boy and a confederate because the last time the bags were seen was when he had picked them up and carried them out onto the field. (Well) The absurdity of such an assumption should have been apparent at once because certainly nobody could have taken those two heavy pieces of luggage away from the airfield without being noticed. Nevertheless, all the native quarters in the town were searched, and the place turned upside down because the authorities were convinced that a theft had occurred. Despite all this hullabaloo, however, no baggage was found.

For three weeks, I was in South Africa without baggage and without money – without purse and without scrip – but this was no great hardship because I ate regularly, my hotel bills were paid, and clothing was purchased, although only the absolute necessities, because I was convinced that my bags would show up, which was a very wrong conviction.

Two nights before I was to leave for India, I sat down to give this whole incident some serious consideration. "This represents a failure on my part. What is that failure? What has gone wrong here?"

He's gonna leave in two days. He has no baggage. He has no—all his personal belongings, probably his books with things that he uses to teach from, probably his underwear, his toiletries – all of that is missing, and he's purchased the bare minimum of replacements because he's sure the baggage is gonna show up. Now he leaves in 48 hours to go to a different country and he's sitting down as you or I would and thinking what's the principle here? What have I missed? So he gets quiet.

I sat in my room, pondering and meditating, finally the answer came:

You notice he didn't say, "I thought it through and figured it out." No, he sat still and he contemplated until that silence came and then into that silent awareness flowed something which he's going to tell us.

...finally the answer came: "This is a spiritual universe,"

Ahh! In other words, this is Spirit! What are you looking for?

(Yes) "This is a spiritual universe, and yet here I am waiting for baggage, when the truth of the matter is there isn't any baggage. All that baggage is, is (a) part of the belief of time and space – space that is occupied by baggage, (and) time in which it could be lost, and space in which it could be lost. (And) Here I am trying to find baggage, when if it were found would only be an evidence that the human scene had been manipulated."

How often does he tell us we're not here to bring about a – to change this bad picture into a good one because that would just be evidence that we manipulated the human scene. That wouldn't be an evidence of God's Spirit. So he says:

"There is no truth to this whole picture because we are living in a spiritual universe where nobody has any need of baggage."

Think about that. Could you sit down 48 hours before your rent is due with no money at all, no purse and no scrip, get silent enough to hear "This is a spiritual universe" and have that inner realization that there's no need for money. Well, that's what he's telling you is required if you're going to live by Spirit, if you're going to transcend these human thoughts.

(No) "There's no truth to this whole picture because we are living in a spiritual universe. Whatever there is of reality is incorporeal, spiritual, and omnipresent; and whatever appears as finite baggage in time and space must be an image in thought, and it can have no reality to it; so I have been fooled into hoping and waiting for material baggage to turn up in a spiritual universe where every idea is [already] omnipresent."

(And) With that I retired.

So he had the inner realization that God already is – harmony, perfection, God's being, Spirit Is omnipresent, and there's no need for anything else. Then he released it, and I'm sure he stood still there until there was a feeling of the presence or whatever came to him that let him know that God was on the field, as he puts it, which is another way of saying that Spirit is omnipresent, and then he went to bed.

(And) The story came to a quick conclusion after that realization. (Because the next morning) *The assistant manager of the airline at the station in Johannesburg was seated at his desk at eight o'clock apparently out of nothing, the thought came to him, "Baggage can't dissolve into thin air. It couldn't disappear between here and there – it has to be somewhere. So where is it?"* (And) *Suddenly another idea struck him, and he went to the hotel where the crew was lodged on*

overnight stops, and there were the two pieces of baggage on the floor where they had been waiting for three weeks. Nobody had thought of that possibility; in fact, nobody thought of any kind of a practical solution until I stopped thinking about baggage.

All right, again, that whole story right there proves this principle in the chapter before:

To heal, it is necessary to transcend thought. Even though a meditation begins as a contemplation of truth, it must, before the healing is accomplished, rise into the higher realm of silent awareness.

Now is that not what he did? He started as a contemplation: This is a spiritual universe and here I am waiting for baggage. Baggage is a part of time and space, time and space in which it could be lost, but this is a spiritual universe, so there's no truth to that picture! Whatever there is of reality is incorporeal and spiritual and omnipresent, so I've been fooled into hoping and waiting for – what did he call it here? – an image in thought to appear, when in fact it's a spiritual universe and every idea is omnipresent, and with that he sat in the silent awareness until he felt that inner movement and then he retired.

Now, the reason why we brought up the two covenants is because one is under the law, the bondwoman. Thought, images in thought come under the law. But the other is under grace. It's a new consciousness, and that comes in silent awareness, and so our movement is all taking place within. There's nothing to do out here. This is an inner movement, a shift, a transformation, a transition in consciousness from thinking thoughts, having images in thought, manipulating images in thought – trying to make this evil image into a good one and seeing this good image turn into an evil one. It's coming out of images, seeing the spiritual universe, standing still in silent awareness beholding that spiritual universe here, now. Not sometime in the future, right here, right now. God Is. And seeing it, not thinking it, because if you're thinking it it's still image in thought. You're still under the law. If you're thinking – well, how does Joel say it? We should not say that; we should let God say it to us. See, there's a difference. One is you're still in the second chapter of Genesis.

Images in thought are in the second chapter of Genesis. They come under the law, but silent awareness is in the first chapter of Genesis and it beholds the I that makes all things new. This is the transformation we're making within. And it must be practiced and must be practiced several times, and every time we fall down and stumble and get caught up in the mental images, we must dust ourselves off, pick ourselves up and practice again because it's staying in the silent awareness which is going to reveal to us our Christ identity. Because Christ identity is God, the Word made flesh, and the Word made flesh is not something that happened 2000 years ago. The Word made flesh is something that happens and is happening now, but it requires your awareness of it for you to experience it, and so that silent awareness is where you behold the Word made flesh or your Christ identity. And he continues to say:

In metaphysics we would think, "Oh, well, the baggage has to turn up" or "It can't be lost." In other words, we would be dealing with an it – an it called baggage. The fallacy of this method of meeting a problem is immediately apparent because in the case of illness, in order to be consistent, we would have to give a treatment that dealt specifically with (your) heart, liver, lungs, stomach, digestion, elimination, head, or foot, but then we would be completely outside the realm of spiritual being.

He says:

We become very sure of ourselves and believe that we are going along in the right direction, and then all of a sudden the hypnotism of human sense can make us think about baggage or the lack of it. Now please understand I was not concerned about the loss of the baggage:

My mistake was that I was sure it would turn up, which is exactly like being sure a person's heart is going to get better, or his sick foot is going to get well; but the principle upon which all our work is based is that of the real creation (ah-ha!) *the first chapter of Genesis in which God made all that was made, and all that He made is good.*

You see it's not enough to repeat that statement, that scripture, is it? You can repeat that scripture over and over and still be living in the second chapter of Genesis under the law, under the Lord God. So when he says *the principle upon which all our work is based is that of the real creation* or living under grace, that's exactly what he means. We need to come out from under that horrible taskmaster called the law, the Lord God. But do you see now that the Lord God is the world mind, and the world mind is the human mind when it's not – well, when it's entertaining images in thought? Your human mind is the Lord God when that mind is entertaining images in thought, and since the human scene has no contact with God – God is not in the human scene was where his spiritual journey started – these images in thought have no contact with God. So if you're standing in those images in thought and you're praying that God change them, "Please God, please send me the rent by Thursday.", "Please help my nephew. He's done nothing wrong. He doesn't deserve this.", "Please, please if you'll just heal my leg, I'll do this and that for you."

Can we not see how ridiculous that is? Images in thought. We're standing there just as insane really as the person that thinks they're Napoleon entertaining images in thought. And we're praying to some God somewhere that God will fix those images in thought, which if they were fixed, now we would have good images in thought instead of bad images in thought. Both of the pairs of opposites exist in the images in thought. That's where you get the law, karma. Ah, but come out from under those images in thought. Transcend, ascend. Use whatever words you want. The experience means come out from under that. Come up over that. Rest in silent awareness. Now where are you? Now you're in the promise, the new Jerusalem. And here in the new Jerusalem you live by grace. You don't live at all; grace lives you.

Think of that. Grace lives you, and this is Christ identity. Now this Christ identity is your identity, has always been your identity and always will be your identity. So why are we bothering with this practicing the principles if this is the absolute truth? Well, it's like my friend from India which I love dearly. He feels that in the absolute we're all God, so why bother, and he goes down the road and he drinks a little too much sometimes and the wife's upset and he chuckles, "It's all illusion." Maybe he's right. I don't particularly want that kind of life, so if I'm consciously aware of my Christ identity, if it becomes an experience, then I live by grace and I don't have that kind of life. I have a life of peace, a life of purpose, a life of fulfillment and harmony.

So I don't care what anybody else's beliefs are in the universe. I know that I have to have the conscious awareness of this in order to experience it. It may be true in the absolute, but it does me no good until I have the conscious awareness of it, and that's why I practice principles. And so getting back to his suggestion here:

The principle upon which all our work is based is that of the real creation as recounted in the first chapter of Genesis in which God made all that was made, and all that He made is good.

Now listen to this line:

The spiritual creation is an incorporeal creation, and the proof of that is that there was light before there was a sun in the sky. If we live and move and have our being (or have our conscious awareness) *in the spiritual creation as set forth in the first chapter of Genesis, we can have everything we need without having baggage.*

However, now we're gonna talk about images in thought.

418

The sense-world, that which we can see, hear, taste, touch, and smell, is the unreal creation described in the second chapter of Genesis — it's a mental image in the mind. If we remember that, (we shall not try to manipulate it) we shall not try to manipulate the human scene or handle the mental image which exists only as a shadow within thought, and then (then when we stand still in that silent awareness, he says) *we shall be witness to the quick dissolution of these mental images.*

Yes, because the awareness — we said that last week or the week before — awareness melts images. Awareness of God, when you have the awareness of the Isness of God right here, right now, images drop away. And as we said before, it's like turning on a light in the middle of the night. You don't know where the darkness goes; you just know it disappears. It's the same here. But he says:

Do not misunderstand what I am saying: I know when we are traveling baggage seems real and necessary. I know [also] that most of the time our <u>concept</u> of body seems real because one thing or another brings it into our awareness, and because of that, there is the temptation to think of it as real.

He's talking about thinking of your mental image of body as real. But then he says:

We do not deny body. It is real.

Yes, but what body is he referring to? Well, he tells you:

What we see as body is not body: It is a mental image within our thought — a universal mental concept, individualized within us.

There is no such thing as a material body.

Now you might want to underline that, put quotes around it or brackets or something or highlight it. He's going to say — he says something else. In the next two pages he'll say something quite like it.

There is no such thing as a material body:

What is this? I'm looking right at it! I'm sitting in it!

(Ah) *There is only a material concept of body. There is no such thing as a material universe: There are only material concepts of the one spiritual universe.*

Well, now there you go. What if you stepped out of the concept of a material body and had the silent awareness of your incorporeal body? Could you not standing in that silent awareness if the Voice said walk, could you not walk on the water? Could you not walk off that cliff and step in thin air? Could you not walk through a wall before the mob closed in on you the way Jesus Christ did? And what if you knew that there was no—if you had no material concept of the one spiritual universe, but you stood in silent awareness beholding the spiritual universe living you? What if you knew that? Could you not do like it says in <u>Life and Teaching of the Masters of the Far East</u> and transport yourself from here to Tibet? Is that not the body that Jesus Christ stood in when the five hundred saw him, but the rest of mankind did not? And the five hundred that saw him, were they not seeing him with that eye that sees and as it stands in silent awareness? I guarantee you, they could not see him if they were in images in thought. Why? The human scene has no contact with God. Says Joel:

I have told you the <u>real</u> secret of life: God is not with mortals. Take it from there.

As long as we accept a material concept of universe, we are under the laws of matter.

Do you not see that standing in the mind and its images and thinking, contemplating, and entertaining those images – you're under the law? Really it's the law of the mind, isn't it? That's Lord God, and you're under the law of the mind. But if you will, if you will come up higher, if you will rest back deeper, if you will ascend or transcend or make the transition out of that mind into silent awareness, which is the whole purpose of <u>The Thunder of Silence</u>, then you shall see. Your eyes shall be opened and you shall be satisfied that Christ is your identity, that the Word is made you.

We are free as soon as we begin to understand we live and move and have our being in the first chapter of Genesis where man is made in the image and likeness of God, or Spirit.

And so you in your true identity, you are made in the image and likeness of Spirit. Now draw me a picture of that! You are made in the image and likeness of Spirit. You can't—you can't draw a picture of that. How can you have a concept of that? You're made in the image and likeness of infinite Spirit. You're made in the image and likeness of infinite, invisible Spirit. You are made in the image and likeness of eternal, infinite, invisible Spirit. You are made in the image and likeness of omnipresence. Draw me a picture of that! You can't. You can't have a concept of that. You might have a picture in the mind of it, but throw it out. That's not it. You must have the experience of it. I AM the Life. I, infinite, omnipresent, eternal Spirit. Be still and know I am Spirit. Be still and know I am you. Be still and experience. Be still and behold. Be still and see. I am come. And so he says:

"Know ye not that your body is the temple of the Holy Ghost" – *not the body as you see it in the mirror, but as it actually is.*

And there he's telling you there's another body, an incorporeal, invisible body of Spirit, and that is what it actually is. But you can't see it while you're standing in mental images praying to an image God to fix an image. No, then you're under the law which has no contact with God. Yes, *"You ask, and receive not, because you ask amiss."* That's right. Who are you asking? An image in thought to fix an image in thought while you live an image in thought and you die an image in thought, and the whole parenthesis in eternity is a series of universal mental images in thought.

Now again, as he says, he understands it's necessary to have baggage when you travel. I understand that it's necessary to use the intellect and the mind when you're programming a computer, when you're balancing your checkbook, when you're filing your taxes, when you're making your budget. I understand that it's necessary to use the intellect and the mind when you're driving your car and taking your driver's examination to get your license. I understand these things. Yes, I understand. But I also understand that mind is the natural mind, the natural man, and it does not receive the things of God.

And so when you're not focused in those areas, you must be focused in your meditation on transcending that mind, or dropping that mind might be a better way of saying it, because you're not really going up or down or sideways. Dropping that mind, being silent and standing in silent awareness, and then Spirit reveals Itself. But that Spirit revealing Itself is you. It's you. It's the I. The I of you, your true identity, is revealing itself to your outer awareness. And eventually, I can tell you, it happens more and more frequently that even while you're taking your driving exam you have the conscious awareness of Spirit. Even while you're planning your budget you have the feeling of the Presence. Even while you're discussing with a roomful of your business associates the plan for the next year for expansion, you're having inner moments of silent awareness.

Rumi says the two worlds have become one. He has learned how to do this.

"And I saw a new Jerusalem,"

"A new heaven and a new earth." The two have become one. John has learned to do this.

"I have overcome the world." Jesus Christ has learned to do this.

And we must, and we will.

Just as my realization that we were not dealing with material baggage, but with Omnipresence, immediately awakened the one man necessary to the demonstration — to understand what (real) body is and what the [real] universe is, is to arrive at a realization that brings the solution:

I live and move and have my being in God; I am in my Father, and my Father is in me. How can I be finite or limited if an infinite Father is within me? How can a finite, limited being have an infinite God within Him? Therefore, I must be as spiritual as the Father that created me.

All being must be spiritual, and into this spiritual creation, nothing finite can enter to limit or create any sense of separation.

Says Joel:

The suffering of this world is due to our looking around for a piece of material baggage — even expecting it to be in its rightful place. That is the error. There is no place for you or me or "he," or "she," or "it," except in the only place where it is to be found and that is Omnipresence, where even that which to human sense seems absent is present.

Again, go back and look at this page:

There is no such thing as a material body: There is only a material concept of body. There is no such thing as a material universe: There are only material concepts of the one spiritual universe.

Says Joel in the book we read last week — I think it was last week — Consciousness Transformed:

It is not easy to stop seeing human beings. But I finally made it!

Yes, the two became one. He stopped seeing a material universe. He stopped seeing human beings. He saw the real spiritual, incorporeal body, the real spiritual universe. He says:

On a cloudy day, the sun seems to be absent when it is merely hidden. Just so, the clouds of human belief (and mental images) and the density of human thought may temporarily hide from us that which is (really) omnipresent, that which is present where I am. And what is it that is present where I am? All that the Father has.

Just think of that. All that the Father has is here flowing and flowing to as the Word made you, but you cannot see it, and you live in these images in thought, and that's no different than the person that is living with the images that they're really Adolph Hitler and thinking that they're supposed to go out and conquer the world and thinking that they're members of the master race, but really they're locked up inside of an institution because they're not safe. They will be a detriment to themselves or other people if let loose on society and so they lock these people up. They have mental delusions.

That's the same thing that we do in the second chapter of Genesis, only we have the illusion I'm Bill and I'm such and so years old and here's my education and I'm limited and I'm lacking because I never had this experience and my environment was this way as a youth and because of that environment now I react this way and it's not my fault. Or my name is Susan and I'm limited because I'm only this age and I'm lacking because I have this physical problem and I can't seem to get my relationships right because of this, that, and the other. Or my name is Mary and I'm just too old to get this thing. I should have done this when I was in my twenties and thirties and now I'm sixty or seventy and I can't possibly make this transition now. It's too hard and I don't want to give up my grandchildren and all these ideas.

Well, these are people that are standing in the images in thought and life is tough because they're coming under the law and there's no contact with God. All the time Omnipresence, all that the Father has is the Word made flesh, but without the silent awareness of it, to all intents and purposes, standing under the law there is no grace. Yet grace is omnipresent, as free as air. It's very strange, isn't it? The second chapter of Genesis is a form of insanity.

"My thoughts are not your thoughts, saith the Lord."

Oh, that is for sure. But in the first chapter of Genesis everything is fine. Yes, and then we decided we wanted our own personal identities, but there was only one way to have a personal identity. No, we didn't want to be one with the Father. No, I want my own, I want my own life! Okay, okay, but there's really no such thing. You're gonna have to imagine it. Okay, then that's what I'll do. I'll imagine it! I'll imagine it. I'll live sort of insane, imagining I'm a human being. Well, okay, if that's what you want to do. Here.

And then we find ourselves living with the pigs, living with the pigs, and even the servants are better off. I want to go home. I just want to go home. So we start the journey. We start taking the steps necessary. Oh, at first we are tricked. We think we're practicing principles so we can double our income here in this imagined, imaginary human life. Or we want to have a better set of lungs or we want to have a better heart or we want to get over these panic attacks or we want to just have a little peace of mind or we want to have a better relationship. We want to find our perfect mate, our soul mate, and so we're practicing principles.

That's how it tricks us. Later in the work that no longer works. Or we can't have the healing we seek, so we go deeper and deeper. What did I miss? What did I miss? Oh, and then it all unfolds before us. It never was about improving these mental images. It's about dying out of these mental images. It's about dying out of that identity. It's about awakening to the Word made flesh. It's about awakening to our Christhood. It's about having the silent awareness of the spiritually real, the realm of Spirit in which Spirit is what I am. Now that's a whole different thing. And here we are. Yes, and before we are halfway home we have this wonderful, beautiful inner experience of the presence of God enfolding us and we feel that kiss on the cheek and we know we're on our way. And we know it won't be long and we'll be standing in silent awareness of Christ living us, as us.

People have sought for a way to transcend mind through a process which has been described as stilling the mind, and they have found that such attempts frequently result, not in achieving spiritual consciousness, but in quite the opposite effect, a dulling of consciousness. There is a way, however, in which we can rise above the mental level of life, although we may not be able to remain there permanently because to do that requires years and years of devotion to this and to nothing else; but we can rise above mind to such a degree that, at least when we are in the world, it will no longer disturb us to any great extent.

So he gives you a little technique here. He says:

A beginning can be made by not attempting to stop our thinking processes.

That's why he's never been keen on trying to just still your mind and stand there. No, he gives us right from Practicing the Presence and The Art of Meditation, he gives us this technique whereby we take a scripture and we contemplate it. Or we take, as he did – why am I failing with this baggage and he looked at it. Baggage, baggage, baggage – until he began to contemplate, but he didn't contemplate the baggage. He contemplated omnipresence which revealed to him there is no baggage. Baggage is a concept of the spiritual universe. So he says here:

We sit and we watch as (the thoughts go by). *No matter what thoughts come, they* (cannot hurt us). *They have no power. If we fear or hate them, we may try to stop them,* (or hold onto them). *So let us not hate or fear* (them) *or love them.*

We let the thoughts come and go while we sit and watch as beholders.

You see? And then he says in his contemplation here:

There is neither good nor evil in what I am beholding: These things (or these thoughts) *are merely pictures, without power. They cannot do anything; they cannot testify to anything; and even if they seem to be good, they are not good because they are only pictures* (images in thought).

If we try this experiment in our meditation, we soon will see that we have suffered because these pictures and thoughts have flooded us and we have become frightened and we try to run away from them and blot them out; and yet; when we are able to see them in the correct perspective, they are nothingness, just shadows.

So again, he takes us through the contemplation to that point of silent awareness. He says:

Let us stop being afraid of these names.

Or let's go up here. He's talking about the images and he says:

This one testifies to false appetite, and this next one is a prophecy of disaster, another one is a fear of lack.

Now these are all thoughts.

...but the truth is that these are only names – terrible names certainly because of their tragic connotation, but nevertheless only names – names that Adam gave to something which he did not understand – only images in thought.

Now remember in your Bible it says that the Lord God came to Adam and said, "Well, what do you want to name these things?" And Adam gave everything a name. Since we know that the second chapter of Genesis is a dream, is a series of universal images, this is Moses' way of pointing out, who gave us that story Noah and the Ark, in this story of Adam and his dream he's showing us how Adam named everything. That mortal mind named everything. Called this one young, this one old, this one sick, this one well, this one lacking, this one abundant, this one male, this one female, this one alive, this one dead. But all of those names were given to images which God did not create.

Let us stop being afraid of these names. Even if it is a picture on an x-ray machine, why should we be afraid of it? It is only a picture, a picture of mind's image. When we no longer have it in mind, it is no longer possible to have a picture of it. We can only take in pictures of that which is being held in mind. If we can see it, hear it, taste it, touch it, or smell it, it is an activity of that human mind, a mental image, the "arm of flesh" – or nothingness - a false creation which God never made.

427

So he says:

All the time we are thinking this, we are still in the mental realm, the realm of knowing the truth; but as we continue in this exercise, looking at the picture, we begin to realize it is a picture without substance or cause. Regardless of how material the condition appears to be, it is not any more material than was my lost baggage, and that was not material: It was a mental image, the realization of that (brought or) revealed Omnipresence.

Eventually (eventually through this contemplation);

Now you must understand here he says: *All the time we are thinking this, we are still in the mental realm.*

Now I hate to break the news to you, but contemplation of spiritual truth is still images in thought, only they help you calm down, which is why Joel says we must use thought to overcome thought. This contemplation, rather than just trying to force the mind to be still, this inner contemplation – just relaxing and contemplating – it brings us to a place where there is no thought, and then we have the silent awareness, and so he's telling you although contemplation is beautiful, contemplating all these truths, you're still standing in the mental images. Not until you go beyond contemplation and that stops and a silent awareness begins – ah, then is when you observe the Word made flesh.

(So) Eventually, we come to a place where there is nothing more to be said or thought. When we achieve complete quietness and peace, the mind is no longer functioning, and we have transcended mind and risen into the atmosphere of Spirit, in which we are receptive and responsive to whatever God imparts. As soon as we become unattached, that is, as soon as we are detached from thought – from hate, fear, or love of objects or people so that they can float in front of our eyes with the utmost indifference to us – (then) we are no longer in the realm of mind (or under the law): *We are then reaching, touching, or being touched by our own Soul, (by Spirit) which is God, and we are in an*

atmosphere where, when God speaks, we can hear Him. When God utters His voice, the earth melts, and all problems dissolve.

Now just so you know that it's not any easier for Joel than it is for you, I couldn't help but notice this part in the chapter before, which is *Henceforth Know We No Man After the Flesh.* Just so you know that it's just as difficult for Joel to step out of that mind and to rest back in silent awareness, he tells you. He says:

Spiritual healing cannot take place on the human plane.

In other words, it can't take place in images in thought.

It can take place only when you have stopped thinking (brief pause) (when you've stopped thinking) *of the person and the disease and the condition and the belief and the claim and have returned to Eden* (or silent awareness) *where there is only God, (or) Spirit.*

Now he tells you just how hard it was for him too.

At one time I was sitting in a room with a person who was to all sense very near death, and I felt the same discomfort that anyone would feel in similar circumstances because I realized there was nothing I could do to prevent his passing. I had no miraculous gifts or any miracle-working words that would prevent the apparently inevitable. Something had to come to me from the depths of within, or there was going to be a funeral. (And) All I could do was to turn within to that still small Voice and wait and wait and wait, and sometimes beg and plead.

Now that sounds like it was sometimes rather difficult, but he knew, he knew he had to transcend the image in thought, and he wasn't doing very good at it. And he waited and he waited and he contemplated. Sometimes he even begged and pleaded in that situation. And finally, finally, for only a moment he transcended that thought, that image in thought or those images in thought of a person dying, and he saw, he caught a glimpse—remember, he's very big in The Infinite Way book in *The New Horizon* of talking

429

about glimpsing, glimpsing the heaven of here and now. He caught a glimpse, because he says:

Finally it came, and (I heard) *"This is my beloved Son, in whom I am well pleased!" (Well) No one would have believed that if he had seen him! Here was disease in its final form; here was a person dying, and yet despite the appearance the Voice said, "This is my beloved Son, in whom I am well pleased." (And) After those words came, it was not long before they became an actual fact in demonstration; and health, harmony, and completeness were restored.*

Or you might say were revealed. You see that?

(Now) On another occasion, (he says) *I was called to my own father's side where he lay in an oxygen tent and, according to the physicians in attendance, he was on his deathbed. I stood there with no words of wisdom that could change this appearance into health;*

Now you see, Joel knows – he knows nothing from the mental realm, no mental thoughts about spiritual truth, no inner intellectual agreement with spiritual truth can reveal Reality. It must come from a deeper source. So he's not going to do that.

I stood there with no words of wisdom that could change this appearance into health; I stood there just as anyone would stand in front of his own father in such a situation—but with this difference: I knew that if God uttered His voice, the earth would melt. Standing there, watching my father breathing (really his last breath) *through that apparatus,* (suddenly) *the words came, "Man does not live by breath alone." In less than five minutes, he signaled for the nurse to take the instrument away, and two days later he was out of the hospital.*

Now that I bring up only not to show you how miraculous Joel is or anything like that or to show you how to practice principles to heal a human being. No, I bring that up just to show you that it was difficult for Joel too. There were situations in which he found it hard to step out of this very active mind, this Lord God showing these images in thought. Yet through his practice, his many really years of meditation and learning to meditate with eyes open, he was able to reach, even though it was a struggle, he was able to step out of that struggle, rest back in silent awareness until he heard the Voice say, "Man does not live by breath alone." "This is my beloved Son in whom I am well pleased."

Now for Joel it came often as words. For you it may not come as words. The words are not necessary. It's the <u>awareness</u>. You see, when he heard that Word, "This is my beloved Son in whom I am well pleased," everything about his being relaxed as that cube of ice in the water, and he rested on a sea of Spirit, and then became silently aware with no personal movement of the harmony of God is'ing and the person showed that harmony in front of him, in front of his eyes. But it wasn't a healing of a person. He was becoming aware of the Isness of God. And standing in front of his own father – that's really quite remarkable because so often we have personal attachments, all these memories, and Joel says:

It is not easy to stop seeing human beings. But I finally made it!

And it's not easy for us to stop seeing a human being when it's someone we're emotionally attached to. Yet somehow he was emotionally attached to his father. He says I stood there the same as anyone would. Yet somehow through his practice he was able to detach momentarily and catch a glimpse of Is, which came to him first, "Man does not live by breath alone," and he rested. He rested in that Word, in that inner – oh yes, okay, ah here's God – and in resting he became silently aware of that Isness of God which appeared in front of his eyes as his father saying I don't need this anymore. I'm breathing fine. You see? Do you see? He beheld Christ where the Father was appearing. He stepped out of for a moment the image in thought and caught a glimpse of the heaven of here and now, of identity, of Spirit, the Word made flesh.

And for me it doesn't come like that, very seldom. Once in a while it comes as a voice, but for me it comes as a flooding of a presence; a spiritual, tingling, vibrant, alive, spiritual energy, but that word doesn't do it justice. Being, but that word doesn't do it justice. Is'ing. And when I feel that come upon me – ah, I relax and I rest and I, too, in silent awareness bear witness to God, to Spirit, to heaven here and now, and it appears as harmony before my eyes of harmony of condition, harmony of being, harmony of place. Just I bear witness to God's harmony and it expresses as person, place, and thing harmoniously. But I know it's really still that invisible, incorporeal spiritual Is'ing.

So you see, is that making sense? I see we're out of time. We're at an hour and five minutes. I think we covered the chapter fairly well, but the point was the principle of stepping out of the images in thought which are under the law, resting back until you feel that inner movement and then standing still in silent awareness as Grace reveals Its harmony, Its being, Its Word manifesting as flesh or appearing. And so we make the movement from law to grace, and in fact, that's what I think the next – let me look.

I can't remember; it's been a while. Yep, part three. After that chapter, *This is a Spiritual Universe*, part three is called *From Law to Grace*. And so you see that really is what this principle of this book is about and hopefully this is the time which Joel referred to when he said this book probably won't be understood for many years to come. Now it's been—well, let's see—this book was done in about 1963, this is 2013, so it makes fifty years. Half a century later are we now finally seeing what this book is really about? Well good! I'm glad!

Thank you for taking the time to listen today with me. Let us have a little silence now just for a minute before we finish.

Stand still and see the salvation of God. Stand still and behold the Isness of I.

[Brief pause]

Be still and know. Be still and experience I, your own identity, Spirit appearing.

Godspeed. May you awaken suddenly, wonderfully, beautifully to the heaven of your own identity here and now. Thank you.

[Silence]

CLASS 26

IMPERSONALIZE GOD

Bill: Good morning.

I was reading something this morning from the book The Mystical I by Joel Goldsmith and the chapter *Impersonalizing God*, and it fascinated me. It just, it brought my thought to a standstill. It brought my mind to a silence, and it says this:

When we impersonalize God then our prayers will not be a mental activity.

Think of that. Think of just how outstanding that is, just how deep that is.

When we impersonalize God then our prayers will not be a mental activity.

And so I started looking at that. It just brought me to a standstill. All I could do was look at that sentence as it began to unfold from within. And wow! You know, we've talked now for a couple of years if not more of rising out of mind, out of the letter and into Spirit, into awareness. And here he says when you impersonalize God, your prayers will not be a mental activity, and so when you impersonalize God, you still step out of the mind. How does that work? What does that mean? Well, he says on the page before this:

God is being, not a being. In fact, the personalization of Spirit is the "veil."

In other words, it came to me that personalizing God is the belief in good and evil. Well, then what does that mean to personalize God? What does it mean to impersonalize God? He says on the next page:

When God has been completely impersonalized, Omnipresence will be... (a real realization.)

It will be a deep inner realization.

When God has been thoroughly impersonalized, Omnipresence will be (an experience). *I have God as Omnipresence only if I am omnipresence.*

Now that's only less than three paragraphs out of this chapter from this book, and yet it just really—it brought my mind to a standstill. It really did because it came to me if you have a personal God, then you are stuck in the mind. If you have a personal God—in other words, there's you and you pray to God, an infinite being. You pray to God, an immortal being.

All that sounds right, doesn't it? God is an infinite being; what's wrong with that? Well, if God is an infinite being, where are you? What are you?

You see, if you have a God and a you, you're in the mind. If you have a personal God, a God of your understanding, and you, you're standing in the mind and that mind contains the belief or is the belief in good and evil. Now we go around a lot, perhaps we say to ourselves in our meditations, "I and the Father are one," but that's not an inner experience. That's a statement. It's emanating from this mind which is personalizing God and personalizing a me, personalizing an I, and so we have an I and a Father, and we say that I and this Father are one. I and the infinite God are one. But while you're saying that, your experience is of two, because that's emanating out of the mind of two, out of the mind of duality, out of the belief in good and evil.

You see, if you have God as a being, then you have God and you. You have perfection and imperfection. You have God and man, God and woman. You have God and this world. You have God and the human mind. And so that's called personalizing God. We have to impersonalize God and then our prayers will no longer be a mental activity. Well, how does that work? Why is that so? I don't understand. Well, he says:

We must make no mental effort to reach God, we are already one with the Father.

Now what if we read this this way:

We must make no mental effort to reach God, we are already one Father.

We must make no mental effort to reach God, we are already Father.

That's no different than what he said on the next page where he said:

I have God as Omnipresence only if I am omnipresence.

And so impersonalizing God and impersonalizing ourselves means coming out of the mind. Again, we started with:

When we impersonalize God then our prayers will not be a mental activity.

You see, if you have a personal God that you pray to, even a personal Father and you, then you have the belief that you have to reach out to this God. There's perfection, which is good, and there's you, which is lacking, which is bad. Do you see this is the belief in good and evil? This is the veil!

On this path called The Infinite Way we must let everything we thought we ever knew fall away in order to come to what Joel calls the Experience. To experience God is'ing we have to get rid of, let go of, drop the belief in a personal God, and that's the same experience that prompted Mary at the tomb to say, "Where have you taken my Lord?"

Listen to this:

"Now upon the first day of the week, very early in the morning, they came unto the sepulchre, bringing the spices which they had prepared, and certain others with them.

And they found the stone rolled away from the sepulchre.

And they entered in, and found not the body of the Lord Jesus.

And it came to pass, as they were much perplexed thereabout, behold, two men stood by them in shining garments:"

Now what do you know so far? What is this saying? This is saying they went to the tomb. What is the tomb? What is the tomb in which Christ is buried? Think about it now. I will tell you that the mind is the tomb because he says when we impersonalize God our prayers will not be a mental activity. So we come within to have a meditation and we're standing before the tomb, and we think that Christ is buried somewhere down in that personal mind, and there's a personal mind and there's a Christ somewhere. There's a personal self and there's a God somewhere. If only I could reach God everything would be better. So we're standing in the tomb of two, and we're looking for Christ.

"And they were afraid, and (they) bowed down their faces to the earth, and they said unto them, (the angels said unto them) *Why seek ye the living among the dead?*

He is not here, he is risen:"

This is what happens in your inner chamber. Eventually you reach the place where God says unto you, which is an angel, that voice, that movement of Spirit says to you, "It is I. Why are you seeking among the dead?" And if you have ears to hear, you realize that God cannot be reached through mental activity. That's seeking the living among the dead. That mind and everything in it is dead. Even the God that you laid in it carefully. You built it piece upon piece, concept upon concept. Even your walk through truth, you built a God and you laid it in that tomb gently, and you go there and you look for it in a certain place in your journey and you're met instead with the Word of God, and It says unto you, *"Why seek ye the living among the dead? He is not here, he is risen.*

And it befuddles you. Like I said, I read this this morning and my mind came to a standstill. Wait – when we impersonalize God our prayers are no longer a mental activity. When we impersonalize God, impersonalize ourselves, our prayers are not in the mind. And when we impersonalize God, impersonalize ourselves, our prayers are an inner experience. Now again, God is being, but not a being. If you have a Being, a God, a Spirit, a Christ – and you – you have not impersonalized God. You have not impersonalized Self. The entire Christ mission, the entire Christ activity, the entire Christ being is impersonal, and it must be not a thought but an experience. So having a personal sense of God or a personal sense of self is the belief in good and evil. That's the veil! He says here:

The personalization of Spirit is "the Veil."

What's the veil? The veil is that which covers the experience, covers – well, it's the stone in front of the tomb, and yet these people in this story which came to the sepulchre, they found the stone rolled away and they entered in. Then they found the shining angel which said, *"Why seek ye the living among the dead? He is not here, but is risen: …"* And I submit to you that in a certain place on this path you come face to face with the fact that your God is not alive; it's dead. And you come face to face with the fact that that God upon which you relied, the God separate from you, the God that you prayed up to or even within to, must be crucified. Must be impersonalized. Then, then you can enter in and you can be instructed by the voice of God, by the angel of God. Then you will be told, everyone of us will be told, *"Why are you seeking the living among the dead? He is not here, he is risen:"* Why are you still personalizing God? Step out of that mental activity.

Make no mental effort to reach God, you are already one with the Father.

You <u>are</u> the Father, God Omnipresence, I Omnipresence, one Omnipresence.

So can you see how when I read this this morning how just incredibly wonderful it was.

Just two pages out of The Mystical I and just two paragraphs and just two sentences.

God is being, not a being, the personalization of Spirit is the "veil."

When we impersonalize God then our prayers will no longer be a mental activity.

It's beautiful! It's wonderful because it's telling us how to commune with that risen Christ. The risen Christ is the experience of Christ, your Christ identity, your Father identity, your God identity. It is time in your journey to bury these concepts of God no matter how wonderful they've been through the years. They prevent you from the experience of the living. While you entertain them and pray up to them and have no answers you are the walking dead. Yet all the time I within you says, "He's not here." This should bring you to a place where your mind comes to a standstill and there is no more mind there, no more personal mind, no more personal self, no more personal God, no more mental activity. And in the silence from a personal self, I reveal Myself, the infinite Self, the only Self, and we hear within, *"It is I; be not afraid."* I am the life, *I.*

You cannot understand I. You will never draw pictures of I. You will never make concepts of I, and yet when there is no more mental activity, I will live you. I am the life. Come unto me. Die to the personal sense. Impersonalize and *"behold, I come quickly."* To those who do this will I give to eat of the hidden manna, the hidden identity. Listen again to what you've probably heard so many times you think you already know it, but realize now that this is Identity speaking. This is the angel in the tomb speaking of the living.

*"In the beginning was the Word **I** and **I** was with God, and **I** was God.*

The same was in the beginning with God.

*All things were made by **I**; and without **I** was not any thing made that was made.*

*In **I** was life; and the life was the light of men.*

And the light shineth in (the tomb) in the darkness; and the darkness comprehended it not."

Why are you seeking **I** in the tomb, in the mental activity?

*"The light, (or **I**), was in the world, and the world was made by **I**, and the world knew **I** not.*

And I come unto my own, and my own receive I not.

*But as many as receive **I**, to them give **I** power to become the living, (the living) sons of God, even to them that believe on **I**:*

*Which are born now not of blood, nor of the will of the flesh, nor of the will of mind, but of **I**.*

*And (**I am**) made flesh, and dwell among you, and we behold the glory of **I**, the only begotten of the Father, full of grace and truth."*

Do you not see the marvelous treasure that is not buried in the tomb of mental activity, but is born as an activity of I living you? Impersonalize God. Impersonalize self. No more mental activity born from the belief in good and evil, in God and you. Only one thing now remains: That you die to all of that. Become silent, a new silence, a silence from personal God, from a personal self. An impersonal silence of being. *"And, behold, I come quickly;"* *"(And) Behold, I make all things new."* And behold, I am the new Jerusalem.

Let us be still now before this temple, for the tomb of mental activity has been transcended and he is risen and I stand before the temple of the living God and I listen and I behold I am the Father. And [Philip], representing the human mind says, *"Lord, show us the Father."* And the Father speaking as Christ says, "Oh (Philip) *Have I been so long a time with thee and thou hast not known me?"* And the angel says to you, *"He is not here: for he is risen."* And the living says to you, "I am here, right here. Have I been here all this time and you never realized I?" Be still. Rest from a personal God. Rest from a personal self. *"(And) Behold, I make all things new."*

Yes, I am the way. I am the Supply. I am the Companion. I am the Life. And when the mental activity, when the personal God and the personal self is buried, then I am resurrected. I come in a moment you think not. And you, you take no thought. I am the way.

I would like to share with you at this time a couple of—well, parts of a couple of the letters received in Herb Fitch's exercise to write to the president. These are quite wonderful, and it shows that this group as a whole is making great progress. This one says:

Dear Mr. President: Cease ye from man whose breath is in his nostrils.

Now is that not what we just said? Cease ye from a personal sense of self.

We have been seeing with our eyes and hearing with our ears and then commenting and reacting to what we see and hear.

Stop It! This is exactly the same as stepping out of the tomb in which we think we will find the living. Stepping out of the mental activity, the human mind activity.

We should be seeing with our inner eyes and hearing with our inner ears with that Christ awareness that judges not by appearances. Then we will know that all of the sin, disease, death, lack, limitation, and chaos in the world today come for only one reason: Sowing to the flesh.

What does that mean? Now we understand that a little differently, don't we? Sowing to the flesh does not mean going out and having a good time on Saturday night. Sowing to the flesh means having a personal sense of self anywhere and a personal God. You did not know personalizing God was sowing to the flesh, did you? And yet it is, because it's a part of the mental activity that creates this fleshly sense of world, of self. Yes, we should be seeing with our inner eyes and hearing with our inner ears with Christ awareness. Yes, yes, yes! *"(But) He is not here: he is risen."* And to come into that type of seeing and hearing is done only when the human mind is still, when there is no mental activity.

Strange, isn't it? When there's no mental activity God reveals Itself. I reveal I.

And so yes, further this person says:

How do we sow to the Spirit? Pray without ceasing. Be still and wait. This is prayer, but know what we're waiting for, and that's to feel Me stirring, fizzing, tingling inside of you. Me is the activity of Christ.

Yes, the activity of the Living. When you rise out of that tomb and there is no mental activity and you are still and waiting upon I, then I take over and that's expressed and felt as a stirring, a tingling, a fizzing, a movement, an activity of Christ, of I.

And so this person says:

Mr. President, this is the ultimate truth. There's nothing left to teach. Come, follow Me. Do not follow Adam and Eve who ate from the tree of knowledge of good and evil and were expelled from the Garden. Come, follow Me, follow Me.

And this is what we are saying in this talk today. Do not follow this mental activity, this personal God. Do not pray to this personal God because it's only praying to a belief. Praying to a belief doesn't work! It's a mental activity. Ah, but says Joel: When you impersonalize God, then the mental activity stops because you don't have a God and a you. You have I, living. You have the living I as an experience.

And so that was one of the beautiful letters and now let's look at a second one, and we won't read all of it, but just touching a few parts. It says:

Dear Mr. President: The answer to every problem of sin, sickness, disease, or death is the same. All appearance is an image, an illusory fabric whose substance is a flimsy dream. Only one world seems evident to the human sense mind and it is fed and maintained by our belief in a selfhood apart from God.

Which is another way of saying it is fed by our belief in a God apart from Self. Just think of the depth of that. If you have a God apart from Self, a God apart from I, then you are standing in this duality.

We have but one true objective, and that is to rise above and see through the sense illusions and all false concepts of people, place, things, and conditions.

Isn't that fantastic and how like the other letter this is? So this letter is saying that we must rise out of the tomb of sense illusions or false concepts of people. In other words, a person, a personal sense of self, a personal sense of God. And down here a little farther it says to the president:

Call for Me at any time or any place and then listen within intently. This is praying without ceasing. Rest, relax. I will answer.

Isn't that just fantastic. Isn't this beautiful? These two people are in entirely different parts of the country of the United States and yet the consciousness they are standing in, this new Jerusalem, is pretty much exactly the same, isn't it? It's wonderful. I find it fascinating.

And so both of these letters are suggesting that what the president and anyone else of us needs to do is to die to this personal sense of self, to go within, to step out of the tomb of mental activity or sense illusions, not pray to a personal God and not be a person praying, but stand so still that the living God, the living water will be poured through us, as us, and I will stand revealed. The I that has stood at the door of consciousness almost seemingly forever, that I will take over and live Itself as you, and then there will not be you and I, you and this I, you and a I. There will be I. *"Be not afraid." "It is I." "And I come quickly;"* and I come whose right it is to live and I am the son of God. And *"I and the Father are one"* because I am Father. See how beautifully this all fits together.

Now let us have a moment of silence and see what else there is before completing this talk.

In order to impersonalize yourself, you are going to find you will have to impersonalize any such concepts as my supply, my companions, my health. Somehow the grace will be granted to you to rise out of that tomb. You really believe you have buried him, the Life that God Is. You believe you buried him into a tomb of humanhood and this human is sixty years old and this human is forty years old. This human is fifty, seventy years old. And this human is male and this human is female. And this human has an education and this human does not. And this human has skills and this human is an artist. And this human is a mother and this human is a father. And this human has children and this human has parents. All, all, all of this is where you think you have laid the Christ inside of this tomb.

Joel's start to his journey was the fact that he realized God is not in the human tomb and will never be. That human tomb in which you think you have cleverly buried the son of God, behold, in the silence, an angel speaks unto you and says, *"Why seek ye the living among the dead? He is not here: he is risen."*

And as you impersonalize God there is not <u>a</u> God. There is I, God. And stand in the stillness, then the living God, the living I reveals grace and truth and lives itself and you have the power to become the son of God. If you will receive I, I will live you. I will be you, and I will make all things new.

Choose ye this day whom ye will follow. As the letter said: Will you follow the fleshly beliefs? Will you sow to the flesh? Will you know everyone as flesh or will you henceforth know no one after the flesh, not even self. Will you have no supply, no family, no companions? Will you have no health? Will you be animated as I living, the living God? Will this be your realization, your experience?

Come. Behold, I am the Way. Behold, I am the Truth. Behold, I am the Life.

Again and again I repeat: *When we impersonalize God our prayers will not be a mental activity.*

I must be that Presence, but if I am going to have a God and a me, I am not impersonalizing. I am setting up a sense of duality. I must have God as Omnipresence only because I am Omnipresence.

Thank you for sending in your letters. Thank you for helping with donations to keep the site up and running with all the Herb Fitch talks and all these talks. And thank you for walking together as one into this new Consciousness, the new Jerusalem, the new Consciousness of I.

[Silence]

EQUAL WITH GOD

Bill: Good morning.

This is Sunday October 20, 2013. I've been thinking a lot about how much the belief in good and evil influences our lives, influences our sense of identity, our sense of the world. Even in such things as our prayer life, our meditation periods, our conduct. This, of course, stems from way back in the early Hebrew days when Moses gave us the law. It was the right and proper thing at that time because the collective consciousness wasn't ready to live by grace. You had, of course, people worshipping many different gods, doing such things as sacrificing – actually throwing living children into the fire or into the volcano or just however they disposed of them, sacrificing them, and then they moved to the sacrifice of animals, and in the early days of mankind this was acceptable.

After Moses left the law and all the rules that went with it, if you lived by that law – and the priests were quick to tell you when you didn't – but if you lived by that law and you sacrificed animals and things to God, then you were a good religious person. And if you didn't, well then, you were condemned. Sometimes people picked up stones and stoned you to death. That's a pretty brutal civilization, if you can call it that. I mean they had houses and they had forms of transportation, chariots and horses, but I don't know if you can call them civilized.

So into that came Jesus Christ, someone that had transcended the law. Where does the law take place for real? The law is part of the letter, or you might say the letter of the law. And all those who believe in the law and practice the law – well, they'll live by the rules, the ten commandments, for instance. In other religions there are other precepts, but they bring an uncivilized, brutal, almost animalistic people into some sense of civilization, and thanks to Moses for doing that because we may not have survived as a species.

But anyway, into this civilization of high priests dotting every "i" and crossing every "t" and telling people what they can eat and how they must wash their hands and how they must wash the food and what they must do on Friday night and Saturday, into this where the sacrifice of a lamb was proper to appease God, into this came Christ Jesus with a different message, a message of love, a message of grace, a message of dying out of all that into being reborn of something called Spirit. And the amazing thing is that he lasted as long as he did, traveling the holy lands in that time period and speaking of these spiritual principles. I'm surprised really that they let him go on for three years. I mean the scribes and the Pharisees and the Hebrews of the time, they must have been completely shocked.

Remember Joel says to us truth is shocking, and it is. It still is because many of us are still being influenced by the law and living by the law, and we don't realize it. We still have a very strong sense of what's evil and what's good.

Now you might agree if someone tells you that a serial killer killing Christians just because they're Christians and maybe killing a hundred of them or more is pretty serious. That's a pretty evil person. Oh, there's probably all sorts of reasons. You could go to the psychiatrist and he would give you one reason, the psychologist another. You might go to the geneticist and he could tell you or she could tell you that the person is predisposed to violence. You might go to the sibling or relative who says, "Well, this person underwent a lot of abuse and now it's showing up in this," but in one way or another you believe this is not good and you see them finally captured and tried on national TV and okay. The murderer, the killer, the serial killer is now being put to death and that seems all right to you or to us.

But what do we have? We have a belief in good, which is not killing, and the belief in bad, which is a serial killer or evil, and the belief in the law and punishment, and if we don't believe in the law as it is in our courts, then we believe in the law of karma: What you sow so shall you reap. And because this person killed a hundred and fifteen people, hundred and fifteen Christians, this is a bad person who sowed some bad things and surely that badness is going to come back around.

Well, these are all concepts that we entertain. Yet, I'm going to tell you something that is shocking when considered deeply. And that is: God doesn't care if you're a murderer. Now that would be even shocking to admit in a church today publicly. Imagine standing at the podium, "My friends, I have discovered God doesn't care if you're a murderer. If you feel like murdering, well fine. God doesn't care." Can you imagine the gasps out in the audience? But it must be true. It has to be true or the spiritual principles are a lie.

Now I was looking at the <u>Realization of Oneness</u> book and a sentence really jumped out at me. It says – if I can find it – it says:

<u>Sin is really the acceptance of a material universe</u>. Just going back to the belief that there are human beings is the sin that throws a person (well, outside the kingdom).

So the original sin is accepting a material universe. The original sin is accepting persons, good or evil. The original sin is accepting human beings.

Now do you believe that God sins? Of course not! God is too pure to behold human beings, so how could God care if one of them is murdering a hundred and fifteen others? If God cared about that picture, He would do something about it, and that's what we ask and many people, all people perhaps, at one point in their lives say, "How can God let this happen!?"

God doesn't care! That's tough. That's a hard one to swallow, isn't it? But it has to be true, because if God cared, God would be hypnotized.

And the proof that God doesn't care about a murderer or murdering, what about one of the greatest saints of all time who had such a profound love of God and such a profound conscious awareness of God that he was able to raise someone from the dead? Now you might think I'm referring to Jesus Christ, but I'm not. I'm referring to St. Paul, the murderer of Christians, the serial killer that systematically killed Christians and their only crime was promoting the Christ message in the middle of a world of law.

How many did he kill? How many did he stop from pouring out this message? We will never know maybe. Yet he's revered. He's a saint. He had one of the most profound spiritual experiences ever recorded in the Bible. So blazing was the light that it made him blind to a material sense of universe. Did God care that he killed a hundred and fifteen or more Christians? No, no. When Paul surrendered Paul, another being took over other than that human being, and that being called itself Paul. Before that it was Saul. So Saul was the serial killer, but God never created Saul, and once Saul surrendered it was immediate. That being called Paul took over, Paul being an emanation of Christ, of God, of Identity. And it was immediate. There's no begging or beseeching. There wasn't even paying back any karma. It was immediate. And so we can see by that one example that God is too pure to behold iniquity.

There was a mystic in the fifteenth or sixteenth century that said God abhors a vacuum. All you have to do is become empty of false sense of self and automatically you're full of God. There's no earning. There's no being good. There's no paying a price first – first you have to pay this penalty. Those are all ideas that stem from the law, from those ancient Hebrews that said it was okay to sacrifice a lamb and before that, earlier than that even, was it Abraham that was willing to sacrifice his own son? But you see, that was the worship of law.

And now here's a very strange proposition. **God did not create the law.** Now if you realize what that means, that means if you go out and kill a hundred and fifteen people there's no penalty because God never made the law. You are just as able to inherit the entire infinite kingdom as the person that devoted their lives to being good. What about the person(s) that devoted their lives to being a monk or a priest or preacher or a nun or a sister of some order. What about these folks that have devoted their lives to doing good in the world? Does God look down and smile upon them? Is there a reward after this in heaven?

Well, I have news – not very good news (chuckles) – **God doesn't care what good you do!** That can be disheartening, can't it?

"Well, I've lived my whole life trying to be good. I've never – I've – you know, I've – I made little mistakes, but I haven't done anything heinous, nothing huge. I didn't murder anybody. I didn't commit adultery. I didn't wipe out a nation or put people in the gas ovens. I lived a pretty good life. I didn't hurt people on purpose and I go to church every Wednesday and every Sunday and especially I go to midnight Mass on Christmas and Easter and I'm up at the daybreak to see the rising of the sun, the dawn on Easter morning. I give part of my money to charity. I've tried to be good my entire life. Oh sure, I admit as a child I lied sometimes. I even stole once or twice. Perhaps I gossiped, but I've been good!"

And I repeat: **God doesn't care.**

Well, can you see how this would be very, very threatening to the Hebrew state of mind which says you must live by the law and dot every "i" and cross every "t" and sacrifice this and do this on Tuesday and this on Saturday and this on Friday and wash your food just so. Can you see that? No, I'm not saying anything against the Jewish race because my ex-wife was Jewish and I have known very beautiful people that are Jewish. But I am only speaking of the Hebrew state of mind in that time when Christ was walking for those three years and spreading a new message.

And think how that state of mind, that rigid, living only by the law and nothing but the law so help you God – think how that must have looked upon Christ Jesus saying, "Well, you know, God doesn't care if you murder. And you know, God doesn't care if you're good. All that has to go."

Why, that must have just scared 'em to death! Why without that we'd go back to being barbarians and uncivilized and without that, without everything Moses gave us we would – we would cease to exist. And yet the timing of Christ is never wrong and so it was time to release gently at first this new message.

God did not create the law, has no interest in the law whatsoever.

God did not create human beings, has no interest in what they do good or bad.

There's no punishment. There's no reward. You're living in a state of mind which sees something God did not create.

And so imagine a person being told that the only sin is the acceptance of a material world. Why this individual must be mad! They must be – they just must be crazy. Let's lock him up. **Let's crucify him!** You can see that perhaps we were there doing the yelling, because it's two thousand years later and we're still just beginning to see the message. So perhaps we were there doing the yelling and now we are here trying to see what was released in consciousness and has gathered momentum ever since then.

Okay, so I also discovered in this book a paper that someone had typed up for me called Joel on Spiritual Healing. It's just five paragraphs. I'm not gonna read the whole thing. He says:

We cannot take the mortal concept of creation into heaven or harmony. We do not bring God to the material sense of existence. We surrender the belief and dream of material living for the life divine. We exchange the sense world for the spiritual formations of divine creation. Does that not say that God doesn't care about your material sense of being, your human being, but that there's a divine creation? [Says Joel]: *To gain the spiritual awareness of life and its perfect formation is our purpose. Bit by bit we are giving up our concern for the structural universe and in proportion as we do that, we gain the awareness of the life which is incorporeal, harmonious, and permanent.*

And I see looking here in the dictionary: Incorporeal (not corporeal, not material, nonmaterial beings without material existence). So when he says that: *Bit by bit we are giving up our concern for the structural universe and in proportion we are gaining the awareness of the life which is not material, nonmaterial beings without material existence, or not made of matter.*

It is impossible for God to care what a human being does.

Now I'm sorry. I know that shatters thousands of years of beliefs and I know it's – it's bitter in the belly. Nevertheless, it **has** to be true. Otherwise, God is just as hypnotized as human beings are.

God does not care if you murder. There is no punishment at any time from God. God does not care if you're good or philanthropic. God doesn't care, because in both cases there's a you and there's a God! There's a material person, a material being, a material universe and God, a spirit. So that means all of the times that you thought quietly when you sit down to pray or meditate, even just briefly thought, "God, I know I haven't been meditating a lot lately, but if you just heal this situation, bring your presence to it and heal it, I will meditate ten times a day. I promise."

Now what did he say? We just read it. He said we cannot bring God to a material sense of existence and we cannot bring a material sense of existence into heaven or to God.

We have to die to any belief that there has ever been a human being created!

Remember what Joel told us, *"It's not easy to stop (seeing) human beings. … But I finally made it!"* Now that includes your human being; you, the human being. You have to stop seeing you where God exists. And you have to let go and die to all the beliefs that are connected to that old Hebraic law and system of law that Moses gave us. We are invited to rise above the letter of the law.

Moses gave us a law, but grace and truth came by Christ Jesus.

How much are you still living by the law? This week perhaps you caught a cold and your thought immediately, immediately goes to what did I do or not do and you have a human being trying to be good, trying not to do evil. You have a human being examining their thought to see what did I – how did I go wrong?

God doesn't care! And you have to get to the place where you don't care, because you're not looking at a material existence anywhere. You see the depth at which this has to go in your consciousness? Even the little things. You stub your toe. Uh-oh, what was I just thinking?

No. **God never created the law.** Look at that. Feel the depth of that. God did not create law, not the law that Moses taught us about. God created spiritual law in which Spirit is perfect, but not this law of good and evil. God did not create that law and so God did not create karma. Who is there to sow and reap? If you have a person that can sow – yes, that person will reap. But it's all in the realm of mental activity and how much we are chained to that. How much we are not free yet. How much we are living by the law. Like I said, you stub your toe and, "Oh, what was I just thinking?" You examine your thought to see if you were thinking something wrong and the wrongness that you were doing was somehow creating this backlash.

It has to be a brand new awareness of a kingdom where no law exists except for God is'ing. There has to be a presence walking, talking where no human exists. There has to be a grace living, being, living Itself where no law exists. Look at Jesus Christ and his responses. Stretch forth your arm. Open your eyes. Nothing about – yes, your parents or your grandparents sinned and this is why—no, nothing. *"Neither do I condemn thee."* Go. You're free. <u>Even in the very act she's caught, in the very act</u>. What does he see? I don't condemn you. I don't even see a human. Go, but stop living as a human.

The sin, the original sin, the only sin that there is anywhere, the only mistake is really the acceptance of a material universe. Just going back to the belief that there are human beings is the sin that throws a person out of heaven. Now that's Joel. Just going back to the belief that there are human beings. You **cannot** influence God. We are taught in The Infinite Way God Is, Is, Is, and you cannot change God, but how many of your prayers are secretly, quietly an attempt to influence God? Even little things. Now I am sitting here and I am practicing being silent like the Kailua study tells me twelve times a day and I expect that pretty soon something wonderful will happen.

Oh really, and who is that something wonderful going to happen to, since God already is? Do you see? We carry our law right into – or we try to carry the law into the kingdom of heaven and it cannot come in. Again, the story about the man who knocked on the gate.

"Who's there?"

"It's me. I'm meditating twelve times a day now. Can I have my spiritual experience, please?"

"Go away! There's no room."

Remember he does that three times over several years and finally at the end he knocks on the door.

"Who's there?"

"Thou." And immediately found himself in heaven.

God doesn't care who you are! (chuckles) Get that through your mind. I know it's really difficult. It's hard! It's a hard saying. What about this loving father? "Oh man, for so many years I've had this belief in a loving father and me." Yes, and that's why you're still standing outside the kingdom of heaven. That must go too. "Oh, but I've had this concept of God as my this and my personal savior and – ." I know. So did Mary Magdalene and that's why she stood in the garden and yet didn't know where she was, and she said, *"They have taken my Lord away"* because she was standing in the kingdom and she didn't know it. She had her Lord and her, and her love was deep. Yet it was the love of a concept.

Our concepts of God must go. Our concepts of self must go. We have to come to God empty, a vacuum. When Joel says we turn in meditation almost a vacuum. That's what he means. And so Mary turned and let that concept go. *"They have taken my Lord."* Yes, they have taken the concept and now Mary turned, and look, in the very garden suddenly her eyes are open. *"Master!"* She sees the Christ.

The two gentlemen on the road to Emmaus talking all the time with the Christ. They think it's a human being. They think there's somebody instructing them and them. Suddenly the concepts disappear and a moment of taking bread their eyes are opened and they see Christ right here, the only presence.

And what about you? Are you willing to make this ultimate sacrifice, the only real sacrifice – the sacrifice that there's <u>you</u> that needs to make a sacrifice? Are you willing to let that go? Are you willing to release man as he puts it in this book, <u>Realization of Oneness</u>? Are you willing to release man? God doesn't care what man, human man or woman does – evil or good – makes absolutely no difference, because if it made a difference God would be just as hypnotized as the person seeing duality. But God is too pure to behold iniquity and canst not look upon evil or good. I think they cut that out. I think it was there originally. Canst not look upon evil <u>or</u> good.

If I walk out the front door right now of the house I'm in and walk to the end of my little walkway and look at the mountain right across the street from me – it starts right across the street and goes up – I can look at the beauty of fall, of autumn. There are golds and reds, greens, purples, yellows, oranges, salmon color. Oh, there are so many beautiful colors. And above it the sky is blue with a few white puffy clouds and there's a gentle breeze blowing and it's beautiful and you can smell – what is that? Oh yes, that's the smell of the first chimney this year. It's gorgeous. And guess what! **God doesn't care!** (chuckles) If I see a material sense of universe, good or evil, I see something God did not make.

Why wait, wait! What – you're taking away my Lord! Yes, I'm taking away your concept.

I'm taking away the entire belief in good and evil. It does not exist. God never made the law. And if He didn't make the law, He didn't make either side of it, not the evil nor the good.

You've taken everything away. There's nothing now but a vacuum. This is where the belief of some of the ancient people went off line or went off course. Being taught by Buddha that the world is Maya or illusion, they just stopped doing anything. Well, if it's all illusion they're like my friend down there in Florida who says, and he's uh – well, I won't tell you his name, but he says that it's all an illusion, so why bother. We might as well just party till we die. And so many of the people sat on the roadside begging alms. Why bother to get a job? It's all so meaningless. Why bother do anything good? It's all so meaningless. I'm just gonna sit here and just lie around, I guess, 'cause it's all karma. I can't do anything about it. Or it's all illusion. I can't do anything about it.

No, both of those approaches are not going to help. So you can spend several lifetimes saying, "Well, this is just an illusion. I might as well have fun. Might as well make a million dollars or I might as well go out and kill some evildoers, have a career in the military. I might as well run for office and try to make some changes in this city, in this county, in this state, in this nation. Or perhaps I'll just do good my entire life and make money, give it away and help poor people. And saying to yourself that this is an illusion and so why bother. I'm just gonna sit by the side of the road and beg alms and as long as I have enough to eat I'm fine. It's destiny, nothing I can do about it. I'm gonna be whatever I'm supposed to be. All of that is the wrong approach. Why?

If you are not consciously aware of strawberry shortcake, you will never have strawberry shortcake. You don't even know that it exists. I remember when I was looking around for a good automobile I finally settled on one with all-wheel drive, which was really nice up here in the mountains in the snow, but I didn't know that particular car existed until it entered my consciousness and I became consciously aware of it. Once I became consciously aware of it – ah, then I saw those cars everywhere. They were part of my consciousness, and it was also true – it's also true of strawberry shortcake. If you come visit – say from Tibet – and you've never tasted any strawberry shortcake, somebody shows it to you the first time – ah, it enters consciousness. Or maybe they give you a pizza for the first time. Ah-ha! It enters consciousness. Now you have it – your consciousness. You can order it; it's a part of you. Right? On a little tiny aspect, a little tiny part.

If you are not consciously aware of Christhood, of your sonship, of God is'ing Itself where you thought you were – if you have not had the experience of God is'ing right here and now, then you still believe you're a human, and the sin is not in trying to be a good human or in trying to be a bad human. The sin is in a belief in a human. The sin is in the belief in a structural universe. The sin is in the belief in a material world.

God doesn't care about it because God never made it. God never made the world or the person or the law in which you've been living. And so trying to bring that to God or bring God to that is the wrong way. And throwing up your arms and saying well, that's it, it's destiny. I can't change it. None of it's real, so why bother. That's the wrong way too.

We want the middle way. We want to awaken consciously. We want to have the conscious living awareness of God is'ing as the I that I am. When you have that, you have overcome the world even if only for a few seconds in your meditation. You have overcome all of those beliefs, all of the belief in the law, all of the belief in good and evil, all of the belief in something you do or don't do can influence God. All of the law that God never made is overcome in the moment you are consciously aware of God is'ing Itself as you.

And then, of course, it's impossible to do anything because God is doing the doing. God is being the being. God is knowing the knowing. And God can't be good and God can't be evil. God can only be whatever God Is, and this you only know by experiencing, by being consciously aware of the Is that is. Then you know what God is.

Several of our precious thoughts and beliefs have to go. We must take away your Lord because if I don't go away, the comforter cannot come. If you don't lose your precious beliefs in a personal God that cares about you or in a God that condemns you and punishes you, if you do not believe those – if you do not let go of and lose – well, *"Loose him, and let him go"* of those concepts – if you do not let go of them you cannot enter the kingdom.

You cannot enter the conscious awareness until you let them go and stand there as a vacuum even though it can be painful because they've been your precious beliefs for centuries. Yet you have said you do not want to remain a child. You want to put aside childish things. You have said that you want to enter the kingdom. You want the conscious awareness of oneness with the God that Is. You want to know God aright so that you can know your own eternal being. And if this is true, then you must let these beliefs and concepts die.

When you see yourself saying, "God, I know I haven't been meditating fully and would you please forgive me?" You must stop right then and remind yourself, "Well, how silly! Who's this me appealing to God? Is that one of those silly human beings that God doesn't even care about? I've got to stop living in that consciousness. I've got to stop! Now into this silence pour Thyself." Or whatever word comes to you to remind you to be the vacuum that beholds and bears witness to **God** in action.

This must be not just in your meditation. Yes, it starts there. It starts there for a few seconds, maybe a minute or two or ten or fifteen. It must become your conscious awareness daily walking, talking, sitting, sleeping.

We must die to the belief in a material universe.

We must die to the belief in a human being including ourself. To gain the conscious awareness of eternal Life and its perfection forming itself, then we must bit by bit give up our concern for a structural universe or person or thing and gain the awareness of eternal Life which is incorporeal.

Incorporeal—is there life under the law that's incorporeal? Could you show it to me, please? All life under the law is material. Think about that. Think about it. All life that comes into judgment under the law is corporeal, material, human, structural. The invisible Is'ing incorporeality of God never touches the law, for the law cannot exist in that being. And so here are the lawyers, the judges, the priests, the high priests, the Pharisees, the scribes, and they come to this man calling himself Jesus and they ask him, "Are you the Christ?" And, of course, he denies it because he knows no human being is anything. There is only the Christ. What do you mean, "Are you the Christ?" That's ridiculous. And he says, *"I and my Father are one." "He that seeth me,"* (that really sees into the invisible and sees the incorporeal me sees the Father, for) *"I, (the incorporeal) and (the) Father are one."* And they take up stones, those scribes and Pharisees and high priests, because he made himself equal with God.

And now I say to you the time perhaps is finally here because I really feel that it was us that picked up the stones. We could not live without the law. We were not ready to renounce humanhood. We were not ready to die. Die and be born again? What are you talking about? Now perhaps we are ready. We are ready to die to humanhood so much so that we'll even give up our concept of good and evil, our concept of the Lord, of God. Our concept of being good enough to enter heaven or being evil enough to stay out. Perhaps we are ready to give up the entire belief in a structural universe, which is the only universe that can be under the law. Perhaps more than just changing – well now, I don't believe in just a structural universe – I believe there's an invisible one too.

Well, that's not enough! You're still a human being with beliefs.

Perhaps now we're willing to become that vacuum, that beholder, that witness. Perhaps we're really ready to let our silence, our silence from any sense of self, be the abiding place of Infinite Spirit, the Incorporeal Self which has never come under the law. That Self, in that Self, in the conscious awareness of that Self, consciously aware of being that I, there is no law. There's nobody to please. There's nothing to prove. There's nothing to earn. There's nothing to be worthy of. There is only grace.

Grace. Even the dictionary calls grace a free gift. You cannot merit it or earn it. Moses gave us the law, but grace came from Christ Jesus, and now after two thousand years, are you ready? Are you ready? Yes, it feels kind of scary, doesn't it? There's no anchors. I'm just floating on a sea of Spirit. Yes, and this you must do. You must launch out into the deep and there you will find buried treasures the likes of which millions and millions have never dreamed.

When you are confronted with any form of humanhood—whether bad or good, whether evil or beautiful—meet it with this moment of incorporeality, this second of silence. Meet it by witnessing God in action and that evil will dissolve and so will that good. And yes, they both must go no matter how precious they are to you – so that you can see – because when you have the conscious awareness of God is'ing as you, then you have overcome the law.

Can it be done? *"Be of good cheer; I have overcome* (this law).*"* Yes, it can. Not by a human being trying to overcome, trying to be good enough, trying to be worthy, trying to stop being critical or stop overeating or stop doing this or that. That's still a human under the law. Even if you overcome that negative character trait, you would still be a human under the law. Something will get you from left field because when you live under the law that's what happens. All humans are born; all humans must die. Yeah, it's true. What I was going to say: All humans are dead, 'cause they are. They're dead to the conscious awareness of Is'ing Spirit, Christhood.

"Come, follow me." I have overcome the law. I live by grace and I tell you, you can too. This is your inheritance. You have one Father. Call no one on earth your father. You're not under anything. You in your silence and the Father are one, one being,

incorporeally, eternally Omnipresence. This is my beloved Son and I love him.

What is? What is the beloved Son? The silence that bears witness to the Father. Anything else, God is too pure to behold. Yes, says Joel, let my silence be Thy abiding place. What a wonderful – well, that's like the Buddhist pointing at the moon.

And so now let us be silent for a moment.

[Brief silence]

Fulfill the one Self that I Is.

Now be still and come to the conscious awareness. Bear witness. Behold, God Is – Is – Is.

[Brief silence]

Well, I see it's been an hour and I could go on, but I think that's quite enough. It may take several listenings to realize the depth of what must be – well, what we must die out of in order to awaken into spiritual identity, Christhood, oneness, Omnipresence.

Thank you and Godspeed.

[Silence]

CLASS 28

THE TEMPLE OF THE LIVING GOD

Bill: Soul to Soul, Spirit to Spirit. Blessings.

I speak today to the group we have gathered which consists of twenty-seven members; (134 now). I also speak to anyone else who may hear this talk. Ye are the temple of the living God and so please listen, Taulere, Bogya, Brian, Eileen, Liz, Heather, Barbara, Joe M., Cheryl, John. Please listen, Kelly, Kahn, Linda, Kim, Laurie, Sylvia, Marian, Pam. Listen, Pat, Rebecca, Kimberly, Bill, Joe S., Susan, Terry, Laura, and Wilhemina.

Ye are the temple of the living God and I, the I within you, the living God send you forth as saints in the spiritual kingdom. Your Consciousness is now a benediction, a blessing, a healer and you must consciously accept the role which I, God, have given you. As saints it means you are now the living God on earth. God through your Consciousness will uplift all. All who come in contact with your Consciousness must feel the lifting up of the I within you, and this is now your work. The days of seeking something, seeking to add something to your individual human life are past. You have been – well, you have been lifted into a new role on earth.

If you have seen the old pictures of saints in ages past or perhaps a picture of Christ Jesus or even of Buddha or Krishna, you will notice that the artists painted an aura around their head.

Why did they do this? Because it was depicting the Presence that enveloped them, the Presence which poured through their Consciousness. They were the living light, that living Presence on earth. This is your work. This is the work now you are given to do. You are to forget your personal self and be an instrument for the grace of God. You are to be a channel for the living waters. Yes, I within you send you forth saints.

How are you to do this? I shall remind you again: If you abide in my Word and let my Word abide in you, you will bear fruit richly. This is how you do it. You must have many periods throughout the day and in the night if you awaken to sit down, remember the specific principles of The Infinite Way, and at the end of the treatment which you will give yourself you will be still and receive the Holy Spirit. The Spirit, then, the living waters, the living God will pour through your Consciousness and make your Consciousness a temple not made with hands, a temple of the living God, and those that come into your Consciousness throughout your day will feel this Spirit. They will feel uplifted. They will receive healings. You may not even know who receives a healing, and then again, you may if they tell you. That is not your concern. Your concern is to be the temple of the living God.

And what are the specific truths you must know when you give yourself a treatment?

All error is impersonal. Anything the eyes, the ears, the nose, the mouth, the touch – anything your senses tell you or show you – this is the error. And it is completely impersonal. It doesn't come from a personal you or a personal him or a personal her.

It is a fabric. It is a series of concepts operating only on the level of the mind belonging to no one. Error is impersonal nothingness.

The Spirit which enters your temple does not uphold these concepts and so the concepts are the arm of flesh or nothingness, and when you give yourself a treatment, you will remember all error is a belief in two powers, a belief in God and something else. But it's only a belief, only a series of concepts. God's not in it or it couldn't dissolve, and so it's nothingness. And this is the treatment that you give yourself.

But this is only using the mind to rest out of the mind. Now Joel is very specific about this in <u>The Art of Spiritual Healing</u> when he says:

When you really begin to comprehend that in healing (or in giving yourself a treatment) *you are not dealing with people, when you learn to eliminate them and their specific claims from your thought, and in every instance deal with the root of the problem which is carnal mind, (or) nothingness; "arm of flesh," (or) nothingness, then you will find how quickly you will be able to become consciously aware of the Spirit within you. This Presence (this Spirit) cannot be felt in your temple until you are free of the barrier: The barrier is the belief in two powers; the barrier is the belief in something apart from God.*

And so again on the next page he says:

(You must) *carry this out in practice,*

And so this is your treatment.

(You must) *carry this out in practice, watching the stone being formed in and of your Consciousness while you stand to one side as a witness or a beholder,* (and as you do this) *eventually a state of peace will come. And you will catch a glimpse of God as Is – just God is. All problems fade out in proportion as you develop this ability to be quiet, to behold, to witness divine harmony unfold.*

And so that is your treatment – to cleanse the temple many times a day and during the night with the specific principles of impersonalization and nothingization and then gain that sense of peace in which you can wait. Just wait until the Spirit infuses your being, your Consciousness, your temple, and when the Spirit floods your temple, your Consciousness, then you are the temple of the living, <u>living</u> God on earth as it is in heaven. Then you are saints in the spiritual kingdom. These are not pretty words. This is the truth of your being and the I within you, the invisible living Presence, I send you forth. And all who enter your Consciousness are touched by the living Spirit. Your Consciousness becomes a law unto all who enter it.

Should you begin to see concepts – for a moment you forget – you see a mailman, perhaps you see a clerk, a waitress – it is time to STOP. Just stop. Remind yourself. No, these are concepts. I am <u>stopping</u>. Enter that rest, that peace, and wait. Wait for the movement of I in your Consciousness, Spirit, and rest and behold what I can do. Then when this so-called clerk, waitress, mailman are looked upon with this Consciousness, this Consciousness will behold Christ and all in range of this Consciousness will be blessed.

Ten righteous men can save an entire city. We have twenty-seven, (134), plus those that hear this worldwide. Again, this is not just pretty, poetic talk. You are being given a commission. Go out as saints in the kingdom. Go out as a temple, a spiritual temple filled with the Holy Spirit. Go out as a benediction, a blessing. Let the Spirit in your Consciousness, the invisible I, flow through and lift up all who touch that Spirit. This is letting the Word abide in you. Your treatment is abiding in the word, or scripture. Your Consciousness is letting the Word abide in you, in your temple.

Joel says this is not a lazy man's work. This is not an easy way of life, and so I would have you know that you must, must work. This is work when you sit down and you give yourself a treatment. But this is beholding when you watch God work hitherto. All of you have reached the place where you are spiritual adults. You are spiritual saints. The living Spirit of God in your temple makes you a saint, and whether you see it or not as you behold the I, this aura is around you.

You must know the truth and the truth will set you free. Now you see that takes place on two levels. You know the truth with your mind so you can drop the mind and stand still and have a God experience, actually feel the Spirit fill the temple of your Consciousness. This is knowing the Truth by an experience, not in the mind. This is knowing I am the truth and feeling it and watching it and bearing witness to It. And so first you know the truth with the mind, but that is not enough. That will help you to rest back out of that mind and then you know the truth with your Soul as Spirit and Soul become one, and this produces the temple of the living God or Christ. Soul, Spirit – they are joined and the birth of Christ takes place. And you stand on earth now no longer just a human being. No, you stand on earth now as a saint.

The living Christ has come to earth again. You are the second coming. Each of you in your community, in your part of the world on this earth are transformed into the living Christ and Christ has come again. And those who have eyes to see and ears to hear will feel it. They may think it's you, but you will know within yourself I of myself can do nothing unless there is this inner movement, this overshadowing by Spirit of my Soul. Nothing will change, but if there is this overshadowing by Spirit, then Soul will be activated. Christ will be on earth. Yes, of myself I am nothing, and yet, through Christ I do all things. And now I stand a little to the side and I behold:

"I live; yet not I, Christ liveth my life."

Abide in the Word and let my Word abide in you. So shall you be my disciples. You are the disciples of the living Christ. And as you move out into the world, saints, and as you behold I, Christ pouring out, filling your Consciousness and making it a true temple of peace, you may hear, *"I have come that they might have life, and life more abundantly."* You may finally see that you – you are ordained to heal the sick, to tell of the good news, to lift up the dead, the dead in Consciousness.

The years that you have studied the truth, no truth was ever given for you and you alone. There is a price to pay for Christhood, for communion. Yes, you may have communion with the I within your Consciousness, but the price is you have to let it out. The price is service to all who have not yet found this inner Presence. And so I, the I of you, sends you forth out into the world to reveal the kingdom is at hand. The Presence is within. The I, the living God, am in the temple of Consciousness.

Let us be still and know that I am God. Let us wait upon the Lord. Let us stand still. *"And, behold, I come quickly;"* Now hear again, listen again to this experience as it was revealed through Joel.

"My mind is filled with the Word of God because I keep my mind stayed on God from rising in the morning to sleeping at night. Always there is some spiritual truth active in my Consciousness, some scriptural passage kept alive within me. My mind is permeated with truth. It is constituted of truth and all who enter the realm of my mind find truth, life, love, eternality, immortality, the grace of God, the benediction of God. My mind imbued with truth is a law of elimination to all discords." But remember, mind imbued with truth does not mean mind imbued with thought. It is mind when it reaches an absolute silence and suddenly has an awareness of truth that is invisible spiritual being. That mind is imbued with truth and *"that mind imbued with truth is a law of elimination to all discords, all inharmonies, all injustices, all sins, all diseases, all false appetites. I of my own self am nothing, but I and my Father are one, and He that is within me is greater than any error that exists in the world. Therefore, when I fill my Consciousness with truth, with love, with wisdom – I am a law of harmony, of healing, of peace unto all who enter my spiritual household, my Consciousness. I can of my own self do nothing, but since I and the Father are one and all that the Father hath is mine, through grace I am given all the dominion, all the healing influence, all of the forgiving influence. When my*

mind, my Consciousness is filled with truth and love – well, neither do I condemn thee. All who enter this temple are forgiven their sins. They come into His grace because my mind is filled with His grace, with His Word, with His truth, and all who enter here enter the divine presence and receive forgiveness and regeneration. They even find that the lost years of the locust are restored to them by the divine grace which God has given me as truth. Man shall not live by bread alone, but by every word of God that proceedeth out of the mouth of God. Every word of truth which constitutes my Consciousness is bread and wine, water, meat, life, and resurrection unto all who enter my Consciousness. Truth is the divine influence. Love is the divine influence. In my mind, in my Consciousness my Soul is filled with truth, spiritual truth and love. All who enter my Consciousness partake of that divine bread, meat, wine, and water, which is Life Eternal. Through the truth embodied in my Consciousness I am a law unto you, a law of healing, a law of forgiveness, a law of grace and benediction, even a law of supply."

And that is Joel's treatment to himself, and then there was the moment, the few minutes of stillness in which he received the Holy Spirit. And then when someone called and he picked up the phone, what did they touch? Did they touch Joel's thoughts? Oh, no, no. No. The Spirit flooded his Consciousness and he became the temple of the living God, and when they called they touched that living God. God Itself on earth as it is in heaven, for the two became one, heaven here and now.

This was what Christ Jesus was trying to show us. The temple, the temple of the living God, the kingdom here, now, closer than breathing, nearer than hands and feet. Don't you know the temple is right here and all those who believed and all those who reached out and touched that Consciousness were healed. Even the woman with the issue of blood followed him. I know if I just touch that Consciousness – and she touched it and was healed – just the edge of that Consciousness. And the I of you, the Holy Spirit, the Christ is sending you forth now as that Consciousness that those who touch you, that those who touch that temple where you are, that presence, will be healed, will be forgiven, will be restored, will be resurrected out of the graves of humanhood.

I recall the story of Lazarus.

Then said Martha unto Jesus, "Lord, if thou hadst been here, my brother had not died. But I know, that even now, whatsoever thou wilt ask of God, God will give it thee."

Jesus saith unto her, "Thy brother shall rise again."

Martha saith unto him, "I know that he shall rise again in the resurrection at the last day."

Jesus turned and said unto her, "I am the resurrection, and the life: he that believeth in me, though he were dead, yet shall he live: And whosoever liveth and believeth in me shall never die. Believest thou this?"

And this is what the Christ of your being is saying unto you. *I am the resurrection.* There's no resurrection down there in tomorrow. There's no resurrection someday. The kingdom of heaven is at hand and I resurrect you into my Self. When you have given yourself a treatment and when you are still and you find that silent place, that secret place of the Most High, I within you, the living Spirit of God, lift you up and you are resurrected out of the grave of mortality and into your Christhood, and then you may say, "Why, I live not; Christ liveth."

I send you forth two by two. Two by two I send you forth into the world, and those two are the mind when it is imbued with truth that you know with the mind, and the Soul, when the Soul becomes so still that it receives within it the Holy Spirit. The mind imbued with truth and the Soul imbued with I, for I am the truth. I send you forth, these two, two by two. And this I, this I is the resurrection. And as you go forth and you stand still and behold

I living Itself, you see I resurrect those who are drawn to you. It's never necessary to speak a single word. It's never necessary to speak this to anyone, but in your temple, in the kingdom of I, the living God, the living water draws up those that come to you.

I, if I am lifted up in Consciousness, will draw unto me, unto my level, and so you become Christ on earth and Christ is the resurrection. And you will see, you will witness those who come to you, who touch this inner water, this inner Consciousness. You will see them lifted out of mortality into Christ. And it will appear as healing, as regeneration, as forgiveness, as blessing. It will appear as supply coming forth from the Invisible. They will point to you, but you will know. No, of myself – that is, of the mind

– I am nothing but a vacuum. But when I am a vacuum, I am one with the Infinite I, and that I makes Consciousness the temple of the living God.

You are instructed now by the I within to go out as disciples of the one I, Christ. You are disciplined. You are a disciple. You are disciplined to know the truth first with the mind and then as an experience in the Soul. You are disciplined to align the two facets – the mind and the Soul – so that Christ may enter in. Yes, you are sent forth as a presence on earth. Henceforth you shall be called friends, for those that do the will of the Father are my friends. They are my brother, my sister. Do not fear to do this, for it is not you, a human. It's not you, a mortal mind. No, it is you when you are imbued with the truth and I am the truth.

So do not fear. Just be still.

Do not speak. Just be silent.

Do not live. Just behold.

And I shall make all things new. And I shall reveal that the kingdom of heaven has come. *"The place whereon thou standest is holy ground"* because it is a temple for the Holy Spirit. Thou art the temple and I am God, and be still and know that I am God.

Now listen one more time to Joel's explanation or definition of those who walk this way:

Above this sense-life (that is, above the mind), *there is a universe of Spirit* (or a temple) *governed by Love, peopled with children of God living in the temple of Truth.*

This world (this kingdom) *is real and permanent* (or eternal): *Its substance is* (your) *eternal Consciousness. In it there is no awareness of discords or even temporary material good.*

(This is) *Reality* – (it is) *the Soul-realm. (And) in this uplifted Consciousness, you are able to see yourselves free.* (You are able to see) *unlimited boundaries of eternal Life and infinite Consciousness.*

He says:

The experience is like watching the world disappear over a horizon.

And this is the experience that you must have. This is the experience of resurrection. I, the Spirit of God in your holy temple called Consciousness do send you forth two by two to be a witness to the living God pouring forth, lifting up, uplifting all who touch this river of life within you. This is your mission. Please accept it now. *"I have come that they might have life, and life more abundantly."* This is your Consciousness. *"Come unto me, all ye that are heavy laden, and I will give you rest."*

This, too, is your Consciousness. *"It is my good pleasure to give you the kingdom,"* and this also is your Consciousness.

No, these are not pretty, poetic words. This is a living, Spiritual Experience. Your Consciousness is the temple of the living God. It is holy ground because it is filled with the Holy Spirit. It is the living Christ on earth, in heaven, one. Yes, long have men awaited the second coming of Christ. You now with your finger on your lips and the inner silence of the Soul, you now behold the secret second coming of Christ. It is your very Consciousness saying to you and to all who enter: *"I am the resurrection."*

Please take this seriously. Your job, your mission if you have accepted it, is to put away childish things. Many times during the day and at night sweep out your temple. Know the specific truths of impersonalization and nothingization. Know that there is no good; there is no evil. Only Christ is, and then be still about that. You've cleaned your temple. Now wait. Open the door unto Me, and I will come in and I will reveal Myself to you. And you shall see such miracles as you never dreamed possible. You shall see the son of God. You shall see the temple of the living God as your very own Consciousness. You are blessed beyond all men, beyond all women. You have been chosen.

And now in this new Jerusalem where you are standing, when Joel stood there his lips said what was in his heart:

"As a beggar have I sought the new Jerusalem and the new heaven and the new earth, and Thou hast made me heir of all.

How shall I stand before Thee but in silence? How shall I honor Thee but in the meditation of mine heart?

Praise and thanksgiving Thou seekest not, but the understanding the open heart Thou receivest.

I now will keep silent before Thee. My Soul and my Spirit and my silence shall be Thy dwelling place. Thy Spirit (Thy Holy Spirit) shall fill my meditation, and it shall make me and preserve me whole. O Thou Tender One and True – I am home in Thee."

Yes, I am home in the living temple, in the infinite temple of Consciousness which houses the living Spirit of God. How shall I stand before Thee but in silence and let my silence be the Consciousness and the dwelling place of the living God. If you hear my voice within you, if you are ready to be Spiritual adults, to be the child of Omnipresence, then you are blessed indeed.

Blessings, far, far beyond any you have ever dreamed. I now will never leave Thee. I am the resurrection.

[Silence]

473

CLASS 29

TO HIM THAT HATH

Bill: Good morning.

Today's principle is going to be the principle of supply. I know this season that we're in and this time economically, let's say, many people are feeling lack and limitation. So it seems to me that perhaps a review of the principle of supply is in order. In this little group there are seven of us [135 now]. I feel it's not necessary to be formal. I feel I can give an informal talk, just be myself and relax and share.

I don't know if you've read Joel's account of when he was in Boston and having a hard time with supply, but he speaks about only having a dime in his pocket and, of course, having bills like the rest of us. And so he looked up the appointments that he had and the meditations and healings that he gave and he sent out bills to the patients and the students and waited, and, of course, he received hardly anything in return. Now Joel, if nothing else, was honest with himself, and so he took a look at that. What could be wrong? And I remember him talking about walking down the street. He didn't have the money to take a bus or a cab, so he had to walk down the street to get home or where he was going and thinking to himself, "What is the nature of supply? What is the nature of supply?"

You remember suddenly the realization came to him: Wait a minute. "I" am supply. I, the I of my being, I am supply. You remember he realized then that supply was not that which came to him; supply was that which flowed out from that I within. And so he tore up the bills and stopped sending bills to anybody, and he said he had a difficult time because it didn't start flowing right away. But he continued to pour out that which he had, which was prayer and meditation and healing, and eventually the flow started to appear.

Pouring out that which he had, it came back, and he realized – in demonstration as his supply began to take form – he realized in demonstration that the I of my being is supply. And the principle is in a wonderful little chapter in <u>Practicing the Presence</u>. I had to hunt for it because I remembered the chapter, but not where it was. And so I'm just going to read a little bit of the beginning because it says it much better than I can and in a lot less words. So this is the chapter in <u>Practicing the Presence</u>, chapter six called *To Him That Hath*. And that's the principle: To him that hath, it shall be given. And so if you are not demonstrating supply or you're not demonstrating a sufficiency of it, then you are not living the principle: to him that hath, it shall be given, because you have to demonstrate that principle that you have, that the I of you is supply, and the only way to demonstrate it is like Joel – to give it away.

So now listen:

When the Master was called upon to feed the multitudes and the disciples told him that there were only a few loaves and fishes, he did not recognize that there was an insufficiency. No, he began with what was available and multiplied that, for he knew that "he that hath, to him shall be given; and he that hath not, from him shall be taken even that which he hath."

You see? If you know that the I of you is your supply, the I of you is all supply, the I of you is supply, I am supply – if you know that and you demonstrate it, then that which flows out is heaped up, pressed down, and running over in your experience. But if you think you're giving from your bank account, Mr. or Mrs. So-and-So; if you're giving from your bank account, from your time, your effort – a personal sense of supply – then, of course, you're going to experience that second part, which is *"from him shall be taken even that which he hath."* It will dry up and run out because you're living through a personal sense of supply.

Now we talked in the last talk here a few days ago about a personal sense of existence, a material sense of life. Well, now we're talking about a personal sense of supply – a personal sense, a material sense of supply. If you live from that material sense you will find that from you shall be taken even that which you have. It'll run out. You'll be on empty and lack and limitation will be exactly what you've sown and are reaping because you're living from a personal sense. But to continue this chapter, it says:

Scripture tells the story of the widow who fed Elijah. Even though she had only a "handful of meal in a barrel, and a little oil in a cruse," she did not say she had not enough to share, but she first made a little cake for Elijah before she baked one for her son and herself. "And the barrel of meal wasted not, neither did the cruse of oil fail." She had little, but she used what she had and let it flow out from her.

Day after day we are faced with the same question: What have we? If we are well-grounded in the letter of truth, the answer is clear and certain:

I have; all that God has, I have because "I and my Father are one." The Father is the source of all supply. In this relationship of oneness, I embody supply. How, then, can I expect it to come to me? I must agree that I already have all that the Father has.

Are we that which receives, or are we that center from which the infinity of God flows out?

I've been saying this for a couple years now in various ways: We either live as the Christ and demonstrate the Christ, or we live as a person and demonstrate all the limitations that go with a person; even that which we have shall be taken.

So he says here:

Are we the multitudes who sat at the feet of the Master waiting to be fed, or are we the Christ feeding the multitudes? In the answer to that lies our degree of spiritual realization. "I and my Father are one" means exactly what it says (period). *We do not ever look outside of our being for our good, we must ever look upon ourselves as that center from which God is flowing. It is* (the function of you and me) *the function of the Christ, or Son of God, to be the instrument as which the good of God pours out into the world:*

So are we ready to make this transition? Are we ready to make the transition from *"man, whose breath is in his nostrils"* to the Christ? Are we ready to make the transition from a personal sense of supply which can be taken and can run out? Are we willing to stand a little to the side and <u>let</u> this Christ, this I of our being, flow out to whomsoever it will?

To him that hath, it shall be given. Now that's a principle, and the only way you prove you have something is by giving it away. Now you have to use a certain amount of common sense. If you have – say right now you're experiencing a sense of lack and you have fifty dollars in the bank and you know that the day after tomorrow you owe forty – it probably wouldn't be prudent to give all fifty away, although I've done that just to prove the principle! It probably would be a little more prudent to take what you can give and give that, but even if you can't give money – oh, there's so much more you can give in so many directions.

I want to tell you a story now because it helped me with this principle. In – well, many, many years ago now I didn't think I had anything to give. I came home one evening and my first wife said to me, "I'm leaving." It was right around, a little before Thanksgiving. She said, "I'm leaving. I found someone else I relate to and I want to be with him." And the next day when I came home from work, the house was empty of all her possessions. Her and our son were gone. I remember I went into the baby's room and it was nothing but blue walls, and I went into our room and all her things were gone. There was not a note, not anything. Just a key. She was gone, and at the time she was my world. I didn't yet have a good conscious awareness of the presence of God. I had just the beginning touch of God, but I didn't have a conscious awareness on a daily basis, and so I pretty much fell apart. I just plopped down on the couch and cried. I couldn't believe that that which I loved more than anything else in the world was gone. And I remember I had a really hard time with it. For a week or two I was just in the most severe, blackest, bleakest place. And, of course, I felt like a failure and so I felt like I had nothing to give.

I talked to a spiritual friend of mine and he said to me, well he said, "There's something in the book The Art of Meditation for you, but he said that I'm going to see if you can find it. I'm not going to tell you what it is," which was a strange thing to say. But I remember I came home and I got down the book off the shelf and I found this chapter called *For Love Is of God*, and reading along here I came to this place where it said:

To those who live in communion with God, serving God through their fellow man, the promise is literally kept: All that I have is thine.

No longer is there a need or a desire for any person or any thing. Every thing and every person become part of our being. What we surrender, we have; what we hold in the grasp of possession, we lose. Every thing we release, we draw to us; every thing we loose, we have; every thing we set free, we bind to us forever. "Loose him and let him go." Let everyone be loosed in Christ.

And I saw that and I put the book down and I meditated on that and I came to the conclusion that I was going to have to find out how to serve God through my fellow man. And indeed this man had told me to find a chapter in The Art of Meditation. He also said that the only way I would get out of this problem was to transfer my feelings to God. And, of course, I said, "Well, how can I do that? I can't see God. I can't hold God." And he said that was for me to discover.

So in the days that followed something miraculous happened. It was such a transforming experience that I've never been the same since. And here's what happened. I made the decision that to the best of my ability I would love God and pour out that love by loving God in every living thing without talking about it. I would just do it. And so I started with a plant that I had in my living room. It was a wandering Jew and each day I would talk to that plant. Nobody was there living with me, so it didn't matter that I talked out loud. And so I would talk to that plant and I would say, "hi, Father – how are you today?" or "hi, God – here, have a drink" and give it a little water. And I can tell you that that plant never got any sun in that living room and yet it flourished. It just flourished. And I had a cat, a black cat named Sufi and Sufi would come from the kitchen and look at me and be about ready to run and jump up on my lap, but I'd be reading The Art of Meditation or Practicing the Presence and I'd put my hand up and say, "Just a minute, Father," and the cat would sit down like a dog and wait. I'd finish the chapter, put the book down and say, "Okay," and then it would come bounding up into my lap, and I talked to God in that cat.

And I began to have some strange experiences, very strange. I can't explain them very well. I'll tell you a couple of them. I went to a diner and I had my – I realized that I could not say to people, "hi, Father – how are you today?" because they would think I was a little eccentric, if not crazy, so I didn't do that. But inside myself whenever I saw a person I would say, "Father, how can I be of service? What do I have to give to you?" And these strange things were happening. I went over to this diner and I ordered my meal and I had a cup of coffee and took the ice out of the water with a spoon and I scooped a little bit of ice into my coffee and before I knew it, this waitress had seen me from way across the restaurant. She came walking up with a glass of ice and set it down there. It was really a strange thing because I was getting – all this love from the universe was coming back and yet I was pouring out all the love to the universe because I was loving God inside of everyone and everything.

Now I'm going to tell you this and this is the absolute truth, and I was there, and I'm not lying. One day I was in my living room and I was reading probably <u>The Art of Meditation</u> and there was a fly flying around living room. You know how they can do. They land on your forehead and you move your hand and they fly away and then they come back and land on your hand and you brush 'em away and then they come back and land on your arm. It was really getting annoying! And finally I thought, "Well, now that's enough. I can't even read a paragraph without this thing landing on my nose or my eyebrow or something," so I got up to get the fly swatter and I stopped dead in my tracks, and I thought, "Now wait a minute. Now wait a minute. God's inside of everyone and everything. God has to be also within this fly." And so I put the book down and I put my hand out, palm up, and I said, "Now, fly. You come over here and land on my hand and I'll put you outside." And it took a couple of laps around the living room and came over, landed right in the center of my palm. I got up and the fly stood there. I didn't move. I walked across the living room to the front door. Still the fly stayed on my hand. I opened the front door. I opened the screen door. I put my hand out and I said, "There you go, Father," and off it flew.

I say I was having some strange experiences like this. And then one night I was reading probably <u>The Art of Meditation</u> and

I set it down and I closed my eyes to have a meditation, and it was a meditation like any other meditation. I got quiet. I repeated the letter to myself a couple times, the letter of truth, and then I listened, you know, with the attitude *"Speak, Lord; thy servant heareth."* Not necessarily words, but the attitude – I was being receptive. And suddenly there was a Presence there with me and I felt it. It touched me on the side of the face. It was a tingling Presence and with it came a sense of peace, and I knew that the Father and I are one because we were right in the same place as one. And from then until now, and that's been forty-two – no, thirty-eight years ago, I guess, thirty-nine years ago [49 years now] – from then until now I've never been alone. That Presence has always been with me.

And so I say this, I bring this up because I learned from this experience that by pouring out into the universe secretly, sacredly, silently – simply recognizing God in the midst of you and everyone I came in contact with – this was pouring out from my cruse of oil. This was sharing. So you see, it didn't have to be money, although I've given a lot of money away over the years too. But if you are right now experiencing a lack and a limitation because you've been trying to pour out your supply, your sense of supply, your sense of money, your personal account, and if it's not working and you don't see any way that you can pour anything out because you haven't got anything physically, it doesn't mean that you can't pour out, because I learned from this experience by loving the One in the many instead of the many in the One, that Life gave it back heaped up, pressed down, and running over.

I have friends today the world over. The world over, good friends. I have a sufficiency of supply and enough to share, and by supply I mean not only just dollars, although I have those too. I mean I share my house with foster children. I share my bedrooms. I share my car by giving people rides when they need them. I share my love by recognizing the Christ in each and every one. I share my meditations when people ask for help and even when they don't. I share my first prayers to the enemy. When we were first informed that at 9/11 that the towers had been attacked and all that, the very first prayers that we gave here in this house were for the enemy because we were told to pray for those that use us, those that hate us, first, and that's what we did here in this house, and then we prayed for the victims.

So what I'm trying to say is the principle is: To him that hath, it shall be given, and I proved that I had supply, that I was supply, by pouring it out in recognition of God inside of everyone and everything and in little acts of kindness and later I poured it out in acts of kindness that nobody could catch me doing. In other words, they were anonymous. And so you see, you prove that you have by giving it away, whether it's love, whether it's prayers, whether it's donations, whether it's charity, whether it's service. You prove that you have by giving it away and you demonstrate that I am supply by going into your closet, becoming quiet, being receptive, and asking that "I" how It wants to pour out. Then the opportunities present themselves. You'll just know when it's right to give and in what way to give. And then you'll demonstrate that "I" am supply and that you never had supply and you never will have supply.

There is no personal supply. That's the problem – living from a personal sense of supply, but the answer is in living by the impersonal I of your being. And so the principle is: To him that hath, it shall be given. And so if you have I as your supply, it will be heaped up, pressed down, and running over in your experience. But to him that hath not shall be taken away even that which he hath, and so if you live by a personal sense of supply, you can pretty much plan on running out.

Now, let's take a look at something else here. Now in the Kailua study series Joel talks about the book The Infinite Way and the chapter *Supply*, and he talks about how he talked of the orange tree, and he gave the principle there of supply and how very few people connected that orange tree up with their existence, so let us see if we cannot enter into this and connect it up the way he was hoping we would. Now he says:

We must understand that money is not supply, money is the result or effect of supply.

You see, if money becomes a part of your experience, it's because the I of you is forming Itself that way. So he says:

Since money is not supply, what is? Let us digress for a moment and look at the orange tree which is laden with fruit.

When I lived in California I had an orange tree in my yard and they were navel oranges and they were quite delicious, and the first year I noticed them there were only two oranges on the whole tree, and I picked them and I ate them and they were wonderful. No seeds, sweet, big, a thin peeling. It was delicious. And so I went out to that tree, knowing that God is inside of everyone and everything, and I thanked that tree, and I said, "Oh, they were so good! They were so delicious. Thank you for sharing." And I didn't think any more about it, although I used to have my meditations on the back porch where I could see that tree quite often. I didn't think any more about it until the next year. The next year when I went out and looked, there were thirty-six oranges on that tree! And so recognizing God and pouring that out to that tree, the tree gave back that love. God is love and by recognizing God in the midst of that tree, it poured back God in the form of love or in the form of oranges.

So anyway, back to this:

Let us digress for a moment and look at the orange tree which is laden with fruit. We know that the oranges do not constitute supply because when they have been eaten, or sold, or given away, a new crop starts at once to grow. The oranges are gone, but the supply remains, because within the tree, there is a law in operation. Call it a law of God or a law of nature – the name of the law is not too important, but the recognition of the presence of the law operating in, through, or as, the tree is very important.

Now in this case, in my case and hopefully in your case, what he is saying is if you look out here – <u>your</u> car, <u>your</u> house, <u>your</u> money, <u>your</u> service, <u>your</u> love – none of these are your supply because **supply is invisible. I am supply**, and if you have I, to him that has I it shall be given. To him that has a personal sense of life shall be taken away even that personal sense of life. You see the principle? If you recognize God in the midst of everyone and everything, especially <u>yourself</u> – if you have I and in your meditation you become still and you feel as we said the other day the living Omnipresence of God, of I, and you let It flow as It will to whomsoever It will – stranger, enemy, or friend, or family – let It flow to whom It will. That's how you demonstrate you <u>have</u> I, and that's the law of supply.

That law operates, (he says) *to draw in – through the roots – the minerals, the substances, elements of the air, water, sunshine and it transforms that into sap, draws it up the trunk of the tree and distributes it through the branches, sent into expression as blossoms and in time* (they turn into) *green marbles and this becomes a full grown orange.*

All right. Now do you see how he wants you to connect this up with your life? This Invisible I is flowing all the time if you don't stop it by trying to live on a personal sense of supply. If you don't stop it by you deciding where and how you're gonna give of <u>your</u> treasures. If you get yourself out of the way and you allow this I, which is supply, to flow to whomsoever it will knowing consciously It – It – that I am supply and watching it, then the world will return it to you in forms of love. Those forms of love can be in acts of kindness coming to you or oranges on a tree or dollar bills showing up in your mailbox that you didn't even expect. But you will recognize the whole time that you're going through these lovely, wonderful experiences that this out here is the effect of that Invisible I demonstrating, forming Itself, and when you have that – and this is what came out of my experience of being alone that Christmas morning so many years ago and discovering that I wasn't alone – that I had I, an Invisible Presence always and forever. That is where I discovered the I, that I is my supply forever. I carry it with me in this world, in the next and the next and the next. I will never leave thee. But this is a conscious experience. It's not a theory. It's not just the letter of truth that I read in this book. It's a very real experience, and when it becomes a real experience and you connect it up as Joel suggests here, then you shall have supply heaped up, pressed down, and running over from all corners of the universe.

And so he says:

Within you and within me, there is also a law – a law of life – and our awareness of the presence of this law is our supply.

You see, it takes – again, like we said the other day in the last talk – it takes your conscious awareness of this I, of this law in operation, of this Life, of this Presence, and it takes your conscious awareness watching It flow out and pour out of Its substance.

(So) *our awareness of the presence of this law is our supply. Money and the things necessary for daily living are the effects of the consciousness of the activity of the law within.*

You're watching. You're no longer living by a personal sense of supply, but you're standing to the side and watching the impersonal I pour out Its supply to the universe in giving money, in giving love, in giving service, in giving recognition of that Presence in the midst of everyone and everything in acts of kindness, in prayer, in service. Your seeing that, understanding that, and being consciously aware of that allows you to take thought off of the things of the world and abide in the consciousness of abundance and it comes to your abiding place and it comes in forms you never dreamed of.

The entire universe pours love at your feet simply by knowing that I am supply.

(So) *The divine or universal Consciousness,* (he says) *your individual consciousness, is spiritual. (And) The activity* (of your consciousness) *is spiritual and therefore your supply in all its forms is spiritual, infinite, and ever-present. What you behold as money, food and clothing, automobiles and homes represents (your) concepts of this invisible supply.*

All right? So finally he says:

Let us agree now to see that just as we need take no thought for oranges as long as we know the source of supply so we need no longer take thought about dollars. Let us learn to think of dollars, as we do leaves on trees or oranges, the natural and inevitable result of the law active.

Let us look at the lilies and rejoice at the proof of the presence of God's love for His creation. Let us watch the sparrows and note how confidently they trust the Invisible. (And) Let us rejoice when we see the flowers in spring and summer because they assure us of the divine Presence.

Do you see the principle of supply? Joel caught it in his, "Oh, I am supply!" and he began pouring without looking for a return. I caught it in my experience of, "Oh, God is inside of everyone and everything, and my job is to love, to recognize, to uphold, to serve, to bless, and to pour out the recognition of that presence in everyone and everything." And I hope you see it in today's talk and in understanding the principle: "To him that hath, it shall be given, and to him that hath not shall be taken away even that which he hath." To you who have the conscious awareness of the living I in your meditation and stand aside and permit it to flow out to whomsoever it will, to you then, you demonstrate I am supply and to you that have not, that still feel you're a person and you have nothing to give and even that which you have is drying up, you are demonstrating the perfect demonstration of a personal sense of life and a personal sense of supply and that which you have shall be taken.

And so I give to you the secret of life, really. This is the secret that Joel talked about when he said in ancient days master Masons were given a password that would allow them to go anywhere in the world and demand a master's wages. This was the secret: I am supply, and now I give it to you, and when you have it, when you've demonstrated it, when you've made it your own, and when you've connected it up for yourself within and witnessed it and bore witness to it flowing, then you can go anywhere in the universe, turn within, and bear witness as it flows – an infinite, eternal abundant supply.

And so, which do you want to be this year coming up? You want to be the person sitting at the feet of Christ and waiting to be fed still after all these years? Come on now. Come up higher. It's time to be the Christ pouring out and then watch the universe pour back to you God in forms of love beyond your wildest dreams heaped up, pressed down, running over. So many you don't have enough storehouses to store them in.

Now let us be still and contact this inner supply, this inner Presence, this inner I.

(Brief silence)

And now we understand that Thy grace is my sufficiency in all things, that Thou art my sufficiency – that I within – I am supply, able to feed five thousand, able to pour out to this universe infinitely. I am supply, the I of you. Is this not perhaps where the original idea of Christmas presents appearing under the tree started? Is not this the experience that Elijah had when cakes were baked on a stone? Is not this the principle that St. Nicholas knew when he gave and gave and poured out and poured out never looking for return? Did he not receive the living Christ as his gift?

And so, my friends, if I do not get a chance to tell you again, Merry Christmas. May you find within yourself the living Spirit of God. May you discover that you have the I and may you discover this Christmas, I am supply.

Blessings.

[Silence]

"All that the Father has is mine." Invisible Supply flowing to and through me from one Source but flowing through instruments of Love everywhere. And the Invisible Comforter, flowing as companions all over the world and beyond from the Invisible Love that permeates the heavens and the earth. And Infinite Invisible Life that flows from Love as my life, as the health of my countenance. All that the Father, my very own Consciousness has is flowing as me, as the I that reads these words. And now I rest here and enjoy the gifts and behold the miracle that is my Christ Life. Thank you Father.

[Silence]

CLASS 30

AS WE FORGIVE

Bill: From The Thunder of Silence, the chapter "As We Forgive".

For nearly two thousand years the world has prayed, "Forgive us our debts, as we forgive our debtors," unaware perhaps that this teaching represents the very core, the very heart and soul, of the good life. Over and over again Jesus extols the virtues of forgiveness.

Therefore, if thou bring thy gift to the altar, and there rememberest that thy brother hath ought against thee;

Leave there thy gift before the altar and go thy way; first be reconciled to thy brother, and then come and offer thy gift.

But if ye forgive not men their trespasses, neither will your Father forgive your trespasses.

Does this not plainly state that as long as any malice, envy, jealousy, revenge, or hatred is entertained in consciousness, just so long as there are blocks in our consciousness which prevents our prayers from being answered.

I think we can look at that now without even going into the rest of the chapter and know almost instantaneously the reason is because we are entertaining a sense of separation from God. We are entertaining a sense of a separate entity. We are entertaining God and someone else. And so if there is any envy, malice, jealousy, revenge or hatred, anger or fear for someone, then there is God and someone. And so, you are back in duality, we're back in duality and in our meditation, we are attempting to commune with a sense of oneness. So naturally entertaining that other in consciousness would block our experience of communion. It has nothing to do with being good or bad.

Only in true prayer is it possible to lose all sense of separateness from one another and from one another's interest. Intellectually, it is practically impossible to convince ourselves that another person's interest is our interest, and that, our interest is his interest or to believe that we are all equally children of God, because material sense testifies to the opposite.

Now material sense is that which you see, hear, taste, touch or smell. That is always, always going to show you two when in fact the reality of this universe is a spiritual universe – One. Therefore, we must shut down, or shut off the senses in our meditation.

It is only in inner communion with God that we find ourselves in inner communion with man. Then we learn that man does not mean white or black, oriental or occidental, Jew or Gentile: Man means man, that which we are, one infinite equal son of God, but that can never be known through the mind: It can only be known when through communion with God it is revealed to us that we are all one.

Do you see, or do we see why the only way we can know God aright is by having an experience, an inner experience of God? We can't know God aright in the mind. Anything that you can know with the mind is not God. Any image you can have in your mind is not God. Even if you have an image that God is Love, well you still have an image and that's not God. And so, it is necessary to transcend the mind. Become so still that even if the mind is still thinking you're not one with the mind you are up just a little higher where you can commune with this Presence, with the Spirit. And in the communion then God reveals to you that we are all ONE. And so, it's an experience, it's an inner experience, it's not sitting and thinking about, well in reality we're all One, and isn't that an interesting concept. No, it's an actual inner glimpse of that Oneness. And that is communion. And that is answered prayer.

Anything that enslaves one enslaves the world; anything that sets one man free tends to free the entire world; anything that impoverishes one man, one race, or one sect impoverishes the world; anything that brings one grain more of supply into the life of an individual, race, or nation tends to set the entire world free from lack. But that, no one can ever accept with his mind, nor could any materialist ever be convinced of its truth. It takes an inner communion with God to reveal why even in the midst of war we should pray for our enemies.

The first thought that comes forth from the materialist when he hears about this radical teaching of praying for our enemies is, "Do you mean that I should pray for my enemy to be successful over me—that he succeed in his deceit, trickery, and conniving?" No, those of spiritual vision would not pray for that at all, but that the enemy's mind be opened and made receptive and responsive to the will of God.

How few people remember that praying for their enemies opens the very doors of heaven, showering its blessings upon them. It matters not whether a nation is an enemy or an ally, the same prayer must prevail, "Open their eyes that they may see with spiritual vision." Whether the offender be personal, national, or international matters not one whit. There must be the desire that all men be awakened to their true identity and to the Source of all being. Even to those who would crucify him, the Master said, "Father,' forgive them; for they know not what they do." To his brethren after they had thrown him into the pit and sold him into slavery, Joseph said, "It was not you that sent me hither, but God." He did not hold them in bondage to their act, but gave them food to carry home, returning good for evil. One of the most important lessons for all of us to learn is that there is no room in the spiritual life for the return of evil for evil—there is no room for anything but a life of forgiveness.

From the moment of waking in the morning until going to sleep at night, there must be periods in the day in which we consciously remember:

I forgive. If I have aught against any man, woman, or child, here and now I forgive— completely, perfectly, entirely. If anyone's misdeeds persist in coming back to my memory, over and over again I will forgive. I seek no punishment for anyone; I seek no revenge; I seek no justice—I lose everyone and let him go.

Father forgive me my trespasses as I forgive those who trespass against me. Father open the eyes of the blind. Father open the eyes of the enemy, whether they are of my household or another's.

An unfoldment on this very subject came to me the night before I was to give two lectures in a midwestern city. I did not have a single thought or idea in my head about what the subject for the next day's lecture was to be, and although I am quite accustomed to that kind of an experience, it is one which I never particularly enjoy. That night, however, as I was meditating, all of a sudden, the word forgiveness flashed into my mind.

The first thought that came to me was, "Am I completely purged? Am I entertaining anything in my thought regarding anyone or any group or any nation that might indicate that I have not completely forgiven them?" As I searched within, I could find no one I was holding in bondage.

Then my thought turned the other way, "Am I really forgiven?" There is not any one of us who has not committed offenses. We may not have considered a particular offense of much significance in our human life, but in the spiritual life things that heretofore have seemed of minor importance take on major significance. And so, I wondered if I had been completely forgiven and purged of any offenses of which I might have been guilty.

There is a secret about forgiveness: There is not anything or anybody that can forgive us. Therefore, there is not any possibility of our ever being forgiven except under one condition, and that is when there is no possibility of the offense being repeated. In other words, no matter what the offense may have been, as long as there is the potentiality within us of its being repeated, we are not wholly forgiven.

Just let us suppose for a moment that we could carry on a conversation with God about our faults. We confess our fault and we seek forgiveness, and to all this God says, "What? Forgiveness to do it all over again?"

"Oh, no, God, it will never happen again. It couldn't happen again. I've realized the wrongness of it."

At the moment, we actually believe that, but let us not forget that God, being God, sees right through to the center of our heart and knows that the same thing that made us guilty of this act once could make us do it again if similar circumstances arose. And so in His omniscience, God says, "Ah, it's still there. There is still a block within you, and you will continue to be under the penalty of it until you are completely purged of it."

And so, we go our way and ponder this response from God. We meditate and look at the situation upside down and from every angle, until all of a sudden we do catch a clear picture not only of the wrongness of what has been done but of the truth that only the state of consciousness that made us commit this offense in the first place could make us do it a second time, and if we find that that state of consciousness does not exist anymore, we have then "died" and have been reborn of the Spirit. Then we can go back again and ask for forgiveness.

This time, God says, "I don't even know who you are any more. I don't see anything wrong in you to forgive."

That is the true idea of forgiveness. There really is no God to forgive. When the state of consciousness that could be guilty of resentment, anger, jealousy, malice, or whatever it may have been "dies," there not only is nothing to forgive, and nobody to forgive, there is not even a remembrance or a memory—not even a "smell of smoke."

It is pure fiction to believe in some God in heaven who is going to look down and forgive us while we are out marauding. True, we can confess our sins and be forgiven instantly, but what about an hour from now when the sin begins all over again? The Master had a sharp answer for that —"lest a worse thing come unto thee." He did not preach a God who permits us to go on our way sinning with impunity and then reassures us with a gentle "I forgive you."

Every time we come to a place in our consciousness where we actually give up our errors of thought and deed, and confess—not necessarily outwardly, but inwardly— to our errors of omission or commission and feel that deep sense of contrition in which we know it cannot happen again, [then] we are washed white as snow. We are never held in bondage to anything once we have recognized it as error and have forsaken it. Every time that we come to a place of inner grief over our errors, we are forgiven. That ends the episode, but it carries with it the command, "Sin no more, lest a worse thing come unto thee."

There is really no such thing as one person forgiving another, or God forgiving us : There is only a "dying daily" to the state of consciousness that accepted good and evil and acted from that premise, and when that old consciousness has been purged or is thoroughly "dead" we come to a place of Self-completeness in God, where we know, "I and the Father are one, and all that the Father has is mine. I am a child of God, an heir of God, and joint-heir with Christ in God."

And remember, we know this as an experience. And so this is not oh well we were thinking about that on Tuesday, this is we come to an inner experience that lifts us up into our Soul-senses our Spiritual faculties and we glimpse, we sense, we have a vision of I and the Father are One and all that the Father has is mine.

Then we can look out on this whole world, and with our new vision behold a world in which there is not a thing anyone has that we want. There is not a sin anyone could commit for which we would hold him in condemnation, criticism, or judgment, knowing full well that the state of consciousness that did it was not really his, but an imposed one, and by imposed I mean a consciousness under the sway of world beliefs and subject to the universal ignorance which characterizes human beings.

When we are fully and completely aware that "I and my Father are one" and when we no longer have any desire for person, place, thing, circumstance, or condition, we are reborn of the Spirit;

We can actually reverse that in order to see when we are reborn, we could say, well am I reborn of the Spirit? Well, if I am reborn of the Spirit then I no longer have any desire for person, place, thing, circumstance, or condition.

We are purged because into that state of consciousness we carry with us none of the desires that could result in sin. It did not take a God to forgive us: It took a dying and a rebirthing, and in this new state of consciousness we need no forgiving, because there is no sin.

Can we see here, can we grasp that the human being has made God in his image, in his likeness, and so we see a parent that needs to forgive us when we are trying to stop being bad and trying to be good? Can we see how that dates way back to the early Hebrews and the law and how we have carried that belief? Well God is punishing me because I did thus and so, or God is rewarding me because I was a good person on Tuesday. No, all that are concepts that have to be dropped. God does not need to forgive you; God does not need to forgive anybody when we have died to the belief in good and evil the consciousness that could commit those acts is not there. And so, who is there? Well, the Son of God, the Spirit of God, Christ liveth within me, and that does not need any forgiveness. You see, it's an inner shift in consciousness, takes care of everything. So, the work is within.

When we come to the state of consciousness that realizes our Self-completeness in God so that we truthfully can live in the full and complete realization of fulfillment, without a trace of desire or need, then there is no block between us and the inner Source of our being, and consequently no block of condemnation, criticism, or judgment, no unfulfilled desire, no greed, lust, or anger. There is only the realization that we are at peace with the Father and with all mankind.

And so, as I continued in meditation another question came to my mind, "Have I died to all that is human? If I have, forgiveness is complete; and if I have not, there must be a continual dying until I have realized my Self-completeness in God. I may not be able to praise myself and declare that I am pure, but this much I can do: I can turn and with an open heart forgive every offense that has ever been aimed at me or mine— at me personally, at my family, community, nation, and the world—and entertain a complete and full sense of forgiveness."

With that realization, I settled down into peace and quiet, and a few moments later had to jump out of bed to make a note, and within the next couple of hours I was up four different times, making the notes that became two lectures, lectures that came out of a heart and mind at peace. There was no barrier—no unforgiveness, no sin, no judgment of anyone—nothing but a purity of vision, and in that purity of vision, there was peace.

And so, it is that I know now that the subject of forgiveness is an important one in our lives. Over and over again, we must forgive, forgive, forgive, and hold no man in judgment, criticism, or condemnation. A heart that is entertaining any judgment of his fellow man is not a heart at peace. It is futile to seek for peace of mind or soul or peace of anything else until we have fulfilled that Christly message of forgiving seventy times seven all those who offend us, of forgiving our debtors as we would have our debts forgiven.

We store up within ourselves the barriers that prevent the kingdom of God from being established in us by our judgments of people and conditions, and by the desires that still remain in us—not merely the sensual desires but even the desires that are considered good. All of *those things operate in our minds to separate us from the realization that that which we are seeking we already are.*

Yes, you can hear the desire for something good. I would like to be a little less criticizing; I would like to be a little more uplifting and positive. Ok, I've just declared that I am incomplete. I can't have that desire and also be realizing that I and the Father are One. And so bad desires, good desires, any desires – they are all human-humanhood, which has to die if we are going to find our real life as spirit.

In other words, God's grace is not something we are going to attain; God's grace is not something we can earn or deserve; God's grace was planted in us from the beginning, since before Abraham was; and it is only waiting to function in us, but it cannot function while we are entertaining a sense of separation from our good. There never is going to be a chance for us to know harmony until we have completely forgiven and been forgiven, and so purged ourselves that we go to the altar purified.

Some period every single day should be set aside for consciously remembering that we are holding no man in bondage to his sins, that we want no man to suffer or even be punished for them. To forgive means much more than to be content with such cant as, "Oh, yes, I don't want any harm to come to anybody." It is not that simple. It is the ability to sit down and face whatever the enemy may appear to be and realize, "Father, forgive him his offenses and open his eyes that he may see."

And if you are in this class, you should have no qualms whatsoever about being able to sit down and realize this about all the insurgents, about all the dictators, about all the men that are involved in what have been termed "the axis of evil". You should have no problem whatsoever praying this prayer, "Father, forgive him his offenses and open his eyes that he may see."

No one need be reluctant to forgive the offender his transgressions in the fear that this will set him free to offend again. True, it will set him free, but that freedom will include freedom from the desire to offend. It is not possible for anyone to receive real forgiveness and then to continue in the offense.

And so we are really praying that they die to their humanhood, aren't we? Now that's a prayer that has power. And if nothing else, it sets you free. If you do not have harmony in your lives, if you are not experiencing this peace that passeth understanding, then you need to pray this prayer.

Father, I come to You with clean hands, holding no one in bondage to a duty, nor anyone in bondage as a penalty for his sins. As far as I am concerned, Father, I am willing for You to forgive him. Whatever the sin, it is past, and let it be done and forgotten; and if he does it seventy times over again, forgive him seventy times over.

I want no revenge and no vengeance. I seek only to keep myself a pure instrument for Your love and Your grace so as to be worthy in Your sight.

I forgive everyone who has ever trespassed against me, consciously or unconsciously, and that forgiveness extends to all those who have trespassed against my religious or political convictions, or my national allegiance. I pray that You, Father, forgive them.

Humanly, there are those who owe me debts of duty and of love. I forgive them also. Henceforth, no one owes me anything, not even the obligation of relationship. What they give out of love, I cheerfully receive, but as a matter of duty I expect nothing, and I expect it of no one. I release my friends and my relatives, and everyone: They owe me nothing. It is my privilege and joy to serve them in whatever way You direct.

I offer myself an empty instrument: Father, use me.

Now in one of the talks that Joel gave I remember that he said that he had a problem with corruption in high places and there were some institutions with which he was having a hard time forgiving them. And I understand that. I've been through something similar with some of the institutions that they call mental health. And he said that in his mediation he was forced to say, "I can't forgive them, Father, you forgive them." And that that set him free. And so, he found a way to pray for even these corrupt organizations and institutions. Forgiveness is not for the other person, it's not really for the corrupt institution. Forgiveness is for us, in forgiving we release the situation, we're not bound to it anymore. Forgiveness sets us free from any kind of karma. And in that freedom, when we are unbound, when we lose them and let them go, then we are receptive. It's no longer a block to grace and grace can function in and through us. And so, forgiveness if for us. Forgiving others, we set ourselves free. You see, when you set someone free, you're really setting yourself free. Because there is only One Self. And so, it is vital that we understand this principle of forgiveness.

And now I will tell you a little story. A true story about forgiveness, and how I have found these principles that we have just read to be true.

When I was a child, I lived in a very abusive home. Both of my parents were alcoholics and they fought all the time. And there was physical violence and just craziness. And while I lived under that umbrella, I suffered a lot of things myself. I had asthma, I was sickly all the time, tonsillitis, I had a speech defect, I had a lot of things while I was under their umbrella, their consciousness. And my Dad left home and ran away really – he ran away from home and I can't say that I blame him. It was pretty crazy around there. He had a couple of other marriages and finally settled down with someone he is still with and he seems to be doing well.

My mother, on the other hand, got worse. And looking around for someone to blame, she found me. I look something like my Dad, and to the best of my ability, I am just assuming that for some reason she directed it at me. And so, I received the abuse.

My brother didn't and my sister didn't, it was centered on me. I was smacked so often, I was beat so often, that I would go to school with purple strap marks across my face and have to explain them to my friends. And I would usually lie and say I bumped into something. I would have nervous attacks at school and have hives and asthma and be sent home. I would be so nervous about getting hit because it would happen so often that when I would be sitting at the dinner table and she would walk by, I would flinch, or duck, or blink, because they would just come out of no where and she would smack me upside the face.

And then there was the emotional abuse. My sister would be in bed, my brother would be in bed and I would have to stand in front of her while she was on the couch having a cup of coffee and a cigarette and she would lecture me about how I was no good, I guess. I don't know, the words would just go on and on. And I used to have to stand there, and I would stand there and listen to her go on and on about how I was no good like my Father, like my Dad, and I remember looking at her until purple dots would come in front of my eyes and finally she would say, "Go to bed" and I would go in and go to bed.

And so that was my early years, going through that torture and there was some other sick things too, which I am not going to bring into this talk, but suffice it to say that by the time I was a teenager, I was hating my Mom. Well, I had one desire – to get the heck out of that house. And so eventually I ran away and never went back. I think I was fifteen.

And so, I have never understood, well, I've understood it – but I've never had the experience of having a close relationship with my Mother. I do not understood what that feels like, because I've never had one. And, I don't understand what it feels like to have a close relationship with my Dad because I've never had one of those either. He wasn't around. And so I do not understand anything that has to do with close relationships with your parents because I didn't experience it.

Now of course it has been several years and through my meeting other people and seeing their relationships and having met my wife's parents who have accepted me pretty well, I understand it somewhat. The point that I am making is that I hated her.

Try to imagine hating your own Mom. And that is where I was as a teenager. Eventually I started a spiritual walk because somebody gave me the *Art of Meditation* and I read it and what was in there resonated with me. And so I came upon this part on forgiveness and I realized that I was going to have to do something about it. And the way that I knew that is that I had had a couple of spiritual experiences and yet I wasn't going any farther. And every time that the phone would ring, and I would pick it up and my Mother was on the other end I would get that twist down in my belly. Something was there and I knew it – I didn't want to really deal with it, but I knew it. And it took nine years before I became willing to do what Joel is talking about here and forgive this person. And finally, what drove me to it was a marriage that wasn't working, and how could it work? – I had a resentment against all, well, half of the human race. Anybody that was female I didn't trust.

Oh, I'm so glad that is gone now, but let me tell you how that happened.

I went to a counselor. She was practicing spiritual principles too, but her job was as a therapist. And I talked it over with her. She said I should go home, and I should write my Mom a letter, but not to give it to her. And so I did that. I went home, I took a day off of work and I started writing. And eventually I got underneath all of the anger down to what I was really feeling was that I wrote down, "Mom, all I ever really wanted was for you to put your arms around me and tell me that you loved me." And then I took this over to the therapist and read it to her and she said, "There you go, now you understand and you have to look at it though an adults eyes and see that perhaps she is a sick person."

Well, I went home, and the phone rang, and my Mom was on the other end and it was still there. Something was missing, something was not solving this problem. That is when I discovered in Joel's writings a part that talked about giving of our first fruits. And I thought, yes, okay, we give of our first fruits, we tithe, we give money to organizations that are helping humanity, but what about if we give of our first prayers? And so I thought about that and I made the decision that if I sit down and mediate I am going to give my first prayers to my Mother because that is the person I am having this resentment against.

And so I practiced that and every day if I mediated three times before I began my first prayers were for my Mother. And it was simple, "God please let her find peace, open her eyes to her true Identity, let your Presence be there." Something simple like that. And of course, in the beginning it felt rather awkward because I was still resenting her while praying for her and I had both things going on at the same time. And so, I felt kind of hypocritical, but I persisted. I had to find a freedom from this. And so, as I persisted, the next day and the next day and the next, pretty soon a month passed and I don't know when it happened but – I sat down to meditate and I gave my first prayers to her and I realized that I meant it. I really did with love want her to find peace within herself and every good thing be hers. I meant it, finally.

A friend of mine said, "Why don't you go see her." And I decided he's right or she's right. And so, I tracked down where she was and by this time she was still drinking quite heavily, and she was in an old hotel and I got her out of that hotel, and she was yellow. I'm pretty sure that she had jaundice by then from too much drinking.

And I put her in my truck and I took her to the park and we sat down on the grass and I just said simply, "Mom, I love you." And do you know I felt it. For the first time in my life I did not have that anger and resentment inside. For the first time ever in my life that I could remember. I did not need to change her; I did not need to make her over. At one point she said, "Would you get my bottle out of my purse?" And I walked to my truck and I got her bottle of vodka and I handed it to her, and I felt perfectly at ease.

You have no idea what a freedom that was. Totally at ease – I was free, and I realized the reality of her was the Presence of God not this thing I was looking at, and that the reality of me was the Presence of God and that that love was one. And as I sat on the grass, I played a few songs for her on the guitar. I let her know I loved her – that was all, that was my whole mission. Just to let my Mother know I loved her, and it was okay no matter what she was. We finished up and I took her back to the hotel, I went back home, and I was free, and I had now established a relationship with the other half of humanity. From then on, I could love men and women and I could trust them both too.

Thirty days after this experience of taking her to the park, I received the news from my sister my Mother had passed away in that old hotel room. She had drunk herself to death. But I was free, for the first time in my life I was free. And I would have missed that day if I had not done the work that we're talking about. And maybe it would still be bothering me but it isn't. My mother was always big on education and when I got my four-year degree I walked across the stage and I kind of closed my eyes briefly and I said, "Mom, this is for you." She always loved pink carnations and now when I have a mediation and she pops into my mind I think of pink carnations because I love her.

And so you see the point of this story is not what I did. The point of this story is that forgiveness is not for the other person.

Forgiveness sets us free so that we might have that relationship of love with God and with his children. We cannot be the instrument for love when we are carrying that.

And so I highly recommend if there is anybody you have not forgiven, please for God's sake, take this message of this chapter and practice it. Practice it and practice it and if necessary, say what Joel said, "Father, I can't forgive him, or her, or them, please you forgive them." And then be still and keep at it until you mean it. I tell you; you will be set free. And you will know a deeper loving relationship with your heavenly Father than you have ever known before. And if you have not had results in practicing these principles, you will begin to have results. If you have not been able to settle down within yourself, you will find that peace has come to you. My peace, the peace that passes understanding.

Now, as we forgive, we are forgiven. We now understand that that does not mean there is some God sitting around keeping score. How ridiculous huh, how childish that concept is. There is no God sitting around keeping score – thank God. No, the reason why we are forgiven when we forgive is because we set ourselves free. Probably one of the finest examples of an expose on this principle is, or on these principles is A Course in Miracles. They really go into the forgiveness part. But all that we need is the experience and to have the experience you must forgive. When you forgive, you are forgiven. It's the same as saying, well okay I am bound to that person over there because I'm angry at them but I'm going to let that go. Well, when you let that go, you are no longer bound. You see? You see how you have the key to your own freedom? Of course, who else would have it? God has made you complete and so you have the key to your own freedom. You have the ability to set yourself free from any bondage, from any karma, from the entire law.

Practice these principles – set your brother free, set your Mother free, set your Dad free, set your sister free, set that employer free, set the employee free, set that nation free, set that man free, set that organization, that institution free, set that law free, set the disease free, set everything free and you free yourself to be the child of God. In this, when you complete this freedom, you will know it. You will have a sense of peace like you have never had before. Your meditations will deepen and broaden. You will have a love that you have never had before. And you will find that God really does give you the power to become the children of God. And that is what we are going to go into next, chapter sixteen, "That you may be the children of your Father."

Bless you all for taking up this study and I just feel a love for all of you.

Thank you.

The End

Ingram Content Group UK Ltd.
Milton Keynes UK
UKHW011813060423
419751UK00004B/182